INDUSTRIALISATION AND THE BRITISH COLONIAL STATE

In memory of John Butler
1913–73

INDUSTRIALISATION AND THE BRITISH COLONIAL STATE

WEST AFRICA 1939–1951

L.J. BUTLER

FRANK CASS
LONDON • PORTLAND, OR

First published in 1997 in Great Britain by
FRANK CASS & CO. LTD
Newbury House, 900 Eastern Avenue, Newbury Park
London IG2 7HH, England

and in the United States of America by
FRANK CASS
c/o ISBS, 5804 N.E. Hassalo Street, Portland, Oregon 97213-3644

British Library Cataloguing in Publication Data:

A catalogue record for this book is available
from the British Library

ISBN 0-7146-4703-9 (cloth)
ISBN 0-7146-4240-1 (paper)

Library of Congress Cataloging-in-Publication Data:

A catalog record for this book is available
from the Library of Congress

Printed in Great Britain by
Bookcraft (Bath) Ltd., Midsomer Norton, Avon

Contents

Abbreviations

AA	*African Affairs*
ACEC	Advisory Committee on Education in the Colonies
ACJ	Arthur Creech Jones Papers
AWAM	Association of West African Merchants
BETRO	British Export Trade Research Organization
BoT/BT	Board of Trade
CAB	Cabinet
CB	Cotton Board
CCAG	Committee on the Conference of African Governors
CCD	(Cabinet) Committee on Colonial Development
CD & W	Colonial Development and Welfare
CDC	Colonial Development Corporation
CDWAC	Colonial Development and Welfare Advisory Committee
CDWP	Colonial Development Working Party
CEAC	Colonial Economic Advisory Committee
CEDC	Colonial Economic Development Council
CEPS	Central Economic Planning Staff
CJH	*Canadian Journal of History*
CO	Colonial Office
CPP	(Colonial Office) Committee on Post-War Problems
CRC	Colonial Research Council
CSSRC	Colonial Social Science Research Council
EAGC	East African Governors' Conference
ECA	Economic Co-operation Administration
EcHR	*Economic History Review*
EPB	Economic Planning Board
EPC	(Cabinet) Economic Policy Committee

FBI	Federation of British Industries
FCB	Fabian Colonial Bureau Papers
HC	House of Commons Papers
IBRD	International Bank for Reconstruction and Development
JAH	*Journal of African History*
JICH	*Journal of Imperial and Commonwealth History*
LP	Lord President's Committee
OAG	Officer administering the government of ...
OCLI	(Colonial) Office committee on encouragement of industry legislation
PD(C)	*Parliamentary Debates (Commons)*
PD(L)	*Parliamentary Debates (Lords)*
PP	*Parliamentary Papers*
PRO	Public Record Office, Kew
T	Treasury Papers
TUC	Trades Union Congress
UAC	United Africa Company
WACCB	West African Cocoa Control Board
WAGC	West African Governors' Conference
WAPMB	West African Produce Marketing Board
WASCO	West African Soap Company
WAWC (CM)	West African War Council (Civil Members' Committee)

Acknowledgements

I have incurred many debts in the course of preparing this book. Special thanks are due to Professor Andrew Porter of King's College London, who supervised the doctoral research on which it is based, and who provided patient encouragement, support and guidance. His interest in the project and refreshing insights sustained me throughout its long period of gestation. The British Academy generously funded much of my research through a major studentship. I am indebted to the staff of the Public Record Office, Kew, for their cheerful efficiency and assistance over many years. I am grateful, too, to the staff of the University of London Library, King's College Library, the Institute of Historical Research, London, the Institute of Commonwealth Studies, London, the School of Oriental and African Studies Library, London, the British Library, the British Library of Political and Economic Science, the Bodleian Library, Rhodes House Library, Nuffield College Library and the Historical Manuscripts Commission. Their assistance has been invaluable. Portions of this work have received helpful criticism from the members of the Imperial History seminar at the University of London Institute of Historical Research. Invariably they have been a generous and receptive audience. The kindness and support of many friends have been expressed in ways too varied and numerous to be listed. Above all, I thank my family for all their efforts to make this book possible.

Crown copyright material in the Public Record Office is reproduced by permission of the Controller of Her Majesty's Stationery Office.

L.J. BUTLER
London, 1995

DIVISION OF RESPONSIBILITIES IN THE COLONIAL OFFICE (JULY 1945)

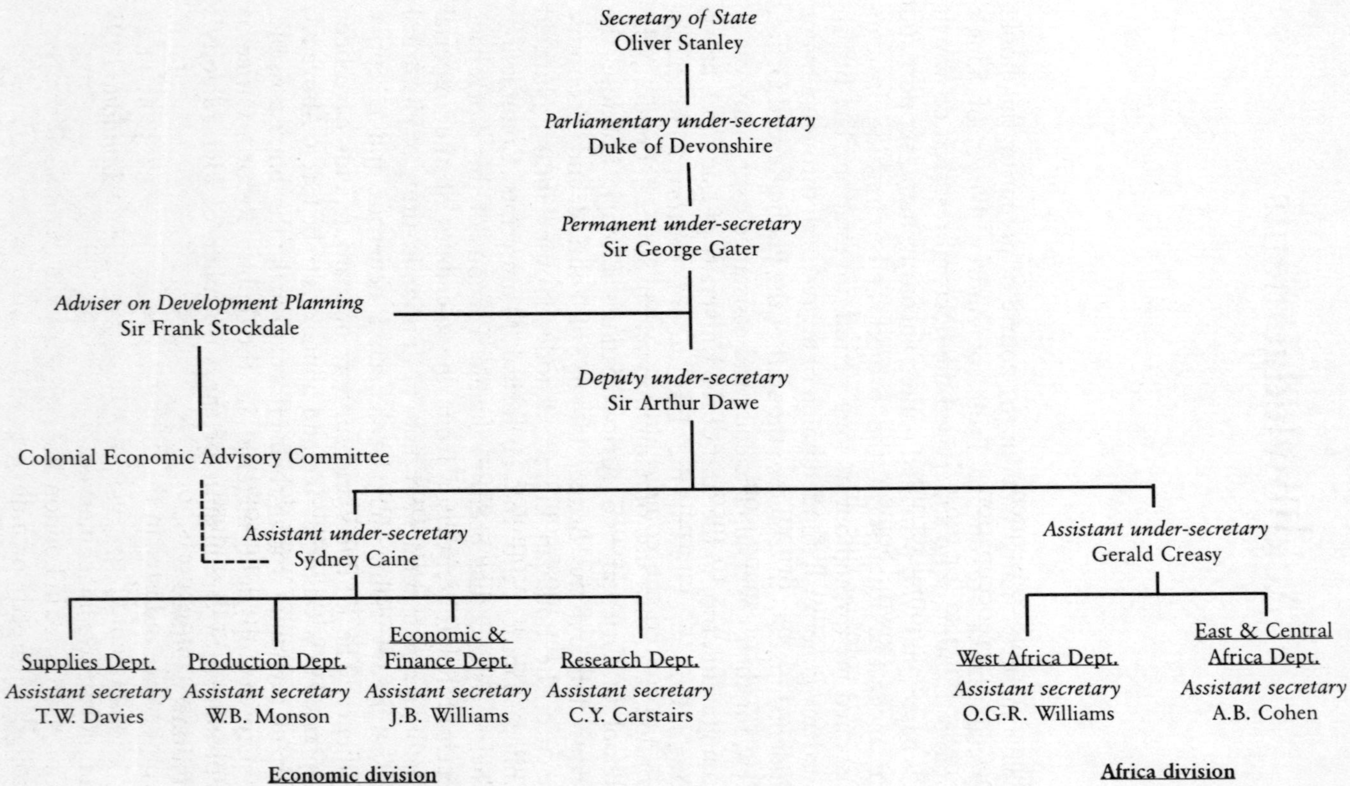

[Derived from Colonial Office *Establishment Branch Notices* in PRO CO 878/26-30]

Introduction

The economic consequences of British colonial rule in Africa have become a preoccupation not only for historians of the British Empire but also for those seeking to explain the apparent failure of former colonial territories to achieve balanced and sustained economic growth.[1] Some writers have detected a clear relationship between colonial rule and the 'structural underdevelopment' of the colonial and post-colonial economies, a condition allegedly engineered by Britain in the interests of the metropolitan economy. For many commentators, the economic function of colonialism was to incorporate underdeveloped regions of the world into the international capitalist economy, to ensure that they produced the commodities needed by the capitalist world and served as secure markets for the developed world's manufactured goods.[2]

One of the most common claims about the impact of colonial rule is that it promoted 'unbalanced' economic development, gearing the colonial economies to the production and evacuation of raw materials while neglecting or obstructing the kind of economic diversification which might have given colonial territories secure economic foundations and the prospect of continuing development after independence.

According to this interpretation, colonial rule not only ensured that the colonies were developed as sources of raw materials and as markets for metropolitan exporters, but also dismantled indigenous craft industries which might have competed with metropolitan exports, or prevented the development of such competitive industry in the colonies.[3]

Fundamental to such arguments is the belief that the administrative machinery of British colonial rule, including the Colonial Office in London and the individual colonial governments, colluded, directly or indirectly, in this process through a series of policies frustrated colonial industrial initiatives. Specifically, it is claimed that colonial administrators either failed to encourage the growth of local manufacturing sectors, or obstructed such opportunities for industrialisation as existed, allegedly in order to safeguard the flow of colonial primary exports and to protect metropolitan manufactured exports from local, colonial competition.[4] This interpretation is central to the influential 'open economy' model of economic relations in West Africa under colonial rule, constructed within the framework of liberal historiography by Professor A.G. Hopkins.[5] Similar conclusions, employing radical perspectives on development, have been reached by R. Howard in her study of Ghana under colonial rule.[6] A growing number of studies of East African conditions share this broad interpretation.[7]

Despite the importance of these assumptions, there has been little detailed, empirical research into metropolitan attitudes and policy-making, especially for the critical period of late colonial rule, immediately prior to the onset of decolonisation in the 1950s. Although the inter-war period has been well served by important studies,[8] there have been few attempts to reconstruct the views of the Colonial Office, which was the junction of relationships between the metropolitan and colonial governments, on economic, as opposed to political, development in the 1940s.

This book aims to provide a detailed historical study of the attitudes of the Colonial Office towards colonial industrialisation in the critical period between 1939 and 1951. It challenges prevailing assumptions by arguing that during this period, the Office attempted for the first time to evolve a coherent and progressive policy on encouraging colonial industry, not simply to meet the short-term needs of war but as part of a broader programme of development intended to prepare colonies for eventual political advance.

As a case study of the general position of officials, the book focuses on policy towards West Africa, a politically advanced region of substantial and growing economic importance to Britain, and one whose special problems increasingly came to dominate the Colonial Office's deliberations in this period. In official discussions, the West African colonies, Nigeria and the Gold Coast, held special prominence. Together representing the largest segment of the colonial empire proper, in size and population, these territories seemed far ahead of Britain's other

African colonies in their preparedness for self-government, arguably the 'model' for the rest of Africa, and therefore increasingly the focus of attention of metropolitan officials. This tendency was reinforced during and after the Second World War when the region became vital, first in maintaining supplies of commodities essential to the war effort and later not only as the linchpin in the Sterling Area's dollar-earning strategy after 1947 but as the test bed for the first phase of controlled decolonisation. For these reasons, a re-examination of London's interpretation of West African conditions appears to be warranted.[9] Moreover, as the book seeks to demonstrate, during the Second World War the West African colonial governments shared, and in part shaped, the Colonial Office's interest in promoting local industry.

Two major factors underline the significance of Colonial Office attitudes in this period. First, against a background of wartime mobilisation of the Empire's resources, metropolitan discussions on post-war reconstruction and the advent of a Labour Government, the colonial State took on new responsibilities in directing local economies, mirroring the growth of collectivism in Britain, and prompting discussions on the State's role in future economic development. Secondly, during the 1940s, the Colonial Office increasingly, if temporarily, became the driving force in colonial policy initiatives, disturbing the traditional balance of power between London and the colonial governments and further exposing weaknesses in local development machinery.

The period after 1939 produced major shifts in the outlook of the Colonial Office, justifying a resurrection of the concept of the 'official mind'. At a time when clear *political* direction in colonial policy was often absent, the continuities and evolution of official thinking were of special importance. Substantial areas of policy were entrusted to an increasingly confident, interventionist and reforming official élite. Moreover, as the very nature of colonial rule became more elaborate, the scope for divergence in the aims of metropolitan and locally based administrators widened – especially the case once the State assumed new responsibilities.[10] From the late 1930s, 'development' became central to the Colonial Office's self-attributed *raison d'être*, the unifying theme in its functions and attitudes.[11] The Office's role had hitherto been largely reactive, shaped by *ad hoc* responses to local developments, cemented by the idea of trusteeship, and limited by a concern to respect the substantial autonomy enjoyed by colonial governments under devolved British rule.[12] The legacy of the Depression, wartime mobilisation, and the need to plan post-war reconstruction, obliged the Colonial Office to be more assertive, to seek above all to anticipate local developments, and to devise new policies, methods and machinery, centred on the single goal of achieving controlled decolonisation at a time deemed appropriate by London. An understanding of the complex processes which constituted decolonisation therefore requires an appreciation of the growing contribution made by metropolitan officials to the formation of policy, despite the reservations of some historians who continue to emphasise the primacy of studying the local impact of colonial rule, from a local perspective.[13]

This was, unquestionably, a period of unusual strains, encompassing war and reconstruction, with their attendant economic dislocations and adjustments, punctuated by metropolitan financial crises and an unprecedented degree of State economic intervention, both in Britain and the colonies.[14] It was also a period when Britain was under increasing pressure to justify its colonial role to domestic, colonial and international opinion.[15] Sandwiched between the inter-war Depression, the experience of which exposed the inertia of traditional colonial 'trusteeship' to criticism, and the early 1950s, when a relative boom in commodity prices (stemming, in part, from the effects of the Korean War), together with concerted opposition to Britain's colonial presence, created new conditions for administrators, these years witnessed a systematic review of policies by the Colonial Office, representing the first, tentative steps towards planned decolonisation.[16]

In particular, officials gathered and digested the unpalatable lessons of the 1930s, when surveys such as those by Hailey and Frankel had revealed the instability of the colonial economies and the extent of colonial poverty.[17] They became preoccupied with the problem of giving the colonies adequate economic foundations on which stable political and social structures could be modelled as the prerequisites for self-government. While the immediate symptoms of colonial economic vulnerability could, it was hoped, be addressed through improved welfare provision, made feasible by successive Colonial Development and Welfare Acts, there remained a long-term need to free the colonies from their crippling dependence on narrow export bases, enabling them to withstand world market fluctuations and to achieve greater economic self-sufficiency.[18] Increasingly, the Colonial Office accepted arguments in favour of economic diversification and devoted considerable effort towards the problem of local manufacturing development. Officials concluded not only that industrialisation was a desirable strategy, but that its promotion both justified and required State involvement. Although this recognition was initially hesitant, it led to the Office becoming more adventurous when, after 1943, in a period which exposed tensions between the political and economic elements in colonial policy, it embarked on planning the post-war resumption of colonial development. The traditional emphasis on minimising the socially disruptive, and hence politically dangerous effects of economic modernisation, enshrined in the pre-war ethos of 'trusteeship', conflicted with a growing need to promote faster development, at first to satisfy colonial and international opinion, but increasingly in response to Britain's post-war financial problems.[19]

This book explores the origins and evolution of the Colonial Office's views on industrial development, analysing attempts to achieve an official consensus on questions including the financing of industrial development, the identification of possible sources of entrepreneurship and the degree to which development should be controlled by the State in the interests of the wider community. These problems triggered an extensive debate on the relative merits of public and private enterprise – a debate affected by officials' awareness of the political sensitivity surrounding the activities of expatriate capital in West Africa. The book also discusses official attitudes on the desirability of tariff protection for 'infant' colonial industries, set against war-time uncertainty over Britain's future commercial policy, itself a core issue in Anglo–American relations.

This book will examine the problems faced by the Colonial Office in implementing its new industrial policy – especially war-time and immediate post-war economic constraints on Britain's ability to supply an adequate volume of capital goods and other exports necessary for colonial development. Arguably more important, however, was the problem of overcoming traditional hostility towards colonial industrialisation from other sections of Whitehall, notably the Board of Trade, which was anxious to defend existing British commercial interests. Here, disagreement focused most sharply on the issue of colonial tariff protection. Increasing contact between the Colonial Office and other departments revealed the former's inability to defend its policy goals in the face of opposition from more influential sections of government, especially after 1945 when the British Government looked to the colonial empire to assist in metropolitan economic recovery.

Although themselves satisfied that industrialisation was an important component of their decolonisation strategy, Colonial Office officials encountered fundamental obstacles to the implementation of their plans. At a practical, immediate level, there was the question of how colonial industries were to be promoted. Throughout this period, local sources of capital, expertise and enterprise appeared to be frustratingly scarce. In West Africa, the most obvious supply of these essential factors seemed to be the large, expatriate firms, such as the United Africa Company, which enjoyed both the necessary funds and a knowledge of local commercial conditions, based on their predominance in the region's import–export trade. Before 1939, however, the firms showed little interest in diversifying their activities into manufacturing, preferring the familiar waters of trade, made even more secure by the fact that they managed to engineer an effective oligopoly during the 1930s.[20] During the war, this conservatism was modified slightly, and several firms put forward proposals to establish manufacturing capacity in West Africa. In part, this may have been a response to the changing commercial environment, especially the introduction and post-war consolidation of state-controlled produce marketing.[21] More important, perhaps, was the firms' desire to improve their relations with the colonial authorities – relations which had been strained by the intense hostility of local opinion to their operations – and to be seen to be adjusting to the recent policy shifts emanating from London. However, the very hostility of West African opinion towards the firms, grounded in bitter memories of the 1930s when produce prices were thought to have been kept artificially low by the firms' buying 'ring', undermined in administrators' eyes the firms' value as agents of economic modernisation.[22] Increasingly, the Colonial Office felt obliged to demonstrate that the State, not the firms, controlled West Africa's economic destiny. In order to minimise political friction, therefore, officials were drawn to consider means of widening the colonial State's role in economic management.

What, then, of the entrepreneurial potential of the colonial governments? The governments of the inter-war years have been accused of indifference, even hostility, towards industrial development – on the one hand because it threatened their chief source of revenue, duties on imports and exports, and on the other because of a deepening preoccupation with restricting the socially disruptive effects of economic development.[23] Concealed behind these motives, allegedly, was a predisposition towards defending British exporters' colonial markets.

The colonial governments before the Second World War have been unfairly condemned for their adherence to *laissez faire* principles.[24] In fact, on the contrary, they were active in promoting export agriculture and the transport infrastructure necessary to evacuate tropical exports, exposing themselves to subsequent criticism on the grounds that they reinforced the colonies' dependence on primary exports and so maintained these territories at a level of underdevelopment advantageous to the metropolitan economy.[25] Certainly, little was done to promote industrialisation: tariff protection for new industries was commonly refused, subsidies and credit were not provided, but here the main concern seems to have been to prevent the erosion of import revenue by import-substituting manufactures.[26] Although limited assistance towards development became available under the 1929 Colonial Development Act, few governments submitted industrial proposals under this scheme.[27] Before 1939, however, the governments' activities never amounted to anything approaching economic 'management': rather, governments saw their role as being to provide essential services which no other agency was willing to provide, in order to create conditions attractive to private investors.[28]

The outlook of local administrators was arguably of greater significance. The largely negative influence of the trusteeship ideology permeated colonial governments long after its hold on the metropolitan official mind had weakened.[29] Notwithstanding their supposed rejection of modern British life and idealisation of African 'tribal' society, colonial administrators had rational, if unsophisticated, motives for conservatism between the wars, grounded in an overriding preoccupation with maintaining political stability, and with doing so as frugally as possible. Confronted with subsistence economies and underutilised resources, colonial governments concluded that African welfare could best be promoted through the expansion of primary production for export.

Confidence in this minimal role for government was shattered by the Depression. Ironically, when State intervention was most needed, if only to provide basic welfare services, colonial governments found their funds disastrously reduced by the decline in revenue from trade. This in itself was a further disincentive to experimentation with revenue-threatening industry. More importantly, the entire notion of development based on private enterprise was shaken.[30]

This experience, together with wartime economic mobilisation, convinced administrators both in London and at the periphery that development required a substantial contribution from government, particularly in its planning.[31] Traditionally, the Treasury-inspired orthodoxy of territorial financial self-sufficiency had been the overriding constraint on greater activity by colonial governments. When this was abandoned, with the promise of metropolitan grant-aid after 1940, together with the possibility of increased revenues from progressive taxation, introduced with London's blessing, the prospects for government-sponsored development brightened.[32] Nevertheless, even when individual colonial governors, such as Burns in the Gold Coast and Bourdillon in Nigeria, favoured industrialisation, the problem remained that colonial governments were poorly equipped to promote development. Personnel shortages were aggravated by retrenchment in the 1930s and compounded by the depletion of staffs and the expansion of work during the war. Only gradually did establishments resume pre-Depression levels in the post-war years.[33]

Faced with the problems associated with the operations of the expatriate firms, coupled to a growing recognition of the inadequacies of existing colonial governments to undertake effective economic development, the Colonial Office explored new means of harnessing the entrepreneurial potential of private capital within politically acceptable structures under public control. Against a metropolitan background of wartime collectivism, the Colonial Office debated the value of public corporations in promoting development. However, what had originally been seen as a vehicle for industrialisation was eventually translated into a Colonial Development Corporation intimately associated with the post-war drive to promote dollar-earning primary production.[34]

Overshadowing the problems of finding the resources needed to develop colonial industry was an even more fundamental obstacle: the long-standing opposition of influential metropolitan interest groups to competitive manufacturing within the colonial empire. This hostility derived not only from specific exporting sectors, such as the Lancashire cotton industry, but also from within Whitehall. The Board of Trade, acting to defend British manufacturers' interests, was the chief obstacle to the Colonial Office's plans for industrialisation. After the war, the Board was joined by the Treasury, which resisted deviations from primary export production designed to earn or save dollars.

Metropolitan policy-makers outside the Colonial Office generally assumed a complementary, non-competitive relationship between the British and colonial economies. In return for their agricultural and mineral exports, the colonies received British manufactured goods, a division of labour claimed to benefit both sides.[35] Proponents of this view, from Joseph Chamberlain onwards, understood colonial 'development' to mean improved primary production for export, confirming the dependence defined in Hopkins' description of the 'open economy'.[36] The Depression, which converted the Colonial Office to a belief in diversifying the colonial economies, also strengthened the attachment of some British interests to 'safe' colonial markets, articulated through the Board of Trade, and accentuated their resistance to competition from indigenous manufacturing.[37]

In 1934, and again in 1937, the Colonial Office attempted to obtain Cabinet authorisation for limited colonial industrialisation. Each attempt was abortive.[38] These experiences shaped the Office's subsequent tactics. The Office learned that little progress was possible without the approval of Whitehall. Despite some encouraging indications of a softening of attitudes during the war, and an apparent willingness by the Board of Trade to adjust to changed post-war trading patterns, this approval eluded the Colonial Office throughout the period under consideration. After the war, when other sections of the metropolitan government were to show an unaccustomed interest in colonial development, the Colonial Office was obliged to set aside the ambitious ideas produced during the reconstruction planning debate, and acquiesce in a short-sighted metropolitan attempt to overcome the sterling crisis by developing colonial resources.[39] This was particularly evident in Britain's control of the supplies which colonial diversification would have required. Wartime shortages of basic development materials were followed not by the expected liberalisation of exports to the colonies, but by a selective policy which considered colonial needs inferior to those of Britain and more lucrative export markets.[40] The Colonial Office's brief experience of relatively untrammelled speculation about the possibilities of colonial development proved to have been founded upon a misconception of the wider goals of the metropolitan government – goals which the Office had little power to influence.

NOTES

1. For surveys of the extensive literature on these problems, see J. Forbes Munro, *Britain in Tropical Africa 1880–1960. Economic Relationships and Impact* (London: Macmillan, 1984); A.G. Hopkins, 'African Economic History: The First Twenty-Five Years', *Journal of African History*, 30, 1, (1989) pp.157–63; C.C. Wrigley, 'Aspects of Economic History', in A.D. Roberts (ed.), *Cambridge History of Africa Vol. VII from 1905 to 1940* (Cambridge: Cambridge University Press, 1986); D. Rimmer, 'The Economics of Colonialism in Africa', *JAH*, 19, 2, (1978), pp.265–73; D.K. Fieldhouse, 'Decolonization, Development and Dependence: a survey of changing attitudes', in P. Gifford and Wm. Roger Louis (eds), *The Transfer of Power in Africa. Decolonization 1940–1960* (New Haven: Yale University Press, 1982).
2. The vast literature on these debates is usefully summarised by D.K. Fieldhouse in 'Arrested development in Anglophone Black Africa?', in P. Gifford and Wm. Roger Louis (eds), *Decolonization and African Independence. The Transfers of Power, 1960–1980* (New Haven: Yale University Press, 1988) pp.135–58, and in the same author's *Black Africa 1945–1980. Economic Decolonisation and Arrested Development* (London: Unwin Hyman, 1986); see also A. Phillips, *The Enigma of Colonialism. British Policy in West Africa* (London: James Currey, 1989) pp.6–10, 161–3.
3. See, e.g., A. Adu Boahen, *African Perspectives on Colonialism* (Baltimore: John Hopkins University Press, 1987) pp.100–03; W. Rodney, *How Europe Underdeveloped Africa* (Washington: Howard University Press, 1982) pp.147–203; R. Howard, *Colonialism and Underdevelopment in Ghana* (London: Croom Helm, 1978) pp.15–26; A.G. Hopkins, *An Economic History of West Africa* (Harlow: Longman, 1973) esp. pp.187–236.
4. See, e.g., R. Austen, *African Economic History. Internal Development and External Dependency* (London: James Currey, 1987) p.181–2; M. Havinden and D. Meredith, *Colonialism and Development Britain and its Tropical Colonies 1850–1960* (London: Routledge, 1993) p.159.
5. Hopkins (1973), pp.262–3.
6. Howard (1978), pp.146–80.
7. E.A. Brett, *Colonialism and Underdevelopment in East Africa: The Politics of Economic Change, 1919–1939* (London: Heinemann, 1973) pp.72, 115–16, 278–81; C. Leys, *Underdevelopment in Kenya* (London: Heinemann, 1975) pp.8–27; N. Swainson, *The Development of Corporate Capitalism in Kenya 1918–1977* (London: Heinemann, 1980) pp.26–7, 40–3; B. Berman, *Control and Crisis in Colonial Kenya. The Dialectic of Domination* (London: James Currey, 1990) pp.178–9, 270–3.
8. Notably S. Constantine, *The Making of British Colonial Development Policy, 1914–1940* (London: Frank Cass, 1984); D. Meredith, 'The British Government and Colonial Economic Policy 1919-1939', *Economic History Review*, 2nd ser., 28, 3, (Aug. 1975), pp.484–99; I.M. Drummond, *Imperial Economic Policy 1917 to 1939: Studies in Expansion and Protection* (London: Allen and Unwin, 1974).

9. On West African developments in this period, see esp. R.D. Pearce, *The Turning Point in Africa: British Colonial Policy 1938–48* (London: Frank Cass, 1982); C.R. Nordman, 'Prelude to Decolonisation in West Africa: the development of British Colonial Policy, 1938–1947', unpublished University of Oxford D.Phil. thesis (1976); R. Rathbone (ed.), *British Documents on the End of Empire, Series B, Volume 1, Ghana, Part I 1941–1952* (London: HMSO, 1993).
10. J.M. Lee and M. Petter, *The Colonial Office, War, and Development Policy. Organisation and the Planning of a Metropolitan Initiative* (London: Maurice Temple Smith, 1982) pp.210–15; J.M. Lee, '"Forward Thinking" and War: the Colonial Office during the 1940s', *Journal of Imperial and Commonwealth History*, 6, 1, (Oct. 1977) pp.64–78; Sir Charles Jeffries, *Whitehall and the Colonial Service: an administrative memoir, 1939–1956*, (London: Athlone Press, 1972), *passim*.
11. Lee and Petter (1982), Ch. 4; Lee (1977), *passim*.
12. Jeffries (1972).
13. A notable example being David Throup's strictures in *Economic and Social Origins of Mau Mau 1945–53* (London: James Currey, 1987) p.1.
14. For the impact of the war, see Sir John Shuckburgh, 'Colonial Civil History of the War' (unpublished; mimeographed typescript, Institute of Commonwealth Studies Library, University of London); see also J. Darwin, *Britain and Decolonisation. The Retreat from Empire in the Post-War World* (Houndmills: Macmillan, 1988) Ch. 2; A.N. Porter and A.J. Stockwell, *British Imperial Policy and Decolonisation 1938–64. Volume I, 1938–51* (Houndmills: Macmillan, 1987) Chs. 4–7; D. Killingray and R. Rathbone (eds), *Africa and the Second World War* (Houndmills: Macmillan, 1986); R.D. Pearce, 'The Colonial Economy: Nigeria and the Second World War', in B. Ingham and C. Simmons (eds), *Development Studies and Colonial Policy* (London: Frank Cass, 1987) pp.264–92; N.J. Westcott, 'Sterling and Empire: The British Imperial Economy, 1939–1951', unpublished seminar paper, University of London Institute of Commonwealth Studies, (1983).
15. E.g. R. Smythe, 'Britain's African colonies and British propaganda during World War II', *JICH*, 14, 1, (Oct. 1985), pp.65–82; Wm. Roger Louis, *Imperialism at Bay: the United States and the Decolonisation of the British Empire, 1941--5* (Oxford: Oxford University Press, 1977) pp.121–286.
16. For the Depression generally, see A.J.H. Latham, *The Depression and the Developing World, 1914–39* (London: Croom Helm, 1981) and C.P. Kindleberger, *The World in Depression 1929–1939* (Harmondsworth: Penguin, 1987); for the Depression's impact on West Africa, see Hopkins (1973), esp. Ch. 7, Roberts (1986), esp. pp.443–54, and B. Ingham, 'Colonialism and the Economy of the Gold Coast 1919–45', in Ingham and Simmons (1987), pp.264–92. On the beginnings of decolonisation, see Pearce (1982); R.D. Pearce, 'The Colonial Office and Planned Decolonisation in Africa', *African Affairs*, 83, 330, (Jan. 1984) pp.77–93; J. Flint, 'Planned Decolonisation and its Failure in British Africa', *AA*, 82, 328, (July 1983) pp.389–411.
17. Lord Hailey, *An African Survey* (Oxford: Oxford University Press, 1938); S.H. Frankel, *Capital Investment in Africa*, (London: Oxford University Press, 1938); see also D.J. Morgan, *The Official History of Colonial Development Volume I* (London: Macmillan, 1980) pp.28–33.
18. On the evolution of British colonial development policy see Morgan (1980) Volume I, pp.44–70; Constantine (1984); Meredith (1975); H. Johnson, 'The West Indies and the conversion of the British Official Classes to the Development Idea', *Journal of Commonwealth and Comparative Politics*, 15, 1, (March 1977), pp.55–75; G.C. Abbott, 'British Colonial Aid Policy during the Nineteen Thirties', *Canadian Journal of History*, 5, 1, (March 1970) pp.73–89; D.G.M. Rampersad, 'Colonial economic development and social welfare; the case of the British West Indian colonies, 1929–47', unpublished University of Oxford D.Phil. thesis (1979).
19. Lee and Petter (1982), esp. Ch. 3; Lee (1977), pp.64–79.
20. P. Kilby, 'Manufacturing in Colonial Africa', in P. Duignan and L.H. Gann (eds),

Colonialism in Africa 1870–1960, Vol.4, The Economics of Colonialism (Cambridge: Cambridge University Press, 1975) pp.488, 491; Fieldhouse (1986), pp.10–11, 46–47.

21. D. Meredith, 'State controlled marketing and economic 'development': the case of West African produce during the Second World War', *EcHR*, 2nd ser., 39, 1 (Feb. 1986), pp.77–91; D. Meredith, 'The Colonial Office, British Business Interests and the Reform of Cocoa Marketing in West Africa, 1937–1945', *JAH*, 29, 2, (1988), pp.285–300; J.H. Bowden, 'Development and control in British colonial policy, with reference to Nigeria and the Gold Coast, 1935–48', unpublished University of Birmingham Ph.D. thesis (1980).
22. Meredith (1986), pp.80–1.
23. Brett (1973), pp.300–11; Meredith (1975), p.260–6.
24. Pearce (1987), pp.266–7.
25. E.g., Brett (1973), pp.300–11.
26. On the development of manufacturing in West Africa between the wars, see Kilby (1975), pp.472–92; R. Olufemi Ekundare, *An Economic History of Nigeria 1860–1960* (London: Methuen, 1973), p.117–85; Hopkins (1973), 262–3.
27. Constantine (1984), pp.195–226; D.G. Meredith, 'The British Government and Colonial Economic Development, with particular reference to British West Africa, 1919–1939', unpublished University of Exeter Ph.D. thesis, (1976), pp.119–26; Meredith (1975), pp.489–94.
28. Pearce (1987), pp.266–7.
29. See, e.g., P.J. Cain and A.G. Hopkins, 'Gentlemanly capitalism and British expansion overseas II: new imperialism, 1850–1945', *EcHR*, 2nd ser., 40, 1, (Feb. 1987), pp.1–26; J.M. Lee, *Colonial Development and Good Government: a study of the ideas expressed by the British official classes in planning decolonization, 1939–1964*, (Oxford: Oxford University Press, 1967); C.C. Ehrlich, 'Building and Caretaking', *EcHR*, 2nd ser., 26, 4, (Nov. 1973), pp.649–67; R.E. Robinson, The Moral Disarmament of African Empire 1919–1947', *JICH*, 8, 1, (Oct. 1979), pp.86–104.
30. P. Hetherington, *British Paternalism and Africa, 1920–1940* (London: Frank Cass, 1978) p.91; W.K. Hancock, *Survey of British Commonwealth Affairs II. Problems of Economic Policy 1918–1939* (London: Oxford University Press, 1940–42) p.323; Lee and Petter (1982), p.26.
31. Ingham (1987), p.251.
32. On wartime taxation policy, see Shuckburgh (II), pp.305–18.
33. Jeffries (1972); Lee and Petter (1982), pp.210–15; R.D. Pearce, 'Morale in the Colonial Service in Nigeria during the Second World War', *JICH*, 11, 2, (Jan. 1983), pp.175–96.
34. M. Cowen, 'Early years of the Colonial Development Corporation: British State Enterprise Overseas during late Colonialism', *AA*, 83, 330, (Jan. 1984), pp.63–75.
35. See, e.g., Meredith (1976), p.129f.
36. Hopkins (1973), Ch. 5.
37. Brett (1973), p.71.
38. Meredith (1976), pp.131–9.
39. For the growing literature on post-war colonial development, see, e.g., Morgan (1980) Volume II; P.S. Gupta, 'Imperialism and the Labour Government', in J.M. Winter (ed.), *The Working Class in Modern British History* (Cambridge: Cambridge University Press, 1983) pp.112–15; R. Hyam, 'Africa and the Labour Government, 1945–1951', *JICH*, 16, 3, (May 1988), pp.148–9; D.K. Fieldhouse, 'The Labour Governments and the Empire-Commonwealth, 1945–51', in R. Ovendale (ed.), *The Foreign Policy of the British Labour Governments, 1945–1951* (Leicester: Leicester University Press, 1984); A.E. Hinds, 'Sterling and Imperial Policy, 1945–1951', *JICH*, 15, 2, (Jan. 1987) pp.148–64.
40. Morgan (1980) II, Ch. 1.

1 Towards 'Development': Colonial Economic Policy Before the Second World War

The 1930s mark the terminal phase in the era of 'classical' colonial rule, sandwiched between a relatively prosperous period of 'consolidation' and the Second World War, which saw unprecedented attempts by Britain to mobilise colonial economic resources and the first serious efforts to shape future colonial policy. Wartime policy discussions were influenced by metropolitan officials' pre-war experiences. The 1930s betrayed unease among administrators that Britain's presence in Africa and elsewhere had not fulfilled the promises of Imperial rhetoric. Deepening self-doubt produced two strands of official thought. The first was a concern to ameliorate the colonial poverty revealed by the Depression. The second was the question of correcting the structural weaknesses of colonial economies, and their vulnerability to fluctuating demand for their exports. An examination of the framework of colonial economic policy in this period reveals that, for several reasons, there was little prospect of colonial economic diversification, helped by the growth of indigenous manufacturing sectors. These reasons included entrenched metropolitan views on the relationship between the British and colonial economies, and British government aversion to potentially competitive manufacturing within the Empire. Superimposed on these were the indifference of expatriate capital to colonial industrial opportunities and a generally unwelcoming attitude from colonial governments. Against this unpromising background, the Colonial Office struggled to clarify its own thinking, less from a belief that industrialisation offered a solution to colonial economic problems than because a workable policy was required in the face of developments on the periphery. The attempt was stillborn, since the rest of Whitehall was unwilling to relinquish control over the colonial economies. While, by 1939, the Colonial Office had secured metropolitan funding of welfare provision in the colonies, little progress had been made in devising policies to promote their economic development.

Metropolitan attitudes to the colonies

Between the wars, metropolitan policy-makers and interest groups assumed a complementary relationship between the British and colonial economies. This, they claimed, brought mutual advantages: from the sale of their exports, colonial producers could buy manufactures, and so improve their living standards; this, in turn, created markets for metropolitan industry. Moreover, to the extent that colonial economic development was discussed, this was generally in terms of improved production of commodity exports, implying a consolidation of the existing division of labour between the world's primary producing and manufacturing regions – a pattern described in Hopkins's celebrated description of the 'open economy' model of colonial dependence.[1]

Although this economic complementarity remained a central argument for Imperial apologists, the colonial relationship was unequal. Whereas individual colonies might depend substantially on British markets, Britain depended very little on any one colony or group of colonies, and her trade with the colonial empire never matched that with the Dominions and the developed world. Thus, in 1924, Britain's colonial trade represented only 6.8 per cent of her total exports, although this figure rose to 10 per cent by 1931. Nevertheless, a small but persistent group of metropolitan politicians, most prominently Leopold Amery, urged the development of colonial resources, much as Joseph Chamberlain had advocated.

Underlying this interest was the belief that, although undeveloped, the colonies offered enormous economic potential as markets and sources of raw materials for British industry. Moreover, unlike the economic policies of the Dominions, which, between the wars, deviated increasingly from metropolitan requirements, colonial development seemed controllable from Britain and could be managed to promote British interests.[2] Such ideas were reinforced after 1918 as Britain's relative economic decline became obvious. The colonial economies, seen as relatively recent initiates to world trade, seemed likely to remain at simple levels of production for many years to come.[3] This unsophisticated conspectus offered little scope for serious consideration of diversifying colonial production.

Between the wars, colonial economic activity continued to concentrate almost exclusively on primary production, and very little diversification into manufacturing occurred. In British West Africa, economic development was characterised by the growth of a narrow range of mainly agricultural exports. For Nigeria, the second largest trading unit in Africa, palm products were especially important, forming the basis of the territory's integration into world trade in the nineteenth century. Palm production was a mainstay of the prosperous 1920s, sometimes amounting to half of Nigeria's total exports. However, the First World War prompted some diversification into groundnuts and cocoa production. By 1937, palm products constituted 37 per cent of Nigeria's exports, with groundnuts totalling nearly 20 per cent and cocoa over 10 per cent. This shift in economic activity demonstrates the dynamism still possible within the colonial economy and the responsiveness of peasant producers to new opportunities, discounting metropolitan prejudices about the supposed economic lethargy of the African.[4] The Gold Coast economy, too, depended heavily on export-orientated peasant production. Here, cocoa was dominant, production having expanded quickly under colonial rule, representing three-quarters of the territory's exports by the 1920s. By the 1930s, nearly half the world's cocoa came from the Gold Coast.[5]

Although West Africa's export trade broadened, little manufacturing capacity developed before the Second World War. In the Gold Coast, for example, a Swiss-owned brewery was established in 1932, but there was no local soap or cigarette production. In Nigeria, by 1939, there was a cigarette factory at Ibadan, cotton ginneries, saw mills, two palm-oil bulking plants, a metal drum plant and a soap works at Lagos (the latter operated by the West African Soap Company, a Unilever subsidiary, using local palm-oil). Thus the region's modest manufacturing sector was concerned largely with processing local produce, and was limited both geographically and in range.[6]

The impact of the Depression

Such narrow economic bases made the colonies, like all primary producing economies, particularly susceptible to recession after 1929. On average, raw material prices fell 50 per cent more than the prices of manufactures. The colonial economies were ravaged by the collapse of commodity prices. For example, the price paid to Nigeria's palm-oil producers dropped by almost 80 per cent between 1928 and 1934, and the total value of Nigerian exports fell from £16,927,000 in 1928 to £8,560,000 in 1933.[7] For the primary producing economies, the Depression involved a deterioration in both the barter and income terms of trade, curtailing their purchasing power. As real incomes fell, producers exported more to maintain levels of import consumption, reflected in Africa's growing share of world trade. A circular problem arose, because when the purchasing power of the primary producing economies fell, so did their ability to buy manufactured imports, bringing depression to the industrial world. In turn, the industrial world's need for African primary produce slumped, compounding the difficulties originally caused by low commodity prices.[8] The Gold Coast paid heavily for its reliance on cocoa, whose price was more than halved between 1929 and 1930. The territory's revenue was derived mainly from export duties on cocoa, from the railways which transported it to the coastal towns and from duties on imports paid for with the income it brought to producers.[9]

Another victim of the Depression was colonial government revenues, drawn largely from customs and excise duties since direct taxation was still embryonic before 1939. Moreover, since much inter-war development was financed by government loans, especially in the brief 'boom' after 1918, the Depression interrupted many development schemes, because declining revenues could no longer service these loans. The Depression therefore drew metropolitan attention to the problem of colonial indebtedness and to the heavy burden which debt charges involved for straitened government resources. Nigeria's problems were typical. By 1934, the territory was devoting almost one third of its gross revenue to debt charges. Declining revenues inevitably affected the quality of government services in the economic and social spheres, as colonial governments embarked on retrenchment.[10]

The review of 'trusteeship'

The impact of the Depression undermined traditional metropolitan claims that colonial rule benefited the dependent Empire by stimulating economic growth through an expanded commodity export trade.[11] The 1930s saw a review, initially hesitant, but becoming more purposeful, of the structures of colonial rule.

Most significant was the tension thus uncovered between the political and economic elements in British colonial policy. Insofar as British colonial rule between the wars had a philosophy, this was 'trusteeship'.[12] Trusteeship implied a responsibility upon the colonial power to 'protect' colonial subjects from the potentially adverse consequences of too rapid an encounter with Western civilisation. Specifically, it meant shielding colonial populations, especially in Africa, from disruption by European economic activity. Its classic statement was Lugard's *The Dual Mandate in British Tropical Africa* (1922), which embraced Joseph Chamberlain's widely shared view that the well-being of Europe and Africa were interdependent, but developed this to emphasise the importance of restricting European penetration in the interests of Africans.[13]

The nebulous character of trusteeship made it a convenient basis for a spectrum of opinions. Particularly receptive was the metropolitan lobby which equated 'development' with exploitation, and which sought to 'protect' colonial societies from the kind of dislocation and distress which industrialisation was perceived to have caused in Britain and Europe. This outlook was not confined to humanitarians, missionary groups, liberals and socialists who championed colonial interests within Britain. It permeated the Colonial Office, too. As far as West Africa was concerned, possibly the key expression of this paternalism was the sustained discouragement by the Colonial Office of European-owned plantation agriculture. It was also seen in the cool reactions of officials in London to the grandiose development schemes for the region proposed by the Empire Resources Development Committee during the First World War.[14]

For much of the inter-war period, then, conservation was the dominant ethos in the Colonial Office. The major practical manifestation of the trusteeship doctrine was the distinctive form of political control generally known as 'indirect rule', essentially a means of governing through existing local elites, or, where these could not be identified, through co-operating groups given legitimacy by the colonial authorities. Obviating the large European official presence required by more interventionist styles of government, indirect rule was cheap, a key consideration for policy-makers in Whitehall. It was equally welcome to colonial governments, hard-pressed during the Depression to maintain even skeleton establishments, as their already modest revenues shrank.

The fact that indirect rule required local co-operating élites gave colonial administrators a powerful incentive to minimise social change, seen as a potential solvent of established patterns of political authority. The desire to 'preserve' colonial societies in turn led authorities to seek to avoid rapid or fundamental economic change, which might disrupt existing social relationships. Reinforcing these ideas were the findings of anthropological research, which, burgeoning between the wars, identified a close interdependence between economic, social and political structures.[15] In practice, this led colonial governments to discourage urbanisation and to prefer labour migration to the mass relocation of population, with the aim of restraining African 'detribalisation'.[16]

Both to satisfy trusteeship's philosophical requirements, and, more immediately, to permit inexpensive administration, the idea of preserving colonial societies from 'undesirable' change developed into an orthodoxy. Here was an effective counterweight to any potential dynamic, metropolitan or local, towards accelerated economic development, and to the modernisation which this seemed bound to involve. Trusteeship therefore created a climate hostile to the development of manufacturing industry in the colonies.

The evolution of colonial development policy

Yet the effects of the Depression highlighted the need to promote economic development, and so a conflict arose between the political and economic strands of colonial policy. While administrators preferred to restrain modernising influences which threatened to undermine the traditional social structures on which colonial rule was based, for economic reasons, including the need to secure metropolitan interests and to tackle colonial poverty, the case for a more vigorous approach to development was increasingly irresistible.

The Depression exposed metropolitan officials' ignorance of basic conditions in the Colonial Empire. An important feature of the 1930s was a deepening understanding, based on systematic study, of how critical these conditions had become. Much new information was amassed, enabling greater coherence to be given to colonial policy, and in itself demanding policy responses in previously neglected areas. The process of fact-gathering began within the Colonial Office, where recognition of the importance of economic questions led to the compilation of the *Economic Survey of the Colonial Empire* (1932) at the instigation of the colonial secretary, Philip Cunliffe-Lister. In 1936, the Office initiated a survey of colonial nutritional standards, with disturbing consequences. In addition a series of financial investigations conducted by Sir Alan Pim, and sponsored by the Colonial Office, concluded that economic and social reforms were necessary in a number of African territories, and buttressed the case for a more active policy of colonial development.[17] Reinforcing the Colonial Office's efforts were milestone studies by Lord Hailey and Professor S.H. Frankel, published in 1938, which both emphasised the need to improve colonial living standards.

Accumulating evidence of fundamental problems in the colonial economies fuelled increasing metropolitan self-doubt about the Imperial role in Africa. Confidence that colonial rule would continue indefinitely remained, but official complacency about its benefits for colonial populations was shaken. Official discomfort was transformed into an urgent attempt to reform colonial policy by two principal developments: the growth of unrest within the colonies, and the resurrection of the 'colonial problem' in international relations, prompted by Germany's renewed interest in acquiring colonial territory.

Conflict within the colonial empire was given sharp and startling focus by the intense economic problems facing its peoples. The most dramatic expression of this were the serious riots in the West Indies between 1935 and 1938, caused primarily by economic distress, the combined effects of a world glut of sugar (the region's chief export), and falling prices.[18] Further potential for conflict was revealed by the West African cocoa 'hold-ups', prompted by the concentration of the cocoa trade in the hands of a few large European companies, bound after 1937 in a buying 'ring' that was regarded by African producers as a device to keep cocoa prices down.

The introduction of the 'colonial problem' into the turbulent diplomatic climate of the late 1930s, in which Germany's appetite for colonial expansion became embroiled in Britain's appeasement policy,[19] prompted closer international scrutiny of the entire question of colonial rule. This interest in colonial affairs, combined with the build-up of unpalatable evidence of conditions in the colonies, encouraged Britain to justify its colonial record and to defend its presence in moral terms. Mounting criticism of

Britain's record, both at home and abroad, demanded evidence of constructive colonial policies and a positive statement of British intentions. Those who justified colonial rule were now obliged to support their traditional rhetoric with practical results. The interim response was MacDonald's Commons statement, in December 1938, that Britain's eventual aim was self-government for the colonial empire. Although vague and lacking any timetable, this was significant as the first formal declaration that the ultimate object of policy for British Africa was self-rule. Of more immediate importance, however, was the rider that, until this became possible, the chief purpose of policy was to secure the 'welfare and progress of all the inhabitants'.[20]

In retrospect, the 1930s seemed to some in the Colonial Office to have been characterised by a 'general aimlessness and drift'.[21] Officials were increasingly disenchanted with trusteeship's apparently negative contribution to colonial well-being. The conservationist approach seemed, after all, to have been a convenient cover for inaction, which no longer appeared defensible. The political, rather than the economic, dimension ultimately enabled MacDonald to extract a commitment from the Treasury to expanded development funding, despite the constraints imposed on metropolitan spending by the rearmament programme after 1938.[22] The undermining of trusteeship was the result not only of external and domestic criticism but also of the recognition that fundamental change was occurring in the colonial economies, such as in the development of the Northern Rhodesian copperbelt and in the organisation of West African trade, and that this was already having social, and potentially political, repercussions, which could no longer be ignored. Colonial theory, such as it was, trailed behind developments on the ground. The Colonial Office had been much impressed with the revelations of recent fundamental research, particularly Hailey's, and, in its eagerness to formulate a new, constructive colonial policy, was receptive to new ideas. Moreover, officials were not immune to the contemporary, extended debate within Britain on the proper role of the State. While State intervention remained a contentious area among senior officials in the Colonial Office, the restlessness of the 'official mind' in the later 1930s encouraged discussions [on the State's economic role during and after the war] – discussions which complemented metropolitan debates on 'reconstruction'. Yet trusteeship, and the values and objectives through which it was expressed, were not easily discarded by a generation of officials for whom the preservation of 'tribal' society had been the touchstone of policy. Long into the Second World War, and beyond, it remained a commonplace in official discussions that beneficial change could safely be brought about in Africa only by evolutionary methods, not by revolution.

Nevertheless, the colonial development policy which emerged in the later 1930s, culminating in the 1940 Colonial Development and Welfare Act, was an important departure, reflecting the Colonial Office's immediate concern to effect palliative measures to tackle the most obvious consequences of colonial poverty. The philosophy which produced the 1940 Act emphasised welfare provision rather than economic development as such. MacDonald's primary aim was to win metropolitan recognition of Britain's duty to provide for recurrent expenditure on colonial social services, as distinct from grants for large-scale capital schemes.[23] Moreover, as Constantine claims,

> Economic advantages to Britain from accelerated development programmes now became the incidental though welcome by-products of a policy conceived for other purposes.[24]

The dynamic of policy, therefore, was a combination of humanitarian concern and a desire to pre-empt international, especially United States, criticism of colonial rule, rather than any grand, neo-mercantilist strategy. Evidence of this was the Colonial Office's eventual decision to entrust responsibility for colonial development and welfare to its new Social Service Department, itself a product of the new thinking, rather than to the Economic Department.[25] Yet, when the development initiative was formally unveiled in February 1940, the need to improve the colonies' *economic* position was emphasised: progress in other spheres was expected to follow from economic development.[26] The argument that economic development would enable colonial governments to provide essential social services was included at Treasury insistence, but found few sympathisers in the Colonial Office.[27]

However, some officials recognised the danger of treating the symptoms rather than the disease. The Office's financial adviser, Sir John Campbell, questioned the concept of putting social welfare before economic expansion.[28] The Treasury, too, sought to maintain the emphasis on economic development embodied in the 1929 Act, fearing that the alternative would be to place the colonies permanently on the 'dole'.[29] At one stage, the Treasury suggested omitting the word 'welfare' from the Colonial Development and Welfare Bill.[30] MacDonald rejected the Treasury's arguments, insisting that traditional ideas on colonial financial self-sufficiency were no longer tenable. Nevertheless, the most important long-term lesson of the Depression for officials was that fundamental economic development in Africa was necessary.[31]

A tension persisted well into the Second World War between advocates of an immediate, 'welfarist' strategy, and those who stressed the importance of tackling the underlying causes of deprivation. Again, both approaches had political rationales. The need to pre-empt international criticism of colonial rule called for immediate, ameliorative responses, especially after the outbreak of war, when it became necessary to smooth Anglo-American relations and to forestall possible Axis propaganda targetting colonial 'exploitation'. MacDonald's success lay in presenting his colonial development and welfare proposals as being politically necessary, essential to the successful prosecution of the war, and a future guarantee of Britain's Imperial status. These political considerations gave the initiative a justification which secured the Cabinet's endorsement in otherwise unpropitious circumstances of war and financial restraint.[32] However, long-term economic development as an issue both raised, and was raised by, the wider question of the long-term goals of colonial policy, and was a central feature of official discussions on the preparation of colonies for ultimate self-government.

Before the outbreak of war the Colonial Office had barely begun to consider long-term strategies to deal with colonial economic problems. Nor did it see any alternative, for most colonies, to a continued dependence on export-directed primary production, despite growing concern at the risks of such specialisation.[33] For example, in February 1939, addressing members of Political and Economic Planning, Hailey advocated raw materials processing and other industries in the colonies, enabling them to produce their own essential goods. He advised against regarding the colonies as exclusive, long-term export markets for Europe, and warned that any area wholly devoted to export production was fundamentally unbalanced in that its entire economy depended upon the fortunes of other countries' economies.[34] MacDonald endorsed this view in June 1939, when discussing the problems of the colonial economies, especially their over-dependence on export commodities. He concluded: 'I am certain that one of the things which we have to do in various colonies is to make the people somewhat less dependent on the return from export crops.'[35]

Yet in practice, MacDonald's officials were at a loss to suggest how the structural imbalance of the colonial economies might be corrected. The head of the Colonial Office's Economic Department, John Calder, argued that priority in development should go to agricultural improvement; diversification into mineral extraction or into manufacturing was very much a long-term prospect.[36] The only palliative offered consistently by the Colonial Office was improved arrangements for marketing colonial produce, intended to achieve stability in producers' incomes.[37] The outcome was the establishment, in 1937, of the Colonial Empire Marketing Board.[38] Here was a translation to colonial conditions of a device already familiar in the economic policy of the National Government, anxious to rationalise domestic agricultural production and marketing.

Pessimism at the scope for diversification stemmed not from a lack of imagination among officials, nor from a casual dismissal of manufacturing's potential contribution to diversification. On the contrary, colonial industrialisation had been much discussed in the preceding decade. It was, however, a highly controversial subject, prone to divide Whitehall and to sour relations between the Colonial Office and the home economic departments as it impinged upon Britain's export interests and the wider question of Imperial economic integration. Colonial industrialisation was also opposed, with varying degrees of frankness, by powerful interest groups within Britain. Furthermore, it remained in doubt whether any practical support for the promotion of local manufacturing was available: the colonies themselves generally lacked the resources to undertake the necessary capital investment, and neither metropolitan-based capital nor expatriate European capital in the colonies seemed interested in its prospects. Finally, few colonial governments demonstrated much enthusiasm for industrial development before the Second World War. In this hostile climate, it is unsurprising that industrialisation appeared irrelevant to the Colonial Office. Each of these apparent obstacles to manufacturing development will be considered in turn, before an attempt is made to account for the Colonial

Office's efforts in the later 1930s to secure a definitive policy ruling from the metropolitan government, and to assess its success.

Whitehall and colonial manufacturing

Before attempting to gauge whether the British government was instrumental in obstructing colonial industrialisation between the wars it is necessary to establish the place occupied by the colonial empire in the government's broad economic strategies, and the importance of markets such as West Africa, to British exporters, whose interests the government has been accused of protecting at the expense of those of the colonies.[39] It is also necessary to determine what steps, if any, the metropolitan government took during the 1930s to protect British manufacturing interests in colonial markets.

Overshadowing the inter-war British economy was the decline of the staple export industries and the contraction of Britain's share in world trade. Because of their dependence on primary producing countries as markets, British exports suffered when the incomes of these economies began to decline. Declining world trade and the lack of competitiveness of Britain's exporters led the metropolitan government to act to support vital British interests, first by attempting to create a more self-sufficient Imperial economic bloc, providing secure outlets for British exports and, secondly, to promote colonial development, thereby creating markets for British capital goods. Neither strategy offered much scope for colonial industrialisation.

The Depression reinforced British interest in the Empire's market potential. Between 1929 and 1932, the volume of British exports declined by over 37 per cent.[40] Exports nevertheless remained vital to the British economy. As late as 1938, they covered nearly 60 per cent of Britain's imports.[41] Hence the attraction of creating a more tightly knit trading system within the Empire, offering some protection from the problems of the international economy. By late 1931, Britain was one of the few major economies that had not yet resorted to protection, leaving the domestic market vulnerable to 'dumping' by foreign exporters.[42]

The idea of strengthening Imperial economic ties had broad metropolitan appeal, spanning the political parties and encompassing both sides of industry. For example, the Federation of British Industry, in which the export trades predominated, consistently sought solutions to its members' problems through protection and the Empire. With the Depression biting deeper after 1930, the Federation saw in the Empire a panacea, a collection of 'soft' markets, offering a permanent solution to foreign competition and providing an alternative to industrial reorganisation and cost-cutting.[43] The Trades Union Congress was equally attracted to Imperial remedies to declining exports and rising structural unemployment. Even before the worst phase of the Depression began, trade union representatives engaged in the Mond–Turner talks had called for machinery to direct investment towards colonial development and the stimulation of colonial markets, to which the Labour government's 1929 Colonial Development Act was in part a response.[44]

The Import Duties Act (1932) formally terminated Britain's free-trading era, and was the basis of the agreements on Imperial Preference negotiated at the Imperial Economic Conference at Ottawa in summer 1932. These introduced reciprocal trade preferences throughout the Empire. Britain secured tariff concessions and increased preference for its products in Dominion markets. In return, most Dominion produce was guaranteed free entry to Britain, and increased margins of preference were granted by the imposition of new or additional duties on certain non-Empire goods which competed with Empire exports.[45] For Britain, the purpose of Imperial Preference was to increase domestic employment levels.[46] The Ottawa Agreements were intended to increase trade within the Commonwealth countries in the face of contracting world trade and increasing economic nationalism.[47] The British Government's fear of overseas manufacturing competition was demonstrated in the post-Ottawa tariff régime, under which the highest rates of duty fell on manufactures and semi-manufactured imports, and the lowest on food and raw materials.[48]

The hopes raised by Ottawa were not, on the whole, fulfilled.[49] Although British exports to the Empire rose, they did not reach metropolitan industrialists' expectations.[50] Instead of increasing Britain's total volume of exports, Imperial Preference diverted exports from non-Empire markets to Empire markets, increasing Britain's dependence on the latter and reducing the incentive for export industries to rationalise and concentrate on producing more competitive lines.[51] Nevertheless, the idea of Imperial autarky proved unrealistic, although it was another 20 years before policy-makers digested this and its implications.

The inherent weakness in Imperial Preference was that the

major economies of the empire depended more on *extra*-Imperial trade than on markets within the bloc, and it proved impossible to find alternative markets within the Empire.[52] Furthermore, it became increasingly apparent that there was little community of economic interest among its members.[53] The central flaw in the Imperial economic system envisaged by Britain was its implicit mercantilism, which assumed a simplistic pattern of trade, with Britain supplying manufactures to the primary producing Dominions and colonies. As such, the strategy arose from the metropolitan government's growing alarm in the later 1920s at protectionism within the Dominions which was geared to safeguard infant industries, a concern which had encouraged speculation between 1928 and 1932 about the possibility of 'Imperial rationalisation' and the sharing of markets.[54] Whereas the Ottawa Agreements enabled the Dominions to secure 'safer' markets for their primary produce, they also made it possible for the Dominions to maintain relatively high protection against British goods and so to reduce their dependence on Britain. While Britain took a larger share of its imports from the empire after 1932, the Dominions did not reciprocate.[55] Moreover, the Agreements did little to curb industrialisation in the Dominions, which may explain London's concern to limit similar developments in the colonial Empire, and to reinforce trading links with the more easily manipulated colonial economies.[56]

In 1933, Imperial Preference was applied to the colonial Empire.[57] The Ottawa Agreements generally benefited the Dominions more than the colonies.[58] However, policy-makers in London appreciated that colonial governments, often heavily dependent on trade-derived revenues, could not be expected to waive the duties they levied on British goods, especially in the light of recurring budgetary crises in the 1930s.[59] The colonies received the same rights of access to the metropolitan market as did the Dominions regarding manufactures. However, they did not enjoy the same privileges as British exports in Dominion and Indian markets, unless specifically negotiated by the British government.[60] The direct effects of Ottawa for the colonial economies were negligible. In particular, little safeguarding was secured for tropical produce, chiefly because Britain's capacity for such imports was limited, and because the Agreements did nothing to limit competition between primary producers *within* the Empire.[61] Moreover, existing treaty obligations curtailed the application of Imperial Preference to the colonies. Thus, in West Africa, the Agreements could be applied to Sierra Leone and the Gambia, but, because of the Anglo–French Treaty of 1898, not to Nigeria or the Gold Coast. In the latter, therefore, both British and foreign goods paid low tariff rates, though it remained open to British colonial authorities to impose quantitative limits, or quotas, on foreign imports.[62] On the other hand, after 1932, exports from all the territories of British West Africa were exempted from duties in Britain.

The consequences of Imperial Preference made possible two broad conclusions. The first was that attempts at Imperial autarky were doomed to failure, given the fundamental divergence of interests between Britain and the Dominions, and that the future lay with a gradual liberalisation of world trade, founded on bilateral trading agreements, for example with the United States. This was, in effect, the broad lesson digested by the Board of Trade in the late 1930s, forming the intellectual framework for that department's re-conversion to multilateralism after 1939.[63]

The second available conclusion was that while it might no longer be politically possible for Britain to manipulate the Dominions' economies in her own interests, it was still possible to safeguard the metropolitan stake in colonial markets. This approach, 'the line of least resistance', appealed to sections of the hard-pressed British export sector, like the cotton industry, which otherwise faced phenomenal adjustment problems if they were to survive against new competition. It was this second conclusion which, consciously or not, underpinned the British government's treatment of the colonial empire in the 1930s. While export markets throughout the world contracted, London not only sought to consolidate those markets which it could control, particularly in the colonies, but also discouraged the development of colonial industries which might further denude the market share of British exporters.[64] Moreover, metropolitan notions of complementarity between the home and colonial economies were actually reinforced in this period. This was expressed in a series of responses whose effect was to create an environment hostile to colonial industrialisation. Against entrenched opposition from the Treasury and the Board of Trade, the Colonial Office, even had it been sympathetic to such development, was virtually powerless to influence policy.[65]

The potential value ascribed to the colonial empire by inter-war metropolitan governments explains the passage of the Colonial Development Act in 1929, specifically designed as a measure to 'aid and develop agriculture and industry in the Colonies, Protectorates and Mandated Territories, and thereby promote commerce with or industry in the United Kingdom'. The Act was consciously intended to create demand for the exports of ailing British industries, and to be a long-term measure to combat domestic unemployment.[66]

The Act provided one million pounds per annum for colonial development, to be administered through a Colonial Development Advisory Committee (CDAC), based in London, which scrutinised applications for assistance.[67] The Act, which embodied Britain's colonial aid policy until 1940, produced disappointing results. The annual grant ceiling of one million pounds was never reached, mainly because of the paucity of schemes submitted by individual colonies. A central weakness in the Act was that the initiative for submitting schemes lay solely with the colonial governments, few of whom had the resources, capital or human, to produce effective development schemes, let alone coherent programmes.[68] This problem continued to be a major theme in the development debate conducted by officials during the late 1930s and 1940s.

Approval tended to be given to a limited range of development schemes, especially those concerning internal transport and communications, and public health.[69] These were not the large-scale projects envisaged by the Act's enthusiasts, the average cost being a mere £27,000. Only a tiny proportion of the total funds distributed, 1.2 per cent, went to schemes for industrial development, although the CDAC rejected only five such proposals. The kind of industrial projects helped were mostly concerned with food processing.[70] Again, the major obstacle seems to have been the failure of colonial governments to put forward proposals for manufacturing rather than any conscious obstruction on the part of the CDAC.

The Colonial Development Act did not, therefore, significantly expand the colonial market for capital goods, which remained small, being confined mostly to materials necessary for agriculture and the extractive industries. A further limiting factor was the decline of colonial government revenues, which reduced the prospects for State-financed 'pump-priming' development, combined with difficulties in attracting investment in primary production at a time of low commodity prices.[71] The colonies were, therefore, principally a market for consumer goods. For instance, West Africa's major imports were textiles, foodstuffs, motor vehicles and petroleum, of which Britain was the main source.[72]

A clear illustration of metropolitan interest in the colonies, and one which led directly to intervention by the British government on behalf of exporters is the West African market for cotton textiles. Textiles were one of the most important sectors of Britain's West African trade. For example, clothing and textiles usually accounted for some 20 per cent of the Gold Coast's total imports, a figure nearer to 30 per cent during the more affluent 1920s. The greater part of this trade was in lengths of printed cottons, from which clothes were made locally.[73]

The decline of the British cotton industry between the wars was largely due to the contraction of traditional export markets and to the presence of new foreign competition after 1918. Between 1929 and 1932 alone, Britain's cotton exports were almost halved. The key problem was the loss of traditional overseas markets, above all India, for cheaper piece-goods such as grey cloths. The Indian market shrank as a local cotton industry developed behind protective tariffs. Politically, devolution in India between the wars made it increasingly difficult for British manufacturers to secure intervention on their behalf. An additional problem, first in India but later elsewhere, was Japanese competition. During the 1930s, Indian imports of cotton goods from Japan exceeded those from Britain but, by then, India's total imports of cottons had fallen significantly. Nevertheless, it was local factory production in India, rather than Japanese competition, that was chiefly responsible for the decline in British exports.[74]

Because of this pressure on their traditional markets, British cotton manufacturers became increasingly sensitive to the further erosion of markets by foreign competition. They were particularly concerned to counter Japanese competition in colonial markets. In West Africa, for instance, rapid inroads were made by cotton goods from Japan in the early 1930s. In 1932, for example, the Gold Coast imported only one per cent of its total cotton goods from Japan. By 1934, the figure had risen to 18 per cent. This alarmed Lancashire interests which sought protection for Britain's market share. The result was the imposition in May 1934 of textile quotas, designed to restrict imports of Japanese cottons into West Africa. These quotas were based on an average calculated from imports during the period 1927–31. On this basis, Japan was given a quota of only two-and-a-half per cent. The result was a considerable reduction in the level of Japanese imports. In Nigeria and the Gold Coast, quotas were extended to imports from all foreign countries in 1937.[75]

The quota system did little to restore Lancashire's fortunes. Although Japanese competition was muzzled, other Asian cotton goods producers, including India and Hong Kong, benefited, since they could produce goods closer in price to the ousted Japanese articles than could Britain. However, although in 1933 only eight per cent of Britain's total exports of cottons went to 'quota' colonies, between 1933 and 1938 these same exports fell by only eight per cent, compared to the 23 per cent decline in the same trade with other Empire countries.[76] Here, then, is the key to Lancashire's continuing interest in colonial markets. While they could not compensate for market losses elsewhere, they were secure markets. As their attraction strengthened, so did Lancashire's desire to keep them secure.

Incidents such as the textile quota case illustrate the seriousness with which sectors of British manufacturing industry viewed the threat of foreign competition in colonial markets. During the 1930s there was also growing concern at the prospect of industries in Britain suffering as a result of competition arising from the development of colonial industries. The immediacy of this danger arose as a result of the Ottawa Agreements. Whereas the Import Duties Act had imposed tariffs on Japanese goods, for instance, these did not apply to colonial manufactures. This had encouraged the production of items such as footwear and tyres for export, notably in the eastern dependencies, such as Malaya and Hong Kong.[77]

In 1934, the Cabinet appointed an inter-departmental committee, composed of representatives of the Colonial Office, the Dominions Office and the Board of Trade, to examine colonial industrial development. The Committee recommended that colonial industries should not be 'artificially' encouraged, and that colonial labour conditions should be brought closer into line with those in Britain in order to tackle competition from 'sweated' labour – an issue which produced constant complaints from British manufacturers.[78]

When the Committee's report came before the Cabinet in June

1934, a confrontation was triggered between the Colonial Office and the Treasury. The Colonial Secretary, Cunliffe-Lister, conceded that colonial industry might affect British export interests but argued that obstruction was pointless since other colonial powers might adopt a more liberal attitude to manufacturing, and then opportunities within Britain's colonies might be missed. However, he saw no reason to give positive encouragement to colonial industrialisation, believing that it was more appropriate for the colonies to concentrate on primary production, which seemed likely to remain their chief activity for the time being.[79] All Cunliffe-Lister sought from the Cabinet was agreement that 'we should endeavour to get all the advantages we possibly could for the Colonial Empire in tariff negotiations provided this involved no prejudice or damage to the United Kingdom.'[80] The Treasury could not accept this. Neville Chamberlain, chancellor of the Exchequer, distinguished between Hong Kong, which already had a substantial industrial sector, and colonies in Africa, which possessed little or no industry, and argued that separate policies were needed for different colonies:

> While it was improbable that west Africa would set up factories to compete with those at home, there was a real and serious danger of such factories being established in Malaya and possibly other parts of the Colonial Empire, and we might well be faced with very serious developments of a problem of industrial competition of which we had already had some experience in the case of India.[81]

The metropolitan government, then, appeared unenthusiastic about colonial industrialisation. Progress with such development seemed, therefore, to require *local* initiatives, whether private or public.

Expatriate capital and colonial manufacturing

The obvious source of entrepreneurial drive was the expatriate trading firms operating in West Africa, the region's largest reservoir of capital and commercial expertise. A small number of firms, among whom the United Africa Company was the largest, dominated the region's economy. As the strongest and most organised expression of private capital in West Africa, the firms seemed to be the natural focus for economic development in the region. However, they remained indifferent to industrialisation before the Second World War, a factor seen by some as having been crucial in retarding such development.[82]

Far from being a dynamic agent of economic development, the expatriate firms had, by the 1930s, become conservative, defending their interests in familiar activities and avoiding diversification and its attendant risks. The firms' operations were relatively unsophisticated, profits depending on maximising trade between Britain and West Africa.[83] Their primary role was to evacuate tropical produce to metropolitan and other industrial markets, in return supplying African producers with European consumer goods.[84]

The firms' lack of interest in manufacturing between the wars arose from the fact that their expertise was essentially commercial rather than industrial, and that manufacturing, in African conditions, was considered difficult and risky. A further disincentive was the possible erosion of the firms' import trade, and the probable decline in income from their shipping interests.[85] Furthermore, while commodity price patterns between the wars were erratic, consumer goods prices, sales of which accounted largely for the firms' profits, rose comparatively steadily in the same period. Crucially, perhaps, the firms saw little evidence before the Second World War that West African markets were large enough to sustain local industry.[86]

Generally speaking, the firms shunned the kind of long-term capital investment required for diversification into colonial industry, preferring the manoeuvrability that was possible with short-term commitments and limiting their local reinvestment to the minimum necessary to secure a satisfactory return. Once these modest goals had been safeguarded by the firms' creation of an effective oligopoly in the late 1930s, the appeal of venturing into unproven and unpredictable activities was slight.[87]

The European firms did not ignore manufacturing possibilities entirely. For example, as we have seen, the antecedents of the UAC, itself formed in 1929 after a succession of mergers, established a soap factory at Lagos in 1923, which used local palm-oil, but this remained a very small-scale operation until the outbreak of war in 1939, after which the rocketing cost of imported soap stimulated local production.[88] On the other hand, the expatriate firms also had important interests in processing primary produce. For example, the UAC's palm-oil interests fed metropolitan soap production by the parent company, Unilever, and local soap production would therefore have affected the latter's export sales. Because produce processing might have formed the basis for local industrialisation, the general indifference of the firms was an important obstacle to such development.[89]

The attitudes of colonial governments

In view of the expatriate firms' apathy, the question remains whether colonial governments might have promoted manufacturing. The inter-war colonial governments have been accused of discouraging the growth of local manufacturing in the interests of securing the colonies as markets for British industry and as sources of raw materials.[90] This interpretation, however, risks over-simplifying the complex metropolitan–colonial relationship, reducing the colonial governments to the status of puppets of London, and ignoring both the interests which territorial governments sought to further in their own right and the considerable freedom of action enjoyed by these governments under devolved British rule.

To examine the possible role that colonial governments might have played in promoting local manufacturing requires an assessment of contemporary thinking on the proper role of colonial administrators in economic management and of the extent to which this may have been changed fundamentally by the experience of the Depression, against a metropolitan background of increased, albeit reluctant, State intervention. In Britain between the wars, there was a growing acceptance of the need for greater government involvement in the economy. This was less an ideological conversion than a sequence of pragmatic responses to changing economic conditions, taken in an *ad hoc* fashion, often in order to protect private investors' interests. Thus measures to encourage rationalisation and cartelisation in agriculture and heavy industry in this period took Britain closer to being a 'mixed' economy, and marked a definite rejection of laissez faire orthodoxy. However, in seeking to restore the profitability of private enterprise, the National Government after 1931 left the administration of many of these measures to private enterprise itself.[91]

As Pearce has argued, the colonial governments between the wars did not adhere slavishly to *laissez faire* ideas.[92] They encouraged new export crops and improved techniques in agriculture, produce inspection, and the provision of rudimentary health and education services. Above all, they provided the basic transport facilities necessary for economic development and for the evacuation of primary export produce. Indeed, a major criticism of the colonial governments has been that they facilitated, and ultimately reinforced, the primary export trade of the colonies, maintaining the latter at a level of 'underdevelopment' advantageous to the metropolitan economy.[93] However, as Pearce again comments, prior to the Second World War, these activities never amounted to anything approaching economic 'management'. Generally, government involvement in economic affairs was reluctant, limited to providing essential services which no-one else seemed willing or able to provide. It has already been noted that the large expatriate firms preferred to avoid long-term investment in West Africa of the kind demanded by the establishment of an infrastructure. An expanded role for the State was therefore unavoidable. As Frankel found, of the total capital invested in the Gold Coast and Nigeria between 1870 and 1936, about half came from public sources. Therefore, even if the sums involved were relatively modest, the contribution of government at least matched that of private enterprise.[94] Nevertheless, the colonial governments saw their role as being to facilitate private investment, which, by stimulating economic development, would ultimately raise local living standards.[95] The corollary of the governments' approach to economics was that they avoided participation in *production*, and, with few exceptions, avoided the public ownership of enterprises.[96]

The Depression challenged assumptions that the colonial economies required minimal State intervention, especially when the modest progress with development since 1918 was effectively halted by the trade slump and the resulting collapse of government revenues.[97] Ironically, State intervention was least possible at the very time when it was most needed.[98] Nevertheless, the lie had been given to the old belief that capital investment in profitable enterprises would naturally stimulate economic development and promote higher standards of colonial welfare. The most important consequence of the Depression was a deepening official belief, shared by a growing number of metropolitan observers, that effective colonial development had to be *planned*.[99] Market forces alone no longer guaranteed prosperity. As (Sir) Keith Hancock remarked, 'Adam Smith seems to be deserting West Africa when he has only scratched the surface of his ... task'.[100] He concluded that the collapse of the commodity market and the demonstrable inadequacy of free trade called for more active policies from the colonial state.[101]

Constraining the activities of colonial governments in this period was the orthodoxy, repeatedly emphasised by the Treasury, that colonial budgets should be balanced and should not place burdens on metropolitan revenues. The belief in locally-financed colonial development was only gradually relinquished.[102] This 'unfortunate tradition of fiscal rectitude'[103] drew particular criticism from Governor Bourdillon of Nigeria, whose own budgetary difficulties led him to canvass the Colonial Office for a revision of development policy.[104] The doctrine of self-sufficiency pre-supposed that the colonies could raise their own capital, the opportunities for which were severely circumscribed. For example, local private resources were meagre, with colonial capital accumulation in its infancy and local banking facilities largely undeveloped. For the more prosperous colonies, the London money markets remained the largest source of loan capital, although they normally functioned without British government assistance. Moreover, during the Depression, many colonies could not afford commercial loans. For example, in the 1930s the Gold Coast had to abandon development financed through foreign loans.[105] Furthermore, sluggish commodity prices deterred British investors.[106] In 1936, British investment in East and West Africa combined amounted to only two per cent of Britain's total overseas assets.[107]

Perhaps the most important restraint on the activities of colonial governments during the 1930s was their declining revenue from trade. The West African governments were dangerously dependent on indirect taxation – especially on export and import duties. This situation was acceptable when commodity prices were buoyant, but when trade slumped, the governments were left perilously exposed. This can be seen from the effects of the trade depression on West African governments' total expenditure. Direct taxation existed in neither the Gold Coast nor Nigeria before the Second World War. A hostile political reaction had caused the abandonment of the Gold Coast's attempt to introduce an income tax in 1932.[108] This unhealthy colonial dependence on indirect revenue troubled the Colonial Office. When the review of development policy was in progress, concern was voiced at the bias towards regressive taxation.[109] Moreover, when Bourdillon proposed to introduce an income tax in Nigeria in 1939, MacDonald and the Colonial Office supported him, despite strong protests from the UAC and representatives of British commercial interests.[110]

Given the colonial governments' dependence on trade revenue, expanded public services seemed to hinge on maximising the commodity export sector. In this context, import-substituting local industry, which would reduce import revenue as well as diverting effort from export agriculture, was inevitably unattractive to colonial governments. Furthermore, the infrastructure needed by industrialisation threatened to place greater demands on public expenditure. Nor was lost tariff revenue likely to be matched by increased income from taxation on industrial wages and profits.[111]

As we have already suggested, the operations of the Colonial Development Act did little to further the development of colonial manufacturing. Fundamentally, the Act was intended to provide *loans* to colonial governments, or to help defray the cost of loans raised by the governments themselves, pre-supposing once again that the latter could borrow. However, many governments entered the Depression heavily indebted and reluctant to increase their debts to sponsor development, let alone industrialisation.[112] A further limiting factor was that for much of this period, colonial governments were ill-equipped for economic intervention – as, arguably, was the Colonial Office itself. A basic problem was the scarcity of personnel, a difficulty aggravated by retrenchment in the 1930s.[113] The gradual development of more interventionist policies in the later 1930s called for a major overhaul of the machinery of government, a task impeded by inadequate revenues.[114] Nevertheless, manpower problems were severe, and establishments only began to resume their pre-Depression levels after 1945.[115] The weakened condition of the colonial governments in this period underlined the inadequacy of the Colonial Development Act, which required the initiative in submitting development proposals to come from the colonial governments.[116]

Compounding these practical obstacles to a more active State role in colonial economies, arguably, was the outlook of administrators themselves. Throughout the inter-war years, this outlook continued to be permeated by the 'trusteeship' doctrine, which retained its largely negative influence even after the weaknesses in traditional colonial rule had been exposed in the later 1930s. However, there were perfectly rational, if unsophisticated, motives for administrative conservatism in economic matters between the wars, grounded in an overriding preoccupation with maintaining political stability as cheaply as possible. From the governments' point of view, when confronted with subsistence economies and under-utilised local resources, African welfare could best be promoted by encouraging primary production for export.

These considerations explain why the colonial governments gave little direct assistance to industrialisation before the Second World War. For instance, governments commonly refused to grant tariff protection to industry, and offered neither subsidies nor credit. To survive, local industry had to compete with imports on equal terms. Moreover, in West Africa, colonial governments restricted the settlement of Europeans and Lebanese ('Syrians'), who were both potential sources of manufacturing enterprise, chiefly because they feared a hostile African response and because of a selectively applied paternalistic desire to 'protect' Africans from foreign competition.[117] Even when metropolitan development funds became available after 1929, few colonial governments submitted proposals for industrial schemes, those which did reach London often being concerned with small food-processing projects.[118] In short, colonial governments made little attempt to overcome the many obstacles to local industrialisation.[119]

The views of the Colonial Office

Because of its demanding role as representative of both British and colonial interests, and as theoretical mediator between them, the Colonial Office's attitudes towards colonial industrialisation are of particular importance. A fundamental question is whether the Colonial Office was sympathetic to local manufacturing, or whether, like other branches of Whitehall and the colonial governments, it was wary of such developments. Opinion on this question is divided. Meredith, for example, has argued that, on balance, the Office did nothing to assist the promotion of colonial industry in this period, for example by providing guidance, training and improved credit facilities or subsidies.[120] Drummond, meanwhile, claims that although the Office did little to assist industrialisation, it did not *obstruct* it, nor did it want to. In his view, the question was largely ignored by the Office, probably because few officials saw much potential for manufacturing.[121]

What seems clear, however, is that the Office feared the risks associated with tariff protection for infant industries, a theme which dominated official discussions on industrialisation. A significant measure of the extent to which opinion in the later 1930s was drifting away from the shibboleths of 'trusteeship', counter-arguments to industrial development on the grounds that it would disturb traditional societies were relatively sparse. It was not industrialisation *per se* which caused official anxiety, but the measures needed to promote it. For example, reviewing development policy in November 1938, Gerard Clauson, the assistant secretary heading the Economic Department, spoke of manufacturing without apparent concern: '*Prima facie* such projects are to be welcomed, if they are really well designed to add to the wealth of the community', although he admitted that judging this was difficult.[122] Generally, where industries occurred 'naturally' and required no government assistance, the Colonial Office raised no objections.[123]

Officials feared 'artificial' tariff protection for two reasons. First, uneconomic industries might be encouraged, unable to withstand normal competition or achieve self-sufficiency, passing on to local consumers the cost of their uncompetitiveness:

> manufacturing industry, which can be established in a colony only at the price of a monopoly protected by a high tariff, ends in producing a locally manufactured article which is too expensive for the primary agricultural producers to buy.[124]

These anxieties persisted well into the war and surfaced regularly in official discussions on post-war development planning. Furthermore, quite rationally, officials, like their counterparts in the field, feared that colonial government revenues, often already threadbare, would suffer from declining import income caused by local industry. Secondly, British manufacturers were bound to oppose the development of protected colonial industry. The Colonial Office's policy was 'to oppose the establishment in the Colonial Empire of a new industry which is likely to affect adversely the interests of established United Kingdom industries.'[125] Whether government revenues or British industry's protests were uppermost in officials' minds, the consequence for policy was the same. Wherever possible, the Office blocked tariff protection to new industries, as in the case of the Ugandan government's request in 1937 for permission to shield a local cotton weaving industry.[126] While the rest of the world abandoned free trade, the Colonial Office still prescribed it for the colonies.[127]

The search for policy guidelines

The question of colonial industrialisation was revived by the Colonial Office towards the end of 1936, having being 'pending' for over two years. It was inconvenient for the Colonial Office to have no clear guidelines when it was being asked repeatedly to sanction industrial projects. Ideally, what was needed was an unambiguous statement from the British Cabinet.[128] Consequently, the Colonial Secretary, William Ormsby-Gore, agreed to appoint a new interdepartmental committee to re-examine the question. However, the whole proposal aroused strong Treasury opposition, and problems were encountered in composing a suitable committee, so that work did not commence until late February 1937.[129] The committee's terms of reference were to 'consider and report how far it is desirable to frame and pursue a policy either to encourage or to discourage the establishment of industrial enterprises in the Colonial Empire.' It was composed of representatives from the Bank of England, the Treasury, the Board of Trade, the India Office, the Dominions Office and the Colonial Office.[130]

Progress, however, was slow. By spring 1938, with no report ready, the Colonial Office grew impatient. The committee examined papers prepared by the Colonial Office, relating to proposed schemes which had caused it concern. The problem common to them all was that they involved fiscal concessions from the local government, whether through tariff protection, the waiving of a countervailing excise or unrestricted imports of a raw material. In each case, both the Colonial Office and the individual government concerned had condoned the concession, and the cumulative effect appeared to be a policy of tacit encouragement of colonial manufacturing. What was necessary was an authoritative ruling on whether this practice should continue.[131]

Eventually, in December 1938, the Colonial Office produced a draft report on the committee's behalf.[132] Based on the findings of the earlier Vernon Committee, it predicted that colonial industrialisation would be slow, handicapped by the small size of colonial markets, their consequent low purchasing power and the resulting barriers to economies of scale, the difficulty of finding overseas markets for colonial manufactures, and the fact that local labour was usually unskilled, a problem which cancelled out the advantage of low wages and actually made labour costs relatively high.[133] Although the report argued that the extent of 'unfair' competition from cheap labour, for example in Hong Kong, was exaggerated, it also considered that competition would be unfair if a colony subordinated welfare to cost-cutting, and that working conditions should therefore be monitored closely. In addressing the labour issue, the Colonial Office may have had two related motives: first, to assuage metropolitan fears, regularly voiced between the wars, of unfair competition from 'sweated' labour and, secondly, to win support from other government departments for the reform of colonial labour legislation which it was anxious to promote both for political and humanitarian reasons (only months earlier the Office had appointed its first labour adviser), and for a more active policy on colonial welfare.

The report said relatively little about ways of promoting colonial industry, except that governments might invest in particular schemes, guarantee the interest on private investments, remit taxation, grant monopoly privileges and provide facilities such as communications. However, it concluded that the most common form of government assistance was likely to remain tariff protection, and it was this controversial question which occupied the greater part of the report. Tariff protection, it was claimed, involved disadvantages – at least initially. First, where a duty was already imposed for revenue purposes, and manufacturing developed behind the shield it unintentionally provided, then imports of the goods involved would probably decline, causing a loss of revenue. Secondly, where a duty was imposed explicitly in order to protect an existing or projected industry, the price of the manufacture concerned was likely to rise, harming the local consumer.

The report doubted whether temporary protection could be applied, until a new industry was established, its labour force became skilled, and the enterprise had reached an economic size. Nor did it accept that, once fully fledged, an industry could bear an excise duty equivalent to any import duty imposed on the type of goods it manufactured, or that temporary protection would enable the price of local manufactures to be pegged at the world level in cases where the welfare of the consumer was of prime concern. On the contrary, 'infant' industries were 'notoriously' slow in reaching maturity, and once protection was granted, it tended to be retained, even if the industry which it supported proved uneconomic. Such an industry might prompt local calls for *further* protection to prevent its collapse. Protection given in these circumstances would perpetuate, or even increase, the disadvantages facing colonial manufacturing. The report therefore concluded that import duties higher than the excise duty on a local product were unjustifiable.

The report was equally cautious about the supposed benefits to primary producers of industries based on local raw materials, thereby providing a more secure market for them than could the export market alone. This in itself did not justify protection:

> Unless the proposed industry has a genuine prospect of standing on its own feet after the initial stages, it may well be argued that some form of direct assistance to the primary producers – for example, a Government subsidy which can be discontinued when the world price recovers – is a surer and less costly method of achieving the desired object.

However, if industrialisation would develop, and not merely maintain, the use of local raw materials, then there was a strong case for protection, provided that the industry was planned on 'sound' lines, and seemed likely, after an initial period, to be able to withstand normal competition. Similarly, where there were 'special considerations', such as the need to find employment for a growing population, or where the strength of 'unofficial' opinion made industrial development politically desirable, government assistance was justified, but only if the proposed development would benefit the whole community, a qualification which the report admitted was difficult to determine. Nevertheless, industrialisation was unlikely to be beneficial unless it was *planned* and promised to become *self-supporting*. Otherwise, government support could 'hardly' be considered.

Turning to Imperial trade, the report saw no need to adjust preferences, although it argued that colonial governments should not encourage hopes that local manufacturers would enjoy indefinite preferential treatment in Britain and the Dominions. Although warning that the imposition of high import duties by colonies in order to encourage local industries might restrict trade within the Empire, damaging the interests of other members, the report took a sanguine view, suggesting that successful colonial industrialisation would increase local purchasing power, indirectly creating new, enlarged markets for Imperial goods, in turn increasing colonial import revenues.

The report's concluding recommendations summarised these arguments. The first suggestion was that colonial governments should impose excise duties on locally manufactured goods equivalent to any import duties levied on similar imported goods, though no excise was considered necessary if the import duty was so small as to provide little protection, or if the administrative costs of levying an excise cancelled out any benefit to the government concerned. Colonial governments were also to warn would-be entrepreneurs that this excise would be payable.

The second recommendation was that colonial governments should monitor industrial development closely. The third was that, where a proposed industry would depend on special government assistance, tariff protection or privileges, then the proposal should be referred for approval to the Colonial Secretary where the constitutional position permitted this. The report gave detailed guidance on the information which London would require, including an assessment of the industry's promoters and the capital at their disposal, details of the capacity and cost of the proposed factory and on sources of raw materials, information on existing import duties and the revenue they yielded, together with a list of the chief sources from which the local market was currently supplied. Details would also be sought on the cost of the manufacture, its potential consumers and relative importance in the average consumer's budget, the colony's likely consumption of the product and any reasons for supposing that this would rise, plus an explanation of how the projected development would benefit the community. This emphasis on close monitoring arose out of concern at previous gaps in London's knowledge of local developments. The report concluded that a co-ordinated policy required full information to be supplied to London in all cases because tariffs imposed for revenue purposes were always potentially protective in effect, and because industries were sometimes established on the assumption that a tariff, once granted, would remain in force, while no corresponding excise would be levied on a local product.

The report's final point was that colonial governments should not discourage industrial development arising from 'natural' growth, since this would contravene the principles of trusteeship. Equally, they ought not neglect colonial welfare, given the potentially unwelcome social effects of industrialisation – for example, on labour relations. For this reason it was thought important that working conditions be safeguarded, for instance by applying the various International Labour Conventions, to avoid the abuses common elsewhere in the early stages of industrial development.[134]

The draft report of the Inter-Departmental Committee faithfully reflected the Colonial Office's *ad hoc* position when dealing with proposals for industrial development, yet it was a disappointment to the Office, which had hoped to extract a much clearer statement of policy from the government.[135] As Sir John Campbell commented:

> It is altogether too dangerous, too full of explosive possibilities, too little susceptible of reduction to clear formulae, for a report which will presumably be circulated generally and will doubtless be published eventually, or leak out eventually.

In the view of Sir Henry Moore, an assistant under-secretary, unusual among his colleagues in that he had formerly been a colonial governor, the report had probably gone as far as was possible, given that 'a more forward policy would alarm the home manufacturers'.[136] Perhaps it had, after all, been too ambitious to attempt to formulate a policy applicable across an extremely diverse dependent empire.[137]

The Treasury, too, was dissatisfied with the draft report, having hoped for a tougher line to be taken on uncounterveiled duties and 'unsound' industrialisation. Against the background of accelerating domestic rearmament, Treasury officials resorted to the traditional argument that since Britain bore the full cost of colonial defence, it could legitimately demand a right to control colonial tariff policy.[138]

In the event, the report was not put before Cabinet. It is not surprising that, late in 1938, the Colonial Office was reluctant to press the matter, because it had already embarked on the delicate process of negotiating with the Treasury a promise to underwrite the new colonial development and welfare policy. As these discussions were bound to be difficult and protracted there was every reason for the Colonial Office to avoid antagonising the Treasury by being inflexible over protection. It is possible, too, that the Board of Trade was reluctant to see this question raised at a time when, following the growing recognition that the policy of

Imperial Preference had failed to expand British trade, negotiations on a liberalisation of trade were in progress with the United States – a country traditionally hostile to the alleged benefits accruing to Britain from its possession of an Empire to which foreign exporters had restricted access.[139]

Yet if the Colonial Office was obliged to exercise great tact when dealing with other departments, irritation could still be vented privately at the treatment of the colonies. In June 1939, for example, Moore attacked his colleagues for their failure to confront opponents at home, complaining of the convention that

> any proposals, whether in the field of industry or tariffs, which give rise to any conflict of economic interest, should be approached from the stand-point that the United Kingdom trade interests must rank first, Dominions' trade interests second, and those of the colonies last.[140]

It is also notable that the report, while discussing the potential *dis*advantages of colonial industrialisation in detail, said little about its potential benefits. This may reflect a lingering ambivalence in the Colonial Office's attitudes towards the entire subject. Although, as has been suggested, the Office did not generally try to obstruct such development in this period, manufacturing was a minor consideration for metropolitan officials, who remained preoccupied with the disposal of colonial primary produce. Moreover, in view of recent international developments, and the likely demands of rearmament at home, the metropolitan funding available for colonial development would probably be less than many officials had previously hoped. It was therefore all the more important that existing resources be put to the best use.[141] This suggested a need to concentrate on agricultural development, and on providing whatever welfare services were possible. The central point, then, may be that on the broad canvas of colonial development, industrialisation remained largely a hypothetical question until agricultural living standards had been substantially improved.[142] Nor was this an exclusively official interpretation. As Fieldhouse has pointed out, Sir Keith Hancock's *Survey of British Commonwealth Affairs*, a monumental exposition of contemporary thinking on colonial issues, second in importance only to Hailey's *African Survey*, was remarkably silent on the possible role of industrialisation. Although published in 1942, Hancock's work was completed before the outbreak of war.

While searching in its analysis of other aspects of colonial economics, it apparently shared the outlook of the Colonial Office, namely that successful industries grew naturally, and were built on the foundations of improved agriculture.[143] On the other hand, in a document such as the draft report of the Inter-Departmental Committee, in which the Colonial Office was trying to secure the acquiescence of departments traditionally hostile to colonial manufacturing, it would have been imprudent for the Office to dwell on the positive aspects of colonial manufacturing. Its purpose was to steer its recommendations as quietly as possible through the machinery of Whitehall, and to avoid giving any impression that a wave of industrialisation would follow.

NOTES

1. Hopkins (1973), esp. pp.167–86.
2. Brett (1973), pp.72, 115–6.
3. Ibid., p.71–2.
4. Pearce, 'The Colonial Economy', in Ingham and Simmons (1987), p.267; Latham (1981), pp.122, 174–5.
5. B. Ingham, 'Colonialism and the Economy of the Gold Coast 1919–45' in Ingham and Simmons (1987), p.229.
6. Kilby (1975), pp.490, 492.
7. Pearce (1987), p.267; Hopkins (1973), pp.237–67.
8. Latham (1981), pp.87, 175–6.
9. Ingham (1987), p.229.
10. Hopkins (1973), pp.184–5.
11. Fieldhouse (1982), pp.491–2.
12. Pearce (1982), p.4.
13. Roberts (1986), p.43.
14. D. Killingray, 'The Empire Resources Development Committee and West Africa 1916–20', *JICH*, 10, 2, (Jan. 1982) pp.194–210.
15. A.D. Roberts, 'The Imperial Mind', in Roberts (1986), pp.48–52.
16. Flint (1983), pp.393–4.
17. Constantine (1984), pp.229–30.
18. Johnson (1977), p.56.
19. A.J. Crozier, *Appeasement and Germany's Last Bid for Colonies* (London: Macmillan, 1988).
20. Hargreaves (1988), p.41.
21. CO 847/25/7, 'Memorandum on factors affecting Native Administration Policy', by Cartland, (n.d., but 1946).
22. Constantine (1984), p.303.
23. M. Petter, 'Sir Sydney Caine and the Colonial Office in the Second World War: A Career in the Making', *CJH*, 16, 1, (Apr. 1981), p.68.
24. Constantine (1984), p.303.
25. Petter (1981), p.68.
26. Cmd.6175 *Statement of Policy on Colonial Development and Welfare*, Feb. 1940.
27. Morgan (1980:I), p.89.

28. Bowden (1980), p.69.
29. Constantine (1984), p.253.
30. Lee and Petter (1982), p.45.
31. Fieldhouse (1982), p.486.
32. Constantine (1984), p.255.
33. Meredith (1975), p.499; this point had been stressed by Frankel in Frankel (1938), pp.13–14.
34. Rhodes House Library, Oxford, MSS. Brit. Emp. s.334, Hailey Papers, Address to P.E.P. 'Development of Colonies', 27 Feb. 1939.
35. *Parliamentary Debates (Commons)*, 348, 443, 7 June 1939.
36. Meredith (1976), p.135.
37. Bowden (1980), pp.37, 76.
38. Meredith (1986), p.80. The Board's life was cut short by the outbreak of war in 1939.
39. E.g. Brett (1973), *passim*.
40. Aldcroft (1986), p.45–6.
41. M. Cowen and N.J. Westcott, 'British Imperial Economic Policy During the War', in D. Killingray and R. Rathbone (eds), *Africa and the Second World War* (London: Macmillan, 1986) p.29.
42. Kirby (1981), pp.65–6.
43. R.F. Holland, 'The Federation of British Industries and the international economy', *EcHR*, 2nd ser., 24, 2, (May 1981) pp.287–9; A. Booth and M. Pack, *Employment, Capital and Economic Policy. Great Britain 1918–1939* (Oxford: Blackwell, 1985) pp.90–1.
44. Booth and Pack (1985), pp.99–100.
45. Aldcroft (1986), p.71.
46. Drummond (1974), pp.425–6.
47. S. Pollard, *The Development of the British Economy. Third Edition 1914–1980* (London: Edward Arnold, 1983) p.121.
48. Aldcroft (1986), p.71.
49. Pollard (1983), p.121.
50. Cain and Hopkins, (1987) p.14.
51. Kirby (1981), pp.65, 75.
52. Pollard (1983), pp.121–2.
53. Kirby (1981), pp.65–6.
54. Drummond (1974), p.439.
55. Aldcroft (1986), pp.81–2.
56. Bowden (1980), p.32.
57. Aldcroft (1986), p.71.
58. Ibid., pp.81–2.
59. Drummond (1974), pp.425–6.
60. CO 852/164/6, Clauson to Sir Cosmo Parkinson, 11 Mar. 1938.
61. Hopkins (1973), p.266.
62. Drummond (1974), pp.429–30.
63. A.P. Dobson, *US Wartime Aid to Britain 1940–1946* (London: Croom Helm, 1986) pp.36–7, 67.
64. Brett (1973), pp.274–5.
65. Meredith (1976), p.137.
66. G.C. Abbott, 'A Re-examination of the 1929 Colonial Development Act', *EcHR*, 2nd ser., 24, 1, (Feb. 1971), pp.68–81.
67. Constantine (1984), pp.195–226.
68. Meredith (1975), p.492.
69. Havinden and Meredith (1993), pp.160–7.
70. Meredith (1976), pp.119–20.

71. Cain and Hopkins (1987), p.15.
72. Howard (1978), pp.79–80.
73. Howard (1978), pp.81–2.
74. A. Redford, *Manchester Merchants and Foreign Trade, Volume II, 1850–1939* (Manchester: Manchester University Press, 1956) pp.237–97; C. Dewey, 'The end of the imperialism of free trade: the eclipse of the Lancashire Lobby and the concession of fiscal autonomy to India', in C. Dewey and A.G. Hopkins (eds), *The Imperial Impact: Studies in the Economic History of Africa and India* (London: Athlone Press, 1978) pp.35–67.
75. CO 554/122/33650/1939, minute by Melville, 8 Feb. 1939.
76. N.K. Buxton and D.H. Aldcroft (eds), *British industry between the wars* (London: Scolar Press, 1979), pp.43–4; Brett (1973), p.155.
77. Drummond (1974), p.440.
78. Constantine (1984), p.286.
79. Drummond (1974), p.440.
80. Meredith (1976), p.137.
81. Havinden and Meredith (1993), p.170.
82. See, e.g., Kilby (1975).
83. Fieldhouse (1986), p.47.
84. Hopkins (1973), p.203.
85. Kilby (1975), pp.488, 491.
86. Fieldhouse (1986), p.46.
87. Hopkins (1973), pp.258–60.
88. Fieldhouse (1986), pp.10–11.
89. Fieldhouse (1986), pp.10–11.
90. E.g. Brett (1973), pp.300–311.
91. Kirby (1981), pp.67–8, 78.
92. Pearce (1987), p.266–7.
93. Brett (1973), pp.300–311.
94. Frankel (1938), p.27.
95. Pearce (1987), pp.266–7.
96. Forbes Munro (1984), p.35.
97. Hargreaves (1988), p.42.
98. Forbes Munro (1984), p.31.
99. Hetherington (1978), p.91.
100. W.K. Hancock, *Survey of British Commonwealth Affairs, Volume 11, Problems of Economic Policy 1918–1939, Part Two* (London: Oxford University Press, 1942) p.323.
101. D. Fieldhouse, 'Keith Hancock and Imperial Economic History: A Retrospect Forty Years On' in F. Madden and D.K. Fieldhouse (eds), *Oxford and the Idea of Commonwealth* (London: Croom Helm, 1982) p.159.
102. Constantine (1984), pp.243–4.
103. Drummond (1974), p.436.
104. CO 583/243/30415/1939, despatch from Bourdillon, 5 Apr. 1939. On Bourdillon's career and attitudes, see R.D. Pearce, *Sir Bernard Bourdillon: The Biography of a Twentieth Century Colonialist* (Oxford: The Kensal Press, 1987).
105. Ingham (1987), p.236.
106. Constantine (1984), pp.294–5.
107. Cowen and Westcott (1986), p.27.
108. Crowder (1968), p.207.
109. CO 852/190/15606, memorandum by Clauson, 'Colonial Development Policy for the next few years', 8 Nov. 1938.
110. CO 583/240/30231/1939 Pt. 1, note by O.G.R. Williams, 16 Mar. 1939; letter from Grundy (President, Manchester Chamber of Commerce) to MacDonald, 13 June

1939; letter from Tobey, (Chairman, Liverpool Chamber of Commerce) to MacDonald, 28 June 1939; replies from MacDonald, 23 June and 4 July 1939; CO 583/240/31231/1939 Pt. 2, despatch from Bourdillon, 12 July 1939.

111. Kilby (1975), pp.491–2.
112. Morgan I (1980), pp.60–1.
113. Havinden and Meredith (1993), p.169.
114. Lee and Petter (1982), p.27.
115. Constantine (1984), pp.228–9.
116. Meredith (1976), pp.120, 126.
117. Fieldhouse (1986), p.46.
118. Constantine (1984), p.286.
119. Fieldhouse (1986), p.46.
120. Meredith (1975), pp.497–8.
121. Drummond (1974), pp.440, 442.
122. CO 852/190/15606, memorandum by Clauson, 'Colonial Development Policy for the next few years', 8 Nov. 1938.
123. Meredith (1976), pp.127–8.
124. Meredith (1975), p.497.
125. Meredith (1976), p.136.
126. Constantine (1984), p.287.
127. Meredith (1975), p.498.
128. CO 852/164/6, minute by Clauson, 11 March 1938.
129. Drummond (1974), p.441.
130. CO 852/164/6, 'Revised draft report of the Interdepartmental Committee on the Industrialisation of the Colonial Empire', 29 Dec. 1938.
131. Drummond (1974), p.441.
132. Meredith (1975), p.497; Drummond (1974), p.441.
133. CO 852/164/6, 'Revised draft report of the Interdepartmental Committee on the Industrialisation of the Colonial Empire', 29 Dec. 1938.
134. Ibid.
135. Bowden (1980), p.45.
136. Meredith (1976), pp.134–6.
137. Bowden (1980), p.45.
138. Drummond (1974), p.442.
139. Pressnell (1986), pp. 5, 16–17, 21.
140. Constantine (1984), p.287.
141. CO 852/190/15606, memorandum by Clauson, 'Colonial Development Policy for the next few years', 8 Nov. 1938.
142. Meredith (1976), p.135.
143. Fieldhouse (1982), pp.158–9.

2 The Impact of War on Development Policy, 1939–42

Between September 1939 and the end of 1942, colonial administrators faced exacting challenges. Initially, colonial economic policy was dominated by the need to reduce demands on metropolitan production through reduced consumption, and to protect sterling through currency controls. Although these concerns persisted throughout the period, and beyond the duration of the war itself, from 1942 they were joined by the aim of maximising the colonial contribution to the Allied war effort through the production and evacuation of valuable raw materials.

These tasks left officials little time to reflect on the longer-term issues involved in economic development. Furthermore, officials in London and West Africa still lacked adequate machinery for economic planning. Although this deficiency was recognised, little had been accomplished by the end of 1942 to equip either London or territorial governments to produce, evaluate and implement the integrated programmes of development which metropolitan officials increasingly saw as essential. Despite this, some consideration was given to post-war reconstruction. It is, therefore, possible to trace the evolution in these years of official attitudes to important development themes, including the potential role of manufacturing in securing more diversified production. These attitudes were often shaped in response to local developments which obliged the Colonial Office to raise the subject of industrialisation with its colleagues in Whitehall, to obtain an authoritative policy ruling for transmission to the colonial governments. In the process the Office revealed its own guarded approval for manufacturing development, but other government departments' responses showed a persisting ambiguity towards this question which formed an unsatisfactory basis for the elaboration of policy.

The impact of war

With the outbreak of war, London immediately urged the colonial governments to retrench. The colonial war economy had three central features. First, colonies were asked to reduce or avoid expenditure of foreign currency, especially dollars. Secondly, they were urged to control imports through licensing systems. Finally, they were encouraged to introduce, or extend, direct taxation.[1] Under wartime conditions the development initiative seemed doomed. MacDonald's successor, Lord Lloyd, briefly considered inserting a clause into the Colonial Development and Welfare Bill suspending its operations for the duration of the war. The Treasury, although interested in the economic contribution the colonies could make to the war effort, remained doubtful about the prospects for advancing the 'social' aspect of development. During the 'Phoney War', a working compromise was reached between the Treasury and the Colonial Office but, as conditions deteriorated in the summer of 1940, the Treasury view prevailed. On 11 June 1940, the parliamentary under-secretary, George Hall, warned that little progress could be expected under the new Act because of the shortage of resources and personnel.[2] In September 1940, stringent criteria were set out restricting applications for metropolitan assistance to schemes with a direct bearing on the war effort, which required only local resources.[3] Consequently, except in the West Indies, whose proximity to the still neutral United States convinced Churchill of the political necessity of progress with development, colonial development and welfare provision was all but suspended.[4]

As the war progressed, concern arose in the Treasury that colonial governments were not doing enough to curb non-essential imports and imports from the dollar area. This concern was echoed in the Colonial Office's Economic Department. By May 1940, the need to economise on shipping space took precedence over concern to limit the spending of foreign exchange, and more rigorous import control by colonial governments was required.[5] Lloyd's successor, Lord Moyne, therefore urged governments to restrict imports still further, to save on scarce shipping space and foreign exchange, and to ease the demands on metropolitan production. He called for stricter import licensing, especially on dollar goods. Moyne also requested measures to reduce consumption through increased taxes. This approach had been introduced in Britain, whose taxation levels the colonies were encouraged to emulate.[6] Since September 1939, officials in London and the colonies had been concerned about inflation, which was being fuelled by the shortage of imported goods.[7] Taxation was seen, primarily, as an anti-inflation mechanism, although its extension during the war had important implications for future colonial government revenues.

Initially, London expected that the colonies' chief wartime role would be to supply raw materials and foodstuffs for Britain and its allies. By summer 1940 this view was being revised.[8] At least until 1942, colonial resources were often more a liability than an asset because of the loss of important European markets and the shipping shortage.[9] Before 1939, over 40 per cent of the exports from Britain's African territories had gone to markets *outside* the Empire, mainly in Europe and the USA. Colonial produce often lay unsold and unshippable because of the disruption of normal trade.

For the Colonial Office, the most important legacy of the 1930s was the belief that steps were needed to stabilise primary producers' incomes.[10] The February 1940 *Statement of Policy* recognised the dependence of many colonies on limited agricultural resources. Colonial governments could not depend upon the secure revenues necessary for sustained development because the value of agricultural produce was liable to fluctuate. This had been the underlying economic justification for colonial development and welfare aid. One consequence of producer insecurity, reinforced by the experience of the West African cocoa 'hold-ups' in 1937–38, was officials' interest in methods of regulating produce marketing. In 1938, the Nowell Commission, which investigated the region's marketing structure, recommended state intervention to ensure fairer prices for African producers. Existing 'pooling' arrangements among the largest European trading firms for buying agricultural produce were seen by African producers as a device to depress the prices they received. Despite the intensity of African hostility towards the firms, and despite the Nowell Commission's recommendations for a statutory marketing scheme, the Colonial Office was unwilling to attempt to loosen the oligopoly's hold. Its steps to reactivate the Colonial Empire Marketing Board were intended to assist the existing export trade, for example through market research and technical advice. Although the Office recognised the economic and ultimately the political problems of agricultural over-specialisation, and of the domination of the export trade by the European oligopoly, it lacked the confidence to create an alternative marketing system, fearing obstruction by the firms. This sense of helplessness in the face of what officials saw as inevitable developments towards larger economic units and reduced competition does not necessarily imply official endorsement of the activities of European traders, but suggests that the Colonial Office had not begun to explore seriously the need to extend State economic intervention.

Increasingly, however, wartime economic mobilisation and, later, the need to plan post-war development, undermined this bias towards non-intervention.[11] The growth of produce surpluses, especially of cocoa and oilseeds in West Africa, gave the region's governments strong political arguments for assisting local producers, in order to avoid unrest in wartime.[12] London established the West African Cocoa Control Board in September 1940, to buy cocoa at a fixed price through licenced buying agents, with African producers being promised 'fair' prices.[13]

An alternative, or complement, to stabilising the West African economies through improved produce marketing was economic diversification into new activities such as the production of food crops for local consumption, the processing of raw materials before export, and the manufacture of consumer goods. At the outbreak of war, the Colonial Office did not see industrial development either contributing substantially to the war effort, or providing a solution to long-term colonial economic problems. However, the Office did not obstruct manufacturing industries that showed promise of long-term viability.[14]

In August 1940, Arthur Greenwood, then Minister without Portfolio, assured the Commons that the question of produce surpluses, and the possible establishment of storage and processing facilities in the colonies, were being considered by a sub-committee of the Cabinet's Economic Policy Committee.[15] The extension of controls on non-essential imports into the colonies also prompted questions on the scope for developing import-substituting industries to help meet import shortages. The Colonial Office was initially sceptical about the potential for local manufacturing, because it seemed impossible to supply the necessary machinery from Britain and because exchange restrictions precluded purchases from the USA.[16] In December 1940, the Parliamentary Under-Secretary, George Hall, admitted that little progress had been made in developing manufacturing for war purposes, mainly because of the shortage of necessary plant. Questioned about measures to compensate for the colonies' loss of overseas markets, for example through local processing and manufacturing, Hall replied that the preparation of a statement would involve an unjustifiable amount of work for officials.[17]

However, guarded encouragement for industrialisation emerged during a major Lords debate on colonial economic policy conducted the day before Hall's speech. Replying to Lord Farringdon, a Labour spokesman on colonial affairs, who stressed the importance of freeing the colonies from their over-dependence on raw material exports and demanded assistance for local industrial development, the Colonial Secretary, Lord Lloyd, expressed interest in manufacturing, recognising Britain's duty to help foster healthy colonial economies:

> They should not merely depend upon one industry or upon the export trade of primary products, but, within the range of what is economically sane and sound, you should try to develop a reasonable number of secondary industries in the Crown Colonies.

Though endorsing the desirability of diversification, Lloyd admitted that such a policy would be difficult to implement, and emphasised the mutual duties between Britain and her colonies: 'the Mother Country, whose taxpayers provide large sums for the defence of the Crown Colonies, must have its interests taken into consideration.'[18] In this context, the British 'interests' were those of exporters of manufactured goods.

Economic diversification: the option of manufacturing

Any sketch of the 'official mind' of the Colonial Office in the period 1939–42 on major questions of economic policy depends upon scattered, and relatively rare, statements. Not only was the pressure of business acute, inhibiting long-term reflection. The Colonial Office was also unaccustomed to codifying its economic, or, indeed, other policies, in an accessible form. Clauson, first head of the Office's Economic Department and assistant under-secretary supervising economic matters since 1940, later commented:

> Ever since the Economic Department was formed in 1934, we have regarded it as one of its functions to endeavour to

> promote a common economic doctrine not only within the Office, but also in the Colonial Empire generally. There was no question, until the out-break of the war, of reducing this common economic doctrine to a stated formula. It was rather a question of dealing with problems as they arose in accordance with certain unstated principles, which were inherent in our general policy.[19]

This reluctance to produce generalised policy statements was reinforced by the tradition of discussing problems on a 'geographical' basis, rather than thematically across the colonies. Although waning, this practice continued to find loyal adherents among conservative senior officials, and contributed to a major division of official opinion on how best to pursue development.[20]

Some indication of the Colonial Office's private views on industrial development is provided by its reactions to a memorandum on export trade policy produced by Lord Stamp of the War Cabinet's Economic Secretariat during September 1940.[21] This attracted the Office's attention because the government had accepted the memorandum's recommendations in principle. Its most pertinent sections explained that in wartime it was necessary to examine whether colonial shortages of imported British goods should be eased by steps to produce similar goods locally. The memorandum favoured encouraging 'reasonably economic' colonial industries, especially those based on local produce, which could be established using mainly local labour.[22]

The Colonial Office sent the memorandum to the colonies, although some senior officials questioned its assumptions, especially the definition of 'economic' industries. Sydney Caine, who succeeded Calder as assistant secretary responsible for the Economic Department in 1940, observed that opinions on this question varied considerably:

> The enthusiasts for local industry will regard anything capable of physical operation as reasonably economic irrespective of its cost, while the believers in strict *laissez faire*, if there are any left, will regard nothing as economic which requires a vestige of protection from outside competition.[23]

Clauson, too, advised caution. He claimed that the Economic Department of the Colonial Office was 'wholeheartedly sympathetic' to colonies which seized the opportunity provided by the war to establish 'sound' secondary industries, but he pointed out that wartime conditions were abnormal, and industries introduced under these circumstances might lose their economic justification after the war:

> It would be a disaster if one of the by-products of the war was a monstrous spawning of uneconomic industries in the Colonial Empire, and we should be greatly and rightly blamed if any part of the responsibility for it could be placed upon our shoulders.[24]

Some of these apprehensions were incorporated in Moyne's covering note which accompanied the despatch in March 1941. Fully agreeing with Stamp's argument that economic industry in the colonies should be encouraged, Moyne emphasised that it nevertheless reflected short-term preoccupations: colonial governments would need to take a long-term view. He stressed that a colony would derive little benefit from establishing an industry which could not produce goods comparable in quality and price to those previously imported. The more dependent an industry was on protection, the more likely it was to be a burden rather than an asset, although he recognised that 'special measures' might be needed to counter attempts to 'stifle' a local industry – for example where competitors resorted to 'dumping'.

Secondly, Moyne reminded the colonial governments that he could not overlook British exporters' interests. Most colonies, he contended, benefited from their links with Britain, notably in the field of defence (a timely example), and he felt that, while local interests remained paramount, industrial development should be tailored to do the least damage to British exporters. Moreover, the entire market of a colony ought not be reserved for local industries: existing British suppliers should retain some business, and local consumers would benefit from the efficiency encouraged by some foreign competition.[25]

More revealing indicators of the Colonial Office's priorities can be derived from the early consideration given to the question of post-war reconstruction. The Committee on Post-War Problems, the Colonial Office's response to the 'false dawn' of reconstruction planning, was established in March 1941 to examine numerous questions expected to arise after the war. The Committee, apparently the first of its kind to be created in Whitehall, was primarily a fact-finding body.[26] However, its discussions enabled the two officials with the greatest experience of economic affairs, Gerard Clauson and Sydney Caine, to speculate on post-war colonial conditions.

Clauson's ideas drew heavily on the experience of developments after 1918. Foreseeing shortages of goods and shipping during the 'transition' period, he considered government intervention essential to prevent a boom followed by a slump:

> After the last war economic forces were broadly speaking left unchecked, and primary producers in the period immediately after the war reaped a rich harvest owing to the high prices which they received for their goods. The consequences, so far as most colonial producers at any rate were concerned, were almost wholly evil. In the first stage they received more money than they knew what to do with; much of it was wasted; and exaggerated ideas of the value of their products and numerous expensive tastes were acquired.

At that time, high raw material prices had raised the price of goods produced from them, a situation which had persisted after raw material prices fell. Wartime government bulk purchase could usefully be continued after the war, enabling colonial governments to control the supply, and hence the price, of raw materials, thereby limiting the scale of the expected post-war 'boom'. Furthermore, colonial governments could reserve profits from selling commodities during the boom to supplement prices paid to producers during the subsequent slump.

> Some rise of price to the producers would of course have to be allowed in order to compensate them for the higher prices which they would have to pay for their requirements; but if any additional profits were earned it would, at any rate in backward places like West Africa, be better to keep them under control and dole them out in the ensuing slump than to let them get prematurely into the hands of the producers.[27]

Clauson subsequently emphasised the need to end the 'wild' short-term price fluctuations characteristic of the inter-war years, prefiguring the paternalistic justifications for the system of State produce marketing eventually created in post-war West Africa.[28]

On post-war development proper, Clauson again drew important lessons from post-1918 experiences. There must be no repetition, he argued, of the 'unco-ordinated' and 'badly conceived' development which had occurred then, with ambitious post-war schemes, initiated during the brief 'boom', in some cases leaving colonies with heavy debt burdens during the subsequent slump. Clauson predicted a three-pronged development strategy. First, the encouragement of economic diversification would continue, for example through the increased production of food for local requirements. Secondly, the 'discreet' policy of encouraging secondary industries on an 'economic' or 'near economic' basis would continue. Here, Clauson's choice of words is instructive, underlining the continuing delicacy of the subject within metropolitan circles. Clauson saw the object of this policy as enabling colonies to supply simple items for themselves, releasing local purchasing power for expenditure on more sophisticated, *imported*, goods. Finally, he envisaged the expansion of commodity production, either in terms of *volume*, where suitable markets could be found, or of *value*, in cases where raw materials could be processed locally.[29]

Like Clauson, Caine was cautious in his predictions. He warned that Britain faced severe financial difficulties and that domestic reconstruction would make substantial demands on metropolitan resources. He believed that colonies should therefore first try to finance development from their *own* resources, using their sterling balances being built up in London as a useful source of development capital. Caine also felt that wartime produce marketing arrangements, increased taxation, and the likely post-war scarcity of consumer goods could be expected to swell government revenues. However, he warned that the supply position would remain difficult, and he showed a degree of prescience seldom shared by metropolitan commentators: 'I think we must count on some appreciable time elapsing before material is freely available from this country for Colonial development.' Not only would the post-war resumption of development probably take longer than many hoped but the expected shortage of metropolitan goods could not be alleviated by the promotion of manufacturing in the colonies. Caine's reasons once again reflect the subject's controversial nature:

> ... a definite policy of promoting any big industrial development would be (a) unlikely to produce any quick results (b) likely to produce a lot of uneconomic industries and (c) certain to produce trouble with United Kingdom manufacturers.[30]

A more positive view of colonial industry surfaced at the Committee on Post-War Problems in May 1941. At its third meeting, the Committee agreed in principle that industrial development should be encouraged despite opposition from British manufacturers, and that more information was needed on the extent of colonial industrial development.[31] A questionnaire was therefore sent to all colonies in an attempt to rectify the Colonial Office's ignorance. The Office possessed nothing to compare with the information on primary production collected for the pre-war *Economic Surveys*. Even at this stage, officials recognised their ignorance as an obstacle to reconstruction planning. Besides requesting information on the scale and type of manufacturing in the colonies, the Office asked whether protective tariffs had been granted or were thought necessary for the survival of these industries, and whether the industries competed, or might compete, with exports from Britain, other parts of the Empire, or the USA.[32] The latter two queries indicate the delicacy of these subjects.

Among the sparse official references to industrial development in this period, the absence of attempts to explore the *advantages* of manufacturing is striking. The Office showed no outright hostility to manufacturing: on the contrary, it welcomed viable industry. However, officials spent little time discussing the promotion of industry. Given the additional work which the war had produced for the Colonial Office, this is unsurprising, but this apparent indifference was not shared by the West African colonial governments, and, the multiplication of proposals to establish industries after 1942 obliged the Colonial Office to re-examine its attitudes, and, most importantly, to air this traditionally thorny issue in Whitehall.

The machinery of economic development

Spring 1941, when Moyne succeeded Lloyd, saw the Colonial Office's first limited exercises in preparing for post-war reconstruction and growing concern within the Office to revive colonial development and welfare policy, an early victim of worsening conditions after the fall of France. The impetus for this came from Churchill's instruction to Moyne, in February 1941, to implement the welfare proposals of the West India Royal Commission, a matter made urgent by the granting of military bases in the West Indies to the United States (Britain had to demonstrate good faith to the United States by pursuing constructive colonial policies in order to stem the tide of American anti-colonialist rhetoric).[33] Moyne, who chaired the Royal Commission, had witnessed colonial poverty, and was convinced of the need for development. He sought to capitalise on Churchill's directive by extending it to the colonies generally.[34] The Colonial Office did not universally share Moyne's optimism. Sir Cosmo Parkinson, 'caretaker' permanent under-secretary between 1940 and 1942, recalled the disappointment when development was curtailed in 1940, and feared that activity might have to be suspended again, 'which would be deplorable from every point of view'.[35] Moyne, however, suspected that the absence of development proposals denoted that colonial governments assumed that the Colonial Development and Welfare Act had been suspended, and he sought to correct this impression.[36]

In June 1941, Moyne addressed the need to balance the maximum use of colonial resources for the war effort with the desire to safeguard the welfare and further development of the colonies. He urged governments not to waste resources so that development would not impede war production. He emphasised the need to maximise the colonial contribution to the war effort, but said little about *how* territorial governments could promote development. Nevertheless, Moyne encouraged them to submit essential development schemes. His references to accelerated development may have been merely a 'sweetener', making palatable the calls for increased taxation and tighter import controls which formed the main thrust of his despatch. Yet, privately, Moyne rejected as 'unthinkable' any suggestion that colonial living standards could be lowered further.[37]

These attempts to reactivate the colonial development and welfare policy also led to renewed discussions on development planning, and on the administrative machinery that this would require. A central feature of the new policy was that future development should be planned. Colonial governments had been invited to prepare development programmes covering a period of years. The intention to give assistance 'primarily towards planned development' was one of the chief differences between the new legislation and the Colonial Development Act of 1929.[38] Echoing Clauson's anxiety, assistant under-secretary Charles Jeffries, soon to take up overall responsibility for colonial development, called for careful planning to avoid the 'undesirable consequences' which would follow the inevitable post-war 'reaction'. Schemes approved under the Colonial Development and Welfare Act would have to complement each colony's general development plan.[39] Moyne also stressed the need to begin planning in readiness to resume development when possible: 'Past experience warns us of the danger of starting work on ill-considered lines for want of the necessary forethought.'[40] Creating the machinery required to co-ordinate planning was more problematic, however. In 1940, the intention had been to establish advisory committees in the Colonial Office to examine applications for assistance. This plan had been deferred indefinitely, since few development schemes were expected. Once colonial governments had been encouraged to prepare development programmes and to apply for grants, in June 1941, the Colonial Office had to examine its existing machinery. Officials believed that at least one of the committees originally proposed should now be established.[41] One factor which convinced officials that an advisory committee should be formed was a desire to placate the ever-vigilant Treasury.[42] Moyne, aware of Churchill's distaste for further expansion among Whitehall's advisory bodies, wanted the new supervisory work to be done by Colonial Office staff.[43] In November 1941, the Colonial Development and Welfare Advisory Committee (CDWAC) was established, comprising five senior officials, including Caine and Sir John Campbell, and chaired by Lord Dufferin, Parliamentary Under-Secretary between 1937 and 1940. It soon transpired, however, that there was insufficient work for the Committee. Hall's confession, in January 1942, that the Committee demanded only one hour per week of Dufferin's attention aroused public criticism, which was itself soon to reach new heights in the wave of recrimination and self-examination following the collapse of Malaya in February 1942.[44] The Colonial Development and Welfare Advisory Committee (CDWAC) was a mere stop-gap. Dependent on proposals from the colonial governments, it was no more capable of seizing the initiative in development than its predecessor, the Colonial Development Advisory Committee, had been. It was not equipped, nor was it intended, to tackle broad policy questions, such as economic diversification, industrialisation, or the economic role of government. The decision to make the Committee entirely official in composition suggests a reluctance to include 'unofficial' advisers in the Colonial Office's discussions.

Similarly, the colonial governments lacked adequate planning machinery. Wartime mobilisation had reduced the strengths of colonial administrations, already depleted by pre-war retrenchment. Hailey believed that the solution was not to recruit academic or commercial 'specialists', but was rather to make familiarity with economic questions, as opposed to subjects such as health or agriculture, a normal requirement of staff recruited into the Colonial Service. He believed that colonial governments should regard economic production as one of their normal activities.[45]

Bourdillon had sought a full-time economic adviser to assist Nigerian development and to take responsibility co-ordinating his government's development activities. He doubted, however, whether a development organisation could be built in Nigeria 'from the bottom upwards', as the Economic Department of the Colonial Office had been, since the Lagos Secretariat lacked the Office's network of contacts. The central problem was the wartime scarcity of suitable personnel.[46] This prompted Bourdillon to argue that too rigid an insistence on the grouping of development schemes into coherent programmes might stifle planning entirely, and that flexibility was necessary if any progress were to be made.[47]

The Colonial Office's apparent failure to create satisfactory supervisory and initiatory machinery attracted criticism within Britain. In June 1942, Conservative MPs called for a 'Colonial Development Board', responsible to the Secretary of State for all existing advisory committees, and for spending the Colonial Office's annual Vote.[48] The Fabian Colonial Bureau (FCB) suggested that a Development and Welfare Commission should be created for West Africa, an idea inspired by the Colonial Office's only wartime exercise in regional development machinery, the West Indies' Development and Welfare Commission in 1940. This body, deemed essential by the West India Royal Commission, was to collaborate with the region's governments in planning development. This step was closely linked to Churchill's concern to placate American opinion by pressing ahead with colonial development and welfare in the neighbouring West Indies. The Commission's work was slow, however, partly owing to shortages of both personnel and materials.[49]

This precedent convinced the FCB that a similar organisation was needed for West Africa. Above all, the Bureau was concerned about the time taken for development schemes to be discussed in the West Indies. The Bureau concluded that development planning for West Africa could not begin too soon if co-ordinated development were to be achieved within a 'reasonable' period of the war's end. This work required a group of full-time commissioners to make enquiries, examine plans, and discuss the needs of each colony with local officials.[50] The fundamental difficulty was to find suitable staff for a commission, but it was also feared that its investigations would create burdens for local administrators, distracting them from war work.[51]

These discussions exposed a problem implicit in development policy since its inception, namely whether the initiative in development should come from London or from the colonies. More conservative officials opposed increased metropolitan intervention. The February 1940 *Statement of Policy* explained that development planning required appropriate machinery and personnel both in the colonies and in Britain, but stressed that their work had to be co-ordinated and collaborative, London's role being to assist and guide, not to dictate policy.[52] Some in the Colonial Office believed that practice had strayed from intention. The assistant under-secretary, Sir Arthur Dawe, head of the Africa Division, thought a Development and Welfare Commission for West Africa would be both more practical and more constructive than the existing system of centralised Colonial Office control of colonial development and welfare expenditure. Future progress would require a means of making funds available to colonial governments without referring detailed individual schemes to London. While the Secretary of State should, in his view, continue to determine broad lines of policy, Dawe saw no reason why colonial governments, which enjoyed considerable latitude in spending their own revenues, should not have similar freedom with colonial development and welfare funds. Addressing the question of machinery, he suggested that if colonial secretariats had to be augmented, regional commissions, on the West Indian model, might be suitable

> But whatever organisation is set up, it should have some roots in the soil and not develop the theorising, unreal and impractical features which seem to be the concomitant of over centralised bureaucracy.[53]

It was precisely the dearth of local expertise which constrained a more energetic approach to development by many colonial governments. Moreover, however much the Colonial Office might have desired a free hand in dispensing colonial development and welfare grants, accountability to the Treasury was a central feature of existing arrangements and, if increased funds were to be obtained in future, Parliament had to be convinced that money was being spent carefully. Some officials therefore saw the requirement that detailed schemes had to be submitted before applications for colonial development and welfare money could be considered as encouraging responsible spending by colonial governments.[54]

Official attitudes towards private enterprise

Whilst the Colonial Development and Welfare Act of 1940 had been portrayed as politically useful by its advocates, especially MacDonald, the sums it provided for development were minute in relation to the tasks facing would-be developers. The urgent need to improve social welfare standards in the colonies using metropolitan funding had been uppermost in the minds of those who devised the colonial development and welfare policy. Although assistance was also to be available for economic development, official thinking on this was less clear. The new policy implicitly assumed that private capital would remain responsible for most economic development. However, Caine had predicted that two wartime policy adjustments would help colonial governments to increase their development resources: first, the new marketing arrangements, which were swelling the colonial sterling balances held in London and, secondly, the introduction or extension of taxation.[55] Moyne also referred to this welcome result of taxation designed to curb consumer spending. He argued that colonial governments should build up reserves for peacetime use:

> It seems to me definitely preferable that Colonial Governments, if they are able to do so, should accumulate surplus balances now which they can use for purposes of reconstruction and development after the war, without having to have recourse to assistance under the Colonial Development and Welfare Act, rather than that such balances should be surrendered now and applications for assistance be made at a later date.[56]

Bourdillon did not share this optimistic view of the financial prospects of colonial governments, and warned that the unspent 'surplus' revenue described by Moyne would not arise in Nigeria, where budget balancing still posed problems.[57]

Official uncertainty about future government aid underlined the importance of private capital, which, in West Africa, effectively meant the large expatriate firms. This raises questions about official perceptions of the relative value of private and public enterprise in promoting colonial economic growth. The depressed 1930s, and the West African cocoa hold-ups, left a legacy of bitterness in the region against the operations of large European firms. The hostility felt by African producers towards the United Africa Company (UAC) was a source of growing concern to colonial governments in the late 1930s. Relations between the Company and the governments were strained. In Bourdillon's view, it was impossible to separate in the minds of local producers the formation of the cocoa trading oligopoly and falling prices.[58] However, he was adamant that where a conflict of interest arose between African producers and the European firms, the government's duty was to support the former.

Late in 1938, MacDonald tried to encourage closer understanding between the West African governments and commercial interests. The responses provided ample evidence of the firms' unpopularity. The principal African grievance was the 'monopolistic' character of the firms' operations. Local officials, however, did not believe that the UAC kept the prices it paid to African producers deliberately low: they assumed it was in the Company's interests to raise African purchasing power, thereby increasing the market for imported goods. Nor did the governments share the view, widespread among Africans, that the 'pooling' agreements between firms and the low prices paid to producers were inextricably linked: instead, officials argued that depressed world prices for primary produce had forced these agreements on the participating firms. However, local administrators agreed that the UAC was 'ruthless' against potential competitors.

The governments were equally unanimous that they could do nothing to improve relations between local populations and the firms without risking their own credibility, as they would be seen to be colluding with the firms.[59] Bourdillon thought that the UAC ought to be more open in its operations, explaining its actions and consulting educated Africans. Governor Hodson of the Gold Coast was more vigorous, calling for a radical change of policy:

'So intense is the feeling of mingled hatred and fear with which the people as a whole regard the Company that no half-measures will suffice to eradicate it.' He believed that the UAC should abandon its selling agreement, and soften its attitude towards competitors.[60]

The reactions of the Colonial Office to this problem offer insights into officials' general opinions on big business. Most apparent is a sense of impotence in the face of an inevitable evolution towards concentration in commerce and industry, and resignation to conflict when modern business methods confronted 'primitive' trading habits. As one official commented:

> The objects of 'big business' and the natural trading instincts of Africans are poles apart, and there is always bound to be resentment and friction where the two meet. This is just one of the problems raised by the impact of European and African civilisation.[61]

Acknowledging that the tendency towards 'monopoly' might not benefit the entire community, and that some relaxation by the UAC of its attitude towards competitors was desirable, officials' comments reveal Darwinian resignation, seeing the struggle being waged in West Africa as both inevitable and necessary. Since Africans had to be integrated into the modern practices likely to be dominant in the future, it was especially desirable that the UAC, for example, should take Africans more closely into its confidence.[62] Above all, the Colonial Office, like the colonial governments, saw little it could do to encourage firms like the UAC to conciliate African interests.[63] Ultimately, the initiative was left squarely with the firms themselves.

The UAC was similarly critical of local administrators in West Africa. Bemoaning the lack of openings for commercial investment in the British colonies, the Company alleged that colonial governments did not co-operate in development with the trading firms. Lord Trenchard, Chairman of Unilever, criticised the governments for being too ready to defend 'native' interests, instead of cultivating trade. Colonial governments, he claimed, had done 'little or nothing' to promote development, for example by encouraging private enterprise, fearing that this would provoke accusations of exploitation. Because of this climate, Trenchard claimed, firms such as the UAC were obliged to seek investment opportunities in non-British colonies.[64] The latter point was of particular concern to the Secretary of State – as, presumably, had been intended.[65] Yet Trenchard's principal grievance appears to have been that commercial representatives in West Africa were not accorded the social status they expected from colonial administrators – evidence, it was alleged, of a continuing official snobbery against 'trade', and of a tendency to dismiss business methods as 'grasping and unscrupulous'.[66]

Trenchard wrote to Lloyd in an apparent attempt to improve relations with the Colonial Office, placing the Company's resources in Britain and overseas at the disposal of the government.[67] However, Caine warned his colleagues to look this 'gift horse rather closely in the mouth': while it might be attractive to use UAC machinery in West Africa, in view of government personnel shortages it was essential to consider the effect on African opinion. To accept the UAC's offer might suggest a surrender by the government to the 'monopoly'.[68] Caine's misgivings were echoed by his senior colleagues, and the Office decided simply to acknowledge the UAC's offer.[69]

Nevertheless, when the bulk purchasing and marketing of West African cocoa began, through the West African Cocoa Control Board, the government sought the firms' help. The Board was staffed by officials from the Colonial Office and representatives of the West African firms. These firms also became the Board's local buying agents. The system of licensing introduced maintained the firms' dominant position in the cocoa trade. The quota system for buying also reinforced the existing oligopoly, since quotas were awarded on the basis of a firm's performance in the years 1936–39. The system benefited the European firms immensely, enabling them to retain their respective shares of the cocoa trade and to preserve their profits and interests generally.[70]

Caine raised a lone voice against the new trading structure, demanding rationalisation of the scheme to permit the entry of new firms, and a more flexible quota system. The WACCB's operations offended his economic liberalism since its allocation of quotas sacrificed efficiency, discouraging cost-cutting by making the margin necessary to cover marketing costs that of the least efficient participating firm. Caine was rare in being prepared to offend European firms by widening the scheme to include African and 'Syrian' traders.[71] Clauson, in contrast, defended the European firms, not only because he feared the consequences of encouraging the formation of a new class of African 'plutocrats', but also because any incursion by 'Syrian' traders might erode British profits.[72]

The position of the European firms was further strengthened by the creation, in May 1942, of the West African Produce Marketing Board, to replace the West African Cocoa Control Board. A consequence of the increased value of West Africa's produce after Allied military reversals in the Far East in February, the new Board was responsible for exports of oilseeds and palm-oil in addition to cocoa. Originally proposed by the UAC, keen to safeguard its future import trade and to exclude potential competitors, the WAPCB continued the firms' advantages.[73]

State-controlled produce marketing was an *ad hoc* response to special conditions: although not recognised as such by officials at the time, it was a basis for greater economic management by government, the implications of which were analysed later in the war. Though temporarily strengthening the position of the expatriate firms, controlled marketing was a particularly important example of State intervention, involving the key sector of most colonial economies: the export of primary produce. It was introduced, however, primarily in order to avoid unrest among the region's producers, emphasising the Colonial Office's pre-war reluctance to reform marketing, and hence to confront the firms' entrenched power.

It is also revealing to note London's reactions to Bourdillon's decision, in September 1940, to invoke the Defence Regulations and veto a UAC scheme to mill flour at Kano except under licence, because he feared the political repercussions of this apparent attempt to stifle African enterprise.[74] Clauson was highly critical of Bourdillon, opposing 'discrimination' in favour of African enterprise. He concluded that it would be 'disastrous' if the Colonial Office favoured the local population,

> for the African has neither the capital nor the experience to go any distance in the development of secondary industries, and if we are to accept the principle that the white man is not to be allowed to develop such industries, they will not in fact be developed, except very slowly and very inefficiently.[75]

Accordingly, Lloyd queried the need to protect African enterprise in the way proposed, adding that competition 'might in some ways be healthy for it'.[76]

In the absence of greater willingness by government not only to intervene in economic affairs, but also to engage directly in production, the burden of future economic development seemed destined to fall upon European firms as the only apparent alternative reservoir of capital and entrepreneurial skill. This may partly explain many senior officials' reluctance to risk offending the firms by confronting them over their activities in West Africa. As Trenchard had reminded the Colonial Office, the firms had the option of transferring their interests to other parts of Africa. Far from confronting the firms, the Colonial Office gave them a valuable role in wartime marketing arrangements. However, the manner in which taxation was introduced in Nigeria, for example, suggests that officials, not only in West Africa but also in London, were becoming aware of the possibilities of drawing on the wealth-creating potential of large concerns such as the UAC for the wider benefit of colonial populations, foreshadowing, perhaps, later arguments on the need to promote healthy, but *controlled*, private enterprise. However, it is hard to detect any substantial shift in official attitudes towards the State's economic role in this period. Officials responsible for economic questions showed little interest in the possibility of State enterprise as an integral component of post-war development: there was little discussion of the scope for government experiments in production, such as manufacturing. It is because officials continued to assume that the initiative in economic development would rest with private enterprise that the relationship of the firms with government is important. As Clauson observed:

> except in the most primitive communities, most impulse and initiative would, and should, come from private individuals, and the role of the government would be rather to indicate the general lines of policy dictated by the economic position of the country, to endeavour so far as possible to direct private initiative into useful channels, and to prevent action definitely contrary to the public interest.[77]

How far did these views represent the opinions of Clauson's colleagues? Reflections on the proper functions of the State by officials during this period are rare. However, the Colonial Office's Economic Department was prompted to record its views in response to a paper commissioned for the Committee on Post-War Problems from the young West Indian economist, (W.) Arthur Lewis, then teaching at the London School of Economics. Lewis's paper, circulated in August 1942, examined the flow of capital into the British colonies. The key problem was that the London capital market, while prepared to participate in certain sectors of colonial economies, especially mineral development, was reluctant to consider 'risky' propositions such as secondary industry. Government policy had concentrated on raising capital for public works rather than for productive enterprise. Moreover, while such local capital as existed tended to be reinvested in agriculture, the little locally owned non-mining industry which had developed in West Africa had drawn heavily on local savings, with the result that most factories were established on a limited scale.

Lewis suggested that government could remedy the problem of financing industry either by guaranteeing private investments or by itself lending capital. A further suggestion, much discussed later in the war, was for the British government to establish a colonial finance corporation to lend capital to approved concerns. Lewis dismissed as irrelevant traditional hostility towards public enterprise based on the argument that bureaucratic management precluded commercial efficiency. This ignored conditions in West Africa, where the choice was between public or private monopolies. Significantly, Lewis did not accept the claim that private firms made excessive profits as an argument for State enterprise. He felt that if this were true, then the remedy lay in effective taxation policies.[78]

Lewis's paper was enthusiastically received. Dawe minuted: 'I wish we could get a few more outside contributors of this intellectual standard'.[79] Clauson regarded the paper as the best yet produced for the Post-War Problems Committee.[80] Caine, however, rejected some of Lewis's assumptions, particularly the criticism that colonial governments, by concentrating their activities on the provision of public works, services, and transport, and by not investing directly in production, had thereby neglected the development of colonial economies:

> It is unduly minimising the activities of colonial governments to suggest that because they have merely spent their money on this kind of thing, instead of investing it in factories, etc., they have done nothing to assist the capital development of their territories. There is still probably a very good deal to be said for the now somewhat old-fashioned view that this is the proper sphere of investment for Governments.

Furthermore, Caine denied that colonial governments had been steeped in *laissez faire* ideology, pointing to their role in providing the infrastructure necessary for development. In his view, it was truer to say that colonial governments had not lived up to the *expectations* of some sections of opinion. By concentrating on the provision of infrastructure, colonial governments, claimed Caine, could enable private enterprise to produce at maximum efficiency.[81]

There is little evidence that the war had, by 1942, altered the Colonial Office's basic assumption that private enterprise was the major agent of colonial economic activity. Hence, the scope for State involvement in production was not examined. This is in marked contrast to the situation in West Africa, where governments showed a growing interest in promoting development, including diversification.

Local proposals for industrial development

Although they received little encouragement from London between 1939 and 1942, the West African governments were increasingly willing to explore the development of local manufacturing, particularly import substitution. Local governors, notably Bourdillon and Burns, were already anticipating the post-war period, unlike the Colonial Office whose first serious efforts at reconstruction planning did not begin until the spring of 1943. In Nigeria, Bourdillon seized the opportunities created by war, aiming to develop food production and processing, and the production of palm-oil. However, he believed that local shortages of capital and expertise demanded government initiative, both in funding and operating new enterprise.[82]

Bourdillon subsequently sought colonial development and welfare funds totalling £50,000 to help establish industries, arguing that in the initial stages of such development, government direction and control were 'essential' if 'sound' industries were to be established. He envisaged that these government-sponsored schemes would eventually be transferred to African management, not to European or Syrian entrepreneurs.[83] The Treasury, however, objected, arguing that the Colonial Development and Welfare Act was not intended to finance potentially economic propositions. The Colonial Development and Welfare Avisory Committee subsequently endorsed the Treasury's view that colonial development and welfare money could not be used for the kind of short-term finance that Nigeria needed.[84]

The Gold Coast government was also interested in industrial development, demonstrated by its reactions to the proposal by Achimota College, put forward in 1942, to establish an Institute of West African Arts, Industries and Social Science. The scheme, first mooted in 1937, was approved by the West African Governors' Conference in 1939, and by the Advisory Committee on Education in May 1940. Responding to the war and the consequent stimulus to local industrial development, Achimota had already created 'pilot' units, including one manufacturing bricks and tiles.[85] The scheme's backers believed that the Institute would help to accelerate local production, provide the trained personnel necessary for manufacturing and contribute to post-war reconstruction planning. A fundamental assumption was that African development would be better served by a large number of small production units, run co-operatively, and spread throughout the country, than by concentrated industrial production in a few centres.[86]

Governor Burns, already considering post-war development, strongly supported the scheme, regarding it as a means of absorbing some of the 'ever increasing' number of youths who left school and could not find employment in the civil service or in commerce. The Institute could help by providing craft and industrial training. In Burns's view, to delay the scheme would be to miss a 'golden opportunity' to provide against what would probably be one of the most important difficulties after the war.[87]

Later, when detailed comments on the scheme were requested from the Economic Department of the Colonial Office, sympathy was expressed with the goal of economic diversification. It was admitted that, in the past, colonies had been vulnerable to world market fluctuations, over which producers had no control. Anything which would broaden West Africa's economic base was therefore considered valuable. The spread of education also called for greater occupational variety than was currently available, as it was thought undesirable that the only opportunities open to educated Africans should be clerical. Doubts were expressed, however, about the apparent bias shown by the Institute's sponsors against large-scale enterprise, and their preference for 'cottage' industry – an outlook thought to derive from the enthusiasm of anthropologists and sociologists for traditional social organisation. It was considered unrealistic to try to shelter Africans from the social evils already witnessed where large-scale development had occurred, for example in the Transvaal or on the Copperbelt. Not only would educated Africans resent such paternalism, but if large-scale enterprise proved to be more economical, then it was bound to develop, as it had done in India, China and Japan.[88]

The Allied military reversals in the Far East early in 1942 placed new demands on West Africa and stimulated local industrial development. There was an increased drive to maximise raw materials production for the Allied war effort. Shortages of commodities replaced earlier surpluses, and in March 1942, London requested the African colonial governors to intensify local production to make good the loss of Far Eastern supplies: '... the foodstuffs and minerals of the African dependencies have become a vast armoury for the war effort.'[89] The most important immediate consequence of this was the major extension of State-controlled produce marketing, and the transformation of the West African Cocoa Control Board into the West African Produce Marketing Board.[90] The West African governors, in turn, were encouraged to examine the question of ensuring that the requirements needed to maintain maximum production were met, including a review of the scope for manufacturing the consumer goods needed to absorb rising African incomes locally, and to act as incentives to greater productivity.[91] There was, similarly, a relative loosening of restrictions on the importation of consumer goods.[92] The Colonial Office recognised that if the colonies were to maintain and increase production, they would have to receive goods in return, and not merely credits. Without some immediate reward, producers were unlikely to keep up their efforts.[93]

The obstacles to local industrial development, and the Colonial Office's responses to them, are illustrated by the proposal, in spring 1942, for Achimota College to manufacture textiles. This was a modest scheme to establish a textile unit of 19 hand-looms and one semi-automatic loom. Its annual output was expected to be about 45,000 yards of 36 inch cloth. Given the Gold Coast's normal minimum imports of cloth – about 25 *million* yards per annum – the Achimota unit posed no serious threat to the import trade.[94] Burns was initially cautious, fearing that Achimota might overreach itself, that the demand for locally-produced cloth might not survive the war, and that unless the local industry received tariff protection, it could not compete with imported British goods.[95]

Nevertheless, when the proposal was formally submitted to London in May 1942, it was backed by the Gold Coast government, which saw the experiment as a means of expanding and improving the small local weaving industry that was facing extinction because of its dependence on scarce imports of machine-spun yarn. It was therefore felt necessary to encourage local cotton spinning. A further advantage of the plan was that it would stimulate local cotton-growing.

The textile unit was initially expected to be supplied with cotton from Nigeria and the Belgian Congo, but it was hoped that this would eventually be replaced by Gold Coast cotton. As the local production of cotton increased, it was planned to establish similar textile units elsewhere in the territory.[96] At first the Colonial Office viewed the Achimota proposal with scepticism. It was thought that African weavers would be slow to learn how to operate and service anything but the simplest type of spinning machinery and hand loom.[97] Clauson's contribution seems particularly inappropriate in view of the technical training currently being given to African military personnel: 'We have no knowledge whether possible mill-hands exist in Nigeria; we do know that many negroes are unfit for the job because their hands are too large + clumsy.'[98]

Clauson had evidently learned little: he used precisely this argument when opposing a proposal from Uganda in 1937 to develop a cotton weaving plant.[99] However, the Achimota scheme was approved in June 1942, and permission was granted for Achimota College to seek funding from the Gold Coast Legislative Council.[100] Among the reasons for the Office's sympathy with the scheme were concern at the ailing condition of local weaving, and the promise that local textile production would help ease the shortage of imported cotton goods.[101] The Colonial Office was also assured by the staff of Achimota that the textile unit could survive without artificial support, such as tariff protection.[102] The Office saw good reasons for proceeding quickly. Not only would the project require little machinery from Britain, and little skilled manpower but, if successful, the unit would demonstrate that manufacturing of this sort was feasible in West Africa.[103] Another reason for official approval was that the proposal was already well known in West Africa: if the Colonial Office delayed the scheme, it risked being accused of putting British business interests before a 'promising' opportunity to help African development.[104]

The Achimota project depended, however, on obtaining the necessary machinery from Britain. Because of the current limits on the export of goods to markets outside the dollar area, the Colonial Office required the Board of Trade's permission for machinery to be earmarked for Achimota. This meant raising the entire question of colonial manufacturing, to which the Board was traditionally hostile. For example, when the Colonial Development and Welfare Bill was under preparation in 1940, the Board urged that the new assistance should not be used to encourage the development of 'uneconomic' colonial industry: it assumed that the Advisory Committee to be created to consider grant applications would bear this concern in mind.[105] Caine thought this reasonable, agreeing that care should be taken, to avoid subsidising uneconomic industries competing with British manufacturers. On the other hand, higher authority in the Colonial Office felt that the Board of Trade should not be the arbiter of what was an 'uneconomic' industry.[106]

Similarly, the Board had been unenthusiastic about the 'Stamp memorandum', already described. One official attacked the Survey's apparent complacency regarding overseas industrialisation, pointing out that unless this process were gradual, it would severely affect British interests. Similarly, the assertion that colonies should be given 'every encouragement' to industrialise was also rejected: wartime encouragement of colonial industries would ignore Britain's post-war requirements for export markets. The fact that Britain was likely to emerge from the war a debtor 'entirely dependent' on its exports was a powerful argument against encouraging overseas diversification.[107] The Board of Trade's continuing concern about the colonies' future as markets for Britain was similarly revealed by its reactions to the Colonial Office's circular telegram of 5 June 1941, which had asked colonial governments to tighten import controls. The Board was annoyed that it was not consulted over so important an issue.[108]

The Board of Trade was inevitably sensitive to foreign textile competition because of Lancashire's pre-war difficulties. The question of the supply of cotton goods to West Africa had already become controversial in Whitehall long before the Achimota proposal. Late in 1940, the Cotton Board urged the Board of Trade to take action to curb Indian competition in colonial markets.[109] The problem was thought to be especially serious in West Africa, where exports of Indian textiles to Nigeria in the first quarter of 1940 were five times the level in the same period in 1939. The Association of West African Merchants (AWAM) believed that India might take 98 per cent of the Nigerian bleached goods market unless London acted (the figure in 1936–38 had been three per cent). The basic problem, as ever, was that Lancashire could not compete with Indian prices. British manufacturers feared for their post-war prospects: by then it could be politically impossible to act, given the seeming inevitability by 1942 of Indian devolution. The Board of Trade agreed that political considerations indicated the need for immediate measures. The President of the Board therefore called for a quota system in colonial markets, and thought that the AWAM might be persuaded to limit its purchases of Indian textiles.[110]

The Colonial Office rejected this proposal, arguing that it was unreasonable to expect West Africa, already suffering from the loss of markets for its main exports, to pay enhanced prices for cloth. Moyne claimed that a fundamental principle was at stake:

> Since the latter part of the 18th Century, when an attempt to reserve the trade of the American Colonies for the benefit of the mother country led to disastrous consequences, it has been the declared policy of H.M.G. not to use the powers of control which it possesses over the Colonial Empire for purely selfish ends.

Moyne explained that the existing quota against Japanese textiles had already given rise to 'considerable resentment' in West Africa, and that the Board's proposal was irreconcilable with the principles of 'trusteeship'; moreover, it would create a dangerous precedent, which it would be difficult to deny to other British industries, where Indian, and possibly even colonial, competition was involved. The Colonial Office feared that a quota system might provoke political unrest, and it doubted whether colonial populations could afford anything but the cheapest goods, given the twin local problems of falling produce prices and the rising prices of essential goods. Moyne concluded that Lancashire's true concern was its post-war future: 'I feel very strongly that, if Lancashire wishes to retain its trade after the war, it should do so by the ordinary commercial means of reducing its prices to a competitive level.'[111] When the Lord President's Committee discussed the question in February 1941, Moyne, supported by the Secretary of State for India, Leo Amery, who was concerned about the possible political reactions in India, convinced his colleagues that the Cotton Board's request was impracticable. Instead, the Committee asked the Treasury and the Board of Trade to investigate other measures to secure Lancashire's colonial markets.[112]

Early in May 1942, the Parliamentary Under-Secretary at the Colonial Office, Harold Macmillan, approached Hugh Dalton, President of the Board of Trade, on the supply of cotton piece goods to Africa to stimulate raw materials production. Acknowledging that West Africa's cotton goods allocation was generous, he claimed that more goods were needed to raise the region's productivity, and that the Colonial Office was considering small-scale, local textile production to supplement British supplies, and sought Dalton's help in obtaining second hand textile machinery.[113] Dalton's reply was discouraging. He argued that West Africa had already received 'generous' allocations of cotton goods (73.6 million square yards in 1941, compared to 82.5 million square yards in 1939), and that an additional eight million yards, originally intended for Asian markets, had recently been diverted to West Africa. He therefore saw no justification for a local textile industry. He foresaw problems in recruiting skilled labour locally, and argued that the reconditioning of second hand machinery in Britain, or the manufacture of new plant, would divert efforts away from essential war work.[114]

While these discussions were taking place, another scheme to produce khaki cloth in West Africa was being considered by the War Office. The proposal involved constructing a textile plant at Abeokuta in Nigeria that would produce one million yards of cloth per annum, thereby saving on shipping space. The necessary cotton would be grown and ginned locally. It was hoped that full production could be reached within a year. The Colonial Office showed little initial interest because it was reluctant to encourage an industry which might have no economic justification after the war.[115] However, officials were subsequently assured by Achimota College that the military scheme complemented its own plans to expand local textile production, avoiding the 'evils' of industrialisation on the usual European model.[116] The military authorities had been persuaded by Achimota that its textile scheme could supply the training needed for the Abeokuta workforce, which led the War Office to ask the Colonial Office to consider the Achimota plans favourably.[117]

On 30 June 1942, representatives of the Colonial Office, the War Office, the Ministry of Supply and the Board of Trade met to discuss these proposals. The key problem discussed was the supply of machinery for the plants at Achimota and Abeokuta. The Ministry of Supply warned that the manufacture of new textile machinery for export was problematic. The Board of Trade added that there would be difficulties in exporting second-hand machinery. One of the undertakings reached in the reorganisation of the British cotton industry, begun immediately before the outbreak of war, was that machinery from factories closed under 'concentration' would not be sold abroad. The Board would have preferred the additional textile production to be in Britain, because of West Africa's importance to Lancashire. Clauson pointed out that other Whitehall departments thought the West African proposals worthwhile, providing insurance against the loss of supplies from Britain and India. He also argued that the schemes would give useful experience of industrial development in West African conditions.[118] Having promised to investigate the question of machinery supplies, the Board subsequently reported that no second-hand machinery was available for Abeokuta, since any proposal to export plant from the 'concentrated' industry would raise a difficult question of principle.[119] Undeterred, the Colonial Office approached the Ministry of Supply. Referring to the Abeokuta project, Gerald Creasy, Caine's successor at the Economic Department, wrote:

> Our position in the Colonial Office is quite clear; we should be very glad to see this industry established and the sooner the better, as it will form a useful guide for the consideration of future developments in regard to textile manufacture in West Africa.

The Colonial Office believed that the necessary machinery could be found in Britain if the project were deemed important to the war effort. However, the Office did not consider it worth pressing for the adoption of the War Office scheme unless 'special wartime considerations' were involved since the output of the plant would be 'trifling' compared to West Africa's total textile requirements. However, the military authorities' interest seemed to derive from the problem of supplying enough cloth from India and Britain. If the Abeokuta project could benefit the War Office quickly, there were grounds for trying to secure the machinery needed from 'concentrated' mills in Britain:

> It will no doubt be possible for the Board of Trade to devise some means of placating the industry, and, even if that proves difficult, it is obvious that in the last resort the industry's post-war position must not be the deciding factor.'[120]

Nevertheless, textile development in West Africa received a fresh blow when the Crown Agents reported that the Board of Trade had vetoed the supply of machinery to Achimota since the larger Nigerian scheme had similarly been refused.[121] The fate of these projects appeared to be sealed only days later when the War Office told the Colonial Office that it had been estimated that the Abeokuta factory would not become operational for nearly two years, rendering the project pointless to the military and the Ministry of Supply. While an alternative scheme to produce cloth in the Belgian Congo would be examined, the War Office intended to postpone a final decision until it had received a full report from its representative in West Africa.[122]

At this stage, the Resident Minister in West Africa, Lord Swinton, intervened. Swinton, later prominent in the reconstruction debate, doubted that West Africa could supply much more to the Middle East theatre than manpower, since all the region's raw materials were needed in Britain and the USA and producing them would demand all West Africa's energies. On the plans to produce cloth for the military, Swinton believed the deciding factor in locating the factory should be how quickly it could become productive. Although he did not dismiss the Abeokuta project out of hand, he thought that in view of the time factor, the most sensible, if politically delicate, choice would be to arrange for increased production from the established textile industry in the Belgian Congo. Swinton acknowledged that there would be hostility in Britain to any extension of textile factories in Africa with British Government funds because this would be seen as subsidising post-war competition. However, the Ministry of Supply could lend the necessary plant. This plant would remain British government property and could therefore be removed after the war. Alternatively, a British firm might be allowed to operate 'shadow' factories in Africa, providing the necessary expertise and personnel.[123] In the event, the military authorities in West Africa advised the War Office that the textile industry in the Belgian Congo should be extended in preference to establishing a new plant in Nigeria, and Swinton endorsed this suggestion.[124] However, the changed military situation in late 1942 persuaded the War Office to abandon the scheme entirely.[125]

Meanwhile, there remained the original Achimota proposal. The scheme's principal advocate, the Art Instructor at Achimota, Meyerowitz, tried to convince the Board of Trade that the project had merits independent of any military textile scheme, and requested the Colonial Office's support.[126] O.G.R. Williams, head of the West Africa Department, was not optimistic: 'I do not believe that the Board of Trade is at present at all interested in post-war textile production in West Africa. Indeed, I should expect them on general grounds to be rather suspicious of it.'

Significantly, he admitted that in exchanges with the Board of Trade, the Colonial Office had emphasised the relation of the Achimota project to the Abeokuta scheme in order to get the Board to consider the former proposal at all.[127] Williams's comments were soon proved to be true when the Board of Trade informed the Colonial Office that 'however meritorious' the Achimota project might be, it was difficult to justify the manufacture and export of textile machinery from Britain, bearing in mind the current policy of restricting exports of machinery to essential war purposes.[128] Williams replied that the Achimota scheme should be considered on its own merits, and that its fate should not depend upon decisions concerning other proposals which had different purposes. He explained that the Colonial Office's chief interest in the Achimota textile unit was its long-term value as an educational project, creating the conditions necessary for the spread of technical knowledge in West Africa. Accepting that these were not considerations which would interest the Board of Trade, he nevertheless argued that the question was 'of great significance' both to Accra and the Office on 'important grounds of policy'. Adding that the proposed plant would ease the cotton goods supply position in West Africa, he asked the Board to reconsider its earlier decision.[129]

Williams's request was reinforced by the personal intervention of Macmillan, who wrote to the Board of Trade in similar terms at the prompting of Sir Keith Hancock, the colonial expert.[130] This initiative produced a markedly different response from the Board of Trade. Harcourt Johnstone, the Secretary for Overseas Trade, told Macmillan that the Achimota project had his Department's sympathy: if reconditioned second-hand machinery were not available, then approval would be given for new textile plant to be manufactured for the project.[131] In the event, no suitable machinery was found and the Board of Trade informed the Crown Agents that orders for new equipment could be placed.[132] The importance of the West African proposals for the development of local industry in 1942 is that they forced the Colonial Office to address specific problems, such as the supply of textile plant, as well as general policy issues, such as the metropolitan government's attitude to colonial industrialisation, and to leave the relative security of internal Colonial Office discussion for the exposed arena of inter-departmental debate.

Towards a policy on industrial development

The Colonial Office was probably encouraged to persevere with this question by developments in the broader consideration given to the issue of colonial industrialisation. Although this matter had been raised on a number of occasions during 1942, the Colonial Office still required an 'authoritative' ruling because of the persistent hostility to the idea among other government departments. Moreover, besides the West African schemes, proposals for manufacturing were being received from East Africa, reinforcing the case for clear policy guidelines.[133] The Colonial Office agreed to refer the subject to the Cabinet Africa Committee, established in 1942 to complement the work of the Resident Minister in West Africa.[134]

At this stage, there is little evidence that the Colonial Office regarded industrialisation as a solution to West Africa's economic problems, nor was the war regarded as an opportunity to cultivate an import-substituting sector in the region. The Office's attitudes to industrial development continued to betray some of the divisions apparent in earlier discussions. However, evidence of official support for limited industrialisation exists. This has already been seen in the West African Department's willingness to defend the Achimota scheme. Earlier, Clauson had emphasised that the purpose of industrial development was to release local purchasing power, which could be redirected towards more sophisticated imported goods. In other words, although industrialisation would reduce imports of simple goods such as soap and matches, this would be balanced by increased imports, for example from Britain, of goods which could not be produced locally. Therefore, provided development was not so rapid as to cause economic dislocation elsewhere (and he saw no prospect of this in practice), Clauson felt that London was bound to support it as essential to the general strategy for raising colonial living standards.[135]

Subsequent discussions revealed that the Board of Trade was less inclined to distinguish between manufacturing designed to broaden colonial import markets, and manufacturing which, more immediately, would erode British export markets, affecting Lancashire especially. The war had not eroded the Board's suspicion of colonial manufacturing, as its resistance to West African textile development suggests.

Privately, the Colonial Office could admit that its ideas on industrial development had evolved gradually. Thus, Clauson could reflect in 1942, on metropolitan policy towards colonial industrialisation:

> Here it is true that views to-day are not the same as they were 8 or 10 years ago, but even then the Government was not preventing, and indeed had not the power to prevent, the establishment of industrial undertakings in the Colonies. What it did have the power to prevent, and did discourage, was the establishment of highly protected industries under the cover of a revenue tariff.[136]

While Clauson left open the question of future policy on protection, suggesting that this would depend largely on any post-war settlement, Caine's ideas were clearer. Although he felt that colonial industries were 'fairly certain' to develop, he believed that 'for a long time' they would be restricted to the 'simpler' kind of factory. On assistance to 'uneconomic' industries, for example by tariff protection, Caine argued that it was 'impossible to challenge the logic of the full free-trade case on the assumption of full freedom in every aspect of the economic process'.

Caine's preference for a general liberalisation of the economic order was accompanied by an understanding that much depended on still unresolved questions of international commercial policy. He was not optimistic that a consensus spanning Whitehall could easily be reached on colonial industrialisation, a question he considered still liable to produce 'violent controversy'. He recalled the Office's recent attempts to compose suitable policy guidelines for colonial governments, noting how they had all failed because interdepartmental agreement in London had proved elusive. Referring to the internal discussions which had preceded the despatch of Moyne's circular in March 1941, Caine remembered how difficult it had been for the Colonial Office to agree on how much of the accompanying 'Stamp memorandum' on export trade policy should be included.[137]

On 16 September 1942, the Cabinet Africa Committee, chaired by the Secretary of State, Viscount Cranborne, discussed a Colonial Office paper on industrial development. Cranborne referred to a widespread impression that London opposed colonial manufacturing, and to the resulting belief that the initiative was left with the colonies. He wanted to reassure the colonies that London sympathised with their aims, and had the necessary machinery to consider the problems involved. Representatives from the ministries of Production and Supply both denied opposing colonial industry. The Board of Trade, similarly, promised not to obstruct any manufacturing scheme beneficial to the war effort, but observed that some schemes, while economic in wartime, might not be so afterwards: some colonies might use the war as a pretext for establishing post-war industries requiring a high degree of protection.[138] After this meeting, there was some support in the Colonial Office for the establishment of an interdepartmental committee to consider proposals for industrial development. The Colonial Office's Permanent Under-Secretary, Sir George Gater, however, agreed with the Ministry of Production that this was unnecessary, since the question could always be referred to the Africa Committee. The deciding factor, however, was Churchill's recent call for a reduction in the number of standing committees in Whitehall.[139]

While there had been some progress towards an agreed Whitehall policy on industrial development in Africa, in that the question was being discussed interdepartmentally after several years of sterile silence, the Colonial Office still had to emphasise, in its advice to colonial governments, that only industries contributing directly to the war effort could be considered. This was the central message of a telegram sent by Cranborne to the East African Governors' Conference in October 1942. However, the Colonial Office promised full support to any project which met this requirement, especially if the project drew only on local resources.[140]

If circumstances seemed unfavourable for discussion of long-term policy, the Colonial Office still needed a clarification of Whitehall's views on more immediate aspects of colonial industrialisation. As the Office told the Africa Committee, the military presence in West Africa, and the shipping shortage, had made it necessary for the region to try to meet military requirements from local resources. Consequently, certain types of industry had been stimulated, and craft skills had been promoted among the local population. However, recent changes in the military situation, notably the Allied victories in north Africa in autumn 1942, seemed likely to reduce the demands made on West Africa. The Office therefore needed to determine how far wartime developments could be harnessed to promote local civilian needs. The Office reminded the Africa Committee that manufacturing in West Africa would assist the war effort by reducing the demand for British goods; moreover, the authorities in West Africa, including the Resident Minister, would appreciate a statement of the British government's attitude to the general policy questions involved, judging from the welcome which greeted the advice already sent to the East African Governors' Conference. Finally, the Colonial Office reassured the Committee that there were no signs of large-scale industrialisation in West Africa. Those industries established to date were modest concerns, mostly based on the processing of local primary produce.[141]

When the Africa Committee discussed the Colonial Office's memorandum in February 1943, the Board of Trade admitted that in peacetime, it 'viewed with a critical eye' any colonial industrialisation harmful to Britain's export trade. However, in wartime, the situation was different, with the fewer demands being made on Britain's exporting capacity the better. This was why the Board had acquiesced in the arrangements made for dealing with industrial schemes in East Africa. Nevertheless, the Board argued that, even where industries could be established that did not require imported machinery, the effects on Britain's post-war export trade had to be considered. The Committee agreed, however, that the kind of industries emerging in the colonies were unlikely to threaten British interests. Inevitably the Board of Trade raised the delicate subject of protection, and warned against long-term assurances to colonial governments on this question. Oliver Stanley, who became Colonial Secretary in November 1942, and who had been President of the Board of Trade from 1937 to 1940, agreed that protection was an important issue, but did not elaborate. Dawe explained that the Colonial Office did not seek to promote industries which could not support themselves, though some industries would require initial protection. The Committee concluded by asking the Colonial Office to prepare a telegram to Swinton, similar to that sent to East Africa, in the light of the Committee's discussion, and in consultation with the government departments concerned.[142] Before this telegram could be drafted, a new phase of the Colonial Office's wartime deliberations on economic development had been entered, with the beginning of a prolonged debate on post-war reconstruction, prompted by calls from Swinton in West Africa for guidelines on future colonial economic policy. This debate and its repercussions form the subject of the next two chapters.

By late 1942 the Colonial Office had not achieved an unequivocal endorsement by the British government of the value of colonial manufacturing development: the limited approval given to such development was conditional, and cannot be divorced from the wartime considerations which produced it. Industrial development, it was agreed, was acceptable in the short term, provided it could demonstrate its value to the war effort. Whitehall, and especially the Board of Trade, remained noticeably reluctant to enter into long-term policy commitments on the question. The Colonial Office had not, therefore, secured the firm policy guidelines on long-term, post-war industrial development that it had sought: these discussions lay ahead. It remained to be seen whether the relative softening of Whitehall's attitudes was more than a temporary policy adjustment.

NOTES

1. For the impact of the war, see *Parliamentary Papers (1946–47) Cmd.7167 x. 403 The Colonial Empire, 1939–1947*; Sir John Shuckburgh, 'Colonial Civil History of the War, Volume I', unpublished manuscript (University of London, Institute of Commonwealth Studies Library); Killingray and Rathbone (1986), pp.1–19.
2. Constantine (1984), p.257.
3. CO 859/41/1, circular despatch from Lloyd, 10 Sept. 1940.
4. Lee and Petter (1982), pp.104–05.
5. Bowden (1980), p.83.
6. *PP* (1940-41) Cmd.6299 viii 1, *Certain Aspects of Colonial Policy in War-Time*, 5 June 1941.
7. Bowden (1980), p.86.
8. CO 852/348/9, minute by Melville, 12 June 1940.

9. Shuckburgh I, p.103.
10. Bowden (1980), p.76.
11. Ibid., pp.29, 36–9, 48, 54–6, 76; Meredith (1988), pp.285–300.
12. M. Cowen and N.J. Westcott, 'British Imperial Economic Policy During the War', in Killingray and Rathbone (1986), p.42.
13. Meredith (1986), pp.77–91.
14. Ibid., p.88.
15. *Parliamentary Debates (Commons)*, 364, 1339, 21 Aug. 1940.
16. CO 852/348/9, minute by Melville, 12 June 1940.
17. *PD(C)*, 367, 518–19, 4 Dec. 1940; 1239–40, 18 Dec. 1940.
18. *Parliamentary Debates (Lords)*, 118, 123–40, 17 Dec. 1940.
19. CO 852/503/7, minute, 2 Sept. 1942.
20. Lee and Petter (1982), p.28; Meredith (1988), pp.286–7.
21. A. Cairncross and N. Watts, *The Economic Section 1939–1961. A study in economic advising* (London: Routledge, 1989) pp.xi, 11–14; A. Cairncross, *Years of Recovery. British Economic Policy 1945–51* (London: Methuen, 1985) p.55; Sir D.N. Chester (ed.), *Lessons of the War Economy* (Cambridge: Cambridge University Press, 1951) pp.3–4.
22. BT 11/1368, P(E & F)(40)115, War Cabinet Survey of Economic and Financial Plans, 'Export Trade Policy', 18 Sept. 1940; CO 852/349/4, circular despatch from Moyne, 22 Mar. 1941; E.L. Hargreaves and M.M. Gowing, *History of the Second World War – UK Civil Series Civil Industry and Trade* (London: HMSO, 1952), pp.70–3.
23. CO 852/349/4, minute, 27 Nov. 1940.
24. Ibid., minute, 28 Nov. 1940.
25. Ibid., circular despatch, 22 Mar. 1941.
26. CO 859/80/3, minutes by Jeffries, 4 Mar. 1941 and Parkinson, 6 Mar. 1941; CAB 117/251, 'CO Committee on Post-War Problems', 15 July 1941; *PD(C)* 373, 593, 16 July 1941. The Committee was chaired by Lord Hailey and comprised four assistant under-secretaries: Dawe (head of the Africa Division), Jeffries, Clauson and Burns, the latter then temporarily 'beachcombing' in the Colonial Office between his governorships of British Honduras and the Gold Coast.
27. CO 852/503/9, CPP 65, 'Colonial economic problems in the Reconstruction Period', 31 Mar. 1941.
28. CO 852/504/5, CPP(123)1, 'The overseas trade of the British Colonial Empire before, during and after the War', 16 Feb. 1942.
29. CO 852/503/9, CPP 65, 31 Mar. 1941.
30. CO 852/503/8, CPP 52, 'Thoughts on reconstruction in the Colonial Empire', (n.d., but probably Apr. 1941).
31. CO 967/13, CRC(41) 3rd meeting, 1 May 1941 (the Committee was briefly known as the 'Reconstruction' Committee).
32. CO 852/368/12, circular despatch, 'Secondary industries in the Colonies', 27 May 1941.
33. Bowden (1980), p.130.
34. Lee and Petter (1982), pp.104–6.
35. CO 852/482/6, Parkinson to Moyne, 28 Mar. 1941.
36. Morgan (1980) I, pp.91–2.
37. CO 852/482/6, minute, 1 Apr. 1941.
38. Morgan (1980) I, p.89.
39. CO 859/80/3, minute, 4 Mar. 1941.
40. CO 852/482/6, minute, 1 Apr. 1941.
41. CO 583/262/30498/1941–43, minute by Jeffries, 17 Sept. 1941.
42. Ibid., minute by Parkinson, 19 Sept. 1941.
43. Ibid., minute by Moyne, 23 Sept. 1941.
44. On the reactions to the losses in the Far East, and the resulting criticism of Britain's

colonial record, see Louis (1977), pp.135–9.
45. CO 967/13, CRC(41) 4th meeting, 6 May 1941.
46. CO 583/253/30463/1940, Bourdillon to MacDonald, 11 Mar. 1940; note of discussion with Bourdillon, 30 Apr. 1940.
47. CO 583/262/30519/1942, record of discussion between Secretary of State, Bourdillon and senior officials in the Colonial Office, 27 May 1942.
48. *PD(C)*, 380, 2025–6, 2032, 2034–8.
49. Morgan (1980) I, pp.137–40.
50. Rhodes House Library, Oxford MSS Brit. Emp. s365, Fabian Colonial Bureau Papers, 67/1 f26, Rita Hinden to Cranborne, 5 Oct. 1941.
51. CO 859/81/8, minutes by O.G.R. Williams, 31 Oct. 1942 and Dawe, 5 Nov. 1942.
52. Cmd.6175, *Statement of Policy...*
53. CO 859/81/8, minute, 5 Nov. 1942.
54. CO 583/262/30519/1942, minute by Gater, 21 Nov. 1942; minute by Macmillan, 23 Nov. 1942.
55. CO 852/503/8, CPP 52, Apr. 1941.
56. Cmd.6299, *Certain Aspects of Colonial Policy...*
57. CO 583/262/30498/1941–43, Bourdillon to Moyne, 17 July 1941.
58. CO 554/122/10/33650/1939, Bourdillon to MacDonald, 16 Feb. 1939.
59. Ibid., memo. by H.T. Bourdillon (summarising replies to MacDonald's despatch of 8 Nov. 1938), 17 May 1939.
60. Ibid., memo. by H.T. Bourdillon, 17 May 1939.
61. CO 554/122/33650/1939, minute by Melville, 20 Jan. 1939.
62. CO 554/122/33650/1939, memo. by H.T. Bourdillon, 17 May 1939.
63. CO 554/122/33650/1939, minute by O.G.R. Williams, 24 Jan. 1939.
64. CO 554/122/10/33650/1939, note of meeting in Colonial Office with Lord Trenchard, 24 July 1939; ibid., Trenchard to MacDonald, 25 July 1939.
65. Ibid., MacDonald to Trenchard, 4 Aug. 1939.
66. Ibid., letter to MacDonald, 25 July 1939; CO 554/125/14/33650/1940, minute by Gater, 16 Feb. 1940.
67. CO 554/125/33649/1940, letter to Lloyd, 23 May 1940.
68. Ibid., minute, 25 May 1940.
69. Ibid., minutes by Dawe, 27 May 1940 and Parkinson, 28 May 1940; letter to Trenchard, 29 May 1940.
70. Bowden (1980), pp.85, 141; D.K. Fieldhouse, 'War and the Origins of the Gold Coast Marketing Board, 1939–1940', in M. Twaddle (ed.), *Imperialism, the State, and the Third World* (London: British Academic Press), pp.153–82.
71. Lee and Petter (1982), pp.87–8.
72. Minute, 5 May 1941 cited in Bowden (1980), p.141.
73. Hopkins (1973), p.259; Meredith (1986), p.81. On the fortunes of the UAC, see Fieldhouse (1992), pp.229–80.
74. CO 852/291/8, Bourdillon to Lloyd, 23 Sept. 1940.
75. Ibid., minute, 30 Sept. 1940.
76. Ibid., Lloyd to Bourdillon, 11 Oct. 1940.
77. CO 852/503/17, 'The problem of raising the standard of living in the British Colonial Empire', 8 Mar. 1942.
78. CO 852/505/3, CPP 152(10), 'Some aspects of the flow of capital into the British Colonies', circulated 4 Aug. 1942.
79. Ibid., minute, 14 Sept. 1942.
80. Ibid., minute, 12 Aug. 1942.
81. Ibid., minute, 13 Aug. 1942.
82. CO 852/269/8, Bourdillon to MacDonald, 30 Nov. 1939.
83. CO 583/262/30498/1941–43, Bourdillon to Moyne, 17 July 1941.
84. Ibid., Syers (Treasury) to Dawe, 3 Dec. 1941, enclosing note on meeting with Treasury,

11 Nov. 1941; minute by Boyse, 18 Dec. 1941.

85. CO 96/775/1/31401/1941, Burns to Moyne, 8 Nov. 1941; Shuckburgh I, pp.300–1.
86. CO 554/130/33685/1942, 'Memorandum on the proposed Institute of West African Arts, Industries and Social Science', 18 July 1942.
87. Ibid., Burns to Moyne, 16 Jan. 1942.
88. Ibid., minute by Carstairs, 15 Sept. 1942. Carstairs was an assistant secretary in the Economic Department, soon to become head of its production branch. The important points that he raised do not seem to have been taken up by his colleagues.
89. Quoted in Cowen and Westcott (1986), p.44. See also Hargreaves (1988), pp.52–3, and N.J. Westcott, 'Sterling and Empire: The British Imperial Economy, 1939–1951', unpublished seminar paper, University of London Institute of Commonwealth Studies, (1983), p.4.
90. Meredith (1986), pp.80–1.
91. CO 852/506/1, Moyne to WAGC , 17 Jan. 1942.
92. Bowden (1980), p.139.
93. CO 852/504/5, CPP 123(1), memo. by Clauson, 'The overseas trade of the British Colonial Empire before, during and after the War', 16 Feb. 1942.
94. CO 852/370/12, minute by O.G.R. Williams, 1 May 1942.
95. Ibid., Burns to O.G.R. Williams, 2 Feb. 1942.
96. Ibid., Acting Governor, Gold Coast to Cranborne, 1 May 1942; ibid., minute by O.G.R. Williams, 1 May 1942.
97. Ibid., minute by O.G.R. Williams, 23 Feb. 1942.
98. Ibid., minute, 30 Apr. 1942.
99. Meredith (1976), p.135.
100. CO 852/370/12, minute by O.G.R. Williams, 16 June 1942; ibid., Cranborne to OAG, Gold Coast, 17 June 1942.
101. Ibid., minute by O.G.R. Williams, 1 May 1942.
102. CO 554/130/33685/1942, minute by O.G.R. Williams, 10 Apr. 1942.
103. Ibid., minute by O.G.R. Williams, 6 June 1942.
104. Ibid., minute by Dawe, 10 June 1942.
105. CO 859/40/7, R.M. Nowell (BoT) to Caine, 3 May 1940.
106. Ibid., minutes by Caine, 7 May 1940, Shuckburgh, 9 May 1940 and Dufferin, 10 May 1940.
107. BT 11/1368, P(E & F)(40)115 War Cabinet Survey of Economic and Financial Plans 'Export Trade Policy', 18 Sept. 1940, with marginal comments by R.J. Shackle, principal assistant secretary.
108. Lee and Petter (1982), p.85–6.
109. BT 175/1, CB 241, Cotton Board 22nd meeting, 12 Nov. 1940; ibid., CB 261, Cotton Board 24th meeting, 26 Nov. 1940. The Cotton Board, created under the Cotton Industry Reorganisation Act (1939) was responsible for streamlining the cotton industry by closing 'surplus' factories. Appointed by the President of the Board of Trade and based in Manchester, the Board, representing employers and workers, supervised a drastic 'concentration' of the cotton industry between 1940 and 1942, when about one-third of working mills were closed. From 1942, the Board was to active in discussions on the cotton industry's post-war prospects. See Hargreaves and Gowing (1952), pp.46–8, 344, 364, 392; Marguerite Dupree (ed.), *Lancashire and Whitehall: the diary of Sir Raymond Streat Volume One: 1931–39* (Manchester: Manchester University Press, 1988) pp.xi–xxi, 47–8.
110. CAB 71/3, LP(41)16, 'Competition between Indian and United Kingdom Textiles in Colonial Markets. Note by the President, Board of Trade', 8 Feb. 1941.
111. Ibid., LP(41)21, 'Competition between Indian and U.K. textiles in colonial markets. Note by the Colonial Secretary', 13 Feb. 1941.
112. CAB 71/3, LP(41) 4th meeting, 14 Feb. 1941. On the Lord President's Committee's responsibilities for major questions of economic policy, see Chester (1951), pp.8–9

and Hancock and Gowing (1949), pp.219–20.

113. CO 852/370/12, Macmillan to Dalton, 4 May 1942.
114. Ibid., Dalton to Macmillan, 15 May 1942.
115. Ibid., Cullen (Ministry of Supply) to Clackson (DDPC), 24 May 1942.
116. Ibid., minute by O.G.R. Williams, 1 May 1942.
117. Ibid., Fisher (War Office) to O.G.R. Williams, 8 June 1942.
118. Ibid., note of meeting held in Colonial Office, 30 June 1942. Since 1941, the Board of Trade had been similarly unenthusiastic towards proposals by the government of Ceylon to develop a textile industry, arguing that new plant was difficult to supply and quoting the undertaking on second-hand machinery given to the Cotton Board. In May 1942, the governor of Ceylon was informed that London could not consider assisting any scheme not of demonstrable value to the war effort. See Shuckburgh I, p.292.
119. Ibid., J.R. Willis (BoT) to Creasy, 8 July 1942.
120. Ibid., letter to Calder (Ministry of Supply), 15 July 1942.
121. Ibid., E. Ringwood (Crown Agents) to O.G.R. Williams, 18 July 1942.
122. Ibid., Maj. F.C. Fawcett (War Office) to Creasy, 22 July 1942.
123. CO 852/502/19, letter to Bishop, 31 July 1942.
124. CO 852/370/12, telegram to Cranborne, 11 Aug. 1942.
125. Ibid., Macmillan to Dalton, 7 Dec. 1942.
126. Ibid., letter to O.G.R. Williams, 5 Aug. 1942.
127. Ibid., letter to H. Meyerowitz, 7 Aug. 1942.
128. Ibid., J.R. Willis (BoT) to O.G.R. Williams, 25 Aug. 1942.
129. Ibid., letter to Willis, 30 Sept. 1942.
130. Ibid., letter to Waterhouse (BoT), 1 Oct. 1942.
131. Ibid., letter to Macmillan, 7 Oct. 1942.
132. Ibid., J.R. Willis to O.G.R. Williams, 16 Nov. 1942.
133. During 1941, import-substituting industries, aimed chiefly at supplying military needs, had developed with support from the East African governments, and the entire question was examined by the East African Civil Supplies Board. See Shuckburgh I, pp.282–3 and Cowen and Westcott (1986), p.55.
134. CO 852/431/1, minute by Carstairs, 2 Sept. 1942.
135. CO 852/504/5, CPP 123(1), 16 Feb. 1942.
136. CO 852/505/3, minute, 12 Aug. 1942.
137. CO 852/503/7, minute, 26 Aug. 1942.
138. CO 852/431/1, meeting of War Cabinet Africa Committee, 16 Sept. 1942.
139. Ibid., minute to Creasy, 14 Oct. 1942.
140. CO 852/480/12, Cranborne to Secretary, EAGC, 19 Oct. 1942.
141. CO 852/480/12, War Cabinet Africa Committee, A(43)2, 'Secondary industries in West Africa', 12 Feb. 1943.
142. Ibid., War Cabinet Africa Committee, A(43) 1st meeting, 19 Feb. 1943.

3 Industrialisation in Colonial Office Reconstruction Thinking, 1943–46

The Allies' improved military fortunes late in 1942 enabled serious metropolitan consideration of post-war planning. The extended debate on reconstruction was both encouraged and focused by the publication of the Beveridge Report on social security in November 1942.[1] The Colonial Office shared the enthusiasm for reconstruction that gripped Whitehall. In contrast to the war's first phase, the period after 1943 required serious and sustained consideration of colonial industrialisation.

A question central to official discussions after 1943 was London's role in development. Early in 1943, Stanley declared that territorial governments would be responsible for detailed planning, with London establishing a broad policy framework and offering advice, funds and expertise, enabling colonial administrations to achieve targets they themselves set.[2] However, concern had grown that neither they nor the Colonial Office were yet equipped to promote development. Early in 1943, Labour's chief spokesman on colonial affairs, Arthur Creech Jones, highlighted problems that were increasingly evident as post-war planning gathered pace. Attacking the Colonial Office for its reticence and failure to publicise its work, he called for more research into colonial problems and a streamlining of the Office's 'cumbersome and slow' machinery. Yet Creech Jones wanted the Office to be more assertive in its dealings with colonial governments, and resisted calls by some Conservative MPs for a 'Colonial Development Board', representing 'big interests'. He defended the colonial secretary's authority from such encroachments, although he endorsed calls for a standing Parliamentary Committee to oversee colonial affairs and make the administrative machine more accountable.[3]

While circumventing such criticism, the Colonial Office recognised the serious gaps in its knowledge of colonial conditions, widened by the war's interruption of routine information-gathering.[4] The Office also understood that its development planning machinery was inadequate. In April 1943, Stanley admitted that the Office lacked satisfactory resources to handle economic questions, and suggested an 'Economic Advisory Council' to advise on development questions.[5]

The Colonial Office's misgivings about the condition of the colonial governments coalesced in February 1943, when Dawe called for study of West Africa's planning machinery. He favoured a regional development staff, supervised by Swinton, to be 'an energising and co-ordinating unit'. Discussions with Frank Stockdale, the Comptroller for Development and Welfare in the West Indies, convinced Dawe that West Africa required a Development Commissioner with the necessary staff to deal with development plans for the whole region – views shared by Sir George Gater and Stanley.[6]

Swinton welcomed the proposal, although he doubted whether a commissioner of Stockdale's abilities could be found for West Africa.[7] However, the West African governments, while keen to proceed with development, and accepting the need for some regional co-ordination, were wary of a Development Commissioner with executive powers, and resented metropolitan encroachments on their authority. Both Lagos and Accra claimed that they already had large expert staffs, and that supplementary expertise was unnecessary – a surprising argument given recurrent indications to the contrary.[8] Swinton suggested instead that a Development Adviser should be appointed to advise him directly.[9]

During 1943, Swinton voiced his misgivings about local officials. He admitted that colonial governments possessed imaginative and experienced personnel, but felt they were poorly employed, partly because they were preoccupied with other problems, and partly due to ineffective communication. This convinced him of the need for a suitably qualified Development Adviser.[10]

The problems revealed as the planning exercise evolved were illustrated by Accra's early attempts to produce a development plan. Early in 1943, Burns sent a summary of the territory's development proposals to London. The Colonial Office was disturbed by their apparent bias towards improving the Gold Coast's social services, rather than its economic development which was seen in London as essential for long-term welfare provision.[11] Bourdillon explained that his secretariat could not produce comprehensive development proposals, yet he opposed the appointment of a Development Adviser, arguing that Nigeria's development should be planned by the officers responsible for implementing it.[12]

Such difficulties undermined the assumption of local initiative in development, challenging the traditional division of responsibilities between the 'centre' and the 'periphery'. Within the Office, loyalty to the primacy of the 'local' initiative was eroded by a belief that progress with development required metropolitan intervention. The case for greater centralisation was advanced by Caine, who had already suggested overhauling the Colonial Office, enabling it to refute 'the constant accusation of dilatory procedure'.[13] In April 1943, Caine succeeded Sir John Campbell as financial adviser, acquiring responsibility for co-ordinating development policy. Subsequent months of frustration convinced him that the existing machinery, lacking personnel and expertise, hampered 'constructive work'.[14] The Colonial Office was equipped to receive and assess development schemes originating from territorial governments, yet few schemes were produced, because the local machinery necessary for 'original and coherent thinking' on development was 'virtually non-existent'. This repeated the warnings Caine had given in August 1942, when stressing the colonial governments' need for expert help in planning.[15] Caine attacked the officially encouraged impression that the wartime hiatus in development would enable individual governments to produce comprehensive plans because no plan yet received in London was adequate. Nor did he see the West Indies' Development and Welfare Organisation as a helpful precedent, since it, too, could only examine schemes submitted by governments. Caine argued that improved regional machinery had to be matched by a strong organisation in London, competent to investigate and initiate development.[16]

Caine's arguments challenged traditional assumptions that were defended by the Colonial Office's geographical departments. Significantly, when the West Africa Department was discussing planning early in 1943, it did not consult the Economic Department.[17] Consequently, it was not always familiar with wider official thinking on economic issues. For example, in April 1943, O.G.R. Williams, head of the Department, confessed his ignorance of any clearly formulated policy on industrial development.[18]

The Colonial Office took steps to improve local and central development machinery in the summer of 1943. In West Africa, the economist Noel Hall was appointed Development Adviser to Swinton to co-ordinate development planning and examine development schemes before their submission to London.[19] However, this appointment was largely nullified by resistance from the West African governments, which were a potential obstacle to greater regional co-ordination of development. Hall's staff found themselves relegated to a consultative role, providing information to experts employed by individual governments. Hall who, like Swinton, doubted the abilities of local officials, resigned late in 1944.[20]

The Colonial Office's major initiative in Britain was to create the Colonial Economic Advisory Committee (CEAC) in September 1943, to advise on economic policy questions, especially those raised by development programming.[21] Among its members were Hailey and Bourdillon, various academics including the economists Evan Durbin, Sir Hubert Henderson and Professor Lionel Robbins, and representatives of British industry and labour. The committee's secretary, until November 1944, was the economist and temporary civil servant, Arthur Lewis.

Early West African initiatives

Despite the poor condition of local machinery, the early initiative in the reconstruction debate came from West Africa, obliging the Colonial Office to address various problems involved in promoting economic development, including industrialisation. Swinton's role was prominent. As Colonial Secretary, he had tried to co-ordinate the Colonial Office's economic policies, overseeing the creation in 1934 of its Economic Department and earmarking the young Sydney Caine for early promotion.[22] In February 1943, Swinton set out his thoughts on future economic policy for West Africa. His chief objective was to help primary producers, through organised marketing and increased production for the internal market. He also sought to encourage industries stimulated by wartime conditions, however, to foster balanced development. This, he believed, would benefit primary producers, whose produce could be processed cheaply for local markets. Industrialisation would also absorb the growing numbers of educated Africans, particularly technically skilled demobilised African soldiers. Since shipping and import shortages would probably persist after the war, Swinton believed that projects least dependent on imported machinery, and which could absorb demobilised troops, should receive priority.[23]

Before the Colonial Office could respond to Swinton's memorandum, it received his request for guidance on tariff protection. Swinton explained that he could plan neither agricultural nor industrial development satisfactorily without knowing whether some degree of protection was acceptable.[24] He felt that colonies should be allowed to develop 'simple' industries and become more self-sufficient in food. Although opposed to 'artificial' protection, he thought that agriculture and industry should be safeguarded against external competition, and that this would benefit British industry because rising living standards would create markets for sophisticated British goods.[25]

Both Lagos and Accra had continued to show interest in manufacturing proposals. Shortly before retiring from Nigeria in 1943, Bourdillon told London that industrialisation was essential to the territory's financial position.[26] As living standards rose and populations grew, he argued, the demand for locally produced food would rise, and so industrial and agricultural development would be complementary. Bourdillon did not advocate 'artificial' industrialisation, but favoured appropriate developments which could be begun quickly, such as the processing of local raw materials, introducing diversification and greater income stability.[27] In the Gold Coast, the government proceeded with plans to establish a West African Institute, one of whose roles would be to examine industrial proposals. The Institute's immediate wartime function was to promote local manufacture of bricks, tiles, pottery and textiles to meet local demand.[28]

A major influence shaping the West African governments' attitudes towards industrialisation in early discussions on post-war planning, was concern to reintegrate returning troops smoothly. The Civil Members' Committee believed that industrial development was vital to the demobilisation and resettlement programme.[29] However, while the repeated impression was that ex-soldiers would seek employment and living standards commensurate with their new skills, the Colonial Office's labour adviser, Granville Orde Browne, who toured West Africa between November 1943 and March 1944, thought differently. Extensive discussions with local administrators convinced him that demobilised troops would not usually demand new employment opportunities, and that their requirements could be exaggerated; furthermore, transport problems would probably delay their return from service abroad, allowing ample time to prepare for their reabsorption.[30]

The Nigerian and Gold Coast governments, however, were less confident. Governor Sir Arthur Richards commented, of the returning Nigerian soldier:

> In the immediate post-war period he will be glad to rejoin his relations at home, but when he has had time to look round and compare his tribal life with what he has seen elsewhere I doubt if he will be satisfied.[31]

Initially, the Accra authorities shared Orde Browne's view. In July 1944, Burns predicted that many demobilised Gold Coast troops would return to their villages and resume their former occupations.[32] By June 1945, however, officials doubted whether the majority would prefer the peasant life to skilled employment and higher wages.[33] In both Nigeria and the Gold Coast, therefore, the prospect of imminent demobilisation remained an incentive to industrialisation.

Commercial policy: Whitehall and protection

The most delicate question raised by Swinton was that of tariff protection for new industries. The Colonial Office's caution in handling this issue arose from continuing uncertainty about post-war commercial policy. Under Article VII of the Mutual Aid Agreement signed in February 1942 with the United States, Britain promised to help secure general tariff cuts and eliminate discriminatory trading practices, casting doubt on the future of Imperial Preference.

This question split the War Cabinet, Iimperial Preference being championed by Beaverbrook and Amery. The uncertainty created by Cabinet disagreements was compounded by Churchill's evasiveness.[34] Throughout the reconstruction debates, future commercial policy remained unresolved. Negotiations with Washington began in 1943, and although both sides agreed on the desirability of lower tariffs and high employment levels to encourage freer trade and on the abolition of quantitative restrictions on trade, no firm decisions were reached.

It was another year before talks resumed, with the Treasury, under Keynes' influence, arguing that Britain's bleak post-war financial prospects required a conciliatory approach to the United States. While Washington believed that Article VII committed Britain to abolishing all preferences, British negotiators sought a matching US offer of substantial tariff cuts.[35]

In July 1944, at Bretton Woods, Britain agreed to the establishment of the International Monetary Fund and the World Bank, the financial bases of multilateralism. However, as late as July 1945, at Potsdam, Churchill could claim that Britain was *not* committed to abandoning Imperial Preference.[36] Only after the abrupt termination of Lend-Lease in August 1945 did Britain ratify the Bretton Woods Agreement in December 1945 in order to secure a fresh US loan. It promised to make sterling freely convertible by mid-1947, and agreed to 'non-discrimination' in trade, involving the removal of quantitative restrictions on US exports to Britain from the end of 1946. Furthermore, Britain and the United States agreed to co-operate towards tariff reductions and the elimination of preferences.[37]

Although future trade policy remained unclear, there were indications of opinion in Whitehall shifting in favour of freer trade. In January 1943, the War Cabinet's Inter-Departmental Committee on Post-War Commercial Policy, chaired by Sir Arnold Overton, the Board of Trade's Permanent Secretary, recommended a general multilateral commercial convention under which existing preferences would be cut to half their 1939 level, a concession believed vital to securing agreement with the United States. It proposed that the protective element in tariffs should be set between 10 and 25 per cent. Moderate state subsidisation of industries, and temporary post-war quantitative import restrictions, were suggested, coupled to the establishment of a Commercial Union to complement the proposed International Clearing Union.[38]

These views were endorsed by the majority of the Committee's members, representing the Board of Trade, the Department of Overseas Trade, the Dominions Office, the Foreign Office and the Cabinet Economic Secretariat. The Treasury, however, remained cool with one of its representatives, Sir Hubert Henderson, being reluctant to dismantle Imperial Preference.[39] The Board of Trade and the Department of Overseas Trade had, however, concluded that future commercial stability depended upon a general liberalisation of world trade. The DOT's Secretary, Harcourt Johnstone, told the Treasury that inter-war experiences suggested that lower barriers would encourage international trade, assisting Britain's recovery. He particularly opposed quantitative import restrictions. While these had benefited British industry before the war, for example by limiting colonial imports of foreign cotton goods, British exporters now regarded them as a serious handicap.[40]

Although the Colonial Office was not represented on the Overton Committee, it appended comments to the Committee's report. The Office welcomed the report's multilateralist recommendations, believing that, if these were associated with schemes to regulate primary production, the colonies would benefit from increased demand for commodities stimulated by freer trade. Hitherto, the Office explained, most colonial tariffs were intended to raise revenue, but a tendency had developed to use them to shelter industries. While the Office's policy had never been defined precisely, it had been customary to accept modest protection. Although the Office believed that the proposed 25 per cent ceiling on *ad valorem* duties was acceptable, it warned of possible colonial hostility. Finally, the Office linked the issue of preference to development finance, arguing that British public opinion was more likely to favour aid if Britain still enjoyed tariff advantages in the colonies.[41] The Colonial Office, however, was moving towards a more explicitly multilateralist position. Thus, in August 1945, Clauson could assert that British and colonial interests would benefit from expanded world trade under freer conditions. While both needed 'moderate' protection, both would suffer from widespread, high protection. However, whereas the developed British economy required limited but comprehensive protection, the colonial economies needed greater protection for fewer emerging industries, although not for basically uneconomic ones. Since freer trade would expand markets for colonial produce, the colonies should make concessions on preferences. Because metropolitan and colonial interests lay in negotiated tariff cuts, the Colonial Office could not obstruct collaboration with the United States over commercial policy.[42]

Uncertainty about the post-war commercial order therefore overshadowed the Colonial Office's discussions on industrialisation. Until major questions were agreed internationally, the Office could not determine long-term economic policy. Nevertheless, tentative attempts were made, late in 1943, to forecast post-war conditions. Generally, officials envisaged continuing demand for most colonial products, but because demand for some commodities might fall, colonial governments were advised to consider promoting other sources of income. Wartime shortages of imports and personnel were expected to continue, at least during the transition to peacetime production. Personnel shortages, it was thought, might be eased by exploiting the technical training received by colonial soldiers. Finally, because import controls would persist, officials believed that local anti-inflationary measures would have to remain, involving price controls and taxation.[43]

If these were the Office's general assumptions about the future, there remained the immediate task of responding to Swinton. Swinton's ideas on economic policy were broadly accepted by the Colonial Office.[44] However, while he concentrated on *post-war* development, the Office was still preoccupied with shorter term developments, and specifically with how industrial development might ease wartime import shortages.[45] Moreover, given the Board of Trade's position, as it was explained to the War Cabinet Africa Committee in 1942, Cabinet approval was needed before territorial governments could be advised on long-term industrial development.[46]

Caine urged caution on the related questions of industrialisation and protection: he felt that while war-related industries should not be obstructed, a long-term policy on industrial development was not yet possible, and no commitments could be made to prolonged protection.[47] Caine's colleagues echoed this view, agreeing that it was too early to provide long-term guidelines.[48] But, pressed by Stanley, officials agreed that some idea of appropriate levels of protection could be derived from the recent Cabinet paper on Post-War Commercial Policy, and that types of industry acceptable in principle might be suggested without consulting other Whitehall departments. Nevertheless, they agreed that colonial governments should be instructed to refer specific schemes to London for approval.[49]

The Colonial Office discussed its response to Swinton's request for guidance on tariff policy against this background of general sympathy for freer trade accompanied by doubts over its precise implications. The most consistent critic of protection was Caine, who, endorsing the Overton Report, saw subsidies as the appropriate alternative. He explained that most of the articles which the Office hoped to see produced by colonial industry were simple. However, if protection kept their prices higher than those of equivalent imports, the burden would fall on poorer consumers.[50]

Stanley's reply to Swinton incorporated these arguments. First, Stanley assured Swinton that no industry that was viable without protection would be obstructed because it competed with British industry. Nor did he envisage 'insuperable' objections to industries requiring 'moderate' protection. However, he warned against highly protected development, geared towards the export trade but effectively subsidised by local consumers. Finally, he repeated Caine's argument that where an industry needed government assistance, subsidies should be considered in preference to tariffs.[51] These comments satisfied Swinton, who reassured Stanley that he had 'strenuously discouraged' any idea of developing protected industries geared to the export trade. He defined an 'economic' industry as one viable *without* high tariffs. Within this definition, he saw much potential.[52]

Given the Colonial Office's emphasis on promoting economic development, what place did industrialisation occupy in its reconstruction priorities? Official thinking on industrial development in West Africa had been underpinned by the belief that the decline in war-related activity, following improvements in the military situation late in 1942 might cause local unemployment. By April 1943 this seemed unlikely in view of proposals to develop an air route between Accra and the Middle East. Local industries would not be needed so urgently to absorb surplus labour.[53] Moreover, the Colonial Office's public and private comments suggest that it still presumed that most colonial economies were, and would remain, primarily agricultural.

Stanley, while keen to promote diversification, harboured no illusions about radical economic restructuring. Higher living standards depended, he thought, upon agricultural improvements.[54] Nevertheless, the view persisted in the Colonial Office that colonial poverty was due, in part, to dependence on primary production, and that industrialisation would raise living standards.[55] However, judgements on the desirability of individual proposals could be blurred under wartime conditions, as Caine warned. He differentiated between the need to secure supplies of particular items, possibly through local production, and the general desirability of industrialisation. He thought it dangerous to confuse these objectives, and warned that promoting local manufacturing for its own sake might impede, rather than stimulate, production of scarce goods.[56]

As the reconstruction debate gathered pace during 1943, the Colonial Office's public pronouncements on industrialisation became more confident. Speaking to Oxford Conservatives in March, Stanley emphasised the need for colonial economic development. Echoing the central thesis of the 'Dual Mandate', he explained that colonial economic growth would benefit local populations and the world. He felt that while the colonies would probably remain predominantly agricultural, the employment-creating potential of industry should not be overlooked. He saw no threat to metropolitan interests in the emergence of colonial industries serving local markets and complementing local agriculture, but warned against 'unnatural and uneconomic' industrialisation behind high tariffs.[57] The West African governments, which endorsed Swinton's ideas, were encouraged by these remarks.[58]

Stanley elaborated these points in his major policy speech of July 1943, though he spoke carefully of limited industrialisation:

> I cannot think of anything more fatal to the economics of the Colonies than a rash, mushroom, industrialist growth, fostered by high protective tariffs unrelated either to local products or to local markets.

He believed that appropriate development might include the processing of raw materials and the manufacture of simple goods that did not require imported raw materials. However, he stressed that in wartime, only industries aiding the war effort could be encouraged. Moreover, while 'moderate' initial protection might be necessary, industries dependent on 'excessive' government help were unwelcome, because of their possible adverse long-term economic effects. Furthermore, he argued that Britain could not rely on Imperial Preference to shield its industry from foreign competition: 'To enable us to compete in the Colonial territories in the cheapest classes of goods would need preferential treatment so great as to question our position as trustees for the territories.' Such preference would be counterproductive because its cost would be passed on to colonial consumers, causing local markets to contract. Thus:

> The more the Colonies are able themselves to supply their

> own cheaper necessities, the more will be available from the surplus for overseas purchase and the more will be available to buy the better class of goods which need skill in their manufacture, and in which, therefore, the export industries of this country will be able to compete on fair terms.[59]

Stanley's July 1943 speech formed the basis of Colonial Office discussions on industrialisation for the remainder of the 'planning' period. Official references to the subject tempered caution with qualified optimism. For example, London's advice to West Africa on post-war planning, issued in August 1943, explained that some questions, including industrialisation, could not be settled during the war, because they involved matters, such as protection, requiring international agreement. The Office believed, however, that Stanley had provided enough interim guidance in his Oxford and Commons speeches.[60]

An important factor contributing to the Office's growing willingness to defend industrialisation was the apparent liberalisation of the Board of Trade's views. The Board's constructive attitude towards several East African industrial schemes early in 1943 prompted Dawe to comment:

> In the past the Board of Trade, as guardian of the interests of home industry, has been our chief obstacle in attempting to establish a wider point of view with regard to the development of secondary industries in the Colonies.[61]

Firmer evidence of the Board's changing views came in a memorandum of July 1943.[62] In this, the Board admitted that in order to protect metropolitan employment, little 'official' encouragement had hitherto been given to British firms to establish industries overseas. While this need remained, wartime overseas industrialisation demanded a review of Britain's role. Obstruction might be counterproductive.

Industrialisation, for example in the Dominions and India, would proceed whether or not British interests participated, but a refusal to help might encourage the promotion of inefficient, uneconomic and highly protected industries.[63] If Britain did not participate, foreign competitors would. Moreover, co-operation would enable Britain to share in the developing world's growing prosperity, partly offsetting the damage done to metropolitan exporters by creating demand for British capital goods, accessories and spares. Non-economic considerations were also relevant:

> From the wider political angle, so far as the Dominions and India are concerned, resistance to local industrial development is bound to lay us open to the charge that we are interested only in our own prosperity and not in theirs.

The Board emphasised that many questions raised by industrialisation in the Empire were unanswerable pending decisions on future commercial policy, but its tentative guidelines assumed that no co-ordinated planning of industrialisation by Empire governments was likely given the degree of State control over private enterprise that this might require. It believed that British firms should hence consider development proposals as they arose. However, the Board's reasoning betrayed signs of a lingering, if camouflaged, scepticism:

> Even where they have good reason to think that the results of such investigations may prove negative, they will stand a better chance of quashing unhealthy projects if they can, as the result of a careful technical investigation, prove them to be so than if they adopt a *non possumus* attitude.

Unco-operative firms would weaken their case for future government help when their interests were threatened by developments overseas. The British government's role, in the Board's view, was to discuss development with other Empire governments, 'and to apply – but very discreetly – a certain amount of "braking" designed so far as possible to delay final *ad hoc* conclusions until the general position is clearer.'[64]

Similar thinking informed the Board's June 1944 submission to the War Cabinet Reconstruction Committee. Surveying British exporters' long-term prospects, the Board concluded that liberalised world trade was essential for revived British exports. Significantly, the domestic textile industry was cited as an export trade whose pre-war decline was likely to continue.[65] If Lancashire's decline was considered inevitable and irreversible, this may explain why the Board's opposition to colonial textile development, evident until 1942, apparently eased thereafter.

Meanwhile, the Treasury argued that care would be needed in Britain's post-war external investments, as it could not be assumed that US aid would continue long after Germany's defeat. On overseas industrialisation, the Treasury echoed the Board of

Trade's position that participation by British interests might be the only means of compensating for the resulting damage to British exports. British participation would establish markets for exports of plant and expertise. The Treasury argued that Britain should not oppose overseas industrialisation, except where it would cause 'violent displacements' to British exports. While 'excessive' tariff or other protection should be resisted, some exceptions were acceptable – enough to safeguard against 'hopelessly uneconomic industrialisation'. Moreover, it was in Britain's interests to see rising standards of living generally, especially where these arose from diversification of overseas economies.[66]

Neither the Board of Trade nor the Treasury had referred specifically to *colonial* industrialisation, suggesting a continuing tendency to assume that metropolitan and colonial interests were identical, or, more likely, that colonial economies were subject to greater metropolitan influence than those of other parts of the Empire. The Board of Trade was clearly referring to industrialisation in the Dominions, whose economic policies Britain could no longer control. It seems likely that this evidence of policy revision by two major Whitehall departments, however vaguely delineated, encouraged Colonial Office tenacity on colonial industrialisation. Nevertheless, it remained to be seen whether the Treasury and Board would extend to the colonial empire the more liberal approach to industrialisation which they seemed ready to apply to the Dominions. It was even more unclear how the Board would react to specific proposals for colonial manufacturing, particularly those for textile industries, given the difficulties already being predicted for the British cotton industry, and the tradition of hostility to such development from Lancashire.

The Colonial Economic Advisory Committee

Industrial development was one of the first matters referred to the Colonial Economic Advisory Committee (CEAC). Officials accepted Arthur Lewis's offer to submit a paper on industrialisation that he had drafted before entering the Colonial Office. This comprehensive survey analysed claims made by proponents of industrialisation and addressed some of the problems involved. Lewis identified four main advantages, beginning with the employment of underutilised labour in agricultural economies. Agricultural improvements would release labour which industry could absorb. Lewis therefore saw a close relationship between agricultural and industrial development. Further, industrialisation would permit a redistribution of external purchasing power, which, together with higher average incomes from more remunerative industrial employment, would raise living standards. Diversification would bring greater economic stability, while enriching communities by introducing new skills.

Lewis did not believe that London had previously obstructed colonial industrialisation, despite promptings by British manufacturers, although little had been done to encourage it. He emphasised the benefits to be derived from economies of scale, and of developing groups of industries simultaneously in the same region, enabling utilities to be provided more cheaply. Instead of a 'gradual evolution', Lewis called for a 'sudden jump' in development, a stance which inevitably alarmed the Colonial Office.

In other respects, Lewis's views were more conventional. For instance, like the Colonial Office, he considered that the best opportunities lay with the local processing of local raw materials and import-substitution. He defended initial, possibly permanent, protection for new industries, but opposed artificial support through high prices, arguing that this would undermine competitiveness.[67]

Caine's willingness to send the Board a copy of Lewis's memorandum, with an invitation to participate in the CEAC's discussions[68] was symbolic of improved relations between the Colonial Office and the Board of Trade over industrialisation. Although the Board judged the case for industrial development to have been 'soberly and convincingly' stated, disquiet remained about the Colonial Office's position. The Board feared that Britain might be required to devote scarce capital to establishing 'redundant and inefficient' plants, justified only by being in the colonies, and that these might secure tariff protection, injuring Britain's exporters and impoverishing local markets.[69] These doubts re-emerged during informal talks, arranged by the Board, with Colonial Office representatives in April 1944. Specifically, the Board asked how far the Office was committed to industrialisation at virtually any cost, and how quickly it would be pursued.

Caine provided the Colonial Office's response. His voice was becoming increasingly authoritative: in April 1944, he became assistant under-secretary with direct responsibility for the Economic Division, retaining supervision of colonial development and welfare planning.[70] Caine reassured the Board of Trade that there was no prospect of 'substantial' wartime colonial industrialisation, and that no decisions had yet been taken on its practical implications. Attempting to dispel the Board's fears, Caine explained that little had yet been achieved in planning colonial infrastructures, let alone industries, and that there had been little response to London's request, in the previous summer, for development plans from colonial governments.[71] This discussion satisfied the Board of Trade that the Office was not 'hatching widespread plans for industrial development'. Relieved that the Office's ideas on development were still 'embryonic', the Board nevertheless declined the invitation to participate in the CEAC's deliberations, which it felt might be 'highly embarrassing' when policy decisions had to be taken.[72]

When the CEAC's detailed discussions on industrialisation began during spring 1944, strong opinions soon emerged. Bourdillon suspected that 'the whole of British industry' opposed colonial manufacturing development.[73] Influenced by his recent Nigerian experiences with the UAC, he blamed British firms for Nigeria's failure to industrialize. Given the past absence of an active government policy on colonial industrialisation, and scarce local resources, such development depended upon British finance and skill, neither of which had been forthcoming. Bourdillon condemned this 'short-sighted' response, which he believed had stifled the growth of a potentially large export market.[74]

One of the most controversial aspects of the CEAC's discussions on industrialisation concerned the proposition that development should be concentrated in the most favourable locations, not spread evenly throughout the colonies. Evan Durbin, backed by Lewis, advocated such concentration, arguing the need to maximise available resources. Instead of gradual development, he favoured the rapid modernisation of a single large area, such as Nigeria.[75] However, Durbin neglected the 'political' argument against selective development, favouring one territory at others' expense. The Colonial Office claimed that it could not ignore local susceptibilities in this way. Yet it is arguable that by concentrating on West Indian development after 1942, prompted by Churchill's concern to appease Washington, the Office had done precisely this.

Between them, early in 1944, Lewis and Durbin were calling for large-scale, 'revolutionary' industrialisation in selected territories. Caine objected, defending gradual development across the colonies according to their potential and needs, which might produce as much development, overall, as any 'concentrated' effort.[76] Durbin and Lewis, however, continued their campaign for radical solutions. Durbin believed that only industrial development could raise the colonies from poverty, and unless Britain promoted it the colonies would be condemned to 'permanent economic and social darkness'. He argued that Britain lacked the resources to develop the whole colonial empire simultaneously, estimating the annual cost of even moderate industrialisation throughout the colonies at £500 million to £600 million. He feared that Britain would waste capital on numerous projects which did not comprise a balanced programme in any single colony.[77] Lewis, too, argued that 'concentrated' development could produce genuinely economic enterprise, whereas thinly-spread efforts would promote uneconomically small industries.[78]

These ideas were circulated to the CEAC's Industry Sub-Committee. Lewis saw Britain's pre-war experiments with trading estates as a model for development, permitting economies of scale in providing industrial infrastructures and ultimately making otherwise unattractive projects economic. He thought it inappropriate to judge schemes on a factory-by-factory basis, since few enterprises would be economic by this criterion. Furthermore, efficient, concentrated development could create competitive new industries, and, being *planned*, could avoid the undesirable effects of industrialisation.[79] However, one reason for the Colonial Office's opposition to concentrated development was the fear that it might raise unrealisable expectations in other territories.[80]

Bourdillon, an ally of Durbin and Lewis in other matters, showed greater concern than them about the social consequences of rapid industrialisation.[81] Caine, although opposed to 'revolutionary' development, was prepared to accept the disturbance of traditional institutions, especially in African societies that were still organised along tribal lines. However, he believed that the impact of industrialisation could be moderated, for example through labour legislation.[82] This, and other observations suggest that Caine did not oppose industrial development from fear of its social consequences. A 'progressive' within the Colonial Office, he repeatedly advocated colonial modernisation.

The Colonial Office urged colonial governments to balance economic and social considerations in promoting development:

> A policy promising rapid increase in income may be unwise

> if it involves the sudden disintegration of an established social system; though, on the other hand, the rigid maintenance of old social habits may be unwise if they impede all economic progress.[83]

At this stage in the planning debate, the Colonial Office offered only this inconclusive formula: ultimately, individual colonial governments would have to determine how much social disturbance would be acceptable. The implications of modernisation, however, remained of concern to the Office. In July 1944, Stanley acknowledged that industrial development in West Africa would have a 'fearful' social impact, and stressed the importance of adequate preparation. Hence his decision to establish the Colonial Social Science Research Council to study the social effects of industrialisation.[84]

The CEAC's report on manufacturing industries was eventually drafted by Caine. Predictably, it encapsulated the moderate views of the Committee's majority and the Colonial Office, omitting radical ideas on concentration. The report assumed that improved colonial living standards required some manufacturing development, but that local interests would not be served by 'artificial' and 'uneconomic' industries dependent on prolonged government protection, whether by tariffs, import controls, or subsidies. It did not recommend particular industries, but favoured those manufacturing goods for export from local raw materials, or goods for local consumption from either local or imported raw materials. The possibility of manufacturing goods for export from imported materials was not excluded. It accepted the case for special assistance to new industries, particularly those temporarily unable to withstand outside competition, preferring subsidies to tariff protection and import controls, and incorporating Caine's argument that subsidies distributed the burden of assistance fairly and that competition stimulated industry and encouraged efficiency.[85]

The Board of Trade considered these guidelines 'impeccable', but could not assume that Caine's opinions would remain dominant. It reserved the right to challenge any deviation by the Colonial Office towards high long-term protection.[86] The CEAC recognised that the social impact of industrial development would have to be 'softened':

> At the same time, we are convinced that a policy of opposing

> any kind of industrial development because of the dangers of such social stresses would be mistaken, and that, provided that due care is taken in smoothing the transition, substantial changes in the social structure must be accepted as a necessary cost of progress.

Finally, the Committee admitted its divisions over the desirable *rate* of industrial development. However, while alluding to the arguments over the relative benefits of 'concentrated' as opposed to evolutionary growth, the report left this question open.[87]

Undeterred by their failure to have their views endorsed by the CEAC, Durbin and Lewis called for more radical policies, elaborating their ideas in a memorandum on planning for the CEAC's Agenda Sub-Committee, of which they were members. This rejected the CEAC's report, and urged the fastest practicable economic development, providing secure foundations for self-government and enabling colonies to finance rapid social development. It advocated complementary agricultural and industrial 'revolutions': agricultural development would release labour for industry, which, in turn, would create cheaper goods and expanded markets for farmers. Work should therefore begin by promoting agricultural change in regions selected as suitable for industrial development. Lewis and Durbin repeated their call for concentrated development, rejecting the widespread development of small, isolated factories, protected behind subsidies, tariffs and so on, as the main Committee's report had suggested, because it was not an economic method of creating necessary infrastructures.[88]

Officials reacted coolly to these suggestions. Caine defended the CEAC's 'moderate' proposals, which would permit 'significant if unspectacular advances'.[89] Subsequently, the CEAC, prompted by Durbin and Lewis, asked Stanley outright whether policy would be to promote 'concentrated' development, or to grant equal facilities to encourage industry in every colony.[90] Stanley replied that industrialisation would probably be determined by local circumstances but that, in future, as much weight should be given to developing a balanced and diversified economy in every colony as to any advantages from 'concentrated' development.[91] Lewis resigned as secretary of the CEAC in November 1944, accusing the Colonial Office of obstructing alternative ideas on development.[92] Durbin, equally frustrated, also threatened to resign. His proposal that Lewis be made a full member of the Committee was ignored.[93]

The Colonial Office circulated an amended version of the CEAC's report to colonial governors. This explained that no attempt had been made to suggest 'rapid' or 'revolutionary' change, and omitted discussion of the desirable rate of development. Instead, it summarised acceptable means of promoting development. In an expanded section on 'special assistance to new industries', Caine emphasised the benefits of government subsidies while minimising the role of tariffs and import quotas. The new version stressed the value of providing, at public expense, training and supervision, and even markets for manufactures in government housing and other schemes.[94] Caine's earlier misgivings about protective tariffs were repeated. Again his argument was that tariffs placed the burden of support for industry on the consuming public, not the taxpayer, so that those least able to pay paid most. Generally, however, the despatch suggested that *ad valorem* duties should not exceed 33 per cent and that, if tariffs were imposed, 'impartial' tariff boards should be established to regulate them. Finally, import restrictions were discouraged on the grounds that they impaired efficiency by reducing competition, and that consumers were left open to exploitation by monopolies or 'rings'.[95] The Board of Trade approved the memorandum but hoped for continuing close liaison between colonial governments and London, adding that governments should avoid decisions prejudicial to the Anglo–American discussions on Article VII.[96]

Local interest in industrialisation

From the positive signals it had received from West African governments prior to 1943, the Colonial Office believed that local administrators were anxious to promote industrial development. The period between 1943 and 1946 witnessed not only planning for post-war development, but also modest attempts to establish manufacturing in the region. In the Gold Coast, Burns's concern to prepare for demobilisation led him to favour industrialisation.[97] Burns assumed that the territory's economic base would remain agricultural, but he believed modest industrialisation would benefit the population.[98] However, planning in West Africa was hampered by inadequate economic information. In July 1944, the Development Adviser confessed that he could not speak authoritatively on the future of industries developed during the war because he was unclear what development had occurred. He concluded, however, that productivity was poor and that low wages did not make local labour cheap. This contradicted pre-war metropolitan beliefs that colonial industry would enjoy unfair advantages from cheap, non-European labour. However, Hall believed the predominance of subsistence economies in West Africa made it difficult to assess the potential role of industry. Thus, local incomes could be raised significantly without great effort, providing little incentive for local populations to succeed in a money economy, a precondition for industrial growth.[99]

The promotion of local textile manufacturing appealed strongly to both Accra and Lagos in this period. Burns reported in July 1943 that experiments had begun in Avatime, southern Togoland, to train weavers, using locally grown cotton. These trials, assisted by the West African Institute, received government funds. The aim was to develop a village-based weaving industry using hand-spun cotton. Initially, the scheme appeared successful, producing high quality cloth which found a ready local market.[100] Progress continued and, in October 1944, the Institute's Textile Officer reported that a new industry had been created. Local hand-loom weavers were described as skilful, easily trained and adaptable to regular working hours. Output per worker had increased more than fourfold, and it was hoped to double this. Production was expected to reach 1000 yards per month early in 1945. Hall consequently revised his earlier comments, concluding that improved methods had transformed African productivity. If this continued, it might radically alter the competitiveness of local industries, invalidating previous estimates of their viability, with important implications for future attempts to promote development.[101] The Colonial Office was optimistic about development of this type.[102] By early 1945, the scheme was apparently thriving. Forty-three looms were operating, and three hundred spinning wheels had been distributed, around half of which were in regular use.[103]

If West African officials and the Colonial Office enthused about the possibilities for textile development, the problem of metropolitan reactions remained. The British cotton industry would inevitably be affected by competitive manufacturing overseas, as inter-war experience of India's textile development demonstrated. Lancashire had been ravaged by wartime concentration and export contraction, losing one-third of its mills and half its labour force. Cotton goods exports in 1943 were one-quarter of their 1939 volume.[104] Late in 1942, the Board of Trade's Post-War Reconstruction Section examined the industry's long-term prospects, concluding that Lancashire could not recover its former export trade. Although increased incomes in India, China and elsewhere would increase demand for cotton goods, the Board doubted that Lancashire would benefit, since these important markets were effectively 'lost' to British manufacturers. Africa, however, was considered a large potential market for cheap cotton goods, but not necessarily Lancashire's products: the African market could not conceivably compensate for the loss of India. Lancashire should therefore use its experience and skilled labour to concentrate on producing high grade goods.[105]

Similarly bleak predictions emerged in a Board of Trade memorandum submitted to the Cabinet Reconstruction Committee in June 1944. Intended to counter optimistic assumptions of Britain's ability to increase its share of post-war world trade, the memorandum concluded that this was unlikely for traditional staple industries unless they became more competitive, and unless overseas markets grew through freer world trade.[106] Against this depressing backdrop, the views of the Cotton Board, inevitably concerned about new overseas competition, are particularly important. To some extent, the Cotton Board shared the Board of Trade's fatalism towards overseas industrialisation. According to a memorandum sent to the Board of Trade and the Colonial Office, the Cotton Board was resigned to industrialisation in the Dominions. However, where the colonies were concerned, the Board believed that 'a more realistic attitude was possible', since no entrenched interests yet existed.

The Board believed that colonial industrialisation would occur regardless of opinion in Britain, and accepted the argument that colonial primary over-specialisation made these economies vulnerable. However, it warned of possible drawbacks including declining village crafts, and the unsuitability of locally-grown cotton for the kinds of industry under consideration. Although it was uneasy about overseas competition, the Cotton Board recognised the likelihood of industrial development, which, given low labour costs, might not require tariff protection. The Board therefore claimed to be prepared to 'participate constructively'.[107]

The Cotton Board's interest in colonial industrialisation had been sharpened by a recent Board of Trade decision to permit exports of second-hand textile machinery to Kenya.[108] It sought clear future guidelines, and called for a 'sane' policy on colonial development. The Board's chairman, Sir Raymond Streat, a former secretary of the Manchester Chamber of Commerce, was prominent in the Board's discussions. From July 1943, Streat developed his contacts with the Colonial Office. He thought it futile to attempt to stifle colonial textile industries, but he believed that the question could be handled in a realistic and constructive spirit, safeguarding British interests. As he told Sir Arnold Overton:

> Any policy evolved by us which would command whole-hearted sympathy in London might be likely to receive criticism from the rank and file, who may take a narrow view, but I think myself that the times and the outlook at large necessitate the taking of a long view by Lancashire.[109]

When Streat approached the Board of Trade for discussions, his priority was to involve Lancashire financially in colonial development, although he understood the need for tact given Lancashire's traditional hostility to overseas competition. Overton agreed to act as an 'honest broker' between the Cotton Board and the Colonial Office.[110]

Streat warned his colleagues that colonial textile development would proceed irrespective of their views. He indicated that demands for protection for colonial industries would arise, obliging the Cotton Board to protest, thus exposing itself to charges of obstructing colonial development. If the Cotton Board participated, however, it could influence the course of development:

> An attempt could then be made to establish the position that only goods which could be made on an economic basis should be produced locally and that Lancashire should supply all other cotton goods. There would then be no need for a comprehensive tariff nor could Lancashire be charged with obstructing Colonial developments.

Constructive co-operation, therefore, offered a means to limit the possible erosion of Lancashire's colonial markets.[111]

Streat's conciliatory posture was evident when he and other Cotton Board representatives met Colonial Office and Board of Trade officials in October 1943. He spoke of the need for a constructive policy on the development of colonial cotton manufacturing.[112] Overton, speaking for the Board of Trade, observed that much overseas industrialisation, stimulated by the war, was 'inevitable'. It was in the interests of Britain's machinery industry, he argued, to encourage and participate in sound development. Against this background, Caine's observation that some colonial industrialisation was likely, necessary and desirable, was largely uncontroversial. Streat proposed the creation of an investment corporation, financed jointly by Lancashire and London, to participate in approved developments. The corporation would co-ordinate the efforts of interested Lancashire firms, avoiding wasteful competition.[113] Here was evidence of a metropolitan interest attempting to accommodate itself to the challenge of colonial industrialisation. It remained to be seen how the Cotton Board would react to specific proposals to establish mills.

While the broad implications of colonial industrialisation were being discussed in Britain, developments in West Africa accelerated, focussing the attention of interested British parties. The first major problem to arise with textile development concerned attempts to foster village textile industries. The output of hand-spun cotton yarn could not meet the demand of more productive weavers.[114] In October 1944, it was predicted that the industry's future depended largely on increased yarn supplies.[115] Although hand-weaving was economically viable, hand-spinning was technically inefficient and unable to support a 'modern' industry.[116] However, as Sir Harold Tempany, the Colonial Office's agricultural adviser argued, having toured West Africa in 1943–44, hand-spinning had other advantages. For instance, in northern Nigeria, it was important for the participation of women in the informal economy and, although it was uneconomic, it produced substantial amounts of yarn.[117] Late in 1944, Accra began to investigate improved methods of spinning cotton in order to safeguard the industry's future.[118] The solution appeared to be powered spinning. The West African Institute agreed to supply machinery and advice, and the Gold Coast government provided £13,000.[119]

In Nigeria, meanwhile, expatriate interests were investigating factory-based textile production. In March 1944, the UAC proposed building a textile mill in Zaria Province, with 5,000 spindles and 200 looms, producing some two million square yards of cloth annually, and employing around 300 people. It was planned eventually to increase the mill's capacity five fold.[120] The UAC sought the Colonial Office's help in obtaining machinery for the project. The UAC needed to be able to satisfy a potential manufacturer that permission to export new machinery would be granted, partly because of Lancashire's expected post-war need for new textile plant, and partly because of the absence of second-hand machinery which would not require extensive re-conditioning.[121] Caine approached the Board of Trade on the UAC's behalf, requesting help in securing the necessary export licence.[122] Although it was sympathetic, the Board of Trade judged the matter to be 'very delicate', and promised nothing until the Cotton Board had been consulted informally.[123]

The Board of Trade told the Cotton Board that it did not believe that export licensing should be used to obstruct overseas orders for textile machinery, and that it would be 'extremely embarrassing' for the British government to be accused of manipulating export controls against schemes such as the UAC's. In the Board's view, this kind of development was inevitable, but suspicions persisted in the colonies that Lancashire could influence the British government over the direction of colonial development.

Streat endorsed the Board of Trade's general policy, and promised not to obstruct the UAC proposal, although he doubted whether suitable machinery would be found for export to Nigeria, and warned of protests from Lancashire.[124] As the Board of Trade told the Colonial Office, however, a means had to be found for the UAC to contact the Cotton Board without creating the impression that schemes such as that for Nigeria were being subordinated to Lancashire's wishes. The Board advised the Colonial Office to inform the UAC that neither the Cotton Board nor the Board of Trade opposed textile development in principle, but that much depended on the precise methods proposed by the Company. However, the Board of Trade added that it hoped that such development would involve the 'least possible interference' with Britain's cotton export trade, 'the importance of which as an asset in our post-war economy His Majesty's Government cannot afford to underrate.'[125]

The UAC's subsequent discussions with the Cotton Board appeared amicable. Frank Samuel, Managing Director of the UAC, explained that the Company did not expect its Nigerian scheme to become profitable quickly but that it wanted to respond positively to the authorities' interest in manufacturing. The Cotton Board, too, promised not to obstruct such developments, or the export of machinery from Britain, but it requested reports on the scheme's progress and sought some influence on development in order to limit the damage to Lancashire's export trade. The Board also sought assurances that the UAC would not seek tariff protection against British cotton imports and that the Company would recognise any trade union organisation which might develop in association with the scheme (a point made at the insistence of the Board's trade union members). The UAC accepted these points, and confirmed that it expected no high tariff protection.[126]

As Streat had predicted, Lancashire was less enthusiastic. This emerged during discussions between the Colonial Office, the Cotton Board, the Board of Trade, and the UAC, held in March 1945.[127] Nevertheless, it appeared that British interests understood that they could not seek the Board of Trade's intervention on their behalf to stop such development. The UAC re-emphasised that its Nigerian scheme might incur substantial initial losses, but it was accepted that this was the logical outcome of its commitment to the Colonial Office's industrial policy. More important was the Company's statement that it did not intend to seek protection for its mill against imported textiles, and that the mill would produce a plain grey cloth that was no longer manufactured in Britain.

Caine warned that Lagos was unlikely to commit itself on the issue of protection, and that it would require a free hand. The Colonial Office, he said, supported the UAC's scheme, believing that Nigeria was an appropriate experimental site, and that only strong reasons should prevent progress. The Board of Trade foresaw no major difficulty in granting an export licence for the necessary textile machinery, but it could not say when this would be because future machinery production would have to be allocated between domestic demand and that of overseas development. Nevertheless, the Board promised that the export licensing system would not be used to hinder colonial industrialisation. The meeting's outcome was that the UAC's scheme secured the 'blessing' of the Colonial Office and the Board of Trade, and the Cotton Board's 'acquiescence'. The UAC was encouraged to make detailed investigations, liaising with the Development Adviser in Nigeria, after which it could apply for the export licence for the machinery that it required.[128]

The process of local consultation in Nigeria revealed obstacles that had not been foreseen by the Company or the Colonial Office, suggesting changing attitudes in Lagos towards the benefits of industrialisation and the desirability of constitutional advance, following the appointment of the conservative Sir Arthur Richards as governor.[129] In November 1944, replying to the Treasury, Richards explained that large-scale industrialisation was not envisaged, although several projects were being considered. F.E.V. Smith, Richards' Development Adviser, saw little point in establishing factories unless their products were cheaper than similar imports. Conversely, he appreciated the potential of a local textile industry, involving perhaps one quarter of a million people in cotton growing. He concluded: 'Industrialisation for its own sake was valueless, but industrialisation with a background of development could be of great benefit'.[130] Over the next two years, Lagos applied increasingly searching criteria in assessing industrial proposals. It initially favoured the UAC's scheme, while stressing that it would not welcome competition with the peasant weaving industry it hoped to cultivate.

Lagos's own plans for a peasant textile industry were outlined in April 1945. A five-year programme, costing over £90,000, was planned, and was expected to employ large numbers of workers both directly and indirectly. Despite the 'primitive' and uneconomical methods to be used, the government believed that, with proper supervision, major improvements in peasant production were possible. Lagos's preference for village industry stemmed partly from the desire to safeguard peasants' incomes by creating spare-time employment for women, and full-time work for men, at times when agricultural work slackened. More fundamental, however, was the government's wish to retard urbanisation and stem the decline of the villages. Eight 'territorial centres' were to be created to conduct research into improved methods, and provide training.[131]

Nigeria's village textile industry, like the Gold Coast's, soon faced the problem that yarn production could not meet local weavers' needs, creating bottle-neck at the weaving stage. A possible solution was to encourage the UAC to produce yarn at its proposed mill[132] but, during spring 1945, the tone of Lagos's statements on the UAC proposal became markedly cooler. Smith told London that the Company's scheme must not compete with the local peasant industry, and that if the UAC wanted a mill in

Nigeria, it would have to co-operate with the government by producing yarn for village weavers.[133] The Nigerian government's purpose in establishing a village-based industry was to prevent a population 'exodus' to the towns, which factory development might encourage but, because hand-spinning threatened to prevent the rapid expansion of the village weaving industry, Lagos would countenance a factory producing yarn in sufficient quantities. This would also obviate purchases of expensive imported yarn from African merchants. The Colonial Office sympathised with Nigeria's plans, and agreed to support them.[134] In August 1945, it approved a colonial development and welfare grant of £53,450 towards the scheme.[135]

Meanwhile, Accra investigated the prospects for local industrial development. In May 1945, the Industrial Development Sub-Committee of the government's Economic Development Committee presented a discouraging report. Its basic assumption was that after the war, the Gold Coast would be a market for overseas manufacturers so, while it was 'desirable on some grounds' to broaden the Gold Coast economy by introducing manufacturing, the report rejected industrial production geared towards an export market (except, perhaps, the manufacture of high quality furniture) and considered that it would be 'dangerous' to promote industries catering for the local market in competition with imported goods.

It argued that there was generally more scope for government assistance to village industries and crafts than to factory production. Even here, the prospects for developing the wartime experiments in import substitution appeared bleak. The Sub-Committee thought it unlikely, for example, that good, locally made bricks could 'ever' compete in cost with other building materials, nor were there grounds for government assistance for tile production. Similarly, although the Gold Coast now produced about half its pre-war soap imports, encouraged by the 50–75 per cent increase in the price of imported soap, the report saw little scope for government action.[136]

The report was equally resolute on the issue of textile manufacturing: 'There can be no question of establishing textile factories in the Gold Coast, but there are possibilities of developing weaving as a village industry', an interest derived from experience of the Avatime project. This experiment was expected to overcome the bottle-neck in yarn supply by establishing powered spinning.[137]

By July 1945, however, there seemed little prospect of the textile machinery needed by West Africa becoming available before late 1946. Soon, however, disquieting reports emerged from the Gold Coast. Concern at the declining quality of cloth produced in Avatime, and fears that existing stocks of cloth were unfit for sale, convinced local administrators that the project required 'competent commercial management' and proper technical supervision. It subsequently became necessary for the government to intervene by purchasing the Avatime cloth and reselling it.[138] In this light, Accra saw the expected delay in securing spinning machinery from Britain as an opportunity to re-evaluate the entire Avatime scheme.[139]

Similarly, early in 1946, there were fresh indications that Lagos was reconsidering the benefits of expatriate-run textile projects. Besides the UAC's proposal, a plan by the Lancashire cotton-spinning firm, Haighton's Ltd, to build a textile mill, was being examined. In January 1946, the Nigerian government told the UAC that if its scheme threatened cotton goods imports into Nigeria, then an excise duty might be levied on locally produced cotton cloth, to compensate for lost import revenue.[140] Richards told Stanley's successor, George Hall, that the UAC's and Haighton's projects required careful investigation, since Nigeria possessed no legislation to control or licence industrial development. Referring to Haighton's scheme, Richards offered detailed objections to factory development. These included the problems of providing adequate housing and food if urban industry developed. He objected especially to factory growth in Lagos, whose existing housing and social problems would, he believed, be aggravated. Richards refuted the defence that textile factories would create employment. He feared not only that textile mills would compete with the embryonic peasant industry, but that the territory's import revenue from cotton goods would suffer. The one point which Richards was willing to concede was that factory spinning of cotton yarn would supply village weavers with raw material.[141]

These views provoked varied reactions in the Colonial Office. In one official's words, the objections listed by Richards constituted a report 'so luke-warm as to amount virtually to rejection'. Moreover, 'small beginnings', if properly regulated, could smoothe the transition from an agricultural economy to a mixed economy. Richards' fears that factories would compete with village industry were rejected: if village conditions were sound, factory development would not necessarily lead to urban migration. Similarly, Richards' fears about falling government revenue, were challenged as this would be a 'transitional' problem: moreover, the goal of industrialisation was to raise living standards, increasing Nigeria's taxable capacity. More serious, in the Colonial Office's view, was the anti-industrial outlook implicit in Richards' despatch. It seemed necessary to decide whether industrialisation was desirable, in which case some urbanisation was inevitable and efforts had to be made to attract reputable and qualified industrialists to undertake development.[142] Another official believed that Lagos sought 'the creation of a rustic economy whose passing in this country is lamented over by writers like G.K. Chesterton', and thought that village industry was compatible with factory development. While factories would have to be sited properly and operate under acceptable conditions, if Nigerian conditions were as difficult as Richards suggested, then an industrial licensing system would have to be introduced.[143]

Caine felt that Richards' arguments vindicated his own warnings of the dangers of entrusting control of industrialisation to colonial governments, which might be more adept at preventing development than encouraging it. He agreed that Lagos's attitude was obstructive and threatened the whole policy of factory-based industrialisation. Precisely for this reason, he believed that the government should not be empowered to control development through licensing. Caine also criticised Lagos's preference for hand-weaving, arguing that it ignored the economics of production and consumers' interests. However, he detected a more serious underlying problem:

> It has been a common place of criticism of Colonial policy in the past that both the home Government and Colonial Governments have prevented the development of manufacturing industries in the Colonies. I have always strenuously denied such a policy and know of no substantial evidence for it in the past. If however the attitude of the Nigerian Government is maintained, it will be impossible any longer to deny that the Government is pursuing a policy directly adverse to industrial development.

If Nigeria had to be protected from the 'evils' of industrialisation, then this should be stated frankly, and not concealed behind an impossibly selective attitude to such development. Caine advocated a liberal economic framework for modernisation:

> Personally, I think it is both economically and socially wrong and politically impossible to prevent a considerable degree of industrial development in a Colony of the size and resources of Nigeria and I think that a policy of the kind now indicated by the Nigerian Government can lead only to the arbitrary building up of special privileges as they select one firm rather than another... as eligible for permission to try their hand at industrialisation; to the preservation of inefficiency and uneconomic techniques merely because they are traditional; and to a permanent retardation in the making available to the consumer in Nigeria of increased quantities of goods at lower prices, in other words, the raising of the standard of living.

Caine concluded that the Colonial Office should tell Richards plainly that his policy was unacceptable.[144]

However, Lagos's misgivings about Haighton's scheme deepened when discussions revealed that the company planned not to use *local* raw materials but to manufacture cotton goods in Nigeria using imported British or Egyptian yarn, more cheaply than it could in Britain. The product could then be exported, possibly to South Africa. This was quite unacceptable to Lagos, which envisaged Nigeria deriving only an unwelcome stimulus to urbanisation.[145]

Meanwhile, the UAC had been both surprised and disturbed by Lagos's threat of a counterveiling excise duty on locally produced cloth, and immediately suspended its project for a mill at Onitsha, a site selected in preference to the original choice of Zaria. The Company conceded that local production would affect cloth imports, but felt that this would probably not occur for several years. Furthermore, although the UAC had not considered asking for protection, it saw a safety margin in the existing revenue duties. Frank Samuel believed that Lagos's thinking was muddled:

> Surely the purpose of the establishment of industry is the raising of the economic level and wealth of the country, thus enabling the people to consume larger quantities of other types of imported goods which will yield their normal import revenue, and greater quantities of heavy duty and excise goods such as cigarettes, beer etc.

No firm, he thought, would invest in a textile industry in Nigeria with the prospect of an excise duty being imposed immediately after its factory started production.[146]

Writing to the UAC in February 1946, the Nigerian government denied being opposed to industrialisation, but stressed its need to consider the long-term value of manufacturing proposals. Since each proposal would have to be judged on its merits, the government was unwilling to issue any general endorsement of industrialisation. Specifically, Lagos doubted that the UAC's scheme would benefit Nigeria as a whole, or that it would generate greater demand for local cotton at higher prices, an issue not previously raised. The Nigerian government felt that, although the scheme might benefit around 2,000 workers, the consequent increase in government responsibilities, stemming from urban growth, might, on balance, make the development a liability. Furthermore, unless the UAC could produce goods locally which were 'substantially' cheaper than imports, the government would not forgo the revenue it derived from import duties on cotton goods.[147]

Trenchard, Chairman of UAC, queried Richards' decision to raise the excise duty question at this stage, together with fundamental doubts about the entire scheme.[148] Richards' reply was conciliatory, assuring Trenchard that his government wanted to examine manufacturing possibilities, and welcomed the UAC's help. He suggested further discussions between the Colonial Office and the Company.[149] The UAC's disenchantment by this stage was understandable. The Company had assumed that Lagos favoured industrialisation, especially the development of textile manufacturing using local raw material, which would find an adequate local market and which required no specific protection.[150]

The Nigerian government's stance evoked unusual sympathy for the UAC within the Colonial Office, where Lagos's arguments against the Company's scheme were considered even weaker than those used against Haighton's project, especially since the former intended to use locally grown cotton.[151] Prompted by these difficulties, George Hall informed Richards that he shared the governor's concern to avoid problems associated with uncontrolled industrial development.

> On the other hand, it seems to me that it is possible for a government to be a little too cautious in its attitude towards

> proposals for new industrial development and by setting its requirements too high to run the risk that no development will take place at all.

Hall requested confirmation that Richards did not oppose factory-based development, since:

> ...there is no doubt in my mind that industrial development in itself offers one of the most promising means we can have of raising the general level of prosperity of the people in a country like Nigeria.

Echoing the advice in Stanley's February 1945 despatch on manufacturing, Hall dismissed the suggestion that a textile mill in Nigeria would be desirable only if it used local raw materials, arguing that if the promoters believed they could operate profitably with imported materials they should not be obstructed.[152]

Richards' response drew on copious counter-arguments. The Governor assured Hall that he did not aim to obstruct factory development, 'provided it does not compete with peasant industry'.[153] Apparently Richards complained for the first time that industrialisation would compete with agriculture for labour. Further, because agricultural living standards were low, industry would be able to obtain labour cheaply, which might encourage accusations that the government was abetting the exploitation of African labour. This, claimed Richards, made him doubtful about industries based on imported raw materials. To be profitable, he believed, these would have to keep wage costs low. Richards may have been affected by the growth of trade unions in Nigeria, a process greatly accelerated by the war, and, specifically, by the general strike called by the Railway Workers' Union in June 1945.[154] Richards concluded with a more immediate problem: the inability of his Secretariat yet to produce a well-considered policy on industrialisation, given that the official whose function this would be had only recently been appointed.[155]

The Colonial Office and officials from Lagos discussed industrialisation between May and July 1946. It became obvious that Nigerian officials feared the social consequences of industrial development. The Development Adviser, F.E.V. Smith, denied being opposed to 'rational' development, citing his government's approval of the UAC's plywood-producing scheme at Sapele, a project first mooted by the Company early in 1943.[156] The essential difference between this and other industrial projects, he argued, was that if the Sapele venture failed, its workers could resume their previous way of life with minimal disruption, whereas a failed *urban* development might create serious housing and unemployment problems. Caine considered such arguments irrelevant. He did not dispute the need to control the location of industry and working conditions: the key question was whether Lagos, unlike the Colonial Office, opposed factory development.[157]

The Nigerian government's counter-arguments to textile factory development continued to be inconsistent. In July 1946, Smith questioned the sincerity of the UAC's interest in textile development, arguing that its proposed mill, whose production could cost Nigeria about £100,000 per annum in lost revenue, would not become profitable for 'at least' ten years. Nevertheless, such development would encourage an influx of British firms and immigrant entrepreneurs, both Indian and 'Syrian', into Nigeria.[158] This was possibly closer to the government's overriding concerns, particularly the need to avoid political friction at a time of major constitutional, economic and social change.

Further insights into Lagos's anxieties emerged in its response to a report by Raymond Firth, secretary of the Colonial Social Science Research Council, who toured West Africa between July and October 1945. Firth noted the rapid post-war increase in urbanisation, especially in the coastal towns. The resulting problems included severe overcrowding, high rents, unemployment, the disruption of families and juvenile delinquency.[159] Richards agreed that a study of labour migration and its effects was necessary. Consistently opposed to constitutional reform, he feared an influx of Ibos into the larger commercial and administrative centres of the Northern Provinces, where the UAC's mill was to be built, threatening to undermine the region's traditional political structures.[160]

Reviewing development policy

Such resistance convinced the Colonial Office that greater metropolitan influence over development was needed. In November 1945, Hall announced that he was considering ways of handling development plans more quickly. It was recognised that if the Colonial Office were to play a more active role in directing development, taking responsibility rather than passively considering plans submitted by colonial governments, its own organisation would have to be reinforced. Hall proposed a small, 'high-powered' committee, with business representatives, to supervise the existing committees and ensure action on their reports. Hall's parliamentary under-secretary, Creech Jones, believed that the key problem was the need to establish guiding principles on economic policy, including industrialisation. He felt that the Colonial Office had hitherto allowed external interests to take the initiative: instead, the Office should itself have positive policies.[161] Subsequent discussions produced the suggestion for a Colonial Economic Development Council (CEDC) to replace the Colonial Economic Advisory Committee, and renewed pressure from Caine for new executive machinery in London capable of initiating development.

The creation of the Colonial Economic Development Council was announced in June 1946. Its function was to advise on the framing and review of development plans and on general questions of economic and financial policy.[162] The Council discussed industrial development in December 1946 and concluded that territorial governments' responses to Stanley's 1945 despatch had been 'disappointing', suggesting a degree of inertia, even of opposition, where this subject was concerned, although the creation of Departments of Commerce and Industry by some governments, including the Gold Coast's and Nigeria's, seemed a 'promising' indication of local initiative. However, the Council added little to the CEAC's original recommendations, other than to stress the importance of selecting industries using local raw materials, and requiring a minimum amount of skilled labour and a maximum amount of unskilled labour.[163]

By 1946, the Colonial Office was less squeamish than the West African governments about the impact of economic development on African societies. Caine called for a more dynamic, modernising approach to development. Existing African patterns of social organisation were, he believed, obstacles to inevitable and irreversible economic change, stifling the emergence of local enterprise. He recalled Lewis's proposals for 'revolutionary' agricultural and industrial change, and the resulting questions about the compatibility of rapid economic change with broader political and social policies. In Caine's view, it was time to reconsider the negative response that the Colonial Office had given Lewis.[164] Endorsing this view was one of the Colonial Office's rising stars,

Andrew Cohen, who was to play a central role in the reorientation of colonial policy after 1946, and who, after his return to the Colonial Office in 1943 after a term as Acting Lieutenant Governor of Malta, injected a progressive, Fabian outlook into the reconstruction debate and a determination to give colonial rule a modernising purpose. Although still Assistant Secretary responsible for the East and Central Africa Department, Cohen was soon to assume charge of the entire Africa Division, and his opinions, if not always unanimously shared by his colleagues, were increasingly authoritative.[165] Cohen believed that 'native' institutions had to be adapted to social and economic change, and that the emphasis in future policy would have to shift from tradition to efficiency.[166] The Development Adviser, Stockdale, commented that colonial policy had reached the 'parting of the ways' in Africa, and that clear guidelines for the future were urgently required.[167] These sentiments were endorsed by Gater, who agreed with Caine that Stanley's responses to the CEAC's questions on future development late in 1944 should be reconsidered:

> Since 1944 a great deal has happened and it is becoming clear that we shall have to face more revolutionary methods if we are to achieve success in raising the standard of living in Colonial Territories.[168]

Stockdale, Cohen and Caine met to discuss this review of development policy in July 1946. They agreed that the most pressing problem was to encourage colonial governments themselves to consider such basic questions as the value of 'concentrated' development, and that it would help governments if they knew that London would listen to radical suggestions.

As demonstrated by its stance over Nigerian development, the Colonial Office remained committed to its industrial policy. The Office was encouraged by fresh indications that industrialisation in the underdeveloped world was accepted by key government departments in a more liberal spirit than before the war. In May 1946, for example, the Board of Trade told the Cabinet Committee on External Economic Policy and Overseas Trade that such development need not ultimately harm British industry as a whole, although it might threaten certain sectors. Overseas industrialisation offered opportunities to some British exporters:

> It must be remembered that if we were to refuse to export

> capital goods in such instances, our competitors among the industrial nations might step in and secure the orders.

This attitude was a pragmatic response to the inevitable. However, the Board continued to oppose the promotion of new 'uneconomic' industries in thinly populated regions of the world, and called for co-operation from the rest of Whitehall.[169]

More sober, if equally fatalistic, conclusions were drawn by the Cabinet Office Economic Section in June 1946. Surveying the overseas economic situation, the Section considered that the post-war 'hunger' for manufactures was temporary, although at the time there was enough demand to absorb most British export production. Overseas industrialisation, however, was a more permanent problem. Although it would increase the demand for capital goods, raw materials and fuel, the demand for consumer goods, especially textiles, was threatened by local import substitution. The growth of incomes and demand resulting from industrialisation could offset the harmful aspects of overseas development by increasing total imports of manufactures in countries with the lowest incomes, for example in Latin America and India. However, the net effect of overseas industrialisation would damage Britain's export trade, involving sectoral changes in British exports away from cheaper textiles and hardware and towards engineering and electrical products. The Economic Section drew some solace from the hope that this would assist Britain's balance of payments because it involved a move away from the production of goods containing a high proportion by value of imported materials, and towards the production of goods that owed much of their value to the skill of British labour.[170]

The Colonial Office continued to seek evidence of interest in industrialisation among colonial governments, despite the hitherto disappointing responses from West Africa. Between February 1945, when Stanley's despatch on manufacturing was issued, and late 1946, the West African governments gave little indication that industrialisation was considered as a developmental priority. Lagos appears not to have responded directly to the despatch, but its attitudes towards industrial development subsequently became clear during the extensive discussions on cotton textile manufacturing. Accra's response was hardly encouraging: the overall conclusion of the government's Economic Development Committee was that few goods could be manufactured economically in the territory.[171]

London's continuing dissatisfaction with the abilities of the colonial governments is evident in the Office's reaction to the draft ten year development plan submitted by Accra early in 1946. Like earlier drafts, this was felt to be too biased towards welfare provision, neglecting the territory's overall development needs. In particular, little mention was made of industrialisation. As one official commented:

> In a colony whose economy relies so largely upon one agricultural crop and on expendable mineral assets, it is essential that larger provision be made – with C.D.+ W. assistance – for establishing and building up new and reliable sources of general revenue.

The plan's 'less urgent' components should, it was felt, be adjusted, giving greater attention to industrial and general economic growth.[172]

During the review of development policy in 1946, however, it became clear that the Colonial Office saw industrialisation as an important but subsidiary aspect of development. As the Office's report for the years 1939 to 1947 stressed, the emphasis in development planning was necessarily on improving agriculture and communications, although 'due regard' was being given to promoting new activities, including industry.[173]

In the official scale of priorities, two considerations underscored agricultural development: the post-war world food shortage, and the scarcity of goods for export to the colonies. Metropolitan concern over world food supplies was especially acute early in 1946, leading Attlee to create a special Cabinet Committee to monitor the situation.[174] The most spectacular, and infamous, consequence of London's anxiety to promote food production was the ill-fated East African Groundnut Scheme, launched in November 1946, to improve supplies of fats. Nevertheless, the British Government's concern to stimulate colonial food production was not yet associated with any grand strategy to utilise colonial resources to reduce Britain's balance of payments problems.[175]

In August 1946, Caine drafted a circular despatch on agricultural productivity in Africa, described by Cohen as one of the most 'encouraging' documents he had seen. Although he recognised that industrialisation was important to African development, Cohen thought it less urgent than agricultural improvement and saw little point in asking colonial governments to examine industrial development while they were addressing questions of agricultural reorganisation.[176] Caine's memorandum, despatched to the African governments in February 1947, stressed the

> vital importance of revolutionary changes in production, particularly agricultural production ... without such changes we shall not succeed in raising, rapidly the standards of living of Africans.[177]

Alongside the growing metropolitan interest in colonial primary production (a tendency not fully revealed until 1947) there remained the problem of meeting the colonies' import requirements for post-war reconstruction and development. The difficulty in supplying West Africa with consumer goods had been the basic motive for examining limited industrialisation early in the war. As peace loomed, however, it became apparent that these supply problems would continue. In December 1944, Stanley admitted the shortage of textiles in the colonies, but, claiming that they received their fair share of available British supplies, he conceded that future colonial demand was causing concern.[178] By early 1945, officials realised that supplies would not improve quickly and that colonial governments needed guidance.[179] The Colonial Office had expected a lengthy 'twilight' period before Japan's collapse, easing the metropolitan transition to peacetime production.[180]

In April 1945, Stanley warned that the supply position might initially worsen after the war because of shipping shortages. He added that 'the position is likely to be most acute with regard to supply of goods of most interest to the mass of colonial populations, i.e. wage labourers and small peasant producers.' The immediate concern was that shortages would fuel colonial inflation. Governments were urged to dispel any 'false' optimism, and to prepare their populations for continuing stringencies.[181] The Colonial Office also warned the Cabinet that the colonies could not endure further import reductions and stressed the 'disastrous effect' which declining supplies of goods such as cotton textiles might have on commodity production and political stability, which might in turn be aggravated by demobilisation.[182] The Minister of Food, eager to increase colonial food production, supported Stanley.[183]

In July, Stanley again told the Cabinet Home Affairs

Committee that colonial food production would suffer unless consumer goods were made available. Inflation was already producing political unrest in parts of Africa. Neither the President of the Board of Trade nor the Minister of Production foresaw any rapid improvement in textiles supplies, although other goods, especially semi-luxuries, might be made available.[184] Paradoxically, when the Colonial Office subsequently unveiled details of the new Colonial Development and Welfare Act, it suggested that increased funding would coincide with greater availability of materials and personnel.[185] In practice, such optimism proved ill-founded.

A year later, the Board of Trade called for cuts in colonial textile supplies, alarming the Colonial Office, which challenged the Board's priorities. As Clauson put it: 'The future prospects of Lancashire's export trade are of course an important matter for this country, but not as important as our political prestige in the Colonial Empire + the food supplies of this country.'[186] The position of consumer goods in West Africa became critically important as the post-war world food shortage impinged upon Britain. As in wartime, there was high-level recognition that such goods were vital to maintain colonial productivity. In February 1946, Attlee personally directed that special efforts be made to meet West Africa's requirements. The Board of Trade, however, opposed the direction of consumer goods to food-producing areas.[187]

What is striking about these supply difficulties is that the Colonial Office did not regard them as an opportunity to promote import-substituting industry in West Africa. The Office encouraged industrial development when proposals arose, but there was no discussion on its role in easing post-war supply difficulties. This is partly attributable to shortages of virtually all the materials required for colonial development, including machinery and other capital goods.[188]

Although wartime controls on British exports were mostly lifted by early 1946, this helped the colonies little since domestic and dollar-earning orders took priority. There was thus a fundamental constraint facing any attempt to ease colonial consumer goods shortages by local production, and this was evident in West Africa's problems in securing textile machinery. Moreover, the Board of Trade's apparent resignation to overseas industrialisation appeared not to apply to individual development proposals, particularly in the colonies. The Board of Trade had seemed co-operative towards West African schemes for textile development, demonstrated by the relatively conflict-free discussions it held with the Colonial Office between 1943 and 1946. However, the Board of Trade remained susceptible to the Cotton Board's anxieties about future competition, amounting to discreet collusion designed to restrict overseas development.

Although the Cotton Board had also appeared to take a constructive view towards colonial textile development, this was less obvious in its stance on similar developments outside the colonial empire, over which Lancashire could expect to have little influence – hence the Board's concern about exports of textile machinery. In mid-1945, the Board of Trade proposed removing controls on textile machinery exports. Deferring to the Cotton Board's policy since wartime concentration, the Board of Trade proposed to retain export licensing for all textile machinery manufactured before 1 May 1941.[189]

In January 1946, however, Streat complained that recent Board of Trade decisions on exports of second-hand machinery amounted to a disturbing trend. He feared that some countries, for example in the Middle East, favoured investment in the production of cotton textiles because of shortages which had created distorted impressions of the true demand for these goods. He thought that such enterprises, once established, would seek tariff protection, harming British export prospects.

Streat urged the Board of Trade to curb export licences for textile machinery. The Board promised to allow the administrative machine 'to function very slowly for the next few months' in handling applications for licences, a suggestion that the Cotton Board accepted.[190] It is unclear whether this decision had direct consequences for West African development although, from the summer of 1945, the textile projects in Nigeria and the Gold Coast encountered particular difficulty in obtaining machinery from Britain.

Against this background, Colonial Office discussions on industrialisation became sparse and incidental. To prevent inflation, and, ultimately, political discontent, the Colonial Office preferred to limit colonial purchasing power through effective taxation and State produce marketing. Central to London's post-war attempts at 'nation building' was the belief that governments should increase their revenues, to promote self-sufficiency and eliminate metropolitan aid. They were encouraged to introduce or extend income taxation, to reduce their past overdependence on revenue from trade.[191]

Nevertheless, excise duties had risen during the war, and net receipts had increased because of the greater value of trade. These duties were seen as having a counter-inflationary function, absorbing the gap between the selling price and the supply costs of consumer goods. The Colonial Office feared that while colonial governments might be tempted to *reduce* wartime taxation levels, the supply problem dictated that taxation might instead have to be *increased*.[192] Yet indirect taxation continued to be important to local administrations. For example, Lagos derived 43 per cent of its revenue from excise duties in 1946: by 1950 this figure had risen to 51 per cent, hence the government's concern, during discussions on the UAC's textile scheme, that local industrialisation might affect revenue from trade.[193]

Through the second element in its anti-inflationary strategy, State produce marketing, the Colonial Office ostensibly aimed to shield producers from violent price fluctuations. The marketing authorities were to accumulate financial surpluses, subsequently payable to producers if world prices fell. During the war, the authorities paid low prices, partly fearing that unabsorbed local purchasing power at a time of import constraints would fuel inflation. While the official justification for State marketing was that it would stabilise producer incomes, the accumulation of ever larger reserves became an end in itself, driven partly by fear of inflation, and partly by the reserves' function in supporting sterling. The Colonial Office was therefore reluctant to see these funds used for development, preferring their exclusive dedication to an ill-defined shibboleth of 'stabilisation'.

During the Office's early discussions on reconstruction in 1941, stabilisation through controlled produce marketing had emerged as a potential rival to arguments for diversification. Early in 1944, Lord Hailey suggested that marketing would be more important than almost any other aspect of post-war economic policy. After 1945, the twin objectives of stabilisation and combating inflation, through state produce marketing and improved taxation, increasingly eclipsed two key arguments for industrialisation current throughout wartime policy discussions: the easing of structural economic instability arising from dependence on primary production, and the immediate danger of inflation due to import shortages.[194]

NOTES

1. J.M. Lee, *The Churchill Coalition 1940–1945* (London: Batsford, 1980) pp.112–41; P. Addison, *The Road to 1945. British Politics and the Second World War* (London: Quartet, 1977) pp.211–69.
2. *PD(C)*, 386, 250, 20 Jan. 1943.
3. *PD(C)*, 380, 2025–2027, 24 June 1942; A. Creech Jones, 'The Colonial Office', *Political Quarterly* (Jan.–Mar. 1943), pp.19–32.
4. CO 852/408, minute by Caine, 20 Nov. 1943.
5. *PD(C)*, 388, 1492, 15 Apr. 1943.
6. CO 852/510/29, minutes, 16 Feb., 19 Feb. and 17 Apr. 1943.
7. Ibid., telegram, 2 Mar. 1943.
8. Ibid., telegram, 10 March 1943; J. Kent, 'The International Dimensions of British West African Policy 1939–1949'. (Aberdeen Ph.D. 1986) pp.335–42.
9. CO 554/132/33718/4/1943, telegram, 10 Mar. 1943.
10. Ibid., letter to Stanley, 1 July 1943.
11. CO 96/776/8/31475/1943, Dawe to Burns, 17 Mar. 1943.
12. CO 583/263/30560/1943, note of discussion between Dawe and Bourdillon, 10 June 1943; ibid., notes of meetings between Stanley, officials and Bourdillon, 22 June 1943 and 2 July 1943.
13. CO 866/16, minute by Caine, 11 July 1940.
14. CO 852/588/2, memo., 16 Aug. 1943.
15. CO 852/505/7, minute, 26 Aug. 1942.
16. CO 852/588/2, memo., 16 Aug. 1943.
17. CO 554/132/33718/1943, minute by Caine, 5 Apr. 1943.
18. CO 96/775/1/31401/1941, minute, 29 Apr. 1943.
19. CO 554/132/33718/1/1943, 'Post-War Planning for West Africa', despatched 31 Aug. 1943.
20. Kent (1986), pp.346–7.
21. Morgan (1980) I, p.184.
22. J.A. Cross, *Lord Swinton* (Oxford: Oxford University Press, 1982), pp.111–13.
23. CO 852/480/11, WAWC(CM)4, 24 Feb. 1943.
24. CO 852/480/11, letter to Stanley, 16 Mar. 1943.
25. CO 852/503/18, WP(43)205, memo. by Swinton, 'Post-War Commercial Policy', 14 May 1943.
26. CO 583/263/30560/1943, note of meeting between Bourdillon and officials, 22 June 1943.
27. Sir B. Bourdillon, *The Future of the Colonial Empire* (London: SCM Press, 1945, pp.51–3; —, 'Colonial Development and Welfare', *International Affairs*, 20, 3, (July 1944), pp.369–80.
28. Ibid., note by H.B. Lawrence, 10 June 1943.
29. CO 554/132/333712/1/1943, WAWC(CM)(15), 7 June 1943.
30. CO 554/139/33764/1944, 'Report on a tour in West Africa November 1943 to March 1944', June 1944.
31. CO 554/139/33764/1945, letter to Stanley, 27 Feb. 1945.
32. CO 96/781/31475/1944, despatch, 26 July 1944.
33. CO 554/139/33764/1945, OAG, Gold Coast, (Gurney) to Stanley, 14 June 1945.
34. C. Thorne, *Allies of a Kind* (Oxford: Oxford University Press, 1979), pp.92–102.
35. M.W. Kirby, *The Decline of British Economic Power since 1870* (London: Allen and Unwin, 1981), pp.93–4.
36. Thorne (1979), p.513.
37. Kirby (1981), pp.95–7.
38. L.S. Pressnell, *External Economic Policy Since the War, Volume I, The Post-War Financial Settlement* (London: HMSO, 1986) p.101; CAB 117/68, 'Report of the

Committee on Post-War Commercial Policy', 6 Jan. 1943.
39. Pressnell (1986), p.102.
40. CAB 123/221, letter, 15 Jan. 1943.
41. CAB 117/68, 'Report of the Committee on Post-War Commercial Policy', 6 Jan. 1943.
42. CO 852/584/1, minute, 21 Aug. 1945.
43. CO 990/2, CEAC(44)11, 'Effects of war-time changes in colonial economic structure and organisation' (n.d.).
44. CO 852/480/11, summary of WAWC(CM)4 (memorandum by Lord Swinton on Economic Policy), Aug. 1943.
45. CO 852/480/11, minute by Creasy, 12 Mar. 1943.
46. Ibid., minute, 15 Mar. 1943.
47. Ibid., minute, 29 Apr. 1943.
48. E.g., ibid., minute by Carstairs, 15 May 1943.
49. Ibid., minute, 24 May 1943 and minute by Carstairs, 28 May 1943.
50. CO 852/480/11, minute, 31 May 1943; CAB 117/68, 'Report of the Committee on Post-War Commercial Policy', 6 Jan. 1943.
51. CO 852/482/2, letter to Swinton, 5 June 1943.
52. CO 852/480/11, letter to Stanley, 22 June 1943.
53. CO 852/480/11, minute by K.E. Robinson, 23 Apr. 1943; ibid., minute by O.G.R. Williams, 27 Apr. 1943.
54. *PD(C)*, 402, 462–3, 20 July 1944.
55. CO 852/578/5, Cmd.6529 *Colonial Products Research Council. First Annual Report 1943–1944*, May 1944.
56. CO 852/482/3, minute, 30 Oct. 1943.
57. CO 875/16/16, speech, 5 Mar. 1943.
58. CO 554/132/33712/1/1943, WAWC(CM), 7 June 1943.
59. *PD(C)*, 391, 66–8, 13 July 1943.
60. CO 554/132/33718/1/1943, 'Post-War Planning for West Africa', (n.d.).
61. CO 852/480/1, minute, 5 May 1943. On developments in East Africa in this period, see Swainson (1980), pp.30–1, 54–5; Berman (1990), p.270.
62. CO 852/409/13, 'U.K. Participation in Empire Secondary Industries', (n.d.).
63. The Federation of British Industries had reached similar conclusions in its report on 'The Future of British Export Trade' (CAB 117/199, 23 Feb. 1943).
64. CO 852/409/13, 'U.K. Participation in Empire Secondary Industries', July 1943.
65. T.J. Miller, 'The Board of Trade and British Economic Reconstruction 1940–49: the regeneration of exporting industries', (M.Litt. thesis, Stirling University, 1986), pp.70–1.
66. CO 852/554/7, 'Overseas investment in the next few years', Jan. 1944.
67. CO 990/1, CEAC 3rd minutes, 15 Feb. 1944; ibid., CEAC(44)15, 'The Development of Secondary Industry in the Colonial Empire', (n.d.).
68. BT 11/2441, letter to Nowell, 7 Feb. 1944.
69. Ibid., minute by Skevington, 22 Feb. 1944.
70. Petter (1981), p.80.
71. BT 11/2441, note of meeting between CO and BoT officials, 4 Apr. 1944.
72. Ibid., 14 Apr. 1944.
73. CO 990/16, CEAC (Industry) 3rd minutes, 17 Apr. 1944.
74. Bourdillon (1945), pp.52–3.
75. CO 990/16, CEAC (Industry) 3rd minutes, 17 Apr. 1944.
76. CO 990/17, CEAC (Industry)(44)5, 'Possible scope for industrialisation in the Colonies', 25 Apr. 1944.
77. Ibid., CEAC (Industry)(44)7, note, 4 May 1944.
78. CO 990/16, CEAC (Industry) 5th minutes, 15 June 1944.
79. CO 990/17, CEAC (Industry)(46)26, memorandum by W.A. Lewis and F.E.V. Meyer,

'The Analysis of Secondary Industries', Feb. 1946.
80. CO 990/16, CEAC (Industry) 5th minutes, 15 June 1944. Comment by Caine.
81. Ibid., CEAC (Industry) 3rd minutes, 17 Apr. 1944.
82. CO 990/17, CEAC (Industry)(44)6, 25 Apr. 1944.
83. CO 96/781/31475/1944, 'The Planning of Social and Economic Development in the Colonial Empire', Apr. 1944.
84. *PD(C)*, 402, 462–3, 20 July 1944; CO 901/1, CSSRC 2nd minutes, 5 Sept. 1944.
85. CO 852/578/5, CEAC(44)32, 'The Development of Manufacturing Industries', 29 Aug. 1944.
86. BT 11/2441, minute by Skevington, 3 July 1944.
87. CO 852/578/5, CEAC(44)32.
88. CO 852/588/2, CEAC(44)38, ASC Third Report, 'Memorandum on Planning', 14 Sept. 1944.
89. CO 852/578/5, minute, 4 Oct. 1944.
90. Lee and Petter (1982), pp.210–11.
91. CO 990/1, CEAC 9th minutes, 19 Dec. 1944.
92. CO 852/586/9, minute, 30 Nov. 1944; Lee and Petter (1982), pp.212–3.
93. CO 852/586/7, letter to Stanley, 22 Dec. 1944; ibid., letter to Durbin, 14 Feb. 1945.
94. Ibid., minute by Caine, 25 Oct. 1944.
95. CO 852/578/6, 'The Development of Manufacturing Industries', 27 Feb. 1945.
96. BT 11/2441, minute by Willis, 19 Dec. 1944; ibid., minute by Shackle, 10 Jan. 1945; CO 852/578/6, letter from Helmore, 13 Jan. 1945.
97. CO 554/132/33718/1/1943, letter to Stanley, 8 Oct. 1943.
98. CO 96/781/31475/1944, despatch to Stanley, 26 July 1944.
99. CO 852/587/4, letter to Clauson, 1 July 1944.
100. CO 852/481/2, letter to Stanley, 31 July 1943.
101. CO 852/574/6, letter to Clauson, 12 Oct. 1944.
102. Ibid., letter to Noel Hall, 18 Nov. 1944.
103. CO 852/574/9, Burns to Stanley, 6 Feb. 1945.
104. D.H. Aldcroft, *The British Economy. Volume 1: The Years in Turmoil 1920–1951* (Brighton: Wheatsheaf, 1986), p.180.
105. BT 11/2021, 'Cotton Industry. Industrial Rehabilitation and Labour Requirements'. (D.R.I.10) Oct. 1942.
106. CAB 87/14, R(I)(44)5, 'Post-War Exports', 23 June 1944.
107. CO 852/482/4, 'Development of Cotton Spinning and Weaving in Empire countries', 14 Sept. 1943.
108. BT 175/2, CB1418a, Cotton Board 96th meeting, 7 Sept. 1943.
109. BT 11/2441, letter, 15 Sept. 1943; Dupree (1987) II, pp.138–41, entry for 28 July 1943.
110. BT 11/2441, letter to Caine, 21 Sept. 1943; Dupree (1987) II, pp.154–5, entry for 17 Sept. 1943.
111. BT 175/2, CB 1468a, CB 97th meeting, 28 Sept. 1943.
112. BT 175/2, CB 1550a, Cotton Board 99th meeting, 26 Oct. 1943.
113. CO 852/482/4, note of discussion, 14 Oct. 1943.
114. CO 852/587/4, letter to Clauson, 1 July 1944.
115. CO 852/574/6, Hall to Clauson, 12 Oct. 1944.
116. Ibid., Clauson to Noel Hall, 18 Nov. 1944.
117. Shuckburgh (I), p.24; CO 852/574/6, minute by Tempany, 31 Oct. 1944; ibid., minute by Caine, 3 Nov. 1944.
118. CO 554/136/33685/1945, letter from Noel Hall to O.G.R. Williams, 20 Dec. 1944.
119. CO 852/574/9, Burns to Stanley, 6 Feb. 1945.
120. BT 175/3, CB 3354a, Cotton Board 129th meeting, 19 Dec. 1944.
121. CO 852/574/6, letter from A.R.I. Mellor (UAC) to Caine, 6 Sept. 1944.
122. Ibid., letter to Nowell, 14 Sept. 1944.

123. Ibid., letter from Caine to Mellor, 13 Oct. 1944.
124. CO 852/574/6, note of meeting between Streat and BoT officials, 26 Oct. 1944.
125. Ibid., Nowell to Caine, 30 Oct. 1944.
126. BT 175/3, CB 3354a, Cotton Board 129th meeting, 19 Dec. 1944; CO 852/574/7, Streat to Helmore, 13 Jan. 1945; Dupree (1987), pp.228–9, entry for 7 Dec. 1944. Streat described his discussion with Samuel as 'an ominously historic interview'.
127. CO 852/574/7, note of meeting, 8 Mar. 1945.
128. Ibid..
129. See, e.g., Pearce (1982), pp.84, 137–8, 179–80.
130. CO 583/271/30572/1944, note of discussion with Treasury on Nigerian development, 9 Nov. 1944.
131. CO 852/574/7, CDWAC No.577, 'Nigeria: Development of the Peasant Textile Industry in Nigeria', 25 July 1944; CO 583/ 288/30572/1948, 'A Ten–Year Plan of Development and Welfare for Nigeria, 1946', 30 Jan. 1946.
132. CO 852/574/7, F.E.V. Smith to Samuel (UAC), 21 Mar. 1945.
133. Ibid., letter to Creasy, 16 Apr. 1945.
134. Ibid., note of meeting in CO, 7 June 1945.
135. Ibid., telegram to OAG, Nigeria, 3 Aug. 1945.
136. CO 852/587/9, enclosure 1 to CEAC (Ind.)(45)21, May 1945.
137. CO 852/574/9, despatch from Burns, 6 Feb. 1945.
138. CO 852/574/9, despatch to Stanley, 22 July 1945; ibid., saving to Hall, 27 Aug. 1945.
139. CO 852/574/9, despatch to Stanley, 22 July 1945.
140. CO 852/574/10, F.E.V. Smith to A.G. Dawson (UAC, Lagos), 11 Jan. 1946.
141. Ibid., saving, 11 Jan. 1946.
142. Ibid., minute, 26 Jan. 1946.
143. Ibid., minute by (W.B.) Leslie Monson, 31 Jan. 1946. Monson became head of the Production Department in July 1944, replacing Charles Carstairs, and so assuming responsibility for industrial development.
144. CO 852/574/10, minute, 6 Feb. 1946.
145. Ibid., F.E.V. Smith to O.G.R. Williams, 20 Feb. 1946.
146. Ibid., Samuel (UAC) to Dawson (UAC, Lagos), 21 Jan. 1946.
147. Ibid., Smith to Dawson, 20 Feb. 1946.
148. Ibid., letter, 28 Mar. 1946.
149. Ibid., letter, 13 Apr. 1946.
150. Ibid., Samuel to Dawson, 29 Mar. 1946.
151. Ibid., minutes by Rosa and Monson, 6 Mar. 1946.
152. Ibid., letter, 12 Apr. 1946.
153. Ibid., letter, 28 May 1946.
154. Ekundare (1973), p.367.
155. CO 852/574/10, letter, 28 May 1946.
156. CO 852/377/3, letter from F. Samuel to Creasy, 21 Jan. 1943; ibid., letter from Acting Chief Secretary, Lagos, to Samuel, 17 May 1943.
157. CO 852/574/10, record of meeting in CO, 30 May 1946.
158. Ibid., note of meeting in CO, 15 July 1946.
159. CO 901/2, CSSRC(45)50, 'Social Science Research in West Africa', 23 Nov. 1945.
160. CO 927/66/1, despatch Hall, 24 July 1946. This interest in a study of West African labour migration was shared by the Gold Coast government, see despatch from Gurney, (Gold Coast) to Hall, ibid., 10 Sept. 1946.
161. CO 852/591/7, minutes by J.B. Williams, 23 Nov. 1945 and 14 Dec 1945.
162. CO 852/586/8, CEAC 16th minutes, 24 June 1946; CO 999/1, CEDC 1st minutes, 7 Oct. 1946.
163. CO 999/1, CEDC 7th minutes, 16 Dec. 1946.
164. CO 852/1003/3, minute, 23 Apr. 1946.

165. On Cohen's early career, see R. Robinson, 'Andrew Cohen and the transfer of power in Tropical Africa, 1940–1951', in W.H. Morris-Jones and G. Fischer (eds.) *Decolonisation and After: The British and French Experience* (London: Frank Cass, 1980), pp.50–72.
166. Ibid., minute, 6 May 1946.
167. Ibid., minute, 21 May 1946.
168. Ibid., minute, 29 May 1946.
169. CAB 134/165, E(46)30, 'Capital Goods Export Policy', 22 May 1946.
170. CAB 132/3, LP(46)149, 'Survey of the Overseas Economic Situation as it affects the United Kingdom', 17 June 1946.
171. Shuckburgh (I), p.300; CO 852/587/9, enclosure 1 to CEAC (Ind.)(45)21, Report of Industrial Development Sub-Committee, Gold Coast, May 1945.
172. CO 96/806/2/31596/1946–47, 'A memorandum on the Gold Coast Ten Year Plan', (n.d., unattributed).
173. Cmd.7167, *The Colonial Empire 1939–1947*, July 1947 *PP*(1946–47), X, 108–14.
174. Morgan (1980) II, pp.177–80.
175. Hinds (1987), pp.151–2; Cmd.7167, *The Colonial Empire 1939–1947*, July 1947, *PP*(1946–47) X, 324.
176. CO 852/1003/3, minute, 24 Sept. 1946.
177. Ibid., despatch to African Governments, 'Agricultural Productivity in Africa', 22 Feb. 1947.
178. *PD(C)*, 406, col.1351, 14 Dec. 1944.
179. CO 852/558/8, minute by Caine, 28 Mar. 1945, and Gater and Stanley, 3 Apr. 1945.
180. Ibid., minute by Clauson, 7 Apr. 1945.
181. Ibid., circular telegram, 21 Apr. 1945.
182. Ibid., minutes by Bentham, 4 May 1945 and Rosa, 5 May 1945.
183. CAB 71/20, LP(45)100, 'Prospective General Supply Difficulties in the Colonial Empire', 10 May 1945; ibid., LP(45)105, memorandum by Minister of Food, 15 May 1945.
184. CO 852/558/8, Cabinet Home Affairs Committee 2nd meeting, 20 July 1945, 'Supply difficulties in the Empire'.
185. Cmd.6713, *Colonial Development and Welfare. Despatch dated 12th November, 1945 from the Secretary of State for the Colonies to Colonial Governments*, *PP*(1945–46), xix, 35.
186. CO 537/1414, minute, 11 Dec. 1946.
187. BT 11/3247, T.W. Davies (CO) to H.J. Habakkuk (BoT), 27 Feb. 1946; ibid., Habakkuk to Davies, 8 Mar. 1946.
188. Cmd.7167 *The Colonial Empire (1939–1947)*, July 1947, paras. 314–315.
189. BT 175/3, CB 3789a, Cotton Board 141st meeting, 19 June 1945.
190. Ibid., CB 4401a, Cotton Board 154th meeting, 15 Jan. 1946.
191. Ibid., circular telegram, 19 July 1946.
192. CO 852/729/2, minutes by Caine, 30 May 1946, and Dawe, 6 June 1946.
194. Meredith (1986), pp.77–91; CO 990/1, CEAC 3rd minutes, 15 Feb. 1944.
193. Ekundare (1973), p.233.

4 Industrial Development: Defining the Colonial State's Role, 1943–46

The Colonial Office's protracted discussions on promoting industrial development accompanied its deliberations on the relevance of industrialisation to West African development in the period from 1943 to 1946. In addition to identifying sources of finance, the promotion of industry involved injecting entrepreneurial and managerial skills into the development process. Official assumptions about the availability of capital changed between 1943 and 1946. Policy-making was hampered by uncertainty about the post-war availability of various forms of finance. For example, it was unclear whether colonial governments would have free access to London's capital markets, or to foreign sources, or even to their own accumulating sterling balances.

Particularly important was growing Colonial Office sensitivity to the political implications of development, an uncomfortable awareness that the operations of European private enterprise attracted charges of exploitation. Discussions on *promoting* industry therefore evolved into a debate on *controlling* development – and on how far the colonial State should intervene in the development process and assume an entrepreneurial role, supplementing private capital with new forms of public enterprise politically acceptable to colonial opinion.

Sources of development capital

Early in the reconstruction debate, the Colonial Office seemed optimistic about the post-war availability of development capital. Officials encouraged two assumptions: first, that many colonies would have amassed sizeable sterling balances; secondly, that colonial governments could borrow on the London money markets.[1] Yet, by spring 1944, the Office, while still promoting optimism, had modified its advice. Colonial governments were now told that three sources of finance would be available. First, governments' own surplus funds, regarded as the 'first recourse' of territories which possessed them. London implied that many colonies could finance substantial development without seeking loans or grants. Secondly, because extended controls on City loans seemed likely, local financial resources would become increasingly important. Finally, officials concluded that colonial development and welfare funds would remain the chief source of development capital for many colonies.[2]

Britain's capacity to promote post-war colonial development remained uncertain long into the 'reconstruction debate'. By 1945, Britain had lost around one quarter of its national wealth, and external liabilities totalled £3,355 million by June 1945. Of this, some £2,723 million was owed to the Sterling Area. In May 1945, Keynes predicted that by the war's end Britain's annual overseas deficit would be around £1,400 million.[3] Nevertheless, late in 1944, the Colonial Office persuaded the War Cabinet to extend the 1940 Colonial Development and Welfare Act, providing £120 million for development over a ten year period. However impressive the gesture, the practical impact of these funds, distributed throughout the colonies, could only be limited. The colonial governments were warned in November 1945 that they would have to supplement their colonial development and welfare allocations from their governments' own resources, or by external borrowing.[4]

The war produced substantial changes in many governments' financial circumstances. This was especially due to new forms of taxation. The Nigerian government's gross revenue grew from £6,113,000 to £13,200,000 during the war, partly due to increased revenue from indirect taxation, especially customs and excise, but also to the introduction of a Company Tax. For the first time, expatriate firms became subject to direct taxation within Nigeria, intended to counteract inflation and stimulate production. More importantly, these changes produced wartime budget surpluses, enabling Lagos to ease some of the public spending limits imposed during the 1930s. Government expenditure rose from £6,499,000 in 1939–40 to £10,693,000 in 1945–46, of which an increasing proportion was available for development.[5] The Gold Coast government was slower in modernising its taxation régime, not introducing an income tax until 1943, following an unexpected revenue deficit for the year 1942–43. Even then, income tax rates in the Gold Coast, regarded widely as a wealthy colony, were lower than in Nigeria. The government preferred to raise Company Tax rates, because the burden of higher personal taxation would have fallen on its own officials. This attitude worried London, prompting doubts about granting colonial development and welfare monies to a lightly taxed colony.[6]

The sterling balances were an important potential source of development capital, to which colonial governments were encouraged to expect access. These credits enabled Britain to import raw materials and pay for services from the Sterling Area. A valuable support to the wartime Imperial economic system, they totalled nearly £3,700 million in 1945. By November 1944, British West Africa was owed £76 million, a substantial figure compared to the region's subsequent colonial development and welfare allocation of £30,400,000 for 1946–56. The growth of West Africa's balances was fuelled by the wartime bulk purchase scheme, and continued State marketing after the war made it likely that the balances generated by the produce boards would continue growing.[7]

The colonial sterling balances complicated Anglo–American relations, however, as Washington saw them giving British exporters unfair advantages since, unless creditors could convert their holdings into 'hard' currency, they could buy only sterling goods. The United States therefore urged Britain to 'adjust' the balances, by reducing them or writing them off, and a promise on Britain's part to discuss this was a condition of the post-war US loan agreement. This was hardly attractive to Britain, which was reluctant to offend creditors or dishonour debts as this would undermine London's standing as a financial centre and weaken sterling's international position.[8]

Pressure on the sterling balances also arose within Britain. In April 1945, Keynes suggested easing Britain's post-war financial difficulties by writing off or appropriating large amounts of the colonial balances. Naturally, the Colonial Office recognised the political difficulties this might create in the colonies.[9] Furthermore, although the Office told the West African governments on several occasions that they could draw on their balances after the war, officials resisted the idea of using these funds – especially those derived from State marketing – for development. Their value in securing price stability was increasingly seen, cushioning primary producers against market fluctuations. For the Colonial Office, therefore, the emphasis was on continued accumulation of balances, justified by the need to avoid a post-war 'boom' similar to that after 1918, 'with all its unhappy consequences', and to provide against future 'lean years'.[10] By late 1946, the long-term fate of the colonial sterling balances remained uncertain but given US opinion, the Bank of England's insistence that 'adjustment' was unethical, and the Colonial Office's private conviction that the balances should be devoted to price stabilisation, the prospects for their use in development were not promising.

The outlook for colonial borrowing was no more encouraging. During the 1930s British overseas investment had shifted markedly towards the Empire. The colonies could raise loans more cheaply in the City than elsewhere, thanks, in part, to prevailing 'cheap money' policies. During the war, however, London imposed rigid control over sterling issues, and colonial governments were encouraged to borrow from local sources, reducing demands on the City.[11] It is unclear whether the Colonial Office expected major post-war relaxations of these controls. The Office's optimism late in 1943 ebbed by the following spring. In June 1945, Caine sought Treasury guidance on future colonial access to London's money markets. The Treasury observed that all overseas borrowers should initially seek local sources of capital to relieve pressure on London and to reduce the likelihood of inflation from heavy expenditure at a time of import restrictions.[12]

During the war, officials apparently gave little attention to the use of foreign capital. During the Carlton Hotel discussions, arranged by MacDonald in October 1939 to encourage constructive thought on colonial policy, Sir Keith Hancock argued that foreign capital was essential for development. Margery Perham, the distinguished Reader in Colonial Administration at Oxford University, considered it essential to harness US capital. For officials, this was a thorny subject, and Clauson dismissed the proposal as 'nonsense'. It had traditionally been British policy to deflect US interests from the colonies.[13]

The war transformed the Anglo–American relationship, however. From late 1942, the strength of the American military presence in Africa prompted concern in the Colonial Office about future US commercial ambitions. London feared that Washington would look to West Africa, a region with which it had only modest pre-war trading links, as a major post-war export market. This anxiety was fuelled by the ambiguous commitments to 'access on equal terms' to raw materials and markets given by Britain in the Atlantic Charter.[14] Nevertheless, interest in American capital's possible role in development grew in Britain as the reconstruction debate accelerated. Paradoxically, this interest was particularly marked among the broad 'Left'. In its 1943 statement on colonial policy, for example, the Labour Party concluded that little development was feasible without large-scale loans of European or US capital.[15]

The Colonial Office discouraged speculation about the role of foreign capital but, in April 1944, Evan Durbin raised the subject of US investment during the CEAC's discussions on industrial finance. Caine countered, blandly, that there should be no discrimination against foreign enterprise interested in establishing factories in a colony.[16] Clauson, more forthright in open debate, saw little point in borrowing foreign capital to finance industrial development, designed to raise living standards, if a consequence of this was that the range of available consumer goods was depleted because of loan repayment costs.[17] Whereas Durbin believed that US aid was the key to development, and that foreign loans might be guaranteed with colonial development and welfare funds, Clauson argued that no country could afford to develop all the colonies to the desirable level, unwittingly repeating one of the central arguments for 'concentrated' industrial development already deployed by Durbin and Lewis. Clauson also warned that, although there was no colonial bias against foreign capital, this might emerge as 'national consciousness' developed.[18]

The CEAC asked whether London would approach foreign governments, or any future international investment fund, for development capital, or whether exclusively private investment was envisaged.[19] Stanley replied that Britain would not seek foreign development loans, and that foreign investment was expected to be largely private. He doubted whether colonial populations would favour development which 'bound' them to a foreign country, and he could not foresee money being lent without 'strings'. Hailey agreed, arguing it would be 'healthier' to encourage private (including local) enterprise than to borrow heavily from abroad, so that industrial development arose from colonies' own resources.[20]

The Colonial Office's reluctance to discuss the role of foreign capital may also have stemmed from Britain's need to demonstrate its intention to take a prominent role in development, a need that was especially strong later in the war when Anglo–American discussions on Britain's future Imperial status were in progress.[21] It was, ultimately, on *political* grounds that Stanley sought extended colonial development and welfare provision, emphasising the need to justify internationally Britain's credentials as a colonial power. These considerations also partly explain the Colonial Office's anxiety to retain control over the development debate, and to limit interference from 'unofficial' enthusiasts, such as the radical wing of the CEAC.[22]

Against this unpromising background, the question of identifying fresh development capital for West Africa led officials in London to conclude that continued and increasing reliance would have to be placed on expatriate firms such as the UAC. Although some officials, including Caine, considered this obvious, others, notably Cohen, became increasingly concerned to harness the capital and expertise of private enterprise within a framework which enhanced the power of the colonial State to control development. This, in turn, aroused official interest in the possibility of giving the State a direct role in promoting development, and hence in explorations of the merits of public enterprise.

Public versus private enterprise

In considering the relationship between public and private enterprise, the Colonial Office needed to reconcile, for public consumption, the experience of European commercial activity in the colonies with a shifting metropolitan intellectual climate. Central to these discussions was a dilemma for officials: on the one hand were the demands of a new, more responsive and interventionist colonial policy, shaped increasingly with reference to international, especially American, sentiment, and on the other, there was the practical question of where the resources for development were to be found. Thus, Lord Hailey, speaking as the Colonial Office's 'unofficial spokesman', defended the record of development under private auspices while conceding its patchy impact. In his view, the 'vitality' of private enterprise would in future have to be supplemented by State action to ensure a broader distribution of development, a responsibility which he thought implicit in the 1940 Colonial Development and Welfare Act.[23] Hailey admitted that problems might arise in privately funded development, notably in the exploitation of cheap colonial labour, but unless all aspects of economic development were to be provided for by the State, he saw no alternative to the continued involvement of private enterprise.[24]

Hailey had identified two related questions which dominated the Colonial Office's consideration of development throughout the reconstruction phase: the need to achieve the optimum balance between public and private enterprise, and hence the cultivation of a constructive partnership between them; and the wider question of government control over development. In July 1943, Hailey suggested that the private sector had a limited role in developing tropical areas and that there was a wide field remaining in which government must henceforth take the lead, promoting secondary industries and organising local marketing, areas 'which a previous generation would have regarded as lying beyond the normal range of government action'.[25]

Caine, although traditionally defensive of private enterprise, recognised the need to accommodate new ideas on the State's economic role. He denied that development was impossible without State planning: 'Nothing is more demonstrably untrue for the Colonial Empire, where tremendous developments have been produced by the planning of private enterprise.' However, he envisaged a future expansion of State economic regulation, with important implications for development. Previously, much development had been financed privately, but future taxation policy and control of the capital markets could diminish the colonies' attractiveness to external investors. Consequently, a much greater proportion of development finance would have to come from the State, which itself would require new skills in 'economic prospecting'.[26]

These comments challenged the development framework being projected by the Office for public consumption. Only a month before, Stanley had delivered his major policy Commons speech, encapsulating the future thrust of colonial policy. Acknowledging that private enterprise's role in post-war development was controversial, he had argued that that role would continue:

> As I see it, the financial resources of the Colonial Governments and the financial assistance which His Majesty's Government are to give under the Colonial Development and Welfare Act, will be fully needed for basic developments and social advances, and I think we shall need and be glad of, the assistance of private capital.

However, private enterprise would have to be controlled, and there would be no place for the entrepreneur seeking rapid returns: 'What I hope is to give a chance to the efficient producer with reasonable security to get a reasonable return.[27]

Despite the caveat, reflecting Stanley's own 'middle way' convictions and sensitivity to public opinion, the message remained that public development funds would be limited. Despite wartime advances, colonial government revenues were not expected to contribute substantially to development, and colonial development and welfare funds would be needed for other forms of development, especially welfare. By late 1943, therefore, it seemed clear to officials in London that most capital for industrial development would have to be provided privately.[28]

Given these assumptions about the importance of private enterprise, the attitudes of potential sources of development capital acquire particular significance. In the West African context, the only likely sources of substantial capital investment were the large expatriate firms, and much depended, therefore, on whether their wartime experiences had eroded their customary indifference to business diversification, and on whether they could be induced to participate in development on terms acceptable to local opinion.

By the onset of reconstruction planning in 1943, signs were emerging of changing attitudes towards industrialisation among the firms. The larger firms in particular attempted to improve their relations with colonial governments, and to appear co-operative towards official development strategies.[29] This was especially true of the UAC. The company supported the establishment of the West African Institute. One of the functions of this institute was research into industrial development, and its Gold Coast manager sat on the Council of Achimota College, the Institute's parent body.[30]

The second largest European concern in West Africa, J. Holt and Co., showed similar interest in diversifying into manufacturing. Early in 1943, the Colonial Office received a copy of an internal company memorandum which declared that industrial development was urgently needed, to satisfy the local élite's expectations and to provide work for demobilised troops. The Company believed that most firms operating in West Africa accepted the inevitability of such development. Since local industrialisation would impinge on the firm's traditional commercial activities, Holt stressed the need to prepare for changing conditions. The Company hoped that industrialisation would ultimately promote new trade based on the export of capital goods to the colonies. Holt therefore sought guidance from government on the role envisaged for the European firms.[31] While the Colonial Office was gratified that the firms appeared to be in a 'co-operative mood', and were looking to government to take the initiative in development, officials were reluctant to comment until Whitehall's attitudes to colonial industrialisation had been clarified.[32]

Besides these expressions of a desire to co-operate in promoting colonial industry, the firms had provided concrete evidence of their interest. The UAC, for example, had increased soap production in Nigeria in response to the wartime expansion of the local market, its sales rising from 4,400 tons in 1937 to 10,643 tons in 1946.[33] As already described, the company also proposed a timber processing mill at Sapele, and was considering cotton textiles production in Nigeria. When the UAC later elaborated its textile proposals, it stressed that apart from commercial motives, it sought to help implement government policy on industrialisation.[34]

The war extended the colonial State's control over private enterprise. For example, the introduction of more sophisticated taxation policies had wider long-term implications for the relationship between colonial governments and the European firms. Thus Nigeria imposed a Company Tax for the first time during the war. As Pearce has commented: 'If the war increased the profitability of expatriate firms in Nigeria, at least colonial policy ensured that the country would share in the profits.'[35] It was probably the strengthened wartime position of the colonial State which encouraged the firms to co-operate. For example, in 1942 the UAC offered to sell its rights to mineral royalties in Nigeria to the colonial government. In 1942, these rights brought the Company payments totalling £155,000, a sum swollen by increased wartime production at artificially high prices. The Colonial Office tried to persuade the Treasury to buy these royalties on Lagos's behalf, to stem the flow of mining profits to British shareholders, arguing that this would improve the international image of Britain's colonial policy. The Treasury refused but, early in 1945, negotiations between the Colonial Office and the UAC began. Although these were inconclusive during the reconstruction period, they suggest that the UAC wanted to improve its standing with the colonial authorities.[36]

The war also had important repercussions on European commercial patterns in West Africa, affecting the firms' outlook and behaviour. Particularly important was the introduction of State-controlled produce marketing. Under this policy, the firms became the State's principal agents, buying produce but selling it to a single buyer, the Produce Marketing Board, which determined prices. The firms benefited from the scheme, which they had been willing to help establish. It was, effectively, an official endorsement of the firms' pre-war 'pooling' arrangements. In return for their co-operation, the firms received preferential treatment in the distribution of import licences, and influenced policy to exclude newcomers (both African and 'Syrian') to West African trade.[37] Yet, although the new marketing policy strengthened the firms' position, it also brought their activities more directly under State control than ever before.[38] Hence, when official interest in continuing State produce marketing grew stronger during 1944, the firms became alarmed. Through their central body, the AWAM, they proposed their own scheme, accepting the need for price stabilisation but arguing that the State Board should guarantee a minimum price above which free competition would be permitted.

Although some in the Colonial Office welcomed this proposal as a means of avoiding confrontation with British and US business interests, the West African governments opposed the scheme, fearing the local opposition which it might produce. Above all, official concern about the local political repercussions of the firms' activities crystallised the decision in 1944 to continue State marketing after the war.[39] Against the combined voices of the Colonial Office, the colonial governments and the metropolitan Treasury, each having its own reasons for preferring State marketing, the firms' opposition was ineffective. Nevertheless, the firms were not entirely without influence over the scheme's implementation: a place on the Gold Coast cocoa board was reserved for a representative of AWAM, the nucleus of the pre-war cartel.[40]

Late in 1943, the Colonial Office told the West African governments that a broad planning framework was envisaged leaving wide scope for private initiative, under the State's 'general direction and supervision'. The governments were asked how far economic regulation was considered to be necessary in the interests of the community, whether adequate basic services for development existed and, if these were not already provided by the State, whether steps were needed to encourage private enterprise to provide them. The governments were also asked to review their powers to promote development and existing safeguards against the exploitation of local populations. The Colonial Office assumed that considerable government economic controls would continue immediately after the war.[41]

The Office's ideas on the scope for government participation in development were elaborated in a memorandum prepared for the CEAC in November 1943. Written by Caine and Clauson, this assumed that government's post-war role would be to produce 'outline' development plans, ensuring the necessary framework for development while leaving ample scope for private initiative. While acknowledging greater opportunity for State action, the paper maintained that colonial governments should concentrate on providing basic services, leaving production largely to private enterprise.[42]

Several members of the CEAC rejected this implication of a minimal State role in production, however. Henderson argued that governments should plan social services in conjunction with their economic planning, on which improved welfare provision depended. Durbin believed that Caine and Clauson were suggesting that government's role was to create conditions favourable to private, and therefore *foreign* enterprise, whereas he stressed the potential for government participation in development.[43] The planning memorandum was revised before being circulated to governors in spring 1944. It now emphasised that the State's role in economic planning should not be minimised, but it still advocated 'outline' planning by government, leaving private enterprise to take the 'bulk' of decisions on development. The essential point was that officials envisaged a *partnership* in development between private enterprise and State planning and control.[44]

Caine's influence is visible here. He had already complained that the Colonial Office's discussions on industrialisation neglected instances of development successfully launched without State assistance, for example in Hong Kong before the war.[45] He warned against overreliance on government to stimulate development, at the cost of minimising the scope for private initiative:

> The part which private enterprise can play in the future as in the past is also vital to active development in the colonies, both economic and social. Wherever possible, government activity should aim at the stimulation rather than the restriction of private initiative, subject to the controls essential to the protection of public interests.

However, government was expected to promote development that was likely to be unattractive to private enterprise. Generally, the Office felt that direct government operation was most appropriate where technical circumstances demanded monopolistic control, for example in order to achieve economies of scale through large-scale production. Since the award of such privileges to commercial firms was controversial, officials concluded that monopolies should be reserved for government operation.[46] Caine suggested that government could offer incentives to private enterprise by providing capital on easy terms, by participating in the formation of companies to undertake development, or by taking on the work itself.[47]

Durbin challenged Caine's suggestion that the State might step in to promote development that was unattractive to private enterprise: he believed that governments should consider participating in every development proposal, not only unprofitable ones. Yet even in mid-1944, lingering official scepticism about the benefits of public enterprise remained. For example, Clauson argued that finance was a barrier to government investment in industry, since the necessary public borrowing, and consequent debt accumulation, was risky and undesirable. In fairness, such views represented not simply a stubborn official attachment to *laissez faire* ideas, but arose from painful inter-war experience, when some colonial governments had over-extended themselves by borrowing heavily during the brief 'boom' after 1918, only to find themselves encumbered with severe debt burdens during the Depression.[48]

In its report on manufacturing industry, the CEAC stressed the importance of governments promoting genuinely economic industries. However, this did not mean that only proven industries should be encouraged: rather, it required 'enterprise and bold experimentation' by government to overcome basic problems such as the lack of local managerial expertise. The report incorporated the arguments of Durbin and Caine on the role of the State. Echoing Durbin, the report urged government not to participate only in ventures whose lack of profit-making potential made them unattractive to private enterprise. It endorsed Caine's suggestion that the State might assist development by providing capital, participating in forming companies, or by operating enterprises directly.

The report did not discuss the administrative machinery required by a more active government role in industrial development except to recommend the creation of Departments of Industry in larger territories, responsible for 'discovering, investigating and promoting desirable industrial development'. It recognised, however, that much depended upon the expansion of government personnel, including the recruitment of staff with non-traditional qualifications.

Subject to unspecified 'appropriate safeguards', the CEAC welcomed the participation of established British companies in industrialisation.[49] The committee's more radical members disagreed: in the Agenda Sub-Committee's controversial planning memorandum they argued that industrial development could not be left to private enterprise. They thought that comparisons between colonial conditions and mature economies like Britain or the United States, where industrialisation had occurred largely without State assistance, were inappropriate, since the latter had enjoyed traditions of entrepreneurship that were considered to be unavailable in the colonies. The Sub-Committee concluded that, unless government were to participate in planning development, very little would occur.[50]

However conciliatory the European firms might have appeared by 1943, and however much officials in London might have recognised that only these firms possessed the capital and expertise necessary to promote industrialisation in West Africa, the problem remained that the firms were profoundly unpopular among key sections of the local population. Moreover, African distrust of the firms was shared by many administrators in West Africa, as demonstrated by the hostility frequently voiced by Governor Bourdillon of Nigeria. Bourdillon estimated in June 1943 that '99 per cent' of the discontent among Nigeria's population was due to economic causes, including the favoured position which the European trading firms were believed to enjoy.[51]

The control of development: industrial licensing

As the Colonial Office's awareness of this situation sharpened during 1943, discussions turned to bringing expatriate enterprise under effective government control. This extended debate was triggered, however, by a separate problem in West Africa, raised by Swinton, involving economic penetration of the region by non-European expatriate capital. This was termed the 'Syrian' problem. In February 1943, Swinton cited the urgent need to curtail the activities of Syrian traders in West Africa as his reason for proposing government licensing for all future industrial development in the region.[52] Swinton's suggestion was prompted by the European firms' concern about Syrian competition – a concern that they had voiced repeatedly. Swinton believed that the small Syrian trading community rather than the European firms, had squeezed African entrepreneurs out of business. While admitting that the number of Syrians involved was small, he was distressed that their growth had been rising since the 1920s, alarming European and African traders, and introducing 'debased commercial standards', seen in the flourishing black market. Syrians were also unpopular because they were suspected of remitting their profits home. Swinton argued that only government control through industrial licensing could deal with the problem.[53] The European firms, anxious to protect their commercial dominance, endorsed Swinton's views. Their wish to restrict potential rivals, requiring government action, may account for their conciliatory posture, increasingly evident during 1943. In return for protection against Syrian competition, the firms seemed prepared to co-operate in the evolving development strategy.

Swinton's sympathies clearly lay with the European firms, with whom he believed colonial governments should establish close working relationships. The firms, he argued, being large, were easier to deal with and to control.[54] He made no secret of his suspicion of government-financed or managed industrial development, although he was interested in encouraging native administrations to take a financial stake in 'sound' local industries.[55] Although he paid lip-service to encouraging African enterprise, using this as a pretext for licensing, it seems likely that Swinton saw expatriate interests as the obvious source of finance, expertise and enterprise.[56] He dismissed critics of British business:

> One school of thought has proposed that industries requiring substantial capital, plant and expert management should be exclusively African, and that they should be financed by government. It desires to exclude all outside capital. I believe this to be thoroughly unsound.[57]

Significantly, Swinton assumed that wartime government economic controls would not continue in peacetime, when policy should aim to allow 'full play for freedom and initiative'. To this extent, he may have regarded licensing as a temporary expedient, unnecessary once Syrian competition had been removed.[58] Swinton had raised a controversial question, and in the Colonial Office, major differences of opinion soon emerged on the use of government controls to limit foreign enterprise in West Africa in favour of locally promoted development.

The incident which prompted Swinton to address London on licensing arose in the Gold Coast. Here, the West African Institute had established a pilot brick-making plant, in line with its policy of encouraging African craft industries. The plant could not, however, produce bricks in quantities large enough to meet wartime demand, so Burns permitted a Syrian company to establish a brick factory and import the necessary equipment. Stanley defended Burns' action, rejecting the argument that Accra should promote exclusively 'local' development, and underlining his preference for a mixed development strategy:

> Whatever may be post-war policy with regard to encouraging the development of secondary industries it seems improbable that it will take the form of limiting development to any single undertaking or institution, even of governmental character, with the consequence of drastic restriction or prohibition of competitive enterprises irrespective of their economic soundness.

Even if, it were compatible with London's future international obligations, such a policy might be criticised as a means of stifling potential competitors of British manufacturers.[59]

Swinton found Burns' response disturbing and contrary to all existing ideas on industrialisation. He dismissed the argument that the Syrian proposal could safely be sanctioned as it was unlikely to remain in business after the war. In his view, Burns had failed to apply basic criteria of desirability, notably whether the firm could be relied upon to follow the government's social and economic policy guidelines.[60]

Swinton's views on controlling industrialisation drew sharp criticism from the Colonial Office. Caine condemned the suggestion that industries could be established only with government approval. Accepting that government might have to assist certain projects, he opposed any system which required government's prior approval of development, believing that this would restrict, and not stimulate, development. Caine cited colonies such as Hong Kong and Palestine, which had achieved some industrialisation through private enterprise unhindered by government. He also detected a serious underlying political consideration:

> I think, moreover, that any system of licensing in normal times would arouse the keenest suspicions that it was being used deliberately to stifle Colonial industrial development in order to prevent competition with U.K. exports.

Significantly, Caine argued that it would be a mistake to contemplate the permanent extension of war-time economic controls whose impact had, historically, been negative.[61]

Implicit in Caine's position were fundamental doubts about the capacity of colonial governments to undertake wide-scale control of development. These misgivings formed the central thrust of his August 1943 memorandum in which he had argued that little progress in development could be expected from the existing administrative machinery.[62] It was natural, then, that he would resist any further extensions in the responsibilities of colonial governments.

Dawe also criticised Swinton's proposals both on economic and political grounds:

> If, in the post-war period, we start attempting to control private enterprise by a system of Government licensing, we shall get into a real mess. On the one side we shall have the U.A.C. pressing us to use the system in one direction, while we shall be exposed to clamour from other interests to use it in another.[63]

This suggests that the Colonial Office sought to avoid too close an association of colonial authorities with specific interest groups, particularly the European firms. However, while senior officials endorsed Caine's views on licensing, they were unsure how to respond to Swinton, concealing their doubts when he visited London in summer 1943.[64] Consequently, Stanley's formal response to Swinton simply noted that the Syrian brick scheme was already in hand and that it was too late to reassess the position.[65]

Swinton's concern to establish clear government controls over industrialisation was shared by the West African governments, although their motives were different. In October 1943, the Civil Members' Committee of the West African Council agreed that industrial licensing was 'essential', favouring legislation giving governments 'absolute discretion' to grant or withhold licences, applicable to existing industries.[66] It encouraged Swinton to request information from London on licensing systems operating in other colonies.[67] Pressure on the Colonial Office for a statement on industrial licensing was simultaneously emerging from other parts of the colonial empire. When the East African Governors' Conference requested guidance on the subject in September 1943, Stanley decided to refer the entire question to the newly established CEAC.

As with tariff policy, discussions on licensing were overshadowed by the continuing Anglo–American commercial negotiations. Opinion in the United States favoured liberalised trading arrangements, and the International Commercial Union then under consideration was intended to cut tariffs and lift import and export prohibitions, a régime in which Washington was keen to secure British co-operation. The Colonial Office was uncertain whether freer trade could accommodate an inherently restrictive system of industrial licensing. The issue was whether colonial industrialisation should be encouraged under free market conditions, or whether territorial governments should control development to curb over-production and the emergence of uneconomic enterprises. As Clauson admitted, there were attractions in controls. The uneconomic competition and consequent failure of enterprises which might arise from unrestricted development could damage the colonies' reputation as sites for investment. Furthermore, licensing could ensure African participation in development through stipulations that a proportion of the capital invested in a project should be held by government for eventual transfer to African investors. Licensing was also thought to be a means of controlling the rate of development, and hence its social impact, enabling urbanisation to be managed through the careful location of new industries, and working conditions to be established. Licensing would therefore facilitate planned industrialisation, corresponding to administrators' social and political objectives.[68]

Despite the apparent attractions of licensing, Caine remained unconvinced, fearing that it would favour 'vested interests', particularly the European firms. Moreover, he believed that licensing was restrictive, conflicting with traditional policies of encouraging private enterprise.[69] Here were echoes of Caine's earlier misgivings at the possibly restrictive consequences of State-controlled produce marketing in West Africa, which benefited firms like the UAC at the expense of newcomers, such as 'Syrian' traders.

The Colonial Office asked both Swinton in West Africa and Sir Charles Lockhart, Chief Secretary of the East African Governors' Conference, to postpone licensing legislation pending further consideration in London.[70] However, officials soon concluded that there was no precedent for licensing suitable as a model for future legislation, as Swinton had hoped.[71] More fundamental misgivings emerged in a letter from Clauson to Lockhart. Clauson explained that the Office was undecided on licensing, but, referring to the pre-war dislocation of international trade, aggravated by widespread protectionism, he suggested that agreement was emerging that post-war prosperity depended upon removing obstacles to trade, requiring concessions on all sides. Consequently, advocates of licensing, a potential barrier to trade, would have to demonstrate that it would generate more development than it hindered.[72]

The Colonial Office had hitherto concentrated on the economic aspect of licensing, but by November 1943, the West African Department was arguing that the question had to be seen in its wider, *political*, context. As early as April 1943, in discussions arising from the Syrian brick-making incident, the Department's head, O.G.R. Williams, emphasised the political and social dimensions to government control over private enterprise, which he thought ought not be subordinated to purely economic considerations.[73] Given that, during 1943, Williams and his colleagues were attempting to construct a framework of long-term colonial policy, their sensitivity to the political ramifications of economic policies under discussion elsewhere in the Office is understandable.

After July 1943 and Stanley's watershed speech to the Commons, London's stated goal was self-government for the West African territories.[74] While this goal was imprecisely defined, officials responsible for it sought to integrate economic and political objectives. If West African populations were to be prepared for self-government, part of their 'training' must include greater economic involvement, and opportunities for self-management: 'To use what are perhaps catch-phrases, economic democracy is an essential concomitant of political democracy.'[75]

For the West African Department, therefore, the priority was to secure the position of Africans in the region. Particularly important was the growing educated class, whose numbers would be swollen by demobilisation: 'It is politically most important that the African should be enabled to show what he can do in the creation and management of secondary industries.'[76] Officials recognised three potential obstacles: the lack of local capital, the shortage of technical and managerial expertise and the presence of non-African competitors. Officials attached great significance to the unpopularity of the European firms since policy-makers looked to private enterprise to provide the major initiative in industrial development and only non-African enterprise seemed to possess the necessary resources. Charles Carstairs, who became head of the Production Department within the Colonial Office's Economic Division in April 1943, observed:

> The European firms themselves, and in particular the United Africa Company, have however much odium to live down… There is a suspicion of the United Africa Company in West Africa which is so strong and so widespread as almost to constitute a mass neurosis.'[77]

All these considerations, especially the presence of the firms, convinced the Department of the need for machinery in West Africa to control industrialisation which

> should not be allowed to develop in W. Africa in ways that are likely to prejudice our policy of encouraging + training the West Africans for ultimate self-government, however remote that goal may be at present. This seems to imply inevitably some form of regulation of the development of industrialisation for which Government must bear the responsibility.[78]

While there was little argument within the Colonial Office on this problem, opinions differed on its significance for licensing policy. There was a division between those in the West African Department, who saw government-controlled licensing as the best means of securing wider opportunities for African entrepreneurs against European and Syrian competition, a concern grounded ultimately in *political* considerations, and those, like Caine, who emphasised the *economic* disadvantages of government regulation. The trend of discussions worried Caine:

> I myself am quite unconvinced of the urgency of the enactment of any licensing legislation, either in East or West Africa, because it seems to me that, in any event in war-time, Government can in practice control any substantial industrial development through its powers of control over the import of machinery and other war-time regulatory powers.

He called for more discussion on promoting, not controlling, development.[79]

Meanwhile, Swinton grew impatient for a response from London, especially after the Syrian brick-makers incident at Accra.[80] He argued that government should promote planned industrialisation, which was possible only if it could control development through licensing. He believed that licensing would ensure that government could approve firms which wanted to develop industries, and satisfy itself that they acted as partners in development. Similarly, governments could control the location of industries, relating them to local primary production, and could manage development, protecting village industries where desirable on social grounds.

Swinton denied that licensing need be restrictive: he believed it would encourage development. He had originally envisaged licensing as applying only to large-scale industry, but believed that in West Africa the Syrians were attempting to 'muscle in' on village industries, threatening administrators' plans for African social development. He stressed that the Civil Members' Committee agreed with him that West Africa required a general licensing system, which need not differentiate between large- and small-scale industries, and could exclude 'undesirable' industries. A general system, he thought, would be flexible, and provide information on industrialisation to those responsible for planning.[81]

Within the Colonial Office, advocates of licensing deployed different arguments. For Swinton, the key point was to tackle the 'Syrian' problem, and it was almost as an after-thought that he claimed that licensing would promote African enterprise. Given his strong views on the need for a constructive partnership between government and the firms, it seems that he saw an African contribution to development as a remote possibility. The West African Department's attitude was entirely different. Its interest in licensing was prompted by the problem of the European firms:

> The violent and universal suspicion against these firms which at present exists creates an atmosphere in which industrial development is hamstrung and paralysed. Our object must be to break down this suspicion and that can only be done by showing that the Governments are the masters. This can only be achieved if the Governments are able to exercise control and licensing seems the simplest and most effective means.[82]

In other words, it had become politically necessary for colonial governments to demonstrate to the populations of West Africa their ability to control the region's economic development. While Swinton appeared insensitive to the political dimensions of development, these formed the cornerstone of the West African Department's outlook.

While Caine felt that the European firms welcomed the licensing proposal precisely because it would benefit them, Cohen doubted this, because so many officials in West Africa shared the local population's anti-firm sentiments.[83] Cohen, who throughout the reconstruction debate championed an enlarged developmental role for the state, believed that the basic problem in West Africa was the strained relationships between the colonial governments, the local populations and the European firms. He shared the West African Department's view that licensing was necessary to demonstrate that the authorities, not the firms, controlled the region's economic life. He conceded, however, that licensing was essentially negative, requiring supplementary, positive government measures to assist development.[84]

When the CEAC discussed licensing, its conclusions resembled Caine's closely. The Committee disliked the prospect of restrictive legislation and was uneasy about the way controls would be implemented. Like Caine, it feared that licensing would in practice obstruct industrialisation. Where licensing was desirable, however, the Committee believed that it should apply only to certain industries agreed by London. There were four cases which the CEAC thought might warrant licensing: first, where a potentially economic industry required initial protection; secondly, where excess capacity might develop without some control; thirdly, where locally owned industries required safeguarding in the territory's wider interests; and finally, to control the location of industry. The Committee saw the purpose of licensing as being to ensure the maximum return from the labour and resources of local populations. Appreciating the issue's importance, the CEAC recommended that the power to grant licences should rest in an 'impartial' authority, and that disappointed applicants should have the right to appeal. Furthermore, licences should be granted for a fixed, but renewable, period, and should be revocable at any time.[85] The CEAC therefore rejected Swinton's call for a general system of licensing.[86]

Swinton was dismayed by the Committee's conclusions. He recognised, however, that since the question of licensing was not related directly to his ministerial remit to co-ordinate the war effort in West Africa, the final decision would rest with Stanley:

> I must, however, make it plain that I could have no part in a plan which, while purporting to accept the principle of licensing, was hedged round with so many conditions and restrictions that I honestly felt it would not work.

To reinforce his case, Swinton claimed that licensing was desirable in the community's interests, a view that his staff at Achimota allegedly shared. Furthermore, the problem remained that those responsible for planning lacked information on what industries were being started in West Africa. As an alternative to licensing, Swinton therefore proposed a scheme of industrial registration. The information which this would provide, he argued, was essential for effective taxation and labour policies and for planning necessary basic services. Furthermore, Swinton believed that the scheme would help in tackling the Syrian problem, by revealing this group's activities in West Africa.[87] The West African Civil Members' Committee shared Swinton's view that there would be little point in pursuing a licensing scheme on the lines advocated by the CEAC, owing to the lack of necessary information, favouring instead a system of industrial registration.[88] Accordingly, the West African governments set about the problem of defining an 'industry' for these purposes.

Swinton discussed the entire question further with Stanley in London in August 1944. Stanley, who disclosed misgivings over the CEAC's recommendations, thought a system of registration was acceptable, although it would not fulfil the same functions as licensing. He arranged for the CEAC to reconsider the question with Hall, Swinton's Development Adviser.[89] The outcome was an agreement that the authorities in West Africa should work out their registration scheme.[90]

Vehicles for growth: development corporations

The momentum behind the debate on licensing and registration apparently dissipated by summer 1944, by which time attention focused increasingly on *promoting*, rather than controlling, development, and specifically on the potential role of development corporations. For the remainder of the 'reconstruction' period, references to licensing were sparse. Early in 1946, the governors of Kenya and Uganda showed enthusiasm for such a system, considering it essential for orderly industrial development.[91] In West Africa, however, interest apparently lapsed. Early in 1946, when Lagos's doubts about factory development were being discussed in London, it was suggested that the territory might need a licensing system to avoid the unwelcome effects of industrialisation.[92] Caine, however, maintained that recent evidence of the Nigerian government's hostility to industrialisation indicated that it would be a mistake to make the government responsible for controlling development.[93] He added that Washington might insist on participating in any licensing system in Nigeria, an opportunity for interference in colonial policy that would be unwelcome to officials and politicians alike in London.

By the time that officials in London had sealed the fate of Swinton's licensing proposals, they had already begun to consider the measures and machinery necessary to promote industrialisation. The emphasis on facilitating a partnership between private enterprise and the State was not new, having emerged in earlier, more nebulous discussions on colonial development. An important breakthrough came with Caine's August 1943 memorandum, which suggested creating an organisation, commercial in form, but not constrained to operate in a purely commercial way – a company acting as the state's agent. Caine believed that a body enjoying the 'comparative freedom of a commercial concern' could undertake, in a relatively informal manner the 'economic prospecting' increasingly seen as essential to successful development.[94]

Even before entering the Colonial Office, Arthur Lewis had speculated on the value of government-controlled corporations working with local and external interests in the larger colonies to promote industrial schemes which private enterprise was unwilling to undertake alone. An alternative suggested by Lewis was to form a single, London-based corporation.[95] Similarly, Cohen complained that official discussions on promoting industrialisation minimised the role of government. At the height of the Office's discussions on industrial licensing, Cohen suggested the formation, with government finance, of a large development company, which could co-operate with private enterprise in specific projects.[96]

The West African governments were initially interested in promoting industry through new organisations, often still termed development companies. These were mentioned, for example, in Accra's outline development plan of July 1944, by which time Lagos was considering similar machinery.[97] Sustained discussion began in August 1944, shortly after Lagos proposed an industrial development corporation. This was discussed when Swinton visited London during summer 1944. Early in August Hall explained that both Lagos and Accra were considering the role of development corporations in promoting industrialisation. Their projected role was still modest, involving the provision of managerial assistance to subsidiary firms; they would not necessarily be prominent in financing development. The principal advantage of machinery of this sort was that it would give governments control over development.

Swinton, who assumed that successful development depended on expatriate capital rather than on the State's entrepreneurial skills, feared that a development corporation might find itself financing 'unsound' schemes. Stanley, however, argued that, in West Africa, only government could provide facilities for small industrial developments, and rejected as impracticable Swinton's suggestion that local co-operatives or the Native Administrations were suitable vehicles for intervention.

These discussions raised a deeper problem: the integration of existing private enterprise into the proposed machinery. It was politically desirable to ensure government control if the European firms were involved in any development corporation.[98] Cohen was enlisted to produce a paper on development corporations in West Africa. Assuming that government policy was to encourage private enterprise to participate fully in development, Cohen noted that only the large firms had the necessary capital and expertise, and that rapid post-war development depended largely on them. However, the 'intense political suspicion' towards the firms in West Africa, shared by Africans and administrators alike, threatened to obstruct progress:

> This suspicion has created a form of economic paralysis which has been serious enough in the past, but is likely to be even more serious in the future when the need for development will be so much greater. It must be the aim of economic policy to put an end to this State of affairs.

As with licensing, Cohen highlighted the *political* dimension to the promotion of development. Cohen argued that governments had hitherto lacked adequate machinery to guide economic development, fuelling African fears that big business, not government, controlled local economic life. This, in turn, had created tensions between government and business, hindering the co-operation between them which development required. Cohen concluded that territorial governments needed machinery equipping them to formulate general economic policies and control private enterprise in the public interest. However, this machinery should not stifle private initiative, but should rather demonstrate to African opinion that government was the 'controlling partner'.

One solution, thought Cohen, was the development corporation, at least half of whose finance should come from colonial governments, either from their own revenues or reserves, or from colonial development and welfare funds. Commercial banks, but not the European firms, should also be encouraged to invest. While he expected local legislatures to decide the broad operating policy of the corporations, Cohen believed the latter should be run on commercial lines. He did not foresee the corporations undertaking projects themselves, but rather envisaged them operating through subsidies, perhaps in partnership with the European firms. However, the corporations would keep overall control through the capital structure of their subsidiaries, and through the appointment of directors. Cohen emphasised the importance of flexibility, explaining that the corporation's degree of involvement would vary from case to case. He believed that the development corporation met the two basic objectives revealed by recent official discussions: control over development, where necessary, and promotional machinery, especially where external finance and managerial skills were needed. Echoing earlier arguments over licensing, Cohen claimed that development corporations would not be restrictive but would facilitate government co-operation in development. A final problem that he identified was that the corporations would require highly qualified and experienced staff, and that to complement these, territorial governments would need economic departments with appropriately qualified staff. Here, Cohen believed that governments' wartime experience could be used.[99]

The idea of improving the machinery for investment and development was strengthened by events in Britain during 1944. In October 1944, the Cabinet Reconstruction Committee approved the Board of Trade's proposal to establish two finance corporations to help fill gaps in metropolitan arrangements for financing industry – gaps perceived as early as 1931 by the Macmillan Committee. The first corporation to be financed by the Bank of England and the clearing banks was to supply investment capital to small businesses. The second, funded by the City and insurance companies, would supply finance for industrial reorganisation. Together, the corporations would have assets of £30 to £40 million, to be increased through borrowing to between £110 and £165 million. Significantly, in the context of discussions on financing colonial development, neither of the new domestic corporations was to receive State capital.[100]

The Colonial Office's discussions on new development mechanisms were not restricted to officials, but included contributions, sometimes unsolicited, from members of the CEAC. The Committee's more radical members proposed sending a commission of industrial experts to investigate colonial possibilities and produce development plans. While this proposal was for an executive body, a problematic suggestion given the delicate relationship between colonial governments and London, evident from earlier official discussions on the creation of a development commission for West Africa, there was nevertheless sympathy in the Colonial Office for the idea of expert investigation of the colonies' industrial potential in preparation for development planning.[101] The dissident members of the CEAC's Agenda Sub-Committee suggested that, having assessed an area's industrial potential, this commission could become a permanent agency, empowered to provide development infrastructures, select appropriate industries for encouragement, negotiate with industry to initiate projects, and, if necessary, arrange for their operation under government control. They stressed that this work was unsuitable for civil servants or economists without practical experience. It criticised the existing local machinery, usually comprising departmental representatives of the colonial governments who could not plan boldly to achieve rapid development because they lacked the necessary skills.

When, in October 1944, the CEAC requested guidance on key development issues, it sought Stanley's views on creating new instruments for industrialisation, including public corporations, possibly with executive powers independent of colonial governments.[102] While Stanley favoured bodies such as departments of commerce and industry, and development corporations acting on a semi-commercial basis with government finance, he warned that any executive powers enjoyed by these corporations would have to be determined by territorial governments, on London's advice.[103]

Development corporations were discussed in October 1944 by senior Colonial Office officials and Nigeria's Development Adviser, F.E.V. Smith. Smith saw the development corporation as the 'commercially executive corollary' of the Department of Commerce and Industry, responsible for promoting industry, which Lagos proposed to create. He envisaged the corporation as a statutory body, financed partly by colonial development and welfare money, and partly by the commercial sector. Like Cohen, Smith saw the corporation operating through subsidiaries in which it had a majority shareholding or voting control. It would finance desirable industries otherwise unattractive to private investors, ultimately aiming to transfer these industries to the producers themselves. The corporation would investigate potential industries and encourage their commercial development while retaining control to prevent 'exploitation' of the local population.[104]

Nevertheless, the government's strategy was essentially facilitative, and there was no intention to supplant private capital.

When Lagos's preliminary development plan was discussed in London in November 1944, Stanley supported its proposal to create a development corporation.[105] He believed there was 'very considerable suspicion of the outside capitalist and a very strong desire to see that development is definitely Nigerian'.[106] The Gold Coast government's Economic Adviser, Professor Richardson was similarly interested in development corporations, acknowledging the need for a 'central nucleus body' to help promote industries by supplying finance and expertise. However, he believed that the corporation's working capital should come from commercial sources, to avoid any local suspicion of government interference.[107]

Interest in the potential for development corporations in West Africa and elsewhere extended beyond the official sphere. In October 1943, Sir Raymond Streat, chairman of the Cotton Board, had proposed an investment corporation, financed by Lancashire and London, to participate in officially approved development, especially projects involving cotton textile production.[108] Having had no response after a year, Streat raised the subject with the Board of Trade, arguing that an investment corporation would enable Lancashire to participate in textile development schemes such as that currently being made by the UAC in Nigeria.[109] Streat persisted, although he understood that his plan raised questions of high policy, and risked hostility from sections of the Lancashire cotton industry.[110]

The Colonial Office had remained non-committal towards Streat's ideas. Eventually, in March 1945, it explained its concern about possible colonial suspicion that the true purpose of Streat's corporation was to stifle local textile development and to ensure that any development would benefit British capital. Caine thought this suspicion might be allayed if the corporation had a broad range of backers, not only Lancashire investors. It was considered important to allow the formal initiative, for example in any approach to Lancashire, to come from the colonies themselves, hence the Office's preference for informal links with Lancashire interests. In any case, the development of colonial cotton industries would involve consultation with the Board of Trade, and hence, indirectly, with the British cotton industry.[111]

If the Colonial Office hesitated over proposals from Lancashire, it was more receptive to a scheme for a development corporation suggested by Barclays Bank (Dominions, Colonial and Overseas) Ltd. In November 1944, Sir William Goodenough,

Chairman of the Bank and a member of the CEAC, told Caine that he perceived scope for an industrial development corporation in Nigeria. Aware of the Colonial Office's current discussions, Goodenough sought to clarify the boundary between the public and private spheres of interest. In his view, the State's function in development should be limited to providing services. He also questioned whether a development corporation could work through subsidiaries, since this might involve the corporation in controversy, for example over the timing of the transfer of subsidiary companies to private enterprise. He stressed that equity interest should normally be provided by private sources. Moreover, Goodenough feared that a powerful government-controlled corporation might encourage unrealistic expectations, although it might do much in the exploratory and research fields. One problem he foresaw was that future Treasury retrenchment might embarrass a mainly publicly operated corporation. He advocated the maximum use of private capital in development, arguing that a government corporation should seek to create conditions to attract it.[112]

Barclays' ideas became clearer early in 1945. The Bank, whose assets expanded substantially during the war, was dissatisfied with the existing financial organisation in the colonies, particularly West Africa, which was especially weak in providing long-term development finance. Barclays therefore proposed a development corporation with authorised capital of £5 million which the Bank would provide. The bulk of the corporation's business would be colonial but this would not preclude involvement in the Bank's most important regions of operation, South Africa and Egypt. The corporation's staff would initially be recruited internally, although local representatives might be included. Barclays expected development to be gradual, and not initially profitable.

The Colonial Office responded warmly to Barclays' scheme, considering it a useful supplement to the machinery already under discussion. The Treasury, while sympathetic, queried whether such a venture should be operated by a single bank. Caine feared that attempts to persuade other banks to participate might delay the entire project.[113] Stanley's reaction was also encouraging. He saw room for both private and public enterprise, and thought that their respective spheres of activity would emerge naturally. However, he felt that Barclays' corporation should co-operate with government corporations to avoid duplicated effort and competition, and he emphasised the importance of securing local participation. He also suggested that Barclays' corporation could be less active in territories that had government corporations.[114]

Goodenough's reply satisfied Stanley that Barclays' organisation would meet the Colonial Office's objectives. It would liaise with any public corporation, work within the officially defined development framework, and accept the Office's guidance. Goodenough explained that he saw private and public enterprise as distinct but complementary, and recognised the political aspect of development and the need to co-operate with colonial governments and encourage local participation.[115] In Caine's view, Barclays' thinking was close to the Colonial Office's. When the Bank of England suggested that other banks should participate, and that Barclays might be trying to outstrip their competitors, Caine argued that it would be wrong to 'stifle an enterprise merely because it may result in the enterprising firm doing better than the unenterprising'.[116]

By March 1945, the Treasury had approved the project on the understanding that the new corporation would consult both it and the Colonial Office on policy matters, and that its beneficiaries would not be confined to Barclays' existing clientele, a condition readily accepted by the Bank. The desire for close liaison stemmed from the Treasury's concern about the absorption of the colonial sterling balances, and about the control of overseas issues generally. In response to the Bank of England's continuing misgivings that other banks with colonial interests were not involved, Barclays explained that because of their 'substantial' surplus in reserves, they could promote development through a subsidiary which, once established, could borrow from other sources. The corporation would engage in all kinds of business, and make medium- or long-term loans. It would be controlled from London, facilitating an economical use of skilled personnel. Barclays also assured the Bank that it would provide for local participation in the corporation, possibly including local banks in the territory concerned.[117] These assurances satisfied the Bank, and late in August 1945, Barclays told the Colonial Office that they were ready to proceed.[118]

The direction of development: central versus local control

While the details of Barclays' scheme were being clarified, the Colonial Office was re-examining its thinking on development corporations. The Office had postponed a decision on the earlier Cotton Board plan, pending both the CEAC's discussions on industrialisation and the Office's own consideration of the proposals already mooted.

By early 1945, there was growing recognition that official views needed sharper definition. Caine's initial interest in the Cotton Board's scheme had given way to doubts. Much had happened since Streat's original suggestion late in 1943, including the Barclays' proposal. Moreover, the Colonial Office was determined to give any new development machinery the 'strongest possible' *local* flavour, avoiding any appearance that it would be controlled by British financial interests. Hence the Cotton Board's proposal, dependent on joint investment by Lancashire and the City, seemed less attractive, as the motives for creating Streat's corporation could be misinterpreted. Instead, the Office had become interested in locally organised, government-controlled corporations in individual colonies playing a substantial, though not necessarily exclusive, role in development.[119]

During the second reading of the Colonial Development and Welfare Bill in February 1945, Stanley mentioned the possible role of development corporations, run by colonial governments, in providing capital and managerial expertise. He also suggested an alternative in which governments could collaborate with external investors to initiate new enterprises, eventually transferring full responsibility for them to private enterprise.[120] Stanley, whose Lancashire connections were strong, had been anxious not to discourage the Cotton Board's initiative, but for wider policy reasons he did not want to involve the Colonial Office in it. The key point was that the Office sought the co-operation of British capital and managerial skill, but in a form which would not stifle the growth of local capital and entrepreneurship, the political importance of which had already emerged during official discussions on licensing. Official concern to give development machinery a genuinely *local* character seemed to demand an emphasis on promoting local development corporations, rather than bodies organised in Britain.[121] Hence, in his February 1945 circular on manufacturing, Stanley advocated corporations, operating commercially but with government capital, as the executive organs of the proposed local departments of industry, to assist in investigating and promoting new industries.[122]

Early in 1945, the Colonial Office still preferred not to consult the CEAC on development corporations, partly to allow time to elicit territorial governments' attitudes, and partly to enable the Committee to gain experience.[123] The Office's internal discussions were taken a stage further with a memorandum by Carstairs analysing the factors affecting the nature and rate of industrialisation and the potential contribution of development corporations. Carstairs concluded that corporations could usefully review matters such as raw material supplies, markets, capital, labour and expertise, and the relationship between them.

A major obstacle to development identified by Carstairs that was not prominent in earlier discussions was the inadequacy of local financial machinery, especially for providing fixed or working capital. Carstairs thought it probable that only government initiative and participation could overcome the absence of a developed system of local issuing houses. This gap could be met either by government credits or by government guarantees for bank loans. In either case, machinery would be needed to examine applications for help.

Carstairs addressed the equally important problem of harnessing the expertise required to bring together capital and 'sound' industrial projects, a question inseparable from the need for entrepreneurship, considered to be scarce in the colonies. Carstairs concluded that government would have to act as a 'catalyst', sometimes undertaking whole operations by providing capital and technicians and initiating projects. Many of these needs, he believed, could be met by establishing an industrial development organisation performing four main tasks. First, it could survey colonies' industrial potential, investigating questions such as raw material and labour supplies. Secondly, it could arrange to fill gaps detected in the factors of production, for example by providing skilled personnel or training. Thirdly, it could supply the missing entrepreneurial element by assuming a managerial role in selected projects, prior to their transfer to local managers. Finally, it could arrange for the supply of capital. Carstairs did not intend his proposed corporation to have a monopoly over industrial development in any colony: rather, it could encourage further private development, eventually becoming an information source rather than an active agent.[124]

Carstairs advocated locally organised and controlled development corporations. This model, attractive to the Colonial Office on political grounds, assumed that colonial governments would themselves take the initiative. Certainly, late in 1944, it had seemed that Lagos and Accra were interested in creating industrial development corporations. Yet by mid-1945, the Colonial Office had not succeeded in inducing either government to explore the subject deeply. Little more, for example, had been heard from Nigeria about the development corporation mooted in the government's development plan of October 1944. While the Colonial Office was considering Barclays' scheme, Lagos showed an interest in the proposal, commenting that the new corporation might be a useful source of development funding. Officials in London, however, saw no reason why Barclays' scheme should delay the Nigerian government's consideration of a corporation of its own.[125]

Lagos's interest in industrialisation had begun to wane late in 1944, with Governor Richards stating that large-scale industrial development was not envisaged. Early in 1945, Lagos was busy shaping its plans for a peasant textile industry. As already described, the Nigerian government was, by now, placing mounting constraints on factory development, affecting particularly the UAC's textile scheme, because of its fear of rapid urbanisation. Given these reservations, it is unsurprising that Lagos apparently lost interest in forming an industrial development corporation.

The situation in the Gold Coast was no more encouraging. Accra dismissed the idea of forming an industrial development corporation, though it had formed an Industrial Development Board to assist promising local industries.[126] As already noted, the Industrial Development Sub-Committee of the Gold Coast Economic Development Committee concluded in May 1945 that the scope for State-assisted industrialisation was limited. Although the Sub-Committee identified some instances of development meriting government assistance, such as textiles and furniture-making, its overall conclusion was that 'none of these projects needs anything like an Industrial Development Corporation'. However, it recommended a government agency of some sort to help initiate and consolidate such industries before their eventual transfer to private enterprise. Instead of a development corporation, the Sub-Committee favoured an Industrial Development Board, operating under commercial, rather than government, principles of accounting.[127]

An even more fundamental question raised by these discussions was whether territorial governments could devise novel forms of development machinery. Officials in London already harboured serious doubts about the ability of colonial governments to play a dynamic role in promoting development. Evidence from West Africa to justify these doubts reached the Colonial Office at an accelerating rate after 1943, undermining what remained of the traditional orthodoxy, still apparent in Carstairs' memorandum, that the initiative in development should rest with the colonial governments. A paradox consequently arose: on political grounds, it was desirable to foster development with an obviously 'local' flavour, minimising scope for allegations of 'exploitation' by Britain; however, concern to accelerate development led officials to consider unprecedentedly centralist solutions, eventually expressed in the plan for a single development corporation based in London.

Unease in the Colonial Office at the capabilities of the West African governments resurfaced following the despatch of Stanley's memorandum on West African planning in August 1943. Governor Burns replied that he proposed to establish a central planning committee for the Gold Coast, over which he would preside, to co-ordinate development plans.[128] The reply from Nigeria was less encouraging. While a Development Branch had been established in May 1943, together with a central Advisory Committee on Economic Development and Social Welfare which had drawn up a programme including industrial development, Lagos complained of an acute shortage of staff to engage in development planning. The so-called 'Development Branch' in fact consisted of one officer. In Richards' view, these staff shortages were a major constraint on the territory's reconstruction planning.[129]

In London, Cohen considered Richards' despatch 'a depressing document'. He felt that Accra, despite similar staffing problems, had made 'considerable' progress with post-war planning, but hoped that the position in West Africa might improve with Hall's appointment as Development Adviser to Swinton. Meanwhile, he thought that the Colonial Office should continue to discuss ways of strengthening Nigeria's development machinery.[130] Similarly, when Caine reviewed Nigeria's initial attempt at development programming, he condemned it as 'simply a collection of scraps, [that] shows no sign of any attempt to review the whole field of what is needed for active and reasonably quick development.'[131]

Resuming the theme implicit in his arguments against industrial licensing, Caine questioned the wisdom of expecting colonial governments to identify industries suitable for development. Traditionally, he believed, colonial governments had been reluctant to experiment with industrialisation, because of pessimism about its prospects, hence machinery was needed to determine which industries should be encouraged.[132]

Strong criticism of the West African governments also came from Swinton. His experiences in the region made him sceptical of the capacity of colonial administrators to make an effective contribution to economic policy and management. He told Stanley 'the more I see of the colonial service, the more I am impressed by the number of misfits, or at any rate of men who just carry on because they are in the groove.'[133] Swinton subsequently warned Stanley that he particularly doubted Accra's ability to undertake any new enterprise affecting the war effort. He was especially critical of the government's 'deplorable' record in cocoa production and other key sectors.[134]

During 1944, however, the West African governments began to establish machinery for development planning, concerned less with Swinton's war effort than with post-war production and demobilisation. Under the direction of F.E.V. Smith, Nigeria produced a comprehensive development plan by the end of the year. In the Gold Coast, Richardson had been appointed Economic Adviser to the government, and an Economic Development Committee was established to consider post-war planning.[135] Nigeria's preliminary development plan, submitted in October 1944, seemed 'inherently sound' to Noel Hall, being calculated to encourage development by both local and external capital and enterprise. In particular, Hall hoped that London would approve the proposal to create a Development Commission or Board in Nigeria to plan and execute the programme, providing 'drive' and checking the tendency towards 'departmentalism' and resistance to outside expertise.[136] Hall had already told the Office that he thought a Development Committee in each colony should be responsible for ensuring that industrial opportunities were taken up in all phases of its development programme.[137]

Although Stanley considered the general outline of the Nigerian plan 'excellent', for political reasons he was less keen on the proposed Development Commission, whose centralising tendency might, he thought, conflict with Nigeria's new constitutional proposals for greater regional autonomy. Another problem was the likelihood of calls for 'unofficial' African representation on the Commission, regarded as impracticable because there was 'no African in Nigeria capable of viewing the interests of Nigeria as a whole'.[138]

The Colonial Office's continuing anxiety about colonial governments' grasp of development planning is also evident in London's reaction to the Gold Coast's outline plan, produced in July 1944. Burns was believed not to have consulted Hall before having the plan drafted, and was even thought to be sceptical towards the entire notion of planning. In one official's view, Burns was 'temperamentally unwilling to consider anything which takes a long time'. If this observation is accurate it may account for the distinct lack of interest in industrialisation which became evident in the Gold Coast government's attitudes by early 1945. Burns's apparently cavalier attitude towards planning was considered particularly worrying, coming from the richest territory in West Africa: 'If investment cannot be made remunerative here then all our Empire is just a hopeless slum.'[139]

Nevertheless, the progress made by Nigeria and the Gold Coast in appointing their own development staff in 1944 gave London a pretext not to appoint a successor to Hall early in 1945.[140] However, it is possible that the Colonial Office was already doubtful that rapid development would automatically follow improvements in the region's administrative machinery (even if personnel shortages permitted this), although London had not yet translated this interpretation into a frankly centralist strategy. Not until summer 1945 did clearer indications emerge that a policy shift was imminent, and even then much remained unresolved.

A final example of the weakness of local machinery was the fate of the West African Institute. Established in April 1943 with a colonial development and welfare grant of £127,000, this body was hailed as a means of investigating potential industries and providing new employment opportunities. Initial progress in fields such as textile production and ceramics, stimulated by the wartime impetus for import-substitution, had been encouraging.[141] Late in 1944, attention focussed on the future relationship between the Institute's activities and government-aided development in West Africa. The Institute did not envisage itself establishing 'pilot' industries which could eventually be hived off, and instead had more modest aims, namely the testing of methods and materials, training and experimentation.[142] Henceforth, it was decided, the Institute should apply itself to 'economic, sociological and technological experimentation and enquiry rather than to day to day supervision of quasi-commercial units and the management of a relatively large labour force.' This would make the Institute's staff more mobile and available to provide specialist advice throughout West Africa.[143]

By mid-1945, problems had become obvious. It was felt in London that the Institute had 'never really got going', chiefly because of staffing problems. This had been aggravated by the 'contempt' in which Nigeria's Development Adviser reportedly held the Institute. Furthermore, Nigeria's own experimental peasant textile industry depended heavily on advice from the Institute's textile officer, and Burns resented devoting the Institute's resources to projects benefiting a single territory rather than West Africa as a whole. Burns concluded that the Institute could not function on a regional basis and told London that he proposed to abolish it, and refound it as a purely Gold Coast concern.[144] By autumn 1945, the Colonial Office considered the Institute 'moribund'.[145]

This mounting evidence of local shortcomings, together with the failure of Lagos and Accra to produce blueprints for development corporations, coincided with acknowledgement in the Colonial Office that its own thinking on corporations was imprecise. Moreover, the change of government in Britain in July 1945 obliged the Office to submit the Barclays scheme for fresh ministerial approval.[146] In August 1945, Leslie Monson, head of the Production Department, suggested that development corporations should be re-examined, particularly since interest in them had been reawakened following a reference by Stanley during a recent Commons speech.[147] Caine interjected that development corporations were of wider interest in relation to development as a *whole*, not only to industrialisation.[148] This was an early indication that the uses envisaged for colonial public enterprise, and even the direction of development itself, were entering a new period of fluidity.

The extent to which official thinking was shifting in the summer of 1945 is demonstrated by a memorandum written by John Rosa in answer to Monson's directive, and by the response it evoked within the Colonial Office. Unlike Carstairs, who had discussed the possible role of territorial development corporations, Rosa advocated a single, large corporation, *centrally* organised in London. Like Carstairs, Rosa identified two basic problems in development: the provision of capital and enterprise in operating individual schemes. He believed that both could be tackled through a development corporation. Of the two problems, Rosa considered the provision of experienced personnel the most difficult. He proposed a 'pool' of expertise in London, from which 'management squads' could be formed to organise schemes, operating them until their transfer to local personnel. A major aim would be to train such staff to take responsibility for projects as soon as possible, releasing the squads for work elsewhere, in a gradual and staged withdrawal. Thus, the squads would themselves acquire valuable experience in development. A practical advantage of Rosa's scheme was that staff could be hired for a limited period, rather than on a possibly less attractive career basis.

In Rosa's opinion, all these considerations suggested that a central corporation was preferable to separate, local corporations. A single body, based in London, would have direct access to a 'wealth of talent and expertise', whereas it would be difficult to find enough qualified people to staff separate corporations. Similarly, local corporations, without access to expert advice, could not assess or initiate development schemes as effectively as could one large corporation. However, Rosa believed that his corporation should work through local subsidiaries, able to examine proposals from a local perspective. The central corporation could then assess the commercial soundness of schemes, taking into account broad questions like the existence of export markets and the prospects of competition with industries in other colonies.

Rosa felt that the corporation would need financial flexibility, and substantial capital of its own, plus wide borrowing powers. The impracticability of raising capital in London for individual projects seemed to Rosa to be another argument for a single corporation. From an investment point of view, a large corporation could also spread its risks, both geographically and among various projects, to an extent impossible for local corporations. This would promote overall operational stability, making it possible to balance failures with successes. Possibly in deference to official sensitivity to the political implications of development, Rosa suggested that the corporation's local subsidiaries could attract local capital, fulfilling the goal of securing local participation. Moreover, Rosa considered this the only way to promote enterprise under local operation.[149]

Meanwhile, a decision was still awaited on Barclays' scheme, which was under ministerial review. As seen earlier, officials in the Colonial Office generally welcomed the plan, which was recommended warmly to ministers.[150] At this stage, the Labour Government's new Parliamentary Under-Secretary, Creech Jones, intervened. He had strong views on the benefits of public enterprise in colonial development. He had championed colonial rights in Parliament since his election in 1935, and was instrumental in founding the Fabian Colonial Bureau with the economist and journalist Rita Hinden. Creech Jones had been closely involved in drafting the Labour Party's 1943 statement on colonial policy, a document which had impressed officials in the Colonial Office, including Caine, with its 'realism' and moderation, and its implicit assumption of a continuing role for private enterprise in development, even if under stricter government regulation than envisaged by the Colonial Office.[151] Creech Jones nevertheless sought to extend government intervention in the colonial economies, and soon made his views plain to officials. In 1944, Creech Jones had written:

> It ought no longer to be the function of colonial governments to hold the ring for alien interests to exploit and develop what natural wealth there may be; to see the surplus wealth drained overseas for the enjoyment of anyone outside the people who produce it or whose natural resources it is; to remain indifferent to the claims of health and education and social advance; to concede little to the people in the way of consultation and collaboration or of political representation and responsibility.[152]

He welcomed the wartime growth of government controls, regarding these as the basis for sound future development. Although more concerned with the immediate problems posed by mining development, Creech Jones also called for public control of industrial development, especially raw materials processing, considering this essential in a planned economy.[153] An index of Creech Jones' commitment to public ownership came when Attlee's Cabinet was divided over steel nationalisation. Creech Jones, Hugh Dalton recalled, was firmly within the pro-nationalisation lobby, possibly influenced by Bevin, who had a regard for Creech Jones not universally shared by his colleagues, and whose parliamentary private secretary at the Ministry of Labour Creech Jones had been during the war.[154]

Like his colleagues in the FCB, who welcomed the development corporation as a means of escaping the 'vicious circle' of colonial poverty, Creech Jones was interested in the potential of this new type of organisation, but felt that the Colonial Office had been precipitate in approving Barclays' scheme before further consideration, and thought that the Office should await the colonial governments' own plans for corporations before sanctioning Barclays' project.

Although acknowledging the role of private capital Creech Jones doubted that colonial development could best be undertaken by private corporations, because they lacked the experience necessary to pursue comprehensive development, or that private enterprise's past reluctance to take risks in the colonies had modified. Moreover, he was concerned about possible colonial suspicion that private corporations would represent exploitation by outside interests. He called for 'safeguards', obliging Barclays Corporation to employ local personnel and to operate within the development framework established by colonial governments. Furthermore, he urged that its work should complement that of any government corporation which might be formed.[155]

Creech Jones' misgivings about Barclays' scheme were not, apparently, shared by his officials. It was felt that initiatives such as Barclays' need not conflict with government measures to establish development corporations. Caine, particularly, stressed the scale of the development task, and doubted whether a single organisation could undertake all the necessary work:

> I believe myself that the greatest need in development of this kind is to get the maximum of enterprise, and that is likely to be best achieved by leaving the field as open as possible and refraining from prohibitions while providing a Government organisation capable of taking up projects which, for one reason or another, had not attracted the attention of private concerns.[156]

Creech Jones, however, was dissatisfied, and insisted that Barclays be reminded of the need for their corporation to co-operate closely with the colonial governments.[157] The Colonial Office also told Barclays of the need for the new corporation to conform to any overall investment plan formulated by London, and for consultation between the corporation and any similar bodies created by government.[158] Barclays' replied that one means of fostering good relations with the colonial governments would be for its corporation to begin by assisting State-approved schemes which lacked finance.[159]

The Barclays Overseas Development Corporation was finally approved by the Treasury's Capital Issues Committee in November 1945.[160] Confusion soon arose over the boundary between projects suitable for government and private finance. Rosa, for example, suspected that Barclays hoped that the State would confine itself to uneconomic enterprises.[161] When Barclays sought clarification, Caine explained that no precise demarcation was yet possible, although it was 'widely agreed' that the two spheres of activity would probably be distinct. He believed the groundwork of development, such as basic research, undertaken by government, would complement and aid private enterprise.[162]

In February 1946, a representative from Barclays was invited to attend the CEAC's discussion. Barclays recognised the valuable work that a government corporation could do in basic research and surveying, but was unenthusiastic about the corporation engaging in industrial enterprise. Caine, however, thought that fundamental research would be too great a burden for a government corporation.[163] Barclays argued that it did not fear competition from a government corporation, but that the bank was unhappy about it engaging in commercial enterprises, possibly in competition with private firms.[164]

When informing the colonial governments about the registration of Barclays Corporation, the Colonial Office also described the organisation's functions and its intention to co-operate closely with both the governments and the Office. It was suggested that the Corporation could provide an additional source of funding for 'remunerative' development, although it did not envisage lending capital to governments. Territorial governments were requested to consult the Office before approaching the Corporation for assistance.[165]

Creech Jones' intervention in September 1945 encouraged the resumption of the Colonial Office's re-evaluation of public development corporations.[166] By now, the discussion papers by Carstairs and Rosa, respectively presenting the case for local and central corporations, had been supplemented by material gathered on similar bodies operating in Puerto Rico and South Africa. By November 1945, the Office at last felt ready to consult the CEAC, which was asked to advise on whether there should be a single, central corporation, or separate corporations in individual colonies. Reference to Barclays ODC was omitted at this stage, although information on it was circulated to the CEAC at Goodenough's request early in December 1945.[167]

Once again, the influence of Creech Jones in accelerating discussions is evident. In December 1945, during talks on the measures needed to strengthen the development machinery, Creech Jones called for more positive policies from the Colonial Office, voicing concern that, hitherto, the initiative had tended to come from external interests. Caine responded by suggesting that an executive organisation was needed, able to accelerate development, including industrialisation.[168]

When referring the subject to the CEAC, the Colonial Office explained to Sir William Goodenough, still a Committee member, that this did not mean there were official plans for a government organisation similar to Barclays. The approach to the CEAC was described simply as a resumption of discussions on promoting industrial development. This suggests a continuing desire among officials, especially Caine, to maintain good relations with private enterprise.[169]

The CEAC's Industry Sub-Committee eventually discussed development corporations in February 1946. The Committee had been asked to advise on whether government should create a corporation to assist industrial development. Welcoming the proposal for a corporation to assist industrialisation, the Committee opted for a central corporation working through local bodies, the course recommended by Caine and Rosa as the most effective means of providing technical expertise. However, it left open the question of whether these bodies should be organised on a territorial basis or on a regional basis. Similarly, no agreement was reached on whether the corporation should be funded publicly or privately. The Committee suggested, however, that a government corporation should not embark on projects competing directly with existing commercial enterprises. This point was underscored by Rosa, who believed that the whole purpose of the new machinery was to encourage industries not yet established.[170]

In official discussions on the proposed corporation's financial structure, the key issue was whether it should be self-supporting. Carstairs, whose role in the wider debate was declining, feared that if the new machinery were expected to be self-supporting, this would defeat its purpose, since if the corporation were too conscious of the financial aspect of its operations, it might restrict itself to 'safe' schemes, from which the private investor would be excluded. Carstairs, supported by the economist Professor Lionel Robbins, a member of the CEAC, thought that the corporation should be free to engage in 'developmental and exploratory expenditure', which, although possibly unprofitable to the corporation, would benefit the territory as a whole by clearing the path for subsequent investors.[171]

However, as Rosa stressed, one argument in favour of a centrally organised corporation was precisely that it could spread its risks widely, and therefore be self-supporting overall. It was therefore important not to overburden the corporation with too many functions, some of which, like basic research, ought to be undertaken directly by government. Equally, the corporation should not have to finance uneconomic schemes simply because they were valuable on other grounds. In Rosa's opinion, if an industry were desirable in the public interest then it should be subsidised directly by government. Rosa concluded that patience would be needed to allow the corporation to achieve solvency and a wide scope of activities. His belief that private enterprise would expect quick results convinced him that the corporation should be operated by government.[172]

By late March 1946, the CEAC had made little progress with its discussions on the form and functions of the proposed corporation. A draft report was therefore compiled for the Committee by its secretary at the suggestion of the Colonial Office's Development Adviser, Sir Frank Stockdale, the CEAC's *ex officio* Chairman.[173] As the Committee's life neared its end during the summer of 1946, officials decided to postpone action on its report until it could be put before the CEAC's successor body, the Colonial Economic Development Council (CEDC).[174] There were, however, additional motives for avoiding further reference to the CEAC. The subject had sensitive political aspects, relating not only to the 'central' versus 'local' debate on the organisation's form but also to whether it should be undertaken on a public or private basis.[175] Caine's lack of enthusiasm for public enterprise was evident from his views on industrial licensing and from his spirited defence of Barclays' initiative. By blocking further discussions by the CEAC, he probably sought to prevent advocates of State operation gaining unchallenged control over the debate on the form the development corporation should take.

The lull in the Colonial Office's deliberations on development corporations seems to have been decisively broken by Creech Jones. Shortly after replacing George Hall as Secretary of State early in October 1946, he told the Commons that he recognised the need to give colonial governments more guidance on industrialisation, and that the whole question was 'under consideration' in the Colonial Office. Admitting that a 'considerable degree' of public enterprise was 'essential' in colonial development, he saw no reason why public and private action should not be complementary.[176]

Balancing his enthusiasm for public enterprise was Creech Jones' interest in improving the machinery of colonial government. Soon after becoming Colonial Secretary, he met his senior officials and advisers and asked whether the Colonial Office's approach to development was sufficiently imaginative and comprehensive. He was concerned that the recent scheme to cultivate groundnuts in East Africa had been produced not by the Office but by a private company.[177] He sought the views of officials on how to achieve the co-operation of local populations in development. Creech Jones questioned whether the existing Colonial Service was qualified for its new responsibilities, for example in the fields of finance, economics and industry. Specifically, he wanted to know how the Colonial Office itself could do more to stimulate development. As one official observed, the problem seemed to be determining how to provide 'instructive direction' from London while fostering local initiative.[178]

Presumably in response to the impetus provided by Creech Jones, Caine suggested that the views of the newly formed CEDC on promoting industrialisation should soon be sought.[179] Creech Jones was particularly keen to have Stanley's February 1945 circular despatch on manufacturing industry reviewed and, if necessary, revised.[180] Accordingly, the CEDC was asked to discuss the despatch and to give its views on the establishment of an Industrial Development Corporation, including its form and structure.[181] The Council considered the incomplete conclusions of CEAC's Industry and Finance Sub-Committees, drafted during summer 1946 in anticipation of the CEDC's creation. These favoured a central corporation, based in London, with local branches in the colonies, and funded publicly. The functions envisaged for the corporation would be to promote industrial development, for example by providing information on opportunities, assessing applications for assistance, and arranging for the provision of capital and managerial and technical expertise. The corporation was also expected to undertake projects itself if necessary. The report had recommended that the corporation should co-operate with any private development corporation established, and that its long-term strategy should be to withdraw its personnel and sell its stake in the projects it had assisted either to colonial governments or local bodies, or to private investors.[182]

In December 1946, the CEDC endorsed CEAC's views as the basis for future action, and proposed to give the question detailed consideration at a later date.[183] When discussions were resumed early in 1947, however, the environment for debate was changing radically. The luxury of speculation, characteristic of the entire 'reconstruction' period, was soon dispelled in the harsher climate of the *annus horrendus*, when all aspects of metropolitan government policy, including colonial development, were increasingly affected by the immediate need to support the domestic economy. In these circumstances, many of the objectives identified by the Colonial Office between 1943 and 1946 had to be reassessed, and some sacrificed.

NOTES

1. CO 990/2, CEAC(43)5, 'Social and Economic Planning in the Colonial Empire', 25 Nov. 1943.
2. CO 852/588 Pt.1, 'The Planning of Social and Economic Development in the Colonial Empire', Apr. 1944.
3. CAB 66/65, WP(45)301, 'Overseas financial policy in Stage III', 15 May 1945.
4. *PP* (1945–46), xix, 35, Cmd. 6713 *Colonial Development and Welfare. Despatch dated 12th November, 1945, from the Secretary of State for the Colonies to Colonial Governments*.
5. Pearce (1987), p.282; Shuckburgh II, pp.310–13.
6. Shuckburgh II, pp.315–18.
7. Morgan (1980) I, p.201; N.J. Westcott (1983), pp.4, 7, 8.
8. Westcott (1983), pp.6–7.
9. Porter and Stockwell (1987), p.45.
10. Meredith (1986), pp.77–78, 87–88.
11. Westcott (1983), p.2; *PP*(1946–47), x, 403, Cmd.7167, *The Colonial Empire (1939–1947)*, para. 401.
12. CO 852/591/3, letter to Brittain (Treasury), 19 June 1945; ibid., A.J.D. Winnifrith (Treasury) to J.B. Williams, 21 July 1945.
13. Louis, (1977), pp.103–5.

14. Hargreaves, (1988), pp.55–6.
15. The Labour Party, *The Colonies: the Labour Party's Post-War Policy for the African and Pacific Colonies* (London: Labour Party, 1943) pp.16–7.
16. CO 990/16, CEAC (Industry) 3rd minutes, 17 Apr 1944; CO 990/17, CEAC (Industry)(44)5, 'Possible scope for industrialisation in the Colonies', 25 Apr. 1944.
17. CO 990/16, CEAC (Industry) 4th minutes, 15 May 1944.
18. CO 990/16, CEAC (Industry) 5th minutes, 15 June 1944.
19. CO 852/588/2, memo. by CEAC to Stanley, 31 Oct. 1944.
20. CO 990/1, CEAC 9th minutes, 19 Dec. 1944.
21. See esp. Louis (1979).
22. Porter and Stockwell (1987), p.43.
23. Lord Hailey, *Britain and Her Dependencies* (London: Longman, 1943) pp.10–6.
24. Ibid., pp.18–9.
25. Rhodes House Library, Oxford: MSS. Brit. Emp. s.335 Hailey Papers, speech to Royal Central Asian Society, 'The Colonies and the Atlantic Charter', 7 July 1943.
26. CO 852/588/2, 16 Aug. 1943.
27. *PD(C)*, 391, 66–8, 13 July 1943.
28. CO 482/2, draft memo. by Carstairs, 'The Control of Secondary Industries in the Colonies, with special reference to East and West Africa', 21 Nov. 1943.
29. Bowden (1980), p.218.
30. CO 554/130/33685/1943, note by H.B. Lawrence, 'The Institute of West African Arts, Industries and Social Science', 10 June 1943.
31. Bowden (1980), pp.218–19; CO 852/480/11, Meyerowitz to Williams, enclosing memo. from J. Holt and Co., 3 May 1943.
32. CO 852/480/11, minute by O.G.R. Williams, 4 May 1943; CO 852/480/11, note of meeting in CO, 12 Nov. 1943.
33. Fieldhouse (1986), p.10.
34. CO 852/574/7, note of meeting in CO with representatives of Cotton Board, BoT and UAC, 8 Mar. 1945.
35. Pearce (1987), p.282.
36. Shuckburgh I, pp.279–81; Robinson (1980), p.58; CO 583/271/30572/1944, note of meeting in CO to discuss Nigerian preliminary development plan, 6 Nov. 1944.
37. Hopkins (1973), pp.259–64.
38. Pearce (1987), p.284.
39. Meredith (1986), pp.85–6.
40. Meredith (1988), pp.286, 295–296.
41. CO 554/132/33718/1/1943, memo. for West African Governments, 'Post-War Planning for West Africa', (n.d.).
42. CO 990/2, CEAC(43)5, 'Social and Economic Planning in the Colonial Empire', 25 Nov. 1943.
43. Morgan (1980) I, p.186; CO 990/1, CEAC 2nd minutes, 9 Dec. 1943.
44. CO 852/588 Pt.1, 'The Planning of Social and Economic Development in the Colonial Empire', Apr. 1944.
45. CO 852/482/3, minute by Caine, 30 Oct. 1943.
46. CO 852/588 Pt.1, 'The Planning of Social and Economic Development in the Colonial Empire', Apr. 1944.
47. CO 990/17, CEAC (Industry)(44)5, 'Possible scope for industrialisation in the Colonies', 25 May 1944.
48. CO 990/16, CEAC (Industry) 5th minutes, 15 June 1944.
49. CO 852/578/5, CEAC(44)32, 'The Development of Manufacturing Industries', 29 Aug. 1944.
50. CO 852/588/2, CEAC (44)38, Agenda Sub–Committee Third Report, 'Memorandum on Planning', 14 Sept. 1944.
51. CO 583/263/30560/1943, note of meeting in CO on Nigerian development, 22 June 1943.

52. CO 852/509/15, WAWC(CM)4, 'Economic Policy in West African Colonies', 24 Feb. 1943. On the Lebanese community generally, see T. Falola, 'The Lebanese in Colonial West Africa', in J.F. Ade Ajayi and J.D.Y. Peel (eds) *People and Empires in African History: Essays in Memory of Michael Crowder* (London: Longman, 1992), pp.121–42.
53. Ibid.; CO 852/482/2, draft memo. by Carstairs, 'The Control of Secondary Industries in the Colonies, with special reference to East and West Africa', 21 Nov. 1943.
54. Kent (1986), pp.340–1.
55. CO 990/1, CEAC 2nd minutes, 9 Dec. 1943.
56. CO 852/509/15, WAWC(CM)4, memo. by Resident Minister, 24 Feb. 1943.
57. CO 852/482/2, WAWC(CM)30, 'Licensing of Industries in West Africa', 9 Dec. 1943.
58. CO 852/509/15, WAWC(CM)4, 24 Feb. 1943.
59. CO 96/775/1/31401/1941, letter to Burns, 2 June 1943.
60. Ibid., letter to K.E. Robinson, 19 Aug. 1943.
61. Ibid., minute, 25 Aug. 1943.
62. CO 852/588/2, 16 Aug. 1943.
63. CO 96/775/1/31401/1941, minute, 27 Aug. 1943.
64. Ibid., minutes by Dawe, 27 Aug. 1943, and Gater, 28 Aug. 1943.
65. Ibid., letter, 28 Aug. 1943.
66. CO 852/480/11, extract from WAWC (CM)29, 4th meeting, 28 Oct. 1943.
67. Ibid., telegram, 9 Nov. 1943.
68. CO 852/480/11, Clauson to Lockhart, 16 Nov. 1943.
69. CO 852/480/11, note of meeting in CO, 12 Nov. 1943.
70. CO 852/480/11, note of meeting in CO, 12 Nov. 1943.
71. CO 852/480/11, minute by K.E. Robinson, 16 Nov. 1943; telegram from Stanley to Swinton, 19 Nov. 1943.
72. Ibid., Clauson to Lockhart, 16 Nov. 1943.
73. CO 96/775/1/31401/1941, minute, 29 Apr. 1943.
74. Pearce (1982), Chs II and III *passim*; Lee and Petter (1982), pp.193–9; J. Flint, 'Planned decolonisation and its failure in British Africa', *AA*, 82, 328, (July 1983), pp.389–411; and Porter and Stockwell (1987), pp.32–8.
75. CO 852/482/2, draft memo. by Carstairs, 'The Control of Secondary Industries in the Colonies, with special reference to East and West Africa', 21 Nov. 1943.
76. CO 852/480/11, note of meeting in CO, 12 Nov. 1943.
77. CO 852/482/2, draft memo. by Carstairs, 21 Nov. 1943.
78. CO 852/482/2, minute by O.G.R. Williams, 27 Nov. 1943.
79. Ibid., minute by Caine, 25 Nov. 1943.
80. CO 852/480/11, telegram from Sandford to Robinson, 23 Nov. 1943.
81. CO 852/482/2, WAWC(CM)30, 'Licensing of Industries in West Africa', 9 Dec. 1943.
82. Ibid., minute by Cohen, 31 Dec. 1943; ibid., minute by O.G.R. Williams, 4 Jan. 1944.
83. CO 852/482/2, minute, 31 Dec. 1943.
84. CO 990/16, CEAC (Industry), 1st minutes, 2 Mar. 1944.
85. CO 852/578/5, CEAC(44)21 (Revised), 'Industrial Licensing', 31 Mar. 1944.
86. CO 852/574/5, Saving from Stanley to Swinton, 13 Apr. 1944.
87. Ibid., Swinton to Stanley, 17 May 1944.
88. Ibid., WAWC(CM) 6th meeting, 6/7 July 1944.
89. CO 554/139/33718/1/1944, note of discussion between Stanley and Swinton, 2 Aug. 1944.
90. CO 852/574/5, CEAC 6th minutes, 29 Aug. 1944.
91. CO 852/586/11, CEAC(45)72, Third statement on action taken on Committee's Reports, 11 Jan. 1946.

92. CO 852/574/10, minute by Monson, 31 Jan. 1946.
93. Ibid., minute, 6 Feb. 1946.
94. CO 852/588/2, 16 Aug. 1943.
95. CO 990/2, CEAC(44)15, memo. by Lewis, 'The Development of Secondary Industry in the Colonial Empire', n.d..
96. CO 852/482/2, minute, 23 Nov. 1943.
97. CO 96/781/2/31475/1944, minute by Carstairs, 11 Oct. 1944.
98. CO 852/578/8, note of discussion in CO, 2 Aug. 1944.
99. Ibid., 'Development Corporations in West Africa', Aug. 1944.
100. CAB 87/9, R(44)174, 19 Oct. 1944.
101. CO 852/578/8, minute by Carstairs, 21 Aug. 1944.
102. CO 852/588/2, CEAC(44)38, Agenda Sub-Committee Third Report, 'Memorandum on Planning', 14 Sept. 1944.
103. CO 990/1, CEAC 9th minutes, 19 Dec. 1944.
104. CO 852/578/8, note of meeting in CO, 24 Oct. 1944; CO 583/271/30572/1944, note on 'Nigeria Development Plan', Nov. 1944.
105. CO 583/271/30572/1944, note of meeting in CO, 6 Nov. 1944.
106. CO 852/578/11, letter to Goodenough, 15 Feb. 1945.
107. CO 852/578/8, note of discussion between Carstairs and Richardson, 6 Dec. 1944.
108. CO 852/482/4, note of discussion in CO with representatives of Cotton Board and Board of Trade, 14 Oct. 1943; Streat had mentioned the idea during an informal discussion with Stanley on 28 July 1943, see Dupree (1987), II, pp.138–41.
109. CO 852/574/6, note of meeting in CO, 26 Oct. 1944.
110. CO 852/578/7, Helmore (Board of Trade) to Caine, 29 Jan. 1945.
111. CO 852/578/7, minute by Caine, 12 Mar. 1945; ibid., J.R. Willis (BoT) to Carstairs, 16 Mar. 1945.
112. CO 852/578/8, letter to Caine, 30 Nov. 1944.
113. CO 852/578/11, minute by Caine, 16 Jan. 1945.
114. Ibid., minute by Gater, 30 Jan. 1945; Stanley to Goodenough, 15 Feb. 1945.
115. Ibid., letter to Stanley, 19 Feb. 1945; minute by Stanley, 20 Mar. 1945.
116. Ibid., minute, 22 Feb. 1945.
117. Ibid., minute by Caine, 13 Mar. 1945; memo. by Barclays Bank (DC & O) Ltd for Bank of England, 'Colonial Development Finance', 24 Apr. 1945.
118. Ibid., minute by Monson, 1 June 1945.
119. CO 852/578/7, minute by Caine, 5 Feb. 1945; ibid., Caine to Helmore, 15 Feb. 1945.
120. *PD(C)*, 407, 2092–2188, 7 Feb. 1945.
121. CO 852/578/7, minute by Caine, 15 Feb. 1945.
122. CO 852/578/6, circular despatch, 'The Development of Manufacturing Industries', 27 Feb. 1945.
123. CO 852/587/9, minute by Caine, 9 Mar. 1945; minute by Clauson, 26 Mar. 1945; Caine to Sir Harold Howitt, 28 Mar. 1945; Howitt to Caine, 6 Apr. 1945.
124. CO 852/587/9, CEAC (Industry)(45)22, enclosure 1, memo. by C.Y. Carstairs, 'Development Corporations', (n.d.).
125. CO 852/578/11, Smith (Nigeria) to Caine, 23 Mar. 1945; ibid., Caine to Smith, 29 Mar. 1945.
126. CO 847/36/2, summary of replies to circular despatch of 27 Feb. 1945, (n.d.).
127. CO 554/139/33718/1/1944, minute by Creasy, 7 Sept. 1944; CO 852/587/9, enclosure 1 to CEAC (Industry)(45)21, 'Report of Industrial Development Sub-Committee, Gold Coast', May 1945.
128. CO 554/132/33718/1/1943, Burns to Stanley, 8 Oct. 1943.
129. CO 583/271/30572/1944, despatch to Stanley, 7 Jan. 1944.
130. Ibid., minute, 27 Jan. 1944.
131. Ibid., minute, 28 Jan. 1944.

132. CO 990/16, CEAC (Industry) 4th minutes, 15 May 1944.
133. Kent (1986), p.336.
134. CAB 104/257, telegram to Stanley, 14 June 1944; J.A. Cross, *Lord Swinton* (Oxford: Oxford University Press, 1982) p.241.
135. Kent (1986), p.343; Shuckburgh I, p.300.
136. CO 583/271/30572/1944, telegram to Stanley, 30 Sept 1944; ibid., 'Nigeria Preliminary Development Plan', 20 Oct. 1944.
137. CO 554/139/33718/1/1944, letter to Creasy, 7 June 1944.
138. CO 583/271/30572/1944, note of meeting in CO, 25 Oct. 1944; see also Pearce (1982), pp.80–3.
139. CO 96/781/2/31475/1944, minute by F.J. Pedler, 29 Sept. 1944.
140. *PD(C)*, 409, 1403–4, 28 Mar. 1945.
141. CO 554/130/33685/1943, ACEC (Advisory Committee on Education in the Colonies) 120th minutes, 14 Jan. 1943; Shuckburgh I, pp.33, 300–01.
142. CO 554/136/33685/1945, letter to O.G.R. Williams, 20 Dec. 1944.
143. Ibid., CRC 154, 'West African Institute of Industries, Art and Social Science', 16 Feb. 1945.
144. Ibid., 'Establishment of Institute', 4 June 1945; CO 852/574/9, note of meeting in CO, 26 June 1945.
145. CO 554/136/33685/1945, note of discussion on future of West African Institute, 30 Oct. 1945.
146. CO 852/578/11, minute by Gater, 29 Aug. 1945.
147. CO 852/578/9, minute, 14 Aug. 1945.
148. Ibid., minute, 16 Aug. 1945.
149. CO 852/578/9, minute, 18 Aug. 1945; 'Industrial Development Corporations'.
150. CO 852/578/11, minute, 11 Sept. 1945.
151. Labour Party, *The Colonies* (1943); Bowden (1980), pp.202–3; Lee and Petter (1982) pp.159–60; P.S. Gupta, *Imperialism and the British Labour Movement, 1914–1964* (London: Macmillan, 1975) pp.275–84; D. Goldsworthy, *Colonial Issues in British Politics, 1945–1961* (Oxford: Oxford University Press, 1971) Ch. 4 *passim*.
152. R. Hinden (ed.), *Fabian Colonial Essays* (London: George Allen & Unwin, 1945) p.12.
153. Ibid., pp.16–17.
154. H. Dalton, *High Tide and After. Memoirs 1945–1960* (London: Frederick Muller, 1962) p.136.
155. Ibid., minute, 18 Sept 1945; *Empire*, 8, 3, (Sept.–Oct. 1945).
156. CO 852/578/11, minute, 25 Sept. 1945; minute by Gater, 25 Sept. 1945.
157. Ibid., minutes by Creech Jones, 26 Sept. 1945, Gater, 13 Oct. 1945 and 15 Oct. 1945, and Creech Jones, 16 Oct. 1945.
158. Ibid., Gater to Goodenough, 16 Oct. 1945.
159. Ibid., note of interview with Goodenough and Crossley (Barclays) in CO, 25 Oct. 1945.
160. Ibid., Goodenough to Gater, 26 Nov. 1945.
161. Ibid., minute, 17 Dec. 1945.
162. Ibid., minute, 16 Jan. 1946.
163. CO 852/587/10, CEAC (Finance) 9th minutes, CEAC (Industry) 11th minutes, (joint session), 12 Feb. 1946.
164. Ibid., Crossley to Stockdale, 13 Feb. 1946.
165. CO 852/578/12, circular telegram, 27 Apr. 1946.
166. CO 852/578/9, minute by Carstairs, 26 Oct. 1945.
167. Ibid., minute by W.A. Morris, 12 Nov 1945; CO 852/587/9, CEAC (Industry)(45)22, 'Industrial Development Corporations', 16 Nov. 1945; CO 852/587/9, CEAC(45)69, 'Development Corporations', 7 Dec. 1945.
168. CO 852/591/7, minute by J.B. Williams, 14 Dec. 1945.

169. CO 852/578/9, minute by W.A. Morris and letter from Caine to Goodenough, 19 Nov. 1945.
170. CO 852/587/10, CEAC (Finance) 9th minutes, CEAC (Industry) 11th minutes, (joint session), 12 Feb. 1946.
171. Ibid.; CO 852/578/10, minute, 11 Mar. 1946.
172. CO 852/578/10, minute, 15 Mar. 1946.
173. Ibid., minutes by Sweaney, 23 Mar. 1946, and Rosa, 5 Apr. 1946.
174. CO 852/587/10, minute by Stockdale, 25 June 1946; minute by J.B. Williams, 3 July 1946.
175. CO 852/587/10, minute, 5 July 1946.
176. *PD(C)*, 427, 393–4, 23 Oct. 1946.
177. Morgan (1980) II, pp.226–319.
178. CO 852/588/3, note of meeting in CO, 29 Nov. 1946.
179. CO 852/587/10, minute, 23 Oct. 1946.
180. Ibid., minute by Gater, 30 Oct. 1946; CO 852/592/3, minute by J.B. Williams, 26 Nov. 1946.
181. CO 852/587/10, CEDC(46)12, 'Note on Industrial Development', (n.d.).
182. Ibid., CEDC(46)12 Appendix III, 'CEAC (Finance and Industry) Joint Report on Colonial Industrial Development Corporation', 15 Nov. 1946.
183. CO 999/1, CEDC 9th minutes, 16 Dec. 1946.

5 The Metropolitan Crisis and Constraints on Colonial Industrialisation, 1947–48

The first 18 months of the Labour government's life provide little evidence of systematic ministerial exploration of colonial solutions to Britain's financial difficulties. The Cabinet largely trusted to multilateral trade and export growth to secure full employment and recovery.[1] The failure of the convertibility operation in August 1947 finally crushed these hopes. The government's problems, however, had been growing since early 1947. The winter brought a crippling fuel crisis and serious disruption of industrial production; the American loan was rapidly depleted; exports grew less quickly than anticipated, and concern mounted at the level of food imports from the dollar area. Against this background, ministerial attention fixed upon colonial resources and their possible role in metropolitan recovery.[2]

Attlee's government succumbed, like none before it, to the myth of colonial panaceas for metropolitan problems. After 1947, it equated colonial development with a drive to maximise colonial commodity production as rapidly as possible. The principal advocate of this strategy, the Foreign Secretary, Ernest Bevin, was convinced that colonial raw materials production could contribute significantly to Britain's balance of payments.[3] He demonstrated a near obsessive faith in Africa's potential, particularly its mineral wealth. In July 1947, he demanded every effort to accelerate colonial production of commodities needed by the United States. His interest in colonial development derived from concern that continued US financial assistance to Britain could not be assumed. Moreover, he was pessimistic about the prospects for recovery based on Britain's former export trade in manufactures, given the wartime stimulus to overseas industrialisation.[4] Similarly, the Deputy Prime Minister and Lord President of the Council, Herbert Morrison, argued that Britain's economic recovery was being 'strangled' by shortages of raw materials, food and fuel, and that without an 'ample flow' of commodities, economic planning would be nullified and crises would recur.[5]

Such attitudes, nascent and largely unco-ordinated early in 1947, were given prominence by the crisis of August 1947 and the suspension of sterling convertibility. Immediately, efforts began to incorporate the colonies in an overall strategy to achieve recovery.[6] The colonies were asked to continue currency accumulation in London in order to strengthen the Sterling Area's position. They were requested to limit their dollar and other hard currency expenditure, and to curb sterling imports, so releasing exports for dollar markets, now vital to Britain. The colonies were invited to help directly by increasing their production of goods which Britain currently bought with dollars, or of dollar-earning goods. From London's point of view, increased commodity exports were the major contribution which the colonies could make to recovery. London described the crisis as an unprecedented opportunity for the colonies to develop their production and trade along lines which would bring advantages both to them and to Britain.[7]

On Bevin's prompting, the Colonial Office was asked to report urgently on prospects for increased colonial exports to the United States.[8] Bevin called for investigations into the raw materials that had been scarce in the United States at the outbreak of the Second World War, and assessments of how far these shortages could be met by colonial exports.[9] However, officials concluded that the only important commodity of which increased supplies could rapidly be made available was rubber, although the supply of other commodities might be expanded if Britain's own imports were cut. Longer-term possibilities included exports of minerals such as tin and lead, although here development was hampered by shortages of capital equipment, a complaint which became familiar over succeeding months.[10]

The creation in 1948 of the Colonial Development Corporation (CDC) was symbolic of the government's new commitment to colonial development and was an example of the brief vogue for applying technocratic and dynamic methods to achieve rapid and efficient colonial development. The idea of promoting development through State action was not contributed directly by the incoming Labour government. Nevertheless, Attlee and his colleagues endorsed it warmly.[11]

As suggested above, the Colonial Office's plans for a

development corporation, supported by local subsidiaries, envisaged a body capable of bringing capital and expertise to a variety of development schemes, embracing both agriculture and industry. The proposal was advanced by the Colonial Office in March 1947. Creech Jones told Attlee that the intention was to

> promote in every possible way increased Colonial production on an economic and self-supporting basis with an eye to the production of foodstuffs, raw materials and manufactures where supply to the UK or sales overseas would assist our balance of payments.[12]

The plan was swiftly approved by Cabinet. In June 1947 ministers agreed to create not only the CDC, but also an Overseas Food Corporation, responsible to the Ministry of Food, to co-ordinate food production and increase supplies to metropolitan consumers.[13] Two factors probably explain the speed with which these proposals were adopted: first, the imminent exhaustion of the American loan; secondly, a growing conviction in Whitehall that Britain derived little immediate benefit from the sums already allocated to colonial development and welfare.[14]

The need to implement the development corporation plan rapidly influenced the Colonial Office's choice of structure. A single, centralised body was preferred to smaller, local bodies, because the latter would take longer to establish, and would deploy scarce expertise less efficiently.[15] The choice of a centralised form probably also reflected the Colonial Office's continuing doubts about the capacity of colonial governments to act dynamically in the field of development. However, while the Office sought greater central control over the corporation, it did not envisage surrendering its overall direction to other branches of the metropolitan government.

The Overseas Resources Development Bill, which created the CDC, gave it borrowing powers of up to £100 million. The Bill, which also created the Overseas Food Corporation, was enacted in February 1948. The CDC's function was to promote schemes either to earn dollars through exports to the United States, or to save dollars by producing raw materials for Britain, thereby continuing the colonies' wartime economic contribution to Britain's balance of payments.[16] The Corporation was expected to judge proposed development schemes according to their value to the Sterling Area. Initially, the Corporation's activities were expected to be biased towards short-term projects requiring a minimum investment of capital goods.[17]

Ministers' enthusiasm for colonial development after the summer of 1947 exposed fundamental weaknesses in Whitehall's co-ordinating machinery. Symptomatic of growing interest, and of mounting demands for development to be integrated into domestic economic planning and located in Britain's general investment programme, was the creation, late in 1947, of an inter-departmental Colonial Development Working Party, which presented its final report in October 1948. This comprised representatives of the Central Economic Planning Staff, the Colonial Office, the Board of Trade and the Ministries of Supply and of Food, and was chaired by Sir Edwin Plowden, the government's Chief Planning Officer. It examined colonial requirements for capital equipment in relation to the needs of metropolitan investment and export, and advised on development programmes in the light of available resources.[18]

Official enthusiasm for development after 1947 inevitably encouraged unrealisable expectations. Development fever was pervasive and infectious. An extreme example was the report by the Chief of the Imperial General Staff, Field Marshal Montgomery, who toured Africa late in 1947. Montgomery, betraying comprehensive ignorance of the realities of post-war Africa, saw 'immense possibilities' in development, and 'almost unlimited quantities' of vital raw materials, which could be tapped to maintain British living standards. Voicing a criticism of the Colonial Office which became increasingly common in Britain during 1947–48, Montgomery attacked what he felt was the current unco-ordinated approach to development, and called for a dynamic 'grand design', with the ruthless elimination of obstacles, human or otherwise.[19]

Montgomery's report drew a predictably defensive response from the Office, which considered his suggestions to be simplistic and impracticable, and contrary to the momentum towards political devolution in Africa: the *political* aspect of development could not be ignored if local goodwill, essential to success in development, were to be maintained. This had long been a commonplace within the Colonial Office: increasingly, other branches of Whitehall had to be convinced of its importance.[20]

Early in 1948, London grew increasingly anxious to accelerate progress with development. Even now, ministers were anticipating the expiry of Marshall Aid. The key point seemed to be that Britain could not assume that it would receive sufficient aid to restore its economic independence. It was therefore essential to give colonial development high priority if satisfactory results were to be achieved before US aid expired.[21] Moreover, ministers felt that previous development planning had been insufficiently integrated with domestic economic policy. For example, no effort had been made to determine what proportion of metropolitan resources colonial development required, and understanding grew that improved arrangements were needed to ensure that the colonies received their fair share of available supplies.[22]

During 1948, the Colonial Office became subject to much direct and oblique criticism over its handling of development. Early in the year, Attlee personally sought reassurances from Creech Jones that the Office was organised to fulfil its responsibilities.[23] Progress with development was reviewed critically in the report of the Select Committee on Estimates of June 1948. This found particular fault with the Colonial Office and its development machinery, calling for stronger co-ordination and centralised planning.[24] Similarly, even late in 1948, ministers remained unconvinced of the Office's capacity to oversee development. They considered this particularly important given the new degree of government participation in the colonial economies, which required the Office to maintain general control over development. Ironically, given their past indifference to colonial interests, ministers now argued that the colonial economies could not be integrated with the metropolitan economy effectively unless the Colonial Office was able to present their case when supplies were allocated and priorities determined.[25]

It took time for the Colonial Office's critics to appreciate the limits to the centralised control of development, a problem aggravated by insensitivity in Whitehall to its political dimension. During the supply debate in July 1948, the Parliamentary Under-Secretary at the Colonial Office, David Rees-Williams, tried to convey the complexities of the colonial relationship:

> We have to recognise the fact that the Colonial Office are very often not in a position to insist upon many things. We can suggest to many of the Colonial Governments, advise them and help them, but in many instances they have the final word and if they do not take our help and advice, there is very little further that we can do.[26]

Since adopting a 'welfarist' outlook regarding development before 1939, the Colonial Office had consistently argued that development should be planned by *local* agencies, with London providing resources and guidance where necessary. This principle had been enshrined in the 1940 Colonial Development and Welfare Act, although, after 1943, the Office became increasingly frustrated and alarmed at the apparent inability of territorial governments to absorb the importance of planning. Moreover, given London's vaunted commitment to progressive colonial devolution, and the need for local co-operation in development, it was politically impossible to impose development plans from Britain. Only repeated explanations of these constraints by the Colonial Office convinced ministers, by late 1948, that development was a complex and delicate process.

Metropolitan insensitivity to colonial political realities was irritating and potentially embarrassing to the Colonial Office. More serious, however, was the virtually exclusive emphasis placed by Whitehall on expanding colonial primary production, especially 1947 to 1948, a bias at odds with the Office's more catholic interpretation of development. This bias was explicitly stated by the chancellor, Sir Stafford Cripps, when addressing the African Governors' Conference in November 1947. Cripps called for the tempo of African economic development to be increased 'out of all recognition', arguing that 'the whole future of the sterling group and its ability to survive depends in my view upon a quick and extensive development of its African resources.'[27]

The Colonial Office appreciated that the key to improved colonial living standards was agricultural efficiency, but it continued to see an important role for economic diversification through industrial development. This was demonstrated, for example, in Creech Jones's despatch to African Governors of February 1947 which called for a 'revolution' in African productivity. According to the despatch, while 'for many years to come', agriculture would inevitably be predominant in African economic development, it was clear, too, that

> the kind of standards aimed at today are impossible of attainment on a purely agricultural basis, and that in the course of years there must be a very substantial development of secondary industry if markedly higher standards are to be achieved.[28]

It became evident during 1947 and 1948 that officials had not lost their wartime interest in industrialisation. Furthermore, the Colonial Office could not ignore growing enthusiasm for industrial development, especially in the African territories, where it was increasingly regarded by emerging political élites as essential for future growth, and symbolic of economic 'maturity'.[29] For the Colonial Office to be seen to be obstructing industrial development would be to risk creating political capital for nationalist (or 'proto-nationalist') leaders.

Fundamental obstacles to industrialisation remained. The immediate problem was the shortage of equipment and other essential supplies. Aggravating this, although it was not then seen as a major limiting factor, was the scarcity of development capital. A third, and arguably critical barrier was the resurgence of antipathy in Whitehall towards colonial industrialisation. The Office's wartime efforts to construct a coherent policy on industrialisation were threatened after 1947 by the weight of opinion in Whitehall which regarded such development as at best irrelevant, or worse, as inherently damaging to British interests.

The supply problem

The dominant obstacle to development in the period 1947–48 was Britain's inability to supply the colonies with the exports they required. Starved of imports during the war, the colonies now found their needs ranking third after those of Britain and dollar markets. Goods not required for metropolitan reconstruction were exported, where possible, to 'hard' currency areas in preference to 'soft' sterling markets.[30] Until August 1947, London tried to dictate colonial import policy in general terms only, with no attempts at detailed controls. After the convertibility crisis, however, colonial governments were asked to estimate their imports from the Western Hemisphere during 1948. These rough estimates were subsequently imposed as 'ceilings' on dollar imports, controlled in London by a Colonial Dollar Drain Committee, comprising representatives of the Colonial Office, the Treasury, the Board of Trade and the Bank of England.[31] In August 1947, the colonies were instructed to limit their imports, especially from hard currency sources, to 'minimum essentials'.[32] Subsequently, wartime import controls were reimposed. Colonial governments were instructed to refuse import licences for goods that would not generate substantial increases in dollar-earning/saving production.[33]

Despite its growing concern to accelerate development, Whitehall was slow to establish machinery to discover precisely which goods the colonies required. The Colonial Development Working Party (CDWP) was formed late in 1947 to remedy this. As pressure grew in Whitehall for the integration of development in domestic economic planning after summer 1947, the Colonial Office proposed to create the Working Party, intended to be a body of recognised authority to examine the allocation of supplies to the colonies and a means of co-ordinating development. Above all, the Colonial Office sought a way of educating Whitehall in the unappreciated problems of development.[34] However, there were early indications of future divisions of opinion within Whitehall. Whereas the Colonial Office saw the CDWP as a means to secure increased supplies for the colonies, others in the metropolitan government, notably Sir Edward Bridges, the Treasury permanent secretary, were keen to limit colonial imports still further.[35]

Not until January 1948 were attempts made to gauge the colonies' needs for basic capital imports such as steel and cement. The accumulation of information on colonial investment plans began with a pilot study of Nigeria's requirements for capital goods in the period 1948–50.[36] Whether colonial needs, once known, could be satisfied, was another matter. When Creech Jones sought Attlee's authorisation to announce that Britain would do everything possible to promote development, not only financially but also with supplies, Attlee responded guardedly that the CDWP might be asked what promises could reasonably be made, though he doubted that the assurances Creech Jones requested could safely be given.[37]

Yet the supply problem's pressing nature soon became clear. Early analyses of achievements in post-war development were disturbing. For example, the CDWP's draft report, produced in April 1948, estimated that colonial exports of many foodstuffs and raw materials during 1946 were *below* 1936 levels, chiefly due to the running down of capital equipment during the war and the scarcity of supplies since 1945. The CDWP subsequently concluded that the major impediment to development was the continuing supply problem. The Working Party concluded that efforts should be concentrated on short-term development possibilities, and on restoring and improving *existing* capital equipment such as railways, avoiding the allure of large new schemes which, while firing the imagination, could not become productive quickly.[38] In effect, this was a call to patch up colonial infrastructures that had been severely stretched by the war, and which, more importantly, were geared almost entirely to the production and evacuation of raw materials. It was, therefore, an implicit call for a bias in development which would benefit Britain rapidly, and ignored the Colonial Office's commitment to economic diversification. Not until summer 1948 did the Colonial Office finally convince Whitehall that colonial import needs should receive the same treatment in the allocation of British goods as those of countries with which Britain had bilateral trading agreements. Although the Office considered this a major breakthrough, it realised that constant pressure would be necessary to make this principle effective.[39]

In this period, shortages of consumer goods were as critical as the scarcity of capital equipment. Wartime experience had demonstrated to officials both in Africa and in London that colonial productivity required adequate supplies of items such as cotton textiles. The shortage of goods, coinciding with rising peasant producer incomes, threatened not only inflation, but also political discontent. As early as August 1947, Lagos warned London of the political risks which might accompany the reintroduction of import control.[40] Such fears were borne out in February 1948 when serious rioting erupted in the Gold Coast. Since the war, the Colonial Office had feared the possible effects, both on colonial productivity and on local political opinion, of consumer goods shortages, warning the Cabinet of the political aspect of the problem as early as May 1945. These warnings were repeated in September 1947 when ministers were told that if the colonies were to make a major contribution to solving Britain's economic difficulties, special attention would have to be paid to their import needs, especially with regard to textiles.[41] The commission of inquiry into the Gold Coast disturbances subsequently identified as the principal cause not the 'communist' conspiracy suspected by some colonial administrators but simple economic discontent, particularly concerning the scarcity and price of basic items.[42]

The British government's response was that, although some shortages persisted, the Gold Coast's total imports in 1947 were approximately 70 per cent higher in value than in 1946, and this would alleviate the inflationary pressure, although it would be offset by any increase in the prices paid to local cocoa producers.[43]

Paradoxically, in its drive to boost exports to the dollar area, London jeopardised its colonial development strategy by restricting exports of incentive goods to the colonies, thus indirectly encouraging local unrest. This was ironic, too, given traditional demands from sections of British industry, particularly Lancashire cotton, for the colonies to be developed as British markets. In March 1948, the President of the Board of Trade explained that the volume of cotton goods exported in 1947 was approximately 32 per cent of the 1937 level, and admitted that Lancashire had been slow to recover from the effects of concentration and other wartime measures.[44] Nevertheless the Board of Trade believed that West Africa fared relatively well in terms of the supplies of cotton goods precisely because it was such an attractive market to Lancashire. Exports of cotton textiles to the Gold Coast in the first seven months of 1948 were 20 million square yards, compared to nine million square yards in the same period in 1947, and 12 million in 1938, and this trend seemed likely to continue. However, the Board concluded that a substantial increase in exports to British West Africa could be achieved only at the expense of other 'equally desirable' markets, such as British East Africa.[45] Unfortunately, it was precisely these cotton goods, along with items such as kerosene and bicycles, for which there seemed to be an 'almost inexhaustible' market, fuelled by rising producer prices and inducements paid to peasant farmers to cut out cocoa trees affected by swollen shoot disease.[46]

Having visited West Africa in 1948, William Gorell Barnes, newly appointed assistant under-secretary in the Colonial Office's Economic Division, stressed the importance of increasing consumer goods supplies to the region in view of the larger cash payments to be made to its cocoa producers. He warned of trouble, particularly in the Gold Coast, unless steps were taken to improve supplies, if necessary by relaxing restrictions on imports from hard currency areas, a move he thought justifiable because ultimately the stability of major dollar-earning territories was at stake. His colleagues, however, doubted that the Treasury would accept a liberalisation on these lines.[47] Arguably more interesting are the Board of Trade's longer-term goals in colonial markets, revealed in reaction to Gorell Barnes's views. The Board felt unable to help implement Gorell Barnes's proposal that counter-inflationary supplies should be deemed 'essential'.[48] Moreover, privately, Board of Trade officials doubted Britain's ability to meet

West Africa's needs for consumer goods so long as local tastes remained conservative. For example, British manufacturers would be unable to supply cotton textiles in sufficient quantities, and London would have to agree to the release of dollars to permit purchases of goods from the United States. However, the Board saw this as an opportunity to stimulate new demand in colonial markets for other kinds of British goods, such as watches, rayon goods, radios, footwear and cameras. As one official observed: 'There is, of course, a tremendous job of export promotion involved, but the opportunities are great, and if missed are unlikely to recur.' There was a further practical consideration, as the same official continued:

> ... I feel that the opportunity of increasing our exports to a very desirable long term market, is a great one. Moreover, it is only if we can provide West Africa with the goods she needs, that we can expect to use the dollars she earns to pay for our own imports.[49]

These supply problems revealed tensions within Whitehall. For instance, the Treasury remained adamant that strict colonial import control was essential to maintain the sterling balances as a support for the pound.[50] The Board of Trade, however, feared that continuing import controls would deprive British exporters of valuable colonial markets. It had been the Board's policy since 1945 to try to maintain at least a 'trickle' of exports to as many markets as possible, hence its concern in December 1947 when the colonies were instructed to reduce their imports from Britain.[51] In September 1947, Cripps presented the Treasury's new 'export plan', a deliberate attempt to direct Britain's exports towards 'hard' in order markets to improve its balance of payments. By December 1947, the Treasury and the Board of Trade had graded overseas markets according to desirability, and this criterion shaped the direction of exports during 1948. Nevertheless, the Board, anxious to safeguard long-term trading interests, was concerned that this policy might damage traditional markets.[52]

A similar divergence of views surrounded dollar conservation. Whereas the unifying theme in Whitehall's policy after August 1947 was the need to reduce dollar expenditure, the Board of Trade considered that it was politically impossible for Britain to continue to 'cream off' the West African producers' return.

Following the increase in the price paid to cocoa producers in the season beginning in autumn 1948, the Board foresaw that the gap between the Gold Coast's exports and imports would worsen, and believed that unless British exports to the territory were increased, absorbing the new local purchasing power, pressure against the Gold Coast's dollar ceiling on imports would become difficult to resist.[53]

In the Colonial Office, the supply problem encouraged fundamental doubts about the strategy of maximising exports to the dollar area. One danger, it was felt, was that unless more consumer goods were diverted to the colonies, the latter might seek to spend *more* dollars on these goods than could be earned by direct British exports to dollar markets.[54] The only way to give the British economy long-term security, it was argued, was to divert more exports to the colonies, so that their wealth and dollar-earning capacity could be expanded, a course which would require Whitehall to consider colonial needs far more seriously than hitherto.[55]

Development finance

Just as the post-war years witnessed a sharp reduction in Britain's capacity to meet the material needs of the colonies, so, too, the period saw the colonial empire being effectively starved of development finance. Although unprecedentedly large amounts of grant aid had been promised under the 1945 Colonial Development and Welfare Act, the supply of investment capital shrank. Colonies were discouraged from borrowing on the London money markets on the grounds that domestic reconstruction took precedence.[56] In August 1948, Creech Jones raised this problem with the Treasury, fearing that restrictions on the colonies' freedom to borrow might be seen as exploitative. In its report, the Colonial Development Working Party subsequently concluded that development loans of up to £60 million over the following three to four years were acceptable, a recommendation later endorsed in principle by the Treasury. The relatively small figure was excused on the grounds that loans were only one of the available sources of funding.[57]

Equally problematic were the colonial sterling balances held in London. The question of the colonies' right to draw on these reserves for development purposes created divisions in Whitehall, with the Treasury advocating the conversion of part of the balances into colonial development and welfare allocations and interest-free loans, and the Colonial Office, vigorously opposed to cancellation, acquiescing in the loan-conversion proposal, and favouring measures to prevent their liquidation. In effect, the consolidation of the Sterling Area after 1947, and London's commitment to maintaining the sterling balances at a high level, meant that the colonies were lending to Britain at a low interest rate.[58]

Even the vaunted colonial development and welfare provision was disappointing. The total allocation of £120 million appeared impressive, but, when distributed among a combined population of over 60 millions and, over a period of ten years, its true significance was modest. Moreover, these sums were not fully utilised: by 1951, only about £40 million had actually been spent, representing approximately one sixth of the net colonial contribution to sterling in the form of loans by colonial governments to London and the sterling balances amassed by the State marketing boards which purchased colonial produce under monopolistic conditions, generally on terms advantageous to the British consumer. Furthermore, the colonial development and welfare grants that were taken up were targeted heavily towards reinforcing existing patterns of production. Economic diversification figured in approved development schemes only to a marginal extent. For example, in the financial year 1946–47, whereas £2.2 million was spent on agricultural schemes, only £3,943 was spent on industrial development.[59]

At the height of post-crisis metropolitan enthusiasm for colonial development, officials in London had discussed the possibility of borrowing dollars to achieve faster progress, for example by enabling colonies to buy agricultural machinery in the United States. Through informal contacts with American officials, Whitehall learned of a growing interest in African opportunities among private US investors.[60] The Colonial Office publicly welcomed foreign private investment in the colonies which complemented existing development plans and observed local welfare and labour regulations.[61] Privately, however, officials were uneasy at the prospect of foreign control over individual development projects. Nor could they afford to ignore the political ramifications of foreign investment, or the sensitive question of the repatriation of profits made in the colonies.[62] Creech Jones in particular was reluctant to see American private capital gaining a dominant position in individual colonies.[63] Similarly, the Colonial Office was cool towards investment either by the United States government or by the International Bank for Reconstruction and Development. International Bank loans were considered too expensive for most colonies, but more important was official concern that 'strings' might accompany these loans, for example giving the Bank the right to monitor how its money was spent.[64] Borrowing directly from the US government was thought to carry the risk that loans towards colonial development might be deducted from Britain's allocation of Marshall Aid, and would almost certainly involve an unacceptable degree of interference.[65] The Colonial Office was not unanimous on this question. Caine, often at variance with his colleagues in the past, warned

> I have very little doubt myself that if we decide not to enlist American aid the absolute limitations of our own resources available for capital development will result in the practical progress made being very much smaller than the vast majority of people are now expecting.[66]

The CDWP eventually concluded that the whole subject of attracting private US capital was problematic. Moreover, International Bank for Reconstruction and Development loans could only be used for purchases outside Britain and the colonies, and, since those goods which Britain could not supply seemed equally scarce in the United States, there seemed to be no advantage in borrowing dollars for this purpose. The conclusion was that, in the short term at least, most external investment in the colonies would have to come from Britain.[67]

Earlier discussions in Whitehall had, however, revealed more fundamental objections to foreign penetration of the colonial economies. The CDWP's interim report had, for example, hoped that any temporary advantage gained from an earlier availability of foreign goods obtained through loans would not deprive Britain of long-term colonial markets necessary to pay for Britain's future imports of colonial produce.[68] Similarly, when the Economic Planning Board met to consider the CDWP's draft interim report, Sir Archibald Rowlands, Permanent Secretary at the Ministry of Supply, argued that it would be a 'profound mistake' to encourage foreign capital into the colonies, given Britain's need to re-create its overseas investment fund and rebuild its 'lost' Empire, adding that 'trade had in the past always followed the flag'. Moreover, since little investment seemed practicable in the foreseeable future, he believed that Britain should concentrate on 'making do' in the colonies until its own economic position permitted it to resume overseas investment. His colleagues on the Board agreed that, since the colonial territories would be required as markets for British capital goods and as a source of investment income, British capital should be invested in the colonies to the maximum extent possible under existing economic conditions, thereby endorsing the CDWP's interim recommendations.[69]

Whitehall and colonial industrialisation

Among the more immediate problems of a shortage of supplies and development finance as obstacles to colonial diversification after 1947 was an increasingly prominent, privately expressed antipathy within Whitehall to colonial industrialisation. This was in marked contrast to the apparent wartime thaw in metropolitan official attitudes, which had encouraged the Colonial Office to adopt a relatively robust position on the subject in its dealings with other departments. The hardening climate of opinion in Whitehall after 1947, fostering an entrenchment of pre-war beliefs in the complementarity of the metropolitan and colonial economies (themselves strengthened by the rise in world commodity prices, which heightened the attraction of colonial produce bought at fixed prices, often on long-term contracts)[70] offered little scope for the development of the Colonial Office's wartime views on the value of limited industrialisation, and the Office found itself outnumbered and outflanked in the Whitehall hierarchy, lacking political weight and poorly placed to withstand concerted pressure to gear development unambiguously towards primary export production, or to confront a Treasury fast regaining control over economic policy after the temporary eclipse of its influence during the war.[71]

An early example of the resurgence of opposition to colonial industrialisation surfaced during the preparation of the Overseas Resources Development Bill in 1947. The Ministry of Food, anxious to press ahead with legislation embodying the East African Groundnut Scheme, complained that a joint Bill, creating both the Overseas Food Corporation and the Colonial Development Corporation, might cause delays, since the CDC was to be empowered to promote secondary industries, a question still considered controversial.[72]

The growing potential for conflict between the policy goals of the Colonial Office and those of other sections of Whitehall is illustrated by the Office's reaction to draft guidelines on colonial investment priorities prepared by the CEPS in 1948 at the CDWP's request and endorsed by the Treasury.[73] The suggested priorities seemed 'almost incredible' to the Colonial Office, since they attached little importance to what would benefit the colonies, concentrating instead on how their resources could benefit Britain, especially in producing dollar-earning and dollar-saving raw materials and food. Moreover, the CEPS had suggested that colonial industrialisation should, in terms of development priorities, 'come third by a considerable margin', and that any such proposals should be considered in terms of their possible effects on British export interests. Similarly, the Treasury argued that colonial labour should be deployed in directly productive activities, and that the minimum possible effort should be deflected from food and raw materials production.[74] The Colonial Office judged such attitudes to be 'deplorable', lending weight to accusations that development policy was essentially exploitative.[75]

During 1948, the CEPS even attempted to justify proposals to curb colonial *welfare* expenditure, arguing that social development could proceed only at a rate warranted by the level of local economic development, otherwise the colonies might incur expenditure commitments beyond their means, and so require British financial assistance, inevitably delaying their progress towards self-government.[76] This was, implicitly, an attempt to return to the discredited pre-war doctrine of colonial financial self-sufficiency, theoretically abandoned with the passage of the 1940 Colonial Development and Welfare Act. Colonial Office protests, however, secured a revision of the Central Economic Planning Staff's (CEPS's) guidelines, giving greater prominence to colonial interests. For instance, the Office argued that if serious political consequences were to be avoided, future development would have to balance economic and social objectives, and it called for greater emphasis on diversification, although it acknowledged that industrial development should not be an end in itself, when primary production was probably, in most cases, more profitable for the colonies themselves. The Office also considered that it could not justify cuts in colonial welfare expenditure when so much progress was being made in this field in Britain.[77]

The Colonial Office's qualified success in resisting the more extreme demands of the CEPS was probably helped by the recent, startling, experience of disturbances in the Gold Coast. While the impact of the Accra riots on London's plans for the colony's constitutional development remains a matter for debate, the incident seems to have made London more sensitive to the political implications of colonial economic policy, leading to a perceptible softening of the development strategy.

Nevertheless, the fundamental conclusion reached by the CEPS was that it was necessary to devote the greatest possible part of available capital resources to highly remunerative projects, and this was recognised as implying a 'bias' in development towards deriving the maximum contribution from colonial resources to the Sterling Area's balance of payments. In deference to the Colonial Office, the revised version of the CEPS's paper stated that this basic objective should be pursued as far as was consistent with progress towards other goals, including the raising of colonial standards of consumption and the promotion of those economic activities, whether primary or secondary, in which individual territories were best equipped to engage.[78]

These adjustments were reinforced in the Colonial Development Working Party's (CDWP's) final report. Stressing the need to secure the mutual advantage of Britain and the colonies, the CDWP argued that both would benefit from the early achievement of a balance of external payments by the Sterling Area. The report endorsed the CEPS's contention that colonial development in turn depended on metropolitan recovery:

> Unless the sterling area as a whole succeeds in restoring the balance of its external payments at a high level, the United Kingdom itself will be unable to provide the overseas capital investment upon which the Colonial territories must rely if their economic development is to be accelerated.

It was, therefore, necessary for the colonies, in their *own* interests, to make the maximum contribution to the recovery of the Sterling Area.

However, the CDWP accepted the Colonial Office's view that investment should not concentrate on highly profitable projects since 'even from the purely economic point of view this would be self-frustrating'. More importantly, the political consequences would be 'most serious'. Development, it was agreed, must be balanced, and must include provision for social expenditure. However, the Working Party accepted the CEPS's argument that capital investment had to be related to each territory's capacity:

> The goal of self-government in the Colonies will be reached more slowly if the burden of maintenance charges for roads, air and seaports, hospitals and schools is so inflated that it cannot be met without external financial assistance wherever economic difficulties are encountered.

On the bias in future development, moreover, the CDWP offered little hope that much progress could be made with industrialisation:

> The main increase in Colonial production within the next few years must, in our view, come from the expansion and improvement of existing agriculture and existing mining enterprises.[79]

The CDWP also suggested general principles to guide colonial production of commodities. First, it was thought preferable to expand production of items which were problematic for *scarcity* reasons rather than for *currency* reasons alone 'since a commodity now in world short supply is likely to have a more assured market than one which is readily available if purchasers have the requisite currency.' Secondly, the commodities produced should be marketable at a competitive price on the world market in the long term. Both of these points echoed the Colonial Office's continuing worries, rooted in pre-war experiences, about commodity disposal, despite the prevailing buoyant market.[80] Nevertheless, in the same month that the CDWP produced its report, Creech Jones warned the Cabinet of the fears expressed by delegates at the recent Africa Conference about the long-term implications of current colonial production. In particular, they were concerned that

> when the immediate demand for increased production of certain dollar-earning and dollar-saving commodities becomes less acute, the local industries would be left to their fate without protection and without adequate markets.[81]

When the CEDC discussed the CDWP's final report in October 1948, Arthur Lewis argued that insufficient attention was being paid to peasant agriculture and to industrialisation. Lewis was still championing the thesis he had put forward during the CEAC's wartime discussions on industrial development, that in many colonies, effective agricultural development required a parallel and complementary drive towards industrialisation. Lewis criticised Rita Hinden for failing to recognise this in her pamphlet *Common Sense and Colonial Development*, which he had read in draft: 'The whole discussion is in terms of either or, as if it were not a historical fact that agricultural and industrial development have always gone hand in hand.[82]

Responding to Lewis, the Council agreed that the importance of agricultural investment should be emphasised. On industrial development, the view was taken that it was premature to assess the adequacy of plans in this field until the Colonial Development Corporation (CDC) was fully operational, as the Corporation was known to be considering a number of proposals. Furthermore, several colonial governments had established local corporations to stimulate secondary industry, and the Council felt that their progress should be awaited.[83]

The CDWP's report was subsequently discussed and endorsed by both the Economic Planning Board and the high-level Cabinet Economic Policy Committee, a small, select body chaired by Attlee, responsible for both home and overseas economic policy.[84] A criticism of the report made by the Board, and later echoed by both Cripps and Creech Jones, was that inadequate emphasis had been given to agricultural development. Sir Graham Cunningham, a member both of the Board and of the CEDC, and a former senior official in the Ministry of Supply, for example, observed that the development plans submitted by colonial governments suggested that the main problem was not to *raise* local living standards, but to prevent them from *falling*, for instance due to soil erosion. In his view, the colonies were basically agricultural, and secondary industries could not be developed for a number of years.[85]

The Colonial Office and industrial development

Against such comprehensive metropolitan indifference, or even hostility, to colonial industrialisation, the Colonial Office had few opportunities to defend the policy goals which it had established during the 'reconstruction planning' period. The Office became notably silent on industrialisation after 1947, provoking a rebuke from Oliver Stanley in the Commons when the annual report on the colonial empire was debated in July 1947. Even privately, there were few discussions in the Office on this controversial subject, in distinct contrast to the period 1945–46, when, for example, officials had been vigorous in defending proposals to develop textile industries in Nigeria. Similarly, although industrialisation was considered by officials in preparation for the African Governors' Conference of November 1947, at which a new course in colonial policy was to be revealed and explained to the assembled administrators, the Colonial Office produced no discussion paper on the subject specifically for the Conference, although numerous memoranda were prepared on other economic matters; instead, officials simply resurrected the circular despatch which Stanley had issued in February 1947. Significantly, the Conference noted this but did not discuss it.[86]

The consumer goods shortage in this period did not, apparently, encourage the Colonial Office to consider systematically the value of local import-substituting manufacture, as it had to some extent during the war. Soon after import controls were imposed following the convertibility fiasco, the Parliamentary Under-Secretary, Ivor Thomas, approached Cripps with a proposal that in addition to producing dollar-earning or dollar-saving commodities, the colonies might produce for themselves some of the goods they needed, thus reducing imports, especially from the dollar area.[87] This idea was not, apparently, developed, probably due to discouraging wartime experiences combined with the cool response of other government departments.

The most important consequence of the scarcity of consumer goods was the threat of inflation, with its attendant risks of political discontent. However, the Colonial Office's response was not an effort to expand supplies, either through exports from Britain or through local production, but rather it encouraged the restriction of the local money supply, for example through revised taxation policies. In West Africa, a key device was State produce marketing, seen by the Colonial Office as 'the most effective' means of countering the effects of large increases in producer incomes.[88] The Office continued to attach importance to accumulation by the State marketing boards of ever greater funds which could be drawn upon to stabilise producer incomes. Moreover, the wartime practice of paying producers prices lower than those current on the world market continued, even after locally organised marketing boards assumed control after 1947.[89]

During 1948, the Colonial Office showed signs of a renewed interest in industrialisation due, chiefly, to a recognition of local enthusiasm for development in this direction. The events in the Gold Coast in spring 1948 appear to have shaken officials out of their lethargy, and discussions on industrial development became more frequent thereafter. When Thomas's successor, Rees-Williams, visited West Africa in summer 1948, he discovered a widespread local demand for industrialisation. He found the local population 'desperately' keen on economic development, and specifically *industrial* development. He concluded that West Africans were even more interested in economic questions than in political matters. However, he considered much of this thinking to be muddled. For example, he found that 'Every territory wants to be self-sufficient in everything, which is absurd.' But while he believed the region would continue to have an agriculturally based economy, he saw room for diversification through processing, light engineering and the production of consumer goods. Rees-Williams noted the start made by local development corporations, but drew attention to the continuing scarcity of African entrepreneurs and managers:

> The African looks for safe jobs where he can wear a white collar. His mendicant outlook blames government for all his shortcomings and believes that it has all the means to provide him with an up-to-date economy with no trouble or work on his part.

One of the major conclusions reached by Rees-Williams in his report on his trip was that a far greater effort was needed to promote industrial development, for example through the provision of finance and training.[90] This interpretation was generally approved at a meeting called by Creech Jones in the Colonial Office early in October 1948. However, it was not thought that any specific action on industrialisation was required from the Office's Economic Division at this stage.[91]

In its sporadic discussions on industrial development after 1947, the Colonial Office felt obliged to concentrate on what seemed feasible, and, given the immense constraints on development, to establish clear priorities so that scarce resources were used as effectively as possible. In this context, effectiveness was measured according to the benefit to the metropole as much as to the colonies themselves. As Rees-Williams put it:

> It is obviously essential that there should be the maximum amount of development in the shortest possible time, otherwise the Government's plan of economic development and the integration of the Colonies with Western Europe and the Commonwealth will fail. If it fails, I cannot personally see how we can get out of our difficulties, and if we go down, the Colonies will go down with us.[92]

To prevent the dissipation of materials and resources, Rees-Williams called on the Colonial Office to prepare a list of priority projects. This list, produced by the Economic Intelligence and Planning Department, itself formed in response to the crisis of 1947, was completed by September 1948, and was reproduced, unaltered, in November and December. The activities judged to have priority mainly involved the production of food and raw materials such as cotton, tobacco, hard fibres and tin, together with experiments in new agricultural techniques, hydro-electricity schemes, communications and education. A separate list, dealing specifically with West Africa, said little about industrial potential, apart from a reference to installing palm-oil mills and the possibility of establishing a plywood factory, also in Nigeria.[93]

The colonial governments and industrialisation

Despite the apparent hesitancy, even ambivalence, in its own attitudes in the face of multiple constraints, the Colonial Office's fundamental faith in industrial development explains its dismay that this area was conspicuously neglected in a number of the development schemes submitted by colonial governments. In its desire to promote modernisation, the Office had to overcome the conservatism of local officials, who were thought to regard London's missives as products of the latest change in fashion in Whitehall.[94] A measure of the colonial governments' grasp of the new urgency informing development policy was the disappointing response to Creech Jones's despatch of February 1947 which called for substantial increases in productivity. By July, only one government (Zanzibar's) had replied.[95] Within the Office, fears persisted that territorial governments gave inadequate priority to *economic*, as opposed to *social*, development in their planning. This theme arose when the Committee on the Conference of

African Governors, created at the beginning of 1947 to prepare the agenda for the African Governors' Conference of November 1947, discussed means of securing more efficient economic organisation in the colonial territories. Caine, chairing the Committee, noted that the development programmes submitted so far by African governments were generally deficient on the economic side of development, a problem he had been warning of since 1943.[96] The Gold Coast development plan, submitted in December 1946, was a case in point. The plan was criticised for being 'unduly conservative' in its financial provision, in view of the territory's healthy excess of revenue over expenditure.[97] As Cohen observed:

> In the Gold Coast we have greater opportunities for development than perhaps anywhere else in Africa. We have good relations between the Government and the people, plenty of money and great economic resources. But little hard thinking seems to have been devoted to the problem of developing the natural resources of the Territory.[98]

Moreover, the Office's development adviser, Sir Frank Stockdale, noted the plan's neglect of industrial development, which he thought 'certainly a matter which requires careful consideration'.[99] Officials believed that the industrial potential of the Gold Coast should be reviewed, together with the government's policy on encouraging industry.[100]

Governor Burns was subsequently asked to review the plan by the Colonial Office, especially its economic components.[101] This proved to be a slow process, however, and as late as November 1948, the Gold Coast government was reported to be beginning to prepare a new ten-year development plan.[102] It is notable in this context that one of the economic causes of the Accra riots identified by the Watson Commission of Enquiry was a local sentiment that the Gold Coast government had not formulated any plans for the future of industry and agriculture, and that it was uninterested in any development apart from production for export.[103]

Fresh evidence that the government was unenthusiastic about industrial development emerged during Rees-Williams' trip to West Africa in summer 1948. During his talks with Gold Coast officials, the question of consumer goods shortages inevitably arose, an issue of special importance in view of the forthcoming increase in cocoa prices and the spur to inflation likely to result. Rees-Williams suggested that the only answer was an increased flow of consumer goods, and promised that every effort would be made to export them to the Gold Coast. However, he also asked local officials whether factories could not be established in the territory to manufacture consumer goods, adding that the CDC would be very interested in this sort of development.[104] The response of local officials was significantly lukewarm. The secretary for Commerce and Industries explained that the Gold Coast had few raw materials other than agricultural produce, and that for industries based on anything else, the raw materials would have to be imported. When told by the secretary for Rural Development that the question of industrialisation had not yet been thoroughly examined, Rees-Williams replied that it was of the first importance, and must be considered carefully. The promotion of industry had already been recommended by the Watson Commission.[105]

Officials in Accra were no more encouraging about the Industrial Development Corporation which the Gold Coast had recently created. The Corporation was expected to concentrate on minor projects, such as the manufacture of starch from tapioca and cassava. Rees-Williams asked whether the Corporation planned to establish and manage any industries itself, but was told that the intention was to foster private enterprise rather than to engage directly in production. As a result of this disappointing exchange it was decided that the possibility of establishing factories for consumer goods should be considered.[106]

The apparent apathy of local officials was particularly worrying for the Colonial Office because of the importance increasingly attached to the colonial State as the engine of development. It also appeared paradoxical, given that contemporary studies suggested that in the colonies as a whole, the State controlled about half the current investment.[107] In Rees-Williams's opinion, the West African territories were confronting the problems of the modern world with little of the machinery or outlook of the modern State:

> Some of the senior officials seem to regard modern planning as just the most recent fad. First it was indirect rule, then social welfare, later mass education and now economic development.[108]

The role of private enterprise

If the West African governments showed little ability to initiate development, what prospects were there for private enterprise to take the lead? The British government's attitudes towards the role of private enterprise in development were summarised by Rees-Williams in July 1948:

> I personally do not believe that private enterprise was ever able to do the job of developing the Colonial Empire, and we do not believe that private enterprise would be able to do the job. That is the whole bedrock of our policy.[109]

Since early 1947, awareness had grown in London that without substantial private enterprise in the colonies, governments would increasingly have to take the place of the private investor, examining available resources, deciding what form development should take, and providing the capital and organisation required.[110] It was, unsurprisingly, at the same time that the Colonial Office's discussions on development corporations were resumed.

Yet the expatriate firms operating in West Africa were not indifferent to development in this period. As in the latter years of the war, they continued to show an interest in diversification into industrial projects. For example, among the schemes submitted to the CDC by Nigeria in the first half of 1948 were two such proposals. The first was a scheme to establish a machine-spinning industry to process locally produced and ginned cotton. This, it was hoped, would encourage the peasant hand-weaving industry by providing increased supplies of better quality yarn. While the Nigerian government did not intend to participate in the scheme, the United Africa Company and other firms were said to be interested. The second scheme was a proposal to establish a factory to make produce bags out of locally grown fibres. This would save expenditure on imported jute sacks and would ensure a supply of bags for Nigeria's own export crops. Again, the government did not intend to participate beyond ensuring an adequate supply of suitable fibres, but the UAC was said to be considering taking part in the scheme.[111]

Although there was continuing evidence, therefore, that expatriate enterprise was interested in local industrial development, the critical impediment remained that local attitudes to firms like the UAC were hostile. Recognition of this problem in London was not confined to the Colonial Office. In its report on colonial development, the Select Committee on Estimates warned that private enterprise could not participate fully in development as long as the belief existed among the colonial peoples that outside firms exploited them unfairly.[112] The Committee took the problem of African hostility to the firms seriously. One of its members, Sir Ralph Glyn, subsequently wrote on the subject to Sir Thomas Lloyd who, in February 1947, had become permanent under-secretary at the Colonial Office. He noted the 'immense' contribution which the UAC had made to Nigerian development, but added that the very fact that the Company was so powerful and virtually monopolistic constituted a deterrent to the emergence of smaller private enterprise:

> I think all of us on the Committee felt that this was a most unfortunate position, and that anything that could be done to attract capital investment in the country by concerns other than the United Africa Company would be greatly to the benefit of the Africans.[113]

The Watson Commission found that, in the Gold Coast the 'monopolistic' position of the importing firms, and the consequent restriction of African enterprise was one of the local grievances about consumer goods.[114] Similarly, Rees-Williams commented on local attitudes towards the European firms following his visit to West Africa, regarding the question as being of the 'highest' political importance: 'Everywhere I met hostility towards the big import houses, especially U.A.C., among Europeans as much as among Africans.' In his view, the Labour government would be judged on its treatment of the firms more than anything else.[115]

Officials in London found that their freedom of action was restricted by the hostility which Rees-Williams described. For example, in July 1948, at an interdepartmental meeting held to discuss the supply of consumer goods to West Africa, the suggestion was made that the problem should be discussed with the expatriate firms trading in the region. These talks were not arranged, however, because Governor Creasy of the Gold Coast feared that they might reinforce local suspicions of collusion between colonial officials and the firms.[116]

Late in 1948, the Labour Party, through its Sub-Committee on

Industries for Nationalisation, was giving active consideration to the case for taking the UAC into public ownership. This case did not rest on allegations that the Company made excessive profits. Since the UAC published no accounts, its profit levels were unknown, but the Sub-Committee accepted, as the Nowell Commission had in 1937, that they were not unduly high. Moreover, nationalisation was not regarded as an appropriate solution to the question of profits, as other controls existed or could be applied if necessary.

More important, in the Sub-Committee's view, were the restrictive effects on development arising from the Company's activities. The UAC, whose primary interest was trade, was alleged to have deliberately stifled industrial development in West Africa. Although the Company might point to the industrial enterprises which it had established and operated in the area, and claim an interest in any similar profitable schemes, this was not felt to evade the basic problem that the Company's need to make a profit meant that it would have to set the profits accruing from local manufacturing against the loss of profits from trade.

Furthermore, the Company was suspected of opposing new developments outside its control, and of hostility to African enterprise.

> What West Africa needs is a great trading organisation that will help to develop local enterprise by offering contracts, advice, and assistance; instead, it gets a great organisation which, by its very nature, must have, and has had, just the opposite effect.

This led the Sub-Committee to what it considered to be the strongest element in the case for nationalisation: the fact that the Company's organisation could then be used to promote economic development, in which industrialisation would be prominent. The UAC structure was seen as the ideal foundation for a consumer co-operative system in West Africa, a system which would have little chance of establishing itself in competition with the Company. Reinforcing these arguments was the *political* case for nationalisation:

> The U.A.C. is thoroughly detested in West Africa, not so much because of its profits (though exaggerated notions are held on this subject) but rather because, in the economic

> sphere, it is widely believed to have sabotaged the development of native enterprise and of secondary industries, and in the political sphere, it has obviously wielded great power in the past, and had excessive influence upon Governors and upon Secretaries of State.

While it was no longer thought that the political charge was applicable, because the hostility of local administrators to the UAC was so marked, Britain could no longer afford, politically, to maintain an institution so resented by local African leaders, to whom

> the U.A.C. is the instrument and the symbol of British economic imperialism, and they will never have full confidence in the British government as long as they continue to see the company's tentacles everywhere that they turn.[117]

Late 1948, however, was an unpropitious time for discussions on nationalising the Company, given the Labour government's shift towards 'consolidation' instead of the further extensions of public ownership. Nevertheless, in light of Rees-Williams's report, and possibly in response to pressure from Labour's colonial specialists, Creech Jones called for a detailed study of the organisation of West African trade, with particular reference to the position of the big trading companies.[118]

The Colonial Development Corporation

Continuing doubts about the adequacy of local development machinery, combined with the problems arising from the activities of private enterprise, account for the importance attached by the Colonial Office to the creation of the Colonial Development Corporation, and for official disappointment with the latter's initial role. The Corporation, intended to be commercial and self-supporting, enjoyed a high degree of operational independence, and wide discretion in judging the commercial soundness of schemes proposed to it.[119] A rift soon developed between the Colonial Office and the Corporation's chairman, Lord Trefgarne, who was determined to preserve his freedom of action, and who took as scriptural the injunction to bind the CDC's activities to strictly commercial principles. Advocates of this commercial role, and of the CDC's bias towards projects of direct benefit to Britain, justified their position by claiming that the immediate developmental needs of the colonies had already been met by successive Colonial Development and Welfare Acts. The Colonial Office was even obliged to resist, successfully, Treasury attempts to use colonial development and welfare funds to finance the new Corporation.[120]

Ironically, the CDC, designed as a vehicle for development that would be acceptable to colonial opinion, itself became a target for colonial criticism, especially in West Africa – to the Colonial Office's dismay. The creation of the Corporation did nothing to reduce intense local suspicion of anything that could be interpreted as exploitation by outside capital, whether its source was private or public investment. The CDC soon came to be regarded as a vehicle for exploitation, not development. A key problem was the Corporation's commercial character, which precluded involvement in urgently required, though not immediately profitable, development projects. The influential Pan-Africanist, George Padmore, described the CDC as

> a system of State Capitalism, operated on behalf of the Labour Government by salaried executives working for a semi-official Corporation rather than for shareholders. This constitutes a new form of Economic Imperialism.[121]

It had been recognised at an early stage in preparing the Overseas Resources Development Bill that the Corporation might be exposed to charges of exploitation. Consequently, particular stress was placed on the *mutual* benefits to be derived from development. Nevertheless, it was acknowledged that the entire question would have to be handled carefully when plans for the CDC were made public.[122] Bevin, especially, was concerned at the international political implications that might arise if Britain's colonial policy appeared to be exploitative. As he told Attlee:

> We must be careful that our plans for the development of our Colonial Dependencies cannot in any way be represented as springing solely from our own selfish interests. It is above all important that in their presentation there is no possible suggestion of exploitation of the colonial populations. In either case we may find ourselves exposed to bitter criticism in the United Nations and be obliged to defend ourselves against quite baseless charges. We know from experience that

> the possibilities of misrepresentation in this field are almost endless.[123]

The Colonial Office's sensitivity to the scope for allegations of exploitation is illustrated by its attitude towards the proposed activities of the CDC's sister organisation, the Overseas Food Corporation (OFC), responsible to the Ministry of Food. The Office was afraid of colonial reactions to a large new body whose primary function was to obtain food for the British consumer. Ivor Thomas warned Attlee:

> There is in many parts of the Colonial Empire, particularly in West Africa, a deep-rooted suspicion of all large-scale enterprises from overseas, a suspicion which may not have been altogether unjustified in the past. A Labour Government should not run any danger of appearing to introduce a new and more potent form of capitalist exploitation.[124]

In this instance, the Colonial Office successfully established the principle that the OFC should not operate in the colonies except at the express invitation of the Colonial Secretary.[125]

In mid-1948, the whole question of the CDC's role was reviewed by Andrew Cohen, a key figure in the evolution of the Colonial Office's thinking on development corporations who, since April 1947, had been assistant under-secretary in charge of the Africa Division. In Cohen's view, the CDC's participation in West African projects highlighted the suspicion felt by local political élites towards external capital. The élites did not always distinguish between State enterprise, which re-invested profits locally, and private enterprise, whose aim was primarily to extract a profit. The result was a tendency to impose conditions on the CDC's prospective operations which discouraged it from entering West Africa. The Corporation's lack of enthusiasm for the region was reinforced by uncertainty over future political developments, especially in the Gold Coast. The CDC, in Cohen's view, had to be reassured. Economically, both Nigeria and the Gold Coast were comparatively poor in terms of the natural resources necessary for heavy industry to develop, but both had great agricultural and other possibilities. Unless all available resources were applied to these territories, which together constituted half the population of the colonial empire, there would be a major gap in the policy of developing colonial economic resources fully. Furthermore,

Cohen noted, the tendency in West Africa was going to be towards rapid political advance, 'more rapid, indeed, than the capabilities of the people would justify on merits', and it would be impossible to decelerate the rate of advance to a pace preferable to local authorities if they enjoyed 'complete discretion'. Therefore, it was essential for economic development to keep in step with political development. The problem had hitherto been that it had not kept pace. In Cohen's opinion, this made it all the more necessary to devise suitable mechanisms for public or semi-public investment.

> I have been pressing for a Development Corporation for West Africa ever since 1943 and now that we have it (and in the light of developments since 1943 both political and economic) I can think of nothing more important to West Africa, or indeed to Africa as a whole, than the devising of proper machinery to enable the Corporation to operate in West Africa.

Moreover, Cohen did not think that political uncertainties or 'theoretical political objections' should prevent the CDC from entering West Africa, and he indulged in a rare piece of speculation on the *economic* implications of decolonisation:

> Political development towards self-government will go forward whatever happens and it seems to me that the future of the British relationship with West Africa demands that as the West African Territories get greater political freedom they should be more closely linked to the United Kingdom economically both for their own advantage and ours.

West Africa, Cohen argued, was 'desperately' short of economic services, technical skill and the apparatus of economic development, and could not progress without outside investment, a point which he believed Africans would come to recognise once they acquired an increasingly important role in the direction of economic policy: 'Provided, therefore, that we play our cards properly, I believe that there is a very real future for United Kingdom investment in West Africa.' However, the problems would be greater if the medium chosen for investment by Britain was private, monopolistic capital. This, thought Cohen, was a further argument for persuading the CDC to enter the region. There remained the problem of devising appropriate machinery. Reviving the original intention when the CDC was being planned,

Cohen suggested the creation of a subsidiary, local corporation, providing for local participation and local directors.[126] The growing importance of associating 'representative local opinion' with the CDC's work was underlined in the fifth report of the Select Committee on Estimates, published soon after Cohen made his analysis.[127]

By summer 1948, relations between the Colonial Office and the CDC were already strained. Officials found the attitude of the CDC's Chairman, Lord Trefgarne, particularly disturbing. Trefgarne had promised to inform the Office of the CDC's intentions, but had made the unacceptable condition that this information should not be passed on to colonial governments, and in practice, adequate information had not been forthcoming. The Colonial Office warned Trefgarne that without details of the schemes being proposed, the CDC's requests for funds could not be considered. As Caine observed of Trefgarne:

> In effect, he is asking that the Corporation be treated as an authority with greater independence of Government control and supervision than any private concern in the country.[128]

When Colonial Office and CDC representatives met in July 1948, Trefgarne announced that the CDC had decided to set up five regional corporations, one to be based in West Africa. This, he explained, was the first step in creating the Corporation's overseas organisation and would not necessarily be permanent. Trefgarne suggested that the West African corporation might be based in Lagos. Caine pointed out the disadvantage of trying to operate new enterprises in the Gold Coast from a base in Nigeria, but Trefgarne replied that conditions in the Gold Coast 'did not seem at all favourable', and that he doubted whether the Corporation would have any substantial undertakings there. It was agreed that care would be needed when the announcement of the new body was made, and that it would be helpful if its form could be agreed with the Governor of the Gold Coast, Sir Gerald Creasy.[129]

Trefgarne had already attracted criticism during a speech at Liverpool in June. Referring to political problems in the colonies, he had warned that the CDC would not invest in territories where there was 'a political obsession against the good faith of the United Kingdom', and suggested that allegations of exploitation stemmed from communist agitation. The Fabian Colonial Bureau reacted strongly to Trefgarne's comments, deploring the implication that political 'strings' might be attached to British investment, and arguing that claims that colonial discontent was the work of communists was 'calculated to drive the colonial peoples into the arms of Communism, and to magnify whatever sense of grievance they already have'.[130] The Colonial Office was particularly concerned when the press announcement of the creation of the CDC (West Africa) Ltd omitted any reference to participation in the Gold Coast.[131] Cohen was led to re-emphasise his belief that

> any impression that we are seeking to squeeze the Gold Coast out of C.D.C. assistance because of alleged anti-British tendencies there can only have a most deplorable effect on the relations between the Gold Coast and this country and that the effect will not, of course, be purely political but will also extend into all economic activities.

Cohen considered a change of policy by the CDC to be essential, together with moves to make good the damage already done.[132] Officials were subsequently mollified by Trefgarne's proposal to reply, if asked, that in accordance with the wishes of the Governor of the Gold Coast, a separate organisation would be established to deal with any large undertaking in the Gold Coast.[133] The importance of stressing to the CDC that Africans required managerial and technical training towards industrial development even more than finance was one of the major recommendations made by Rees-Williams on the basis of what he had seen in West Africa in summer 1948. In his view, it was necessary to convince the CDC that it was the Africans' 'great hope', and that there was no need for the Corporation to fear operating in the Gold Coast.[134]

Proposals for industrial development

During 1948, developments at the local level obliged the Colonial Office to turn its attention from the general principles of industrial policy to specifics. An appropriate example was the case of textile development in West Africa. As during the war, the possibilities of developing textile industries in the region received continuing attention. When the Colonial Office reviewed development opportunities early in 1948, Stockdale singled out this sector's potential, based on locally grown cotton.[135] It was subsequently acknowledged that a proposal to establish a cotton textiles factory in Nigeria 'some years ago' (presumably a reference to the Haighton's scheme discussed earlier) had collapsed because the government refused to guarantee that the factory's products would not be subject to an excise duty equivalent to the import duty levied on cotton piece-goods.[136]

In November 1948, Arthur Lewis put forward a proposal which, he said, gave the British government an opportunity to implement its often-stated desire to assist colonial industrialisation and to demonstrate that it did not intend to maintain the colonies as sources of cheap raw materials. Prompted by the serious colonial shortage of textiles, and by reports that peasants were in consequence refusing to grow more, Lewis suggested that some of the textile machinery made idle by the current labour shortage in Lancashire could be obtained cheaply and used to develop colonial textile industries. His argument was that much of this machinery would never again be used in Lancashire, partly because of the labour shortage and partly because British cotton manufacturers were anxious to re-equip with modern plant. Anticipating the likely reaction that this would endanger British interests, Lewis claimed that Lancashire was resigned to losing much of the colonial market for cotton goods once Indian, Chinese and Japanese production regained momentum. Furthermore, he argued, the future of Lancashire lay with producing quality goods, and if colonial cotton industries developed, mass-producing countries would feel the impact most rather than Britain.[137]

Lewis believed that local cotton industries would not only stimulate agricultural production but would also provide work in colonies where unemployment was a problem – for example in the West Indies – and would improve these economies by diversifying them and creating new opportunities for talent. Moreover, he judged this a rare instance where surplus British plant existed and could be delivered immediately, and argued that colonial demand for textiles was such that local manufacturing would be bound to pay its way, at least in the short term. Although some expertise would have to be supplied, Lewis observed that this would be true of *all* development. He suggested that the CDC might take the initiative in starting industries, possibly in partnership with an experienced private entrepreneur, withdrawing after an initial period. He advocated establishing fully integrated manufacturing, incorporating weaving, knitting and finishing. Weaving and knitting were relatively simple processes, and the CDC could quickly pass on its interests in them once local enterprise was proficient. Spinning, however, was a large-scale operation, responsibility for which, Lewis thought, would have to remain with the Corporation for a longer period.[138]

The Colonial Office's response was to circulate among the CEDC a memorandum describing two colonial textile projects under consideration, both in Nigeria. The first was the scheme, referred to previously, submitted to the CDC by Lagos to establish a mechanised spinning industry to process locally produced and ginned cotton. A site for a spinning mill had been chosen at Onitsha, on the Niger. The mill would consist of 8,600 spindles, increasing by 1949 to 17,500 spindles, and would require one million pounds of cotton per annum initially, rising to two million pounds. The Nigerian government estimated that the necessary plant and equipment would cost £215,000. The second scheme was a plan being contemplated by the Commonwealth Investment Trust Ltd to build a spinning mill with a capacity of 15,000 to 20,000 spindles. The intention was to form a subsidiary company with capital of £250,000, in which the Nigerian government had agreed in principle to participate up to a limit of £150,000. This company would include representatives of the government and local 'unofficials'. The government had also suggested that the CDC might invest in the Trust's subsidiary company, leaving the company in control, and was also keen to enable Nigerian investors to subscribe to the subsidiary's capital. Negotiations, explained the Colonial Office, were being conducted by the CDC and the Commonwealth Trust. However, the Trust's managing director had revised the costs of the scheme dramatically, estimating that the spinning machinery alone for a factory of 20,000 spindles would cost about £300,000, and that the equipment for a 600 loom factory would cost around £100,000. When additional costs, such as power and housing, were taken into account, it was judged that a scheme on the scale contemplated would cost between £750,000 and £1,000,000. In reply to Lewis's proposal to use redundant plant from Lancashire, the Colonial Office claimed that this had been considered but that, although a great deal of surplus machinery existed, not all of it was suitable for use in the colonies. However, it was conceded that in some cases the advantage in price and early supply might outweigh the disadvantage of not obtaining modern equipment.

Furthermore, because colonial industries would have to

compete in the world market, it was argued that they should be equipped with the most modern machinery available. It was therefore felt that colonial industries would be disadvantaged if equipped with machinery which, although adequate at present, was soon liable to become obsolete and would have to be replaced with new plant. The Colonial Office's conclusion perpetuated the arguments which had dominated the debate on industrialisation since the late 1930s:

> To establish industries in the Colonies which are not likely for one reason or another to be able to compete successfully, as soon as they have been properly established, is liable to do more harm than good in the long run to the cause of developing secondary industries in the Colonies.[139]

When it discussed the Colonial Office's paper in November 1948, however, the CEDC stressed the importance of seizing opportunities for textile development and suggested that the Cotton Board's views should be sought.[140] The Board's subsequent discussions demonstrated that Lancashire's traditional hostility to overseas textile industrialisation had not abated. Sir Raymond Streat considered that in the existing 'unsettled' state of the world, it would be undesirable to promote such development. The Board sought to persuade the Colonial Office of the need for prior consultation before any steps were taken to stimulate the development of colonial textile industries.

The Board's dismissal of Lewis's belief that Lancashire saw its future in exporting high quality textiles was particularly interesting: the colonies, it seems, were still regarded as valuable outlets for cheaper lines. The Board emphasised that where such development was proposed in order to raise colonial living standards, it should proceed along lines least damaging to Britain's export trade.[141] These attitudes suggested little progression in Lancashire's thinking since the war: indeed, they were evidence of a considerable *regression* since the mid-war years when Streat had appeared to be seeking a constructive means for Lancashire to adjust to changing world conditions.

More disturbing, perhaps, was the Colonial Office's brief response to the Board, disclaiming any intention of pursuing the general question of cotton textile development at that stage.[142] Two factors may be relevant here. First, given the continuing physical constraints on industrial development, together with recent confirmation that the subject was still controversial, it was easier for the Office to deal with proposals to establish manufacturing industry as they arose, rather than to risk generating consolidated opposition from Whitehall and from British exporters by airing the question in terms of general policy. Secondly, the supply of textiles to West Africa improved significantly during 1948. Thus, total cotton piece goods imports into Nigeria rose from 104,852,000 square yards in 1947 to 124,969,000 square yards in 1948, chiefly due to a massive recovery in supplies from Germany and Japan. Similarly, in the Gold Coast, cotton piece goods imports rose from 42,651,000 square yards in 1947 to 62,324,000 square yards in 1948.[143] It was precisely the resurgence of German and Japanese competition in textile exports which reinforced the Cotton Board's resistance to the encouragement of local colonial industries which might erode Britain's market share still further. With the relative easing of the supply problem during 1948, one pressing incentive for the Colonial Office to explore the scope for local manufacturing in West Africa had been removed.

By late 1948, opinions outside the Colonial Office on what was achievable in development were noticeably more sober than they had been 18 months earlier. This was reflected in the Colonial Development Working Party's broad conclusions, which seemed to vindicate the Colonial Office by acknowledging the need to promote a wider view of development. One lesson learned from the CDWP's efforts was that any attempt to introduce major schemes for rapid economic development might seriously disrupt the colonial economies.[144] This view, as already noted, was accepted by the high-ranking Cabinet Economic Policy Committee, which endorsed the Working Party's three main conclusions: first, that development plans needed to maintain a proper balance between economic development and social welfare; secondly, that the rate of development would be severely limited by shortages of plant and materials in Britain and by problems of adjustment created by large-scale economic development in 'primitive' communities; and finally, that while resources were scarce, they were best applied to restoring and improving existing capital and equipment rather than initiating *new* development schemes.[145] A new sense of realism had supplanted the reckless optimism shown in some quarters in mid-1947. The Colonial Office had patiently explained why the approach to development favoured by Montgomery, the Select Committee on Estimates, and others was impracticable.

In addition to the greater realism evident in London late in 1948, there was growing government recognition of the scope for allegations that its actions in the colonies were exploitative. This encouraged a fresh official emphasis on the advantages which both Britain and the colonies could derive from development. The acknowledged bias in development towards schemes for quick, dollar-earning production acquired a new justification at the hands of the Treasury and the CEPS: a 'temporary' bias in development was claimed to be necessary to improve Britain's balance of payments, restoring the metropolitan economy to a condition in which it would be able to devote more resources to colonial development.[146]

Several Cabinet ministers understood the scope for charges of exploitation. Bevin was especially sensitive on this point, and was keen to avoid criticism of British colonial policy in the United Nations, notably from the Soviet Union. The CDC, for instance, appeared to be a prime candidate for criticism. The Bill to create the Corporation was deliberately combined with legislation to form the Overseas Food Corporation because it was thought that the latter, designed to serve British interests, might attract adverse comment in the colonies and in the United Nations.[147] This sensitivity surfaced again early in 1948, when ministers expressed general support for the rapid development of African resources in order to reinforce Britain's political and economic position. This prompted the Cabinet Secretary, Sir Norman Brook, to remind Attlee of the potential difficulties of defending such a policy, which could easily be interpreted as 'imperialism', adding that it was important for a Labour government to be able to justify its actions and not alienate its supporters or 'enlightened' public opinion.[148]

NOTES

1. Cairncross (1985), pp.21–2; Gupta (1983), pp.105–6.
2. Cairncross (1985), pp.21–2; R. Hyam, 'Africa and the Labour Government, 1945–51', *JICH*, 16, 3, (May 1988), pp.148–9; R. Hyam (ed.), *British Documents on the End of Empire, Series A, Volume 2, The Labour Government and the End of Empire 1945–1951* (London: HMSO, 1992), pp.xlii–xlix; A.E. Hinds, 'Sterling and Imperial Policy, 1945–1951', *JICH* 15, 2, (Jan. 1987), pp.151, 155.
3. CO 537/3047, letter to Attlee, 13 Sept. 1947; letter to Attlee, 16 Sept. 1947; Gupta

(1983), pp.101, 106; Hinds (1987), p.153; Hyam (1988), p.149.
4. CAB 130/19, GEN.179/5th meeting, 28 July 1947; GEN.179/14th meeting, 20 Aug. 1947; CO 537/3047, letter to Attlee, 16 Sept. 1947; Gupta (1983), p.106.
5. CAB 124/1079, 'Planning for Expansion', 31 May 1947 (final version CP(47)169).
6. CO 852/870/2, circular telegram, 6 Aug. 1947.
7. Ibid., T 236/693, circular telegram, 20 Aug. 1947.
8. CAB 130/19, GEN.179/15th meeting, 21 Aug. 1947.
9. Ibid., GEN.179/14th meeting, 20 Aug. 1947.
10. CAB 128/10, CM(47)74, minute 2, 25 Aug. 1947.
11. PREM 8/457, Creech Jones to Attlee, 26 Mar. 1947; Attlee to Creech Jones, 26 Mar. 1947; CO 537/2002, Creech Jones to Dalton, 28 Apr. 1948.
12. CO 537/2002, letter to Attlee, 26 Mar. 1947.
13. CAB 128, CM 53(47)5, 10 June 1947; Gupta (1983), pp.106–7; PREM 8/457, Portal to Attlee, 10 Apr. 1947; CAB 129 CP(47)175, 'The Development of Colonial Resources'.
14. Bodleian Library MS Attlee dep.48 (Attlee Papers) fols. 116–19, Portal to Attlee, 17 Dec. 1946.
15. CO 852/867/1, CEDC(47)7, note by Chairman on formation of a Colonial Development Corporation, (n.d.).
16. Ibid.; CO 537/2002, Creech Jones to Attlee, 26 Mar. 1947.
17. CO 852/875/1, 'The Colonial Development Corporation. Method of Operation', 5 Dec. 1947.
18. Morgan (1980) II, p.18; the Central Economic Planning Staff had been established in March 1947, as an inter-departmental, but non-executive 'think-tank', and was also chaired by Sir Edwin Plowden; see Aldcroft (1986), p.242; Cairncross (1985), p.53.
19. T 220/17, 'Tour in Africa in November–December 1947' by Field Marshal the Viscount Montgomery of Alamein, 19 Dec. 1947.
20. Ibid., Watson (CO) to Fogarty (Treasury), 6 Jan. 1948; CAB 130/31, GEN.210 1st meeting, 9 Jan. 1948.
21. CAB 130/31, GEN.210 1st meeting, 9 Jan. 1948.
22. Ibid.; CO 537/3030, Creech Jones to Attlee, 5 Feb. 1948; Hinds (1987), p.159.
23. CO 537/3030, letter to Creech Jones, 29 Jan. 1948; Creech Jones to Attlee, 31 Jan. 1948.
24. H.C.181, *Fifth Report from the Select Committee on Estimates. Session 1947–48. Colonial Development*, 30 June 1948.
25. CAB 134/216, EPC(48)35th meeting, 9 Nov. 1948.
26. *PD(C)*, 454, 611, 22 July 1948.
27. CO 852/1000/3, address by Cripps, 12 Nov. 1947.
28. CO 847/36/2, despatch to African Governors, 22 Feb. 1947.
29. See, e.g., CO 537/3226, report by Rees-Williams, 'West African Tour – 1948', 27 Sept. 1948.
30. Westcott (1983), p.8.
31. CO 852/889/3, memo. by Gorell Barnes, 'Economic Planning in the Colonies', 3 Aug. 1948.
32. T 236/693, circular telegram, 6 Aug. 1947.
33. T 236/688, circular telegram, 'Import licensing policy', 5 Sept. 1947.
34. CO 852/871/1, minute by Caine, 10 Nov. 1947; minute by Rees-Williams, 11 Nov. 1947; Creech Jones to Cripps, 22 Nov. 1947; minute by Caine, 24 Nov. 1947; CO 852/831/1, minute by T.W. Davies, 11 Nov. 1947.
35. CO 852/831/1, minute by T.W. Davies, 11 Nov. 1947.
36. T 229/220, Strath (CEPS) to Plowden, 22 Jan. 1948; CO 852/875/1, telegram from Beresford-Stooke (Nigeria) to Caine, 24 Jan. 1948; CO 852/871/1, circular telegram, 27 Jan. 1948.
37. CO 537/3030, Creech Jones to Attlee, 31 Jan. 1948; Attlee to Creech Jones, 15 Feb.

1948; Attlee to Rees-Williams, 27 Feb. 1948.

38. CO 852/868/3, CEDC(48)2, CDWP draft Interim Report, 12 Apr. 1948.
39. CO 852/889/3, telegram from Poynton to Rees-Williams, 18 Aug. 1948; ibid., Poynton to Rees-Williams, 20 Aug. 1948.
40. T 236/688, telegram to Creech Jones, 26 Aug. 1947.
41. CAB 71/20, 'Prospective general supply difficulties in the Colonial Empire', 10 May 1945; CO 537/1414, minute by T.W. Davies, 11 Dec. 1946; CO 537/2007, CM(47) 75th conclusions, 9 Sept. 1947.
42. Col.no.231, *Report of the Commission of Enquiry into Disturbances in the Gold Coast, 1948*, 8 June 1948; see also Hargreaves (1988), pp.114–15.
43. Col.no.232, *Statement by His Majesty's Government on the Report of the Commission of Enquiry into Disturbances in the Gold Coast, 1948*, 8 June 1948.
44. *PD(C)*, 448, 1398, 11 Mar. 1948.
45. BT 11/4089, minute by Reardon, 27 Aug. 1948.
46. CO 537/3226, report by Rees-Williams, 'West African Tour – 1948', 27 Sept. 1948.
47. CO 852/801, telegram from Gorell Barnes to Creech Jones, 20 July 1948; CO 852/874/7, CDWP(48)9th meeting, 27 July 1948; Morgan (1980) II, p.15.
48. CO 852/801, letter from Harris (BoT) to Gorell Barnes, 29 July 1948, cited in Morgan (1980) II, p.15.
49. BT 11/4089, minute by Dyson, 3 Aug. 1948.
50. Morgan (1980) II, pp.53–63.
51. CO 537/3095, CD(47)7, Dollar Drain Committee. Colonial Empire. Progress Report by the Treasury, 10 Dec. 1947.
52. Miller (1986), pp.317–38.
53. BT 11/4089, minute by Harris, 5 Aug. 1948.
54. CO 537/3146, CDWP(48) 5th meeting, 8 Apr. 1948.
55. CO 852/889/3, memo. by Gorell Barnes, 'Economic Planning in the Colonies', 3 Aug. 1948.
56. Morgan (1980) II, pp.46–52.
57. CAB 134/65, Report of the Colonial Development Working Party (Revised), 11 Oct. 1948.
58. Morgan (1980) II, pp.53–62.
59. D.K. Fieldhouse, review of Morgan (1980) Volume II, *English Historical Review*, Apr. 1982, pp.386–94.
60. CO 852/875/1, Trefgarne to CO, 12 Jan. 1948; CDWP(48)5, 12 Jan. 1948; CO 852/877/1, Makins (FO) to Caine, 15 Aug. 1947.
61. Morgan (1980) II, p.100.
62. CO 852/877/1, Caine to Makins, 18 Aug. 1947.
63. CO 537/3030, draft note, 'Economic Development in the Colonies', Feb. 1948.
64. CO 852/877/1, Rowe-Dutton (Treasury) to Caine, 18 Sept. 1947; minutes by Eastwood and Ivor Thomas, 18 Sept. 1947.
65. CO 852/875/1, CDWP(48)20, memo. by CO, 'Investment of foreign capital in the Colonies', 9 Mar. 1948.
66. CO 852/877/1, minute by Caine, 6 Nov. 1947.
67. CAB 134/65, Report of the CDWP (Revised), 11 Oct. 1948.
68. CO 852/868/3, CEDC(48)2 CDWP draft Interim Report, 12 Apr. 1948.
69. CO 537/3146, EPB(48) 6th meeting, 15 Apr. 1948. The EPB was a purely advisory body, comprising the Chief Planning Officer, the permanent under-secretaries of several government departments and representatives of the CEPS, the employers' organisations, and the TUC.
70. Porter and Stockwell (1987), pp.48–9.
71. Lee (1980), pp.102–3, and Cairncross (1985), pp.50–6.
72. CO 537/2003, note of meeting at Ministry of Food, 30 May 1947.
73. CO 852/876/1, Grant (Treasury) to Croome (CEPS), 9 Aug. 1948.

74. T 236/696, Rowe-Dutton (Treasury) to Caine, 5 Feb. 1948.
75. CO 852/876/1, K.E. Robinson to Gorell Barnes, 9 Aug. 1948; minute by Gorell Barnes, 10 Aug. 1948; note of meeting held in CEPS on 'Principles of Colonial Investment', 11 Aug. 1948.
76. CO 852/875/3, CDWP(48)50, memo. by CEPS, 'Principles for the Guidance of Colonial Investment', 14 Sept. 1948.
77. CO 852/876/1, note of meeting with CEPS, 11 Aug. 1948.
78. CO 852/875/3, CDWP(48)50, memo. by CEPS, 'Principles for the Guidance of Colonial Investment', 14 Sept. 1948.
79. CAB 134/65, Report of the CDWP (Revised), 11 Oct. 1948.
80. Ibid.; CO 852/878/1, EPB(48) 13th meeting, 21 Oct. 1948.
81. CAB 129/30 CP(48)237, 'The African Conference. Memorandum by the Secretary of State for the Colonies', 12 Oct. 1948; see also Gupta (1983), p.109.
82. CO 852/868/5, CEDC(48) 5th minutes, 19 Oct. 1948; FCB 32/4, f23, Lewis to Hinden, 2 Dec. 1948.
83. CO 852/868/5, CEDC(48) 5th minutes, 19 Oct. 1948.
84. G.D.N. Worswick and P.H. Ady (eds), *The British Economy, 1945–50* (Oxford: Oxford University Press, 1952) p.348; Cairncross (1985), p.51.
85. CO 852/878/1, EPB(48) 13th meeting, 21 Oct. 1948; CAB 134/219, EPC(48)92, 1 Nov. 1948.
86. CO 852/860/2, Record of the proceedings of the Conference of African Governors (8–21 November 1947), Nov. 1947.
87. CO 537/3027, Thomas to Cripps, 17 Sept. 1947.
88. CO 852/1041/2, memo. by Research Section, Economic General Dept., CO, 'Survey of inflationary and deflationary tendencies in the Colonies', 21 July 1949.
89. Meredith (1986), pp.77–91.
90. CO 537/3226, 'West African Tour – 1948', 27 Sept. 1948.
91. CO 537/3561, minute by Poynton, 7 Oct. 1948.
92. CO 852/888/4, minute, 27 May 1948.
93. Ibid., 'Priority Development Projects October 1948', 24 Sept. 1948.
94. CO 537/3226, 'West African Tour – 1948', 27 Sept. 1948.
95. CO 852/1003/4, circular despatch, 13 July 1947.
96. CO 847/36/2, CCAG 2nd meeting, 11 Feb. 1947.
97. CO 96/806/3/31596/1948, note by A.P. Rogers, 25 June 1948.
98. CO 96/806/2/31596/1946–47, minute, 27 Feb. 1947.
99. Ibid., minute, 8 Feb. 1948.
100. Ibid., 'Comments on Gold Coast Draft Ten Year Plan', (unsigned, n.d.).
101. Ibid., Lloyd to Burns (Accra), 3 Mar. 1947.
102. CO 537/3227, 'CO Internal Report', Nov. 1948.
103. Col.no.231, *Report of the Commission of Enquiry into Disturbances in the Gold Coast, 1948*, 8 June 1948.
104. CO 852/801/1, minutes of meeting held by Rees-Williams in Accra, 22 Aug. 1948.
105. Col.no.231, *Report of the Commission of Enquiry into Disturbances in the Gold Coast, 1948*, 8 June 1948.
106. CO 852/801/1, minutes of meeting held by Rees-Williams in Accra, 22 Aug. 1948.
107. CAB 134/65, Report of the CDWP (Revised), 11 Oct. 1948.
108. CO 537/3226, 'West African Tour – 1948', 27 Sept. 1948.
109. *PD(C)* 454, 611, 22 July 1948.
110. CO 847/36/2, CCAG 2nd meeting, 11 Feb. 1947.
111. CO 537/3031, 'Schemes submitted by Nigeria to the CDC', 9 June 1948.
112. H.C. 181, *Fifth Report of the Select Committee on Estimates. Session 1947–48. Colonial Development*, 30 July 1948. On the firms' attempts to improve their image, see S.E. Stockwell, 'British business, politics and decolonisation in the Gold Coast, *c*.1945–60', unpublished University of Oxford D.Phil. thesis (1993).

113. CO 852/855/4, letter, 12 Sept. 1948.
114. Col.no.231, *Report of the Commission of Enquiry into Disturbances in the Gold Coast, 1948*, 8 June 1948. A detailed examination of these questions is provided in S.E. Stockwell, 'Political Strategies of British Business during Decolonisation: The Case of the Gold Coast/Ghana, 1945–57', *JICH* 23, 2, (May 1995) pp.277–300.
115. CO 537/3226, 'West African Tour – 1948', 27 Sept. 1948.
116. Morgan (1980) II, p.15.
117. Rhodes House Library, MSS Brit.Emp.s332, Creech Jones Papers, ACJ 45/1, ff13–14, Labour Party Sub-Committee on Industries for Nationalisation, 'The United Africa Company', Oct. 1948.
118. CO 537/3561, minute by Poynton, 7 Oct. 1948.
119. CO 852/875/1, 'The Colonial Development Corporation. Method of Operation', 5 Dec. 1947.
120. CO 537/2002, note of informal discussion at Treasury, 14 May 1947.
121. *Empire*, Nov. 1948.
122. CO 999/1, CEDC 13th minutes, 10 Mar. 1947.
123. PREM 8/456, letter, 4 Oct. 1947.
124. Ibid., 'Definition of functions of Colonial Development Corporation and Overseas Food Corporation', 1 Oct. 1947.
125. Ibid.
126. CO 537/3033, minute, 17 June 1948.
127. H.C. 181, *Fifth Report from the Select Committee on Estimates. Session 1947–48. Colonial Development*, 30 June 1948.
128. CO 537/3031, minute, 26 June 1948.
129. CO 537/3033, note of second monthly meeting with CDC, 12 July 1948.
130. FCB 51/2, ff17–18, Hinden to Creech Jones, 6 July 1948.
131. CO 537/3033, minute by Gorell Barnes, 9 Aug. 1948.
132. Ibid., minute, 9 Aug. 1948.
133. Ibid., minute by Gorell Barnes, 12 Aug. 1948.
134. CO 537/3226, 'West African Tour – 1948', 27 Sept. 1948.
135. T 220/26, CDWP(48)7, 'Possible development projects in the British Colonies', 14 Jan. 1948.
136. CO 852/875/2, CDWP(48)28, note by CO, 'Control of capital investment in the Colonies', 3 May 1948.
137. CO 852/896/1, CEDC(48)32 Annex A, 'Colonial Textile Industries. Suggestion by Professor Lewis', 8 Nov. 1948.
138. Ibid.
139. Ibid., CEDC(48)32 Annex B, note by CO, 'Colonial Textile Industries', 8 Nov. 1948.
140. Ibid., CEDC(48) 6th meeting, 15 Nov. 1948; ibid., CEDC(48) 7th meeting, 20 Dec. 1948.
141. BT 175/5, CB 7330a, CB(1948) 17th meeting, 14 Dec. 1948.
142. Ibid., CB 7420a, CB(48) 21st meeting, 4 Feb. 1949.
143. *Statistical Abstract of the British Commonwealth*, No. 71, (1951).
144. CO 852/878/1, EPB(48) 13th meeting, 21 Oct. 1948.
145. CAB 134/216, EPC(48) 35th meeting, 9 Nov. 1948.
146. CAB 134/65, Report of the CDWP (Revised), 11 Oct. 1948.
147. E.g., PREM 8/456, Bevin to Attlee, 4 Oct. 1947.
148. CAB 21/1690, minute by Norman Brook, 14 Jan. 1948.

6 The Threads of Policy Resumed, 1949–51

The improvement in Britain's balance of payments apparent late in 1948 proved to be temporary, and in 1949 a fresh sterling crisis developed, culminating in the devaluation of the pound in September. During 1948, Sterling Area exports rose rapidly, while import controls continued. Although this eradicated the overall balance of payments deficit, the Sterling Area's dollar deficit persisted. 'Marshall Aid', operative from mid-1948, covered this deficit until April 1949, but thereafter, Sterling Area exports to the United States declined both in volume and price. Throughout the first half of 1949, US imports fell, largely because the immediate post-war demand released by the abolition of wartime controls diminished. Consequently, between April and June 1949, Britain's deficit with the dollar area grew from $330 million to $632 million. In July, Herbert Morrison warned his colleagues that exhaustion of Britain's gold and dollar reserves was imminent.[1] In these circumstances, London saw no alternative to devaluing the pound by 30.5 per cent in September 1949. This not only ended speculation against the pound but also led to an expansion of Sterling Area exports, and, ultimately, to the virtual elimination of the Area's dollar trade deficit.[2]

Following devaluation, Britain's overseas trade figures and balance of payments improved. By 1950, stability was achieved, with the first post-war surplus, and an acceptable trade deficit with the dollar area. As exports to the Western hemisphere grew, Britain's reserves continued to rise until 1951.[3] During this period, aggregate colonial dollar earnings grew, reaching an annual rate of $560 million in the second half of 1950, compared to approximately $200 million in 1948–49.[4] The period ended with a new balance of payments crisis in 1951, resulting from rearmament, spurred by the Korean War, and from the increased import prices which the war encouraged. These price increases, fuelled by United States strategic stockpiling, drew Britain's dollar balance out of a £308 million credit in 1950 into a deficit of £561 million in the second quarter of 1951.[5] The developing US recession led to a reduction in imports from the Sterling Area. The colonial dollar export surplus, which had reached a monthly level of between $15 million and $20 million in April and May 1949, was wiped out, threatening a major cut in colonial export incomes.[6]

As in 1947, so again in 1949, Whitehall examined the colonies' possible role in easing Britain's dollar problems. One working party charged with supplying information to the Economic Cooperation Administration proposed examining the scope for stimulating colonial dollar exports.[7] The Colonial Office was unlikely to welcome any crude policy of boosting colonial dollar exports. Experience over the previous two years convinced officials that despite the crisis of 1947, colonial production had *not* been geared purely to earning dollars, because the metropolitan government had seen the colonies primarily as a source of supply for Britain, either of dollar-saving commodities, or of commodities which it could not otherwise acquire. An important consequence of this had been that the colonial price structure had been influenced by that in Britain. It seemed unlikely, therefore, that any substantial increase in production for export to the USA could occur unless the colonies accepted US, rather than British, prices. This, however, was problematic so long as colonies were expected to buy from Britain at relatively high price because of the dollar shortage. As one official observed, the CEPS was, by mid-1949, concluding that the solution might lie not in forcing the colonies to sell at lower prices to the USA than in Britain, but for the latter to reduce its purchases from the dollar area and from the Sterling Area.

Accepting the apparent logic of this conclusion, the Colonial Office nevertheless feared that it would nullify most of the assumptions governing recent colonial production policy, especially the assumption that Britain would remain a stable, long-term market for colonial produce. This would represent a *volte face* in Britain's moral commitments to the colonial economies.[8] Nor was the Office convinced that a renewed colonial 'dollar drive' was practicable. Officials saw little scope for centralised action since the problem was ultimately one of selling more colonial commodities in dollar markets.[9] Any attempt to give 'absolute' priority to dollar exports, as the Cabinet Committee on Exports appeared to favour, would raise another fundamental problem. As Creech Jones told Cripps in October 1949, if exports otherwise intended for the colonies were diverted to the dollar area, the risk would be that relatively small, if immediate, returns would be achieved compared to the potentially much greater dollar return possible if the same exports went to the colonies. Moreover, the success of Britain's continuing attempts to curb colonial dollar expenditure would depend largely on the home economy's ability and willingness to replace colonial dollar imports with its own goods. As Creech Jones asked, in terms echoing the Colonial Office's pre-war and wartime concern to achieve market stabilisation: 'Is it wise to withhold these exports from what is almost certain to be a permanent dollar-saving market for a more precarious expansion in direct dollar earnings[?].' In addition, there might be *political* repercussions if the recent improvements in the colonial supply situation were not maintained.[10]

The supply problem

Despite Creech Jones's reference to recent improvements, the supply problem continued to overshadow development policy. It was one of the subjects most frequently discussed by the Cabinet Committee on Colonial Development, created late in 1948 at the suggestion of the Colonial Development Working Party (CDWP), and charged with reviewing development plans in relation to wider economic policy.[11] When London took stock of the situation up to May 1949, it was admitted that the overall achievement in development fell short of original hopes, mainly due to shortages of materials and personnel, and that some colonial governments might need to consider whether their initial goals had been realistic given these continuing constraints.[12]

Early in 1949, the Colonial Office decided to convene a conference of colonial supply officers in London to discuss import programming plans and the need for continued restraint, and to examine the relative desirability of different countries as sources of supply.[13] Whitehall feared that a conference, through which details of the dollar ceilings on each colony's imports would for the first time become generally known among the colonial governments, might encourage combined opposition to the system of import controls.[14]

Meanwhile, problems had arisen over price differentials in colonial imports. The dollar ceilings imposed on colonial imports during 1948 meant that goods from 'hard' currency sources were generally excluded, even when they were cheaper than 'soft' currency equivalents. The Colonial Office, fearing political complications, noted that while Britain imposed fixed prices for colonial produce, it did not reciprocate with fixed prices for sterling exports to the colonies. The question was referred to the Cabinet Committee on Colonial Development (CCD) in March 1949. The Colonial Office did not envisage governments being authorised to buy 'hard' goods wherever prices of 'soft' imports were higher by a given percentage: instead, officials favoured asking colonial administrations to report instances where, under existing instructions, they would have to buy soft imports at unjustifiably high prices compared to similar hard currency items, and believed that London should adjust colonial dollar ceilings accordingly.[15]

The Colonial Office considered the existing instructions on import licensing, issued in September 1947, too restrictive, for example in forbidding licences for imports unlikely to yield 'substantial' earnings or savings of dollars. Officials wanted dollar imports required for development to be permitted, regardless of whether the development would promote dollar earning or saving (but in keeping with the CDWP's guidelines) provided the supplies were unavailable from soft sources, or only at substantially higher prices and after long delays.[16] The Office hoped to establish a level of price difference beyond which the colonies should not be pressed to buy from Britain. The CCD believed that if full political value were to be derived from any concessions made, these should be publicised and any special arrangements applied to the *whole* colonial empire.

Whitehall recognised the need to forestall any suspicions that Britain was protecting her colonial markets through import controls. Consequently, the CCD stressed that colonies should regard *all* soft currency sources, and not only Britain, as the alternative to dollar supplies. Moreover, the Committee considered that British export promotion in the colonies should be undertaken through separate channels, such as the Board of Trade commissioners, who should be ready to seize the opportunities at hand.[17]

The period 1949–51 saw continuing evidence that colonial markets were highly prized, at least by certain sectors of British manufacturing industry, for example, Lancashire cotton. Although Lancashire's fortunes had improved following the war, with demand exceeding the industry's capacity to meet, fears of German and Japanese competition in overseas markets soon re-emerged. Moreover, US exports remained much greater in volume than they had been before the war. Thus, although total world exports of cotton goods had reached some 89 per cent of their pre-1939 level, Britain's share of this had declined from 27 per cent to 15 per cent.[18] At the Colonial Supplies Conference in June 1949, Sir Raymond Streat told delegates that the colonies were 'most important' to Lancashire's future, offering the most 'assured' markets, given their rising populations and the improved living standards expected to result from development. According to the Cotton Board's estimate, total world exports in 1952 would be 15 per cent below their pre-war level; however, total *colonial* imports would be some 16 per cent *above* the pre-war figure. Before the war, Lancashire had enjoyed about one third of this trade, and hoped to secure at least half of it in the future. Whereas before the war, 15 per cent of Britain's cotton exports had gone to the colonies, by 1949 40 per cent of all orders on hand were for these territories. Nevertheless, the recent decline in colonial orders alarmed Lancashire, and Streat emphasised that the metropolitan cotton industry would 'never' be able to compete in prices with Japan. If the colonies were to choose their imports according to price, he explained, Lancashire would be finished.[19]

The Nigerian representative at the conference spoke of feelings in West Africa that Lancashire had missed a 'tremendous opportunity' to expand its post-war trade. Since 1947, when the system of allocating supplies was abolished, imports from Britain had declined: of 125 million square yards of cloth imported into Nigeria, for example, only 35 million square yards were from Britain. This, it was claimed, was resented by the local population, who allegedly disliked Japanese goods, and without measures to restore trade with Britain, the problem might have political consequences.[20]

In September 1949, Streat warned the Cotton Board that it was 'vitally' important for Lancashire to increase supplies to colonial markets, arguing that as other markets became less penetrable, colonial markets would grow in value. Unless Lancashire increased its supplies to these markets, it would lack a stake in them large enough to warrant the colonial authorities acting to protect British interests, risking a loss of colonial trade and further contraction at home.[21]

Although, in May 1949, the CCD was informed of the 'very satisfactory' colonial gold and dollar surplus of $260 million, some $50 million higher than the 1948 figure, the overall sterling area position soon eclipsed this hopeful indicator. At the end of May, the CCD was told that the (Cabinet) Economic Policy Committee had endorsed the suggestion by the Official Committee on Economic Development that all dollar expenditure, except Britain's own dollar imports, should be reviewed with the goal of further economies. The Colonial Office, with one eye on price differentials, considered that the entire field of dollar saving should be examined, and that any cuts should not fall solely on the colonies, dependent as they were on dollar imports if soft supplies were unavailable. With the Treasury urging every effort to ensure that dollar expenditure in 1949–50 was the 'absolute minimum', the Colonial Office argued that colonial spending had already been reduced to essentials and that any further attempts to switch from dollar to soft sources would accentuate the price differential problem, and it warned that an 'excessively stringent' attitude on London's part might create political difficulties in the colonies, undermining the entire purpose of the exercise. The CCD accepted that a cut in colonial dollar expenditure would be defensible only if a similar amount were deducted from the estimates of colonial dollar receipts, which were themselves based on optimistic assessments. Even the CEPS, previously insensitive to colonial needs, conceded that there was little prospect of cuts being made without lowering colonial living standards, especially since food imports represented around 40 per cent of total colonial imports.[22]

In July 1949, the CCD was told that the colonial dollar balance of payments surplus, hitherto between $15 and $20 million per month, had virtually disappeared, owing largely to the recession in the United States and its effects on US purchases of colonial commodities. This threatened not only to reduce colonial earnings from dollar exports, but also to increase expenditure by the independent sterling area to take advantage of currently falling American prices. According to the Treasury's estimate, the probable gap between earnings and expenditure would require a cut of some 25 per cent in the Sterling Area's total imports. The Colonial Office, accepting that the colonies had to contribute to dollar economy, doubted how far this could be done by arbitrary cuts in imports. Nevertheless, the CCD concluded that colonial governments should be asked to undertake no further dollar commitments unless 'absolutely essential' until further notice, and that in view of falling prices and the increased availability of supplies from Britain, every effort should be made to economise on current dollar ceilings.[23] The Colonial Office requested governments to suspend dollar import licences, except where 'grave effects' would result, and asked for estimates of dollar import reductions in 1949. The Office hoped, and encouraged colonial governments to believe, that by mid-August, the standstill on dollar import licensing might be removed. Nevertheless, the CCD recommended that the colonies be warned that further reductions in their dollar expenditure would be necessary in the first half of 1950 if the overall Sterling Area target of a 25 per cent cut were to be achieved.[24]

Any hope of relaxing controls was dashed, however, by the progressive deterioration of Britain's dollar balance during summer 1949, leading to devaluation. This step was extended automatically to colonial governments, and the Colonial Office sought to avoid any impression that the consequences for the colonies had been ignored. The principal effect of devaluation was to reduce the real external purchasing power of the Sterling Area. However, as the Office pointed out, the repercussions were likely to vary considerably between Britain, with its vast industrial and agricultural output, and the colonial economies, which lacked this protective cushion. For example, colonies which imported virtually all their manufactured goods and exported a limited range of commodities were likely to be markedly affected by devaluation. Similarly, the consequences were likely to be far greater for colonies where average incomes were low, if not at subsistence level, than for Britain, with its relatively high incomes.

Furthermore, Britain was in a stronger administrative position to alleviate the impact of devaluation than were many colonies. Since the sterling cost of all imports from the United States increased, the immediate consequence would be a rise in colonial costs of living, especially in colonies heavily dependent on dollar imports, such as the West Indies. More generally, much would depend on the effects of devaluation on sterling and other soft currency prices, together with Britain's ability to supply colonial needs.[25] This last point concerned the Colonial Office particularly, since Britain supplied by far the greater proportion of colonial non-dollar imports. It seemed likely that Britain's exporters, encouraged by the Board of Trade, would try to increase their exports to the dollar area, if necessary at the expense of other markets. This led the Colonial Office to warn the CCD that any deliberate policy of directing exports away from the colonies would not only create political difficulties, since the colonies would then be obliged to buy essential items from now relatively expensive dollar suppliers, but it would also require administrative controls in the colonies to ensure that supplies from the sterling area were not obtained by indirect means, and the Colonial Office doubted whether such controls could be imposed.

The general supply problem raised the issue of Whitehall's attitude to colonial policy and to colonial needs. Early in 1949, the Colonial Office complained to the CCD that some British manufacturers were refusing to accept colonial orders, allegedly on instructions from government departments to reserve their output for the domestic market. This, argued the Colonial Office, conflicted with the notion that the colonies should be treated as integral parts of the British economy. The Board of Trade and the Ministry of Supply replied that this affected only a small range of items, including (ironically) agricultural machinery, and that it was impracticable to consult the Colonial Office over every case. In their view, the colonies generally received fair, even favourable, treatment.[26] In March 1949, the CCD established that colonial orders should receive equal treatment to home orders.[27] Creech Jones subsequently raised this problem with Cripps, arguing that while Whitehall's views on colonial affairs were improving, they still fell short of what was desirable. He requested a directive from Cripps, or from the appropriate Cabinet committee, that colonial and metropolitan orders should receive equal treatment. Cripps, however, countered that time was needed to allow the new procedure to take effect.[28]

When the CCD's Sub-Committee on Import Programmes reported in April 1949, it proposed dollar ceilings for the colonies totalling $202.8 million, $45 million less than the colonial governments had requested. Although the report urged that colonial governments should be reminded of the need for continuing dollar economy, it conceded that overall expenditure had fallen from $436 million in 1947 to $380 million in 1948.

Furthermore, the Sub-Committee recognised that the colonies needed Britain's help in limiting their dollar expenditure. It was understood that much of the reduction in colonial dollar spending since 1947 had been due to revived supplies of Japanese and German cotton textiles, which were often cheaper than imports from Britain. To complicate matters further, some US cotton textiles were now cheaper than Japanese goods.

The supply problem demonstrates the paradoxical character of metropolitan economic policy towards the colonies in this period. At a time when British government directives sacrificed colonial needs to Britain's immediate balance of payments requirements, longer-term official concerns persisted at a submerged level. In April 1949, for example, alarmed at the rapid recovery of Japanese and German exports, the CCD urged the UK production departments to remind British exporters of the need to maximise current opportunities to entrench themselves in colonial markets, by striving to meet colonial requirements at competitive prices.[29] Whitehall understood the danger of Britain being seen to be using import controls to protect its colonial markets, but an anxiety over the future of long-term markets remained a recurring theme in its discussions.

The supply problem also revealed contradictions in metropolitan policy. For instance, not long before the danger to British exporters from Japanese and German competition was attracting comment in Whitehall, the CCD noted with apparent satisfaction that the colonies in general were maximising on these 'soft' sources of supply, enabling them to reduce their consumption of dollar imports, the question which remained of overriding immediate concern.[30]

When the Colonial Supplies Conference opened in London on 8 June 1949, earlier fears at the prospect of convening a gathering of potentially restless colonial administrators proved largely groundless. Little hostility was expressed to the colonies' membership of the Sterling Area, or to the Treasury's broad strategy, although concern surfaced that Britain had limited its own dollar spending less strictly than the colonies were being urged to do.[31]

The issue of price differentials in colonial imports was more contentious, however. This problem had been accentuated by the US recession, which had depressed American export prices, increasing their competitive edge over sterling and other soft supplies. Furthermore, the deteriorating sterling balance of payments position, also a product of the US recession, created obstacles to effective action on price differentials. The Colonial Office optimistically hoped that the recession might ease the problem since colonial dollar allocations would go further as dollar prices fell, although it recognised that continuing dollar economy was necessary. The Colonial Office proposed writing to territorial governments after the Supplies Conference, explaining that the price differential question might worsen if the US recession continued, and that the Office had suggested a modest relaxation of dollar ceilings. However, conference delegates feared that any relaxation would encourage a 'flood' of applications, making it impossible to restrict additional hard currency licensing to the level envisaged by Whitehall. Since then, however, the dollar situation had made it even less possible for Britain to contemplate any adjustment which might expand hard currency spending. But because falling dollar prices would mean that existing dollar ceilings would go further than expected when set, the Office hoped that revised arrangements might not be necessary after all.[32]

As Britain's dollar position deteriorated in July 1949, colonial governments were asked to stop issuing dollar import licences and were told not to expect increased dollar ceilings, to resolve the price differential problem or for any other reason. The Colonial Office sugared this pill by suggesting that the developing world recession, with the emergence of a buyer's market, would increase the availability of non-dollar goods.[33] Perhaps unrealistically, Creech Jones later told the colonial governments that he hoped, by mid-August 1949, to be able to withdraw the standstill on dollar import licences.[34] Circumstances prevented this, however, and late in August the original instruction was confirmed. A contributory factor was the fact that discussions were then in progress in the Organization for European Economic Co-operation over the distribution of Marshall Aid. As Creech Jones explained, any suggestion that curbs on dollar import licensing were to be relaxed might 'most seriously' affect the allocation of aid, and thus the total amount of dollars available to the Sterling Area as a whole.[35]

The colonies had responded to the 4 July telegram by volunteering cuts in their dollar import ceilings totalling $15 million, leaving the overall ceiling for 1949 at $215 million.

When special provision was made for purchases of petroleum products, and when known overspending during the year – especially by Malaya – was taken into account, a total projected expenditure of $250 million was calculated. Yet in the first half of 1949 alone, colonial dollar imports had totalled around $150 million, and it seemed unlikely that spending could be kept within the target set.[36]

Following devaluation in September 1949, fresh calls were made for the 1950 colonial ceilings to be reduced. The CCD's Sub-Committee on Imports, which set these ceilings, decided that in view of the improving supply position, the 1950 target should be fixed at $169 million, compared to the figure of $196 million set before devaluation. The main CCD, however, believed that there was little scope for further cuts in the dollar ceilings, acknowledging that pressure might arise for *increases* in some cases. There were striking disparities in the distribution of dollar ceilings among the colonies. For instance, of all the ceilings proposed for 1950, 50 per cent were allocated to the West Indies and 24 per cent to Malaya, but only 8.5 per cent to West Africa.[37] Even allowing for the special circumstances of the West Indies, heavily dependent on neighbouring dollar suppliers for essential imports, and for Malaya's post-war reconstruction needs, it is ironic that West Africa, a major dollar-earning region, received so little of what it earned, underlining the inequitable character of the controls operated from London.

A paper produced for the CCD in June 1950 demonstrated the effects of these controls on colonial dollar expenditure since 1947. In 1947 the colonies had imported $390 million worth of goods, a figure reduced to $355 million in 1948. It was estimated that the 1949 figure would be $248 million, with a forecast for 1950 of $206 million. In West Africa's case, the target for 1950 represented a 45 per cent cut since 1947, from $42 million to $23 million.[38] The Colonial Office now felt confident that colonial governments understood the objectives of dollar limitation, and considered that detailed programming of their dollar imports for 1951 was unnecessary.[39]

The continuing supply problem was reflected in swollen colonial cost of living indices, estimated to have doubled between 1939 and the end of 1948. This rise was attributed chiefly to the increased prices being paid for colonial exports. Colonial governments responded by trying to counteract the resulting inflationary tendency through taxation and budgetary policies, but above all through produce marketing arrangements. It was recognised that the supply position had been improving steadily. For instance, since inflationary pressures had become noticeable late in 1947, supplies appeared to have increased at a faster rate than incomes, creating a relatively stable relationship between the supply of goods and the money supply. A key indicator of this was the fact that colonial cotton piece-goods imports were higher in volume in 1948 than in any year since 1937. With the emergence of a buyer's market by mid-1949, and the halt in the increase in export prices from the main supplying countries, officials in London confidently expected an easing of colonial inflationary pressure. However, the Colonial Office realised that increased supplies of consumer goods would be needed as local incomes rose. Officials considered that one means of combating inflationary tendencies might be to increase the volume of local goods production for the domestic market.[40] Although the idea was apparently not developed, the fact that such a suggestion could be aired helps to illustrate the renewed importance increasingly attached to industrialisation by the Office.

By late 1950, the Colonial Office was becoming concerned at the consequences of the rapidly accelerating metropolitan rearmament programme for the colonial supply position. The Office had already raised the implications of rearmament for the colonial economies generally with the Cabinet Economic Steering Committee. Officials were particularly worried by increased colonial earnings from raw materials exports resulting from price rises, fuelled by high world demand; nearly all colonial exports had increased in price in the previous year, but this development had not been matched by a corresponding rise in colonial imports. Evidence for this was the growth of the colonial sterling balances (of which West Africa's share was 30 per cent by the end of 1950) from £670 million in December 1949 to £850 million a year later.[41]

The Colonial Office feared that, combined with the effects of rearmament, and especially the danger of fresh shortages of capital goods, this situation would have inflationary consequences in the colonies, stimulating the accumulation of unspent balances, a potential source of embarrassment, implying that colonies could not draw on their own resources for development. It was also feared that this would retard economic development, and, more importantly, increase the risk of local political discontent. The impact of events in the Gold Coast in 1948 on the official mind in London had evidently been deep and long-lasting. The Colonial Office warned the Cabinet Economic Steering Committee that fiscal measures taken by colonial governments could have only a limited effect in curbing local spending power. The Committee, however, was unmoved: accepting that unchecked growth of the sterling balances was 'undesirable', it considered that these might provide the colonies with 'a most valuable cushion' against any future difficulties. Ironically, the Colonial Office was now being obliged to digest the official rationale for continued accumulation which it had promoted since the latter years of the war.[42]

Rearmament had further implications for the colonial supply position. The switch to soft currency sources, evident in 1950, continued in the 1951 dollar expenditure programmes, but it seemed increasingly likely that the colonies would have to be allowed greater latitude in their dollar spending, not only because rearmament was liable to affect dollar goods prices in 1951, but also because it was improbable that goods that were scarce in Britain as a result of the rearmament programme would be any less scarce in the United States. Aggravating this was the threat of inflation as raw material prices rose. Accordingly, the CCD's Sub-Committee on Imports concluded that its parent committee should realise that the colonial dollar ceilings being proposed for 1951 might be inadequate.[43]

During summer 1951, the Colonial Office was reminded of the political delicacy of the supply question. To accompany his estimate of the imports the Gold Coast would need for development in the period 1951–60, over and above its normal requirements, Governor Sir Charles Arden-Clarke warned of the serious political consequences which might follow if the capital resources necessary for development were not forthcoming. This danger appeared greater following the elections recently held under the Gold Coast's new constitution, which brought to power a party calling for rapid, large-scale economic and social development.[44] As the Colonial Office put it to the CCD:

> If the present harmonious relations between the new African Ministers and their official colleagues in the Gold Coast Executive Council are to be maintained, and the pressure of

> the more extreme nationalist elements for full and immediate self-government is to be neutralised, it is imperative that every possible effort should be made to enable the Gold Coast development programme to be implemented to the fullest possible extent. Failure in this respect will inevitably lead to a breakdown in the working of the constitution with serious consequences for the whole future of His Majesty's Government's relations with the Gold Coast.[45]

The Colonial Office emphasised that as development programmes gathered momentum, colonial supply needs would grow (a problem not unique to the Gold Coast) and that special action to help that territory would in itself raise problems, especially if, as a result, other colonies were deprived. The Office lacked information on the demand which other colonies' development programmes would create; moreover, many colonial administrations were reluctant to predict their needs beyond a twelve-month period, and found it even more difficult to predict the likely requirements of the local private sector.

The CCD considered it unlikely that the world availability of capital goods would increase over the next few years, and warned that supplies might even decline. Because of Britain's rearmament programme and raw materials shortages, it was also unlikely that Britain would be able to maintain the current level of engineering exports, and the same appeared to be true of the United States. The Committee accepted that, except possibly for a brief period during 1949–50, many colonies had effectively been investing in Britain since 1939, and that if this situation continued, there might be 'very serious' political difficulties, and the success of the experiment in 'controlled transition to self-government' might depend largely on whether the colonial governments then in office could demonstrate achievements in economic development. The Committee conceded, moreover, that colonial needs were not excessive, in that the African territories' development plans could apparently be implemented up to 1956 provided the 1950 level of expenditure, at 1950 prices, was maintained. Nevertheless, the CCD concluded that nothing like the ten-year commitment to a given level of supplies requested by Arden-Clarke was possible, suggesting instead that the colonies could attempt to plan for the three-year period covered by the present rearmament programme.[46]

Development finance

If the supply position continued to present difficulties in the path of broad-based colonial economic development, constraints on the provision of development finance also persisted. The relative easing of Britain's own difficulties in 1949–50 encouraged some reflection among officials in London on progress made since 1945. A firm conviction remained, however, that finance was not the major limiting factor on development. Even with the temporary improvement in Britain's financial position by 1949, the prospects for any substantial, immediate increase in British investment in the colonies were slight. Creech Jones, having informed the colonial governments of his earlier appeal to Cripps for a relaxation of loan policy, added that, on the basis of the CDWP's final report, it seemed unlikely that there would be any 'appreciable' increase in the rate of colonial investment from British sources over 'the next few years'.[47]

It became clear after devaluation in September 1949 that the provisional loan ceiling of £60 million accepted by the CDWP was unlikely to be increased, although the Colonial Office believed that this figure would, in practice, suffice for most colonial governments until March 1952.[48] Attention shifted from possible metropolitan sources of funding to local, colonial resources, and, once again, to foreign investment. Local resources were still depressingly limited. It appeared to the Colonial Office that the majority of banks operating in the colonies, such as the Bank of British West Africa, were willing to finance small industries, although generally only against adequate security. However, the Office saw little evidence of interest in this kind of development among banks based in Britain, with the exception of Barclay's. The fundamental problem was that while 'sound' commercial undertakings, regardless of size, could normally attract loans through commercial channels, difficulties arose when the would-be borrower was inexperienced. Yet it was precisely the *local* entrepreneur whom officials, both in London, and especially in West Africa, were most concerned to encourage, and as the momentum towards political devolution developed, so did the perceived pressure to provide development with a secure indigenous base.

It was in these circumstances that officials looked again, after prolonged distractions, at Barclays Overseas Development

Corporation, whose creation in 1946 had largely shaped the Colonial Office's thinking on development corporations. Little had been heard of the Corporation since its formation. In 1947, the Corporation proposed to allocate a small part of its resources for use as a 'revolving fund' to finance small development schemes proposed by West Africans. The distribution of this fund was to be delegated, in each West African territory, to a local representative of the Corporation and a representative of the territorial government who together could make advances of up to £1,000. The Gold Coast government welcomed this proposal and agreed to co-operate with the Corporation through its own Industrial Development Corporation. Lagos, however, agreed to the proposal only on condition that it should not itself incur any financial liability, a proviso which Barclays understandably found unacceptable. Therefore although the Colonial Office understood the scheme to be operating in the Gold Coast early in 1950, there seemed in practice to have been little demand for its services.[49]

In June 1950, Creech Jones's successor as Colonial Secretary, James Griffiths, advised the colonial governments to give priority to important development projects, especially where these would strengthen the governments' future reserves. He simultaneously revived the possibility of colonial borrowing from the International Bank for Reconstruction and Development (IBRD), which was now made more attractive by being only about half a per cent more expensive than London loans. Nevertheless, the basic obstacle remained the fact that IBRD loans could not be used to make purchases in sterling or colonial currencies. At a time when continuing calls were being made for dollar restraint, this stipulation eroded the usefulness to colonial governments of IBRD funds. Griffiths had only been induced to remind the colonies of this possible resource by the prevailing uncertainty over the availability of metropolitan loan finance. This fear was confirmed very soon by the Treasury's announcement that some 'postponement' of colonial borrowing in London was inevitable.[50]

The Colonial Office reviewed the position towards the end of 1951, informing the CCD that the total amount approved by the Capital Issues Committee in respect of colonial enterprises during 1951 had been approximately £8.5 million. But, as the Office pointed out, this figure did not represent British private investment in the colonies. Since April that year, a number of applications to the CIC had concerned the capitalisation of reserves, rather than the raising of additional capital. The Colonial Office saw this as a demonstration that little fresh capital was actually being raised by private enterprise in Britain for colonial investment.[51]

The question of foreign, and specifically American, investment in the colonies re-emerged following President Truman's inaugural address on 20 January 1949, in which he outlined his 'Fourth Point', promising US aid to the underdeveloped world. As Truman put it: 'We must embark on a bold new program for making the benefits of our scientific advances and industrial progress available for the improvement and growth of underdeveloped areas.' The Fourth Point, a product, like the earlier Marshall Plan, of a deepening Cold War was presented as a wholly new approach to development: 'The old imperialism – exploitation for foreign profit – has no place in our plans. What we envisage is a programme of development based on the concepts of democratic fair-dealing.' The British ambassador in Washington saw in the Fourth Point great opportunities for Anglo–American relations, provided Britain responded quickly and favourably. He thought it clear that Truman envisaged assistance primarily to Latin America and the Far East, especially China, and he cautioned against any attempt by Britain to 'grab the proceeds' for Africa. As the ambassador hoped, Ernest Bevin's reaction to the Fourth Point was enthusiastic.[52]

The Colonial Office felt that US private investment in the colonies was beneficial both to the colony concerned and to the Sterling Area provided it earned or saved dollars and that it complied with exchange regulations and local welfare and other legislation. However, officials believed that while some of their prominent US counterparts were interested in promoting US private investment in overseas territories, investors themselves were nervous. Anticipating calls that London should actively encourage foreign investment by indicating appropriate spheres of development, the Colonial Office outlined some of the accompanying difficulties. Not only would the balance of payments implications have to be considered, but Britain could hardly contemplate easing financial and 'social' restrictions on colonial investment since this would be incompatible with the declared policy of 'protecting' the interests of colonial populations. If anything, officials felt, pressure was likely to develop in favour of more stringent restrictions, for example through immigration controls and assurances about training local personnel. Furthermore, the possible repercussions of US investment on the interests of British, Dominion and other foreign investors had to be considered. Finally, the condition of colonial governments themselves, particularly their lack of expertise in economic planning, was thought to be a constraint on expanded investment: officials considered that there was a limit to the extent to which colonial development could be accelerated without risking local administrative collapse. Given these problems and the potential for allegations of exploitation, the Colonial Office questioned the political practicability of stimulating US investment.[53]

On the Fourth Point proper, that is, direct US Government involvement, the Colonial Office was equally cautious. The acknowledged deficiencies of colonial administrations could encourage proposals for US control over development projects, which neither Westminster nor territorial governments were likely to accept. Even less attractive, in the Office's view, was the possibility of Washington opting for international control of development, which revived officials' wartime fears concerning the internationalisation of colonial rule. A final counter-argument was that US aid to the developing world might involve cuts in Marshall Aid, and hence affect metropolitan interests. The Colonial Office's objections to US investment were therefore broadly similar to those raised in 1948.[54]

Creech Jones had already told the colonial governments, in February 1949, that London was drafting guidelines on colonial investment for the benefit of foreign governments and investors, and he had solicited local administrators' views. The accompanying note pointed out that many foreign concerns were already operating in the colonies and that the creation of the CDC and OFC was not intended to preclude further foreign investment. The draft note advised interested investors to become familiar with local legislation and regulations. It reminded them of existing controls, for example over marketing, and explained that foreign exchange was available for the remittance of dividends and interest, but not for the repatriation of capital invested for less than ten years.[55]

For colonial governments, the fundamental problem was to reconcile foreign investment with limitations on foreign competition with local populations both in employment and enterprise. This impinged on other sensitive areas of policy, such as controls on immigration into the colonies, particularly in West Africa. For instance, Nigeria's policy was to exclude any potential competitors with local entrepreneurs.[56] In the Gold Coast, however, policy was unresolved; in 1949, proposals were under discussion to control immigration on economic grounds, but these were regarded as 'non-discriminatory' in that they distinguished between the population of the Gold Coast and *all* others, British or foreign.

In the discussions prompted by the Fourth Point, it became obvious that the Colonial Office was unenthusiastic about private US investment. While the maximum possible US investment in the Sterling Area was desirable on balance of payments grounds, the existing controls on investment, together with investors' expectations of large returns where their risks were high, had tended to counteract this. Moreover, officials recognised that any preferential treatment to such investors would not only be unfair to other investors, but might result in a net loss to the Sterling Area if it involved a relaxation of exchange controls and import licensing. Officials concluded that the US should be told that private investment, on conventional terms, would contribute little to colonial development, and that aid without the 'strings' which might attach to the Fourth Point was preferable, as this would prepare the way for 'orthodox' private investment.[57]

The Colonial Office's reservations were incorporated in a CCD report produced in April 1949, and subsequently endorsed by the CEDC. The Committee concluded that political, social and balance of payments considerations dictated that existing controls on foreign colonial investment could not be lifted.[58] Furthermore, the Committee believed that measures to attract US capital might involve risks. An interesting counter-argument to private investment was now introduced: private investment depended on adequate basic services in the colonies, now identified as the main factor impeding development. Whereas private investment had traditionally provided these services to the 'minimum degree essential', social, labour and other standards had risen, and adequate provision by private enterprise no longer seemed practicable. Increasingly, private investment could flourish only after the State had developed basic services, and it was considered that US assistance might be useful here, although not in the form of commercial loans.[59]

The Colonial Office's underlying disquiet was, however, revealed by its reactions to a draft report, 'Investment opportunities in British Africa', prepared by the US Chamber of Commerce. This was described by one official as a 'poor' document, unlikely to encourage American firms to invest in Africa, although, significantly, he added 'As we ourselves are not enthusiastically attempting to encourage American private investment this is perhaps all to the good.'[60]

This view was not, however, shared universally within the British government. In June 1949, the Lord President of the Council, Herbert Morrison, suggested to Attlee that the possibility of attracting US investment for colonial development should be considered.[61] In July, Creech Jones put a memorandum on foreign investment to the Cabinet Economic Policy Committee. This was essentially the same as the note circulated to the colonies in February, and explained that foreign investment was welcome provided that it complemented the colonies' own plans, and was devoted to productive, long-term purposes beneficial to the colonies and the Sterling Area, and provided that investors conformed to local regulations governing commercial undertakings.[62]

When Cabinet discussed the question, Treasury concern surfaced over alterations in exchange control policy to facilitate US investment, a concern that the Colonial Office shared. The Cabinet decided to postpone any public statement until the Anglo–American financial discussions, due in September, were completed.[63] It is clear, however, that the Treasury foresaw no sizeable influx of foreign private investment, given the disincentive of inadequate basic services.[64] A major consequence of the Washington talks was a new emphasis on the importance of encouraging foreign investment, especially dollar investment, in the colonies. The Colonial Office therefore proposed an inter-departmental examination of policy on foreign private investment, and the CCD agreed that the CEPS and the Treasury should consider the question urgently.[65]

Accordingly, an inter-departmental committee, formed in October, reported in January 1950.[66] It recommended that the existing selective policy on US investment in the Sterling Area should continue, based on the criterion of dollar earning or saving, or increased productivity, bearing balance of payments considerations in mind. It also recommended that this policy should be made public. Having read the draft statement of policy requested in the committee's report, Dugdale, sensitive to the danger of a hostile response from the Labour left and the Tory right, commented:

> The more I look at it, the less need can I see for the House of Commons to have to listen to a glorified company prospectus asking people to invest in 'British Colonial Empire Limited'.

In his view, such statements might be counter-productive. In response to Dugdale's request for an alternative to a Commons statement, Hugh Gaitskell, the Minister of Economic Affairs, suggested that the Colonial Office and Treasury statements could be incorporated in a letter from Britain's ambassador in Washington to the US Secretary of State, and that this letter could be given whatever publicity was necessary in North America.[67]

Eventually, however, a Commons statement was made in the form of a written answer by Thomas Cook, the Parliamentary Under-Secretary. This explained that while current policy, in general, was to welcome US investment in the colonies, it was necessary to remember the dollar liability arising from the remittance of dividends or profits, together with the ultimate liability for the repatriation of capital. Therefore, as long as the dollar problem persisted, policy would have to remain selective, and any project would have to promise a net saving or earning of dollars, or be so economically beneficial to the colony concerned as to justify any loss of dollars involved.[68]

Colonial government machinery and attitudes

This was the unpromising background against which colonial governments sought to formulate their own policies on industrial development. There was, in this period, a growing sense of urgency among local officials about the need to present a constructive attitude towards industrialisation, a need sharpened by rapid developments at the political level, especially in West Africa. This was one aspect of a broader evolution in policy that was even more noticeable in the Colonial Office. At least as far as West Africa was concerned, officials were increasingly obliged to review, and even reverse, traditional priorities in colonial policy in which economic and social development had been seen as a necessary, and probably lengthy process, designed to provide constitutional advance with secure foundations. After 1948, and particularly after the rapid sequence of events following the Accra riots, the need to maintain local political goodwill became the touchstone of development policy, expressed in an official anxiety to promote economic development so as to retain the co-operation of local political elites. Among the emerging political forces in West Africa, economic development, and industrialisation, were potent slogans to which colonial authorities felt obliged to respond. The manifesto of the Convention Peoples' Party, produced for the general election of February 1951, stated that industrialisation was one of the Party's principal objectives as a means of raising living standards, adding:

> Imperialism is incompatible with industrialisation of a colonial country. It is only under self-government that this country can be industrialised in the way that it should.[69]

As already suggested, a recurring theme in the development policy debate had been doubts over the capacity of colonial governments to tackle new responsibilities and functions. Such doubts persisted into the later 1940s. For example, in 1949, Arthur Lewis wrote:

> most colonial administrations have not yet begun even to recognise the nature of their most important economic problems, let alone to make provision for dealing with them.[70]

Yet it was towards the end of the period covered in this study when the idea of State-led development gained fresh impetus, particularly after the influx of new ministerial blood after the February 1950 general election in Britain. The re-examination of the role of public enterprise by the Colonial Office was associated especially with Dugdale, but was apparently also encouraged by James Griffiths. The discussions initiated by ministers in the Colonial Office embraced a wide range of development issues, the most prominent being mining and industrial development. In this, there is a sense of the enthusiasm of Creech Jones, clear from 1945 onwards. It was truncated, *inter alia*, by the crisis of 1947 and its aftermath, but was rediscovered during 1950.

Dugdale, who had been advocating planned industrial development in the colonies since the early 1930s, expressed a concern still prevalent among ministers, and shared by some senior officials, that colonial development should take place 'in an orderly manner, and that it should not be the old scrambles of early capitalist development in this country.'[71] Citing the Nigerian example, Dugdale suggested that colonial governments be encouraged to promote industrial development through local development boards, to include representatives of the local population, rather than by direct government action. Generally, however, he thought that assisted schemes should remain under the permanent management of these boards, and not be transferred after an initial stage to private ownership. He was also keen to protect such schemes from unfair competition, for example from expatriate firms, if necessary by legislation.[72]

When officials in London examined the steps taken to promote development by colonial governments since the war, the pattern which emerged was uneven. The Gold Coast government, for example, had established an Industrial Development Corporation in 1947, to initiate and operate industrial undertakings, and to 'facilitate, promote, guide and assist' the financing of new projects. It had capital resources of £100,000, which were increased in 1950 to £350,000. Although fully operational since 1949, progress had initially been slow, but by mid-1951, some £190,000 had been taken up.

The Corporation's activities represented almost the entire Gold Coast government's contribution to industrial development. The government was the Corporation's sole shareholder, and was to receive any dividends payable. The IDC assisted printing, soap-making, timber and weaving enterprises, and various craft industries such as carving and furniture-making, chiefly by centralised marketing produce. The responsible minister in the Gold Coast did not, however, believe that the Corporation had developed as originally intended. Specifically, he felt the new machinery was concerned too much with providing finance, to the neglect of the investigative and technical aspects of development, largely due to staff shortages, a persistent problem to which no resolution appeared likely in mid-1951.

More fundamentally, the government considered that the recent high world price of cocoa had been an obstacle to industrial development which had discouraged local diversification. The government also doubted whether it would be economical to develop industries for which both power and raw materials would have to be imported. Looking ahead, however, it was thought that the scope for industrialisation would increase once the Volta River hydro-electric project was developed.[73]

The Nigerian government, in contrast, appeared to be more positive about industrialisation. Early in 1949, Governor Macpherson reassured Creech Jones that it was his administration's 'declared policy' to encourage new industrial enterprises beneficial to the territory in spheres not already fully exploited.[74] Similarly, the government claimed that its policy was to provide 'all possible opportunities' for Nigerian businessmen to play an increasing role in the country's commerce, and to develop secondary industries on the widest possible scale by methods ensuring the maximum participation by Nigerians.[75] By May 1950, the Nigerian Director of Commerce and Industry believed that local pressure for industrial development was 'extremely strong', that the available machinery for dealing with these problems was 'quite inadequate', and, in particular, that territorial governments lacked the expertise necessary for more rapid progress.[76]

Lagos's Department of Commerce and Industries was intended chiefly to establish new industries and to recruit qualified expatriate staff. It was not expected to manage enterprises permanently: rather, once financially 'sound', they were to be transferred to African control. Following pressure from the Nigerian Finance Committee, the Department was expanded and given the function of breaking 'new ground so that others can follow'.[77]

The Nigerian government had not been idle since 1945. Having established a Local Development Board in 1946 to provide loan capital to promote a wide range of development schemes, the government decided in 1948 to accelerate development, and encourage small schemes, including industrial projects such as brick and tile-making, soap production, spinning, and weaving.[78] In keeping with the trend towards political decentralisation in the territory, it was also decided to regionalize the development board machinery. This was investigated by Rees-Williams during his trip to West Africa in 1948, his conclusion being that the existing central Board had promoted very few schemes.[79] In the Colonial Office's view, the original body had been on 'too high a level', and was too inaccessible to local entrepreneurs.[80]

In 1949, therefore, Development Boards were established for Nigeria's northern, western and eastern territories, with a total budget of £100,000 per annum, while the Colony Development

Board had a limit of £50,000. The purpose of these boards was not to engage directly in enterprises, but to provide finance.[81] The funding of the boards by the territory's existing marketing boards was itself significant, representing an important break with the previous tendency to reserve funds derived from State marketing for price stabilisation.[82]

Lagos's continuing interest in industrialisation can be seen in its encouragement of a local textile industry, partly in response to growing enthusiasm among local entrepreneurs. Government assistance was provided to two local companies which decided in 1949 to erect textile mills, in Lagos and Kano respectively. These small units were to be capable of rapid growth on the weaving side, and were initially expected to produce up to one-and-a-half million yards of cloth per year. The Kano mill was to be operated by the Kano Citizen Trading Company, partly financed by a loan of £35,000 from the Northern Regional Development Board, with the Department of Commerce and Industries providing technical assistance. The scheme was equipped with reconditioned British looms, made available by the re-equipment of the metropolitan industry.[83] The mill at Lagos was a purely private development, about half the size of the Kano unit, but also receiving assistance from the Department of Commerce and Industries. Both the Nigerian government and the private investors soon realised, however, that if a local textile industry were to expand, it would require the participation of an overseas textile firm in order to obtain adequate capital and expertise.[84] In the government's view, a fundamental problem remained:

> There are no Nigerians at present competent to run textile mills or to undertake the training of operatives and none possess the banking, legal and accounting knowledge which is essential for the successful establishment and running of a mill.[85]

In 1949, the government's own textile development scheme was revised to include powered weaving. The government, still enthusiastic, foresaw the development of a substantial local mechanised industry and established research and training centres. It was hoped that mechanically produced cloth could compete with imported goods. Handweavers were expected to retain their market position and, as the supply of yarn improved, would enjoy lower costs. It was recognised, however, that a much larger market was open to powered weavers, and that handloom weaving would therefore have to take second place. By September 1949, of the eight textile training centres envisaged in the development plan, six were in operation. The training they provided was thought to result in better quality weaving and a higher output, and it was considered necessary to extend training to the skills required in textile mills. Official optimism was shaken when, midway through the territory's ten-year development plan, a review of government sponsored handloom weaving revealed that the effects of training were only temporary and that, when the weavers returned home, they resumed their former, inefficient practices, a problem which indicated a need for greater government supervision of the scheme.[86] Nevertheless, early in 1950 the Governor of Nigeria told the Colonial Office that the training centres' work was stimulating interest in textile production as a village industry throughout the country.[87]

The Colonial Development Corporation

Given the importance of attracting external enterprise to promote development, recognised by both the Colonial Office and the colonial governments, the role of the Colonial Development Corporation in this period is of particular interest. Alhough its initial concern seemed to be with schemes to accelerate raw material and agricultural development, the Corporation gradually began to explore industrial proposals. An early problem, however, was that the CDC preferred larger industrial schemes, geared towards an export market, rather than small units designed to meet local needs; these, it was felt, were the concern of local enterprise.[88] Although the Corporation was theoretically empowered to finance small industries, without itself becoming involved in their control, in practice it was inclined only to deal in large projects, securing the right to participate in their management. Thus, by the end of 1949, capital sanction had been sought for only one scheme involving less than £100,000.[89]

One of the most important West African industrial projects in which the CDC became involved was a textile manufacturing scheme at Onitsha, Nigeria. The plan was to produce sacks, and to establish a cotton-spinning plant. The scheme won Lagos's warm support, being seen as 'an important step in industrialisation', and one which would operate in the interests of the local population.[90]

Initial investigations were made into the possibility of manufacturing twenty million sacks per year from imported jute, enough to meet all West Africa's needs. The Corporation's cotton-spinning plan began with exploratory discussions on co-operation with a British firm, Calico Printers.[91] Under the proposals which subsequently emerged, the CDC would undertake the initial work of establishing a small spinning factory; once the stages of weaving and finishing had been reached, the British firm would become involved.[92] Significantly, relations between the Corporation and the Nigerian government seemed to have improved.[93] The government was so keen to see the Onitsha project started that it offered to collaborate with the CDC if Calico Printers proved to be unwilling.[94]

Yet by late 1949, the CDC was reconsidering its position, following investigations by an independent specialist. The plan was now thought 'too ambitious', precisely because it depended on jute imported from India or Pakistan. Instead, the Corporation chose to consider a smaller project, based on locally grown fibres.[95] In August 1950, Trefgarne, the CDC's chairman, told the Colonial Office that the Corporation proposed to build and operate the combined sack factory and cotton-spinning plant in co-operation with the local marketing boards. This, it was hoped, would provide the boards with the sacks they needed, as well as replacing all the cotton yarns currently imported. In addition, the scheme was expected to promote local production of jute and raw cotton.[96] The scheme secured Treasury approval and, in the Colonial Office, Griffiths was enthusiastic.[97]

Once again, however, difficulties arose. By mid-1951, it was apparent that the project would require considerably more finance than originally envisaged. The CDC therefore chose to reassess the scheme and the likely profitability of both jute and cotton mills.[98] Fundamental problems were subsequently revealed. In the CDC's view, the cotton-spinning scheme was 'a washout' because, contrary to the Nigerian government's prediction, no market could be found for the grey yarn it was to produce. The proposed sack factory had also reached an impasse, since the Nigerian government refused to promote local fibre production, on which the plan depended, until there was a mill to process the produce. The CDC, for its part, refused to erect a mill until it was assured of sufficient supplies of raw material, a caution born of the Corporation's concern at the apparent apathy of the local population towards fibre production. While sympathising with the CDC, the Colonial Office was disappointed, having been very interested when the project was first proposed.[99]

The review of industrial policy

It was while the CDC was investigating West Africa's industrial potential that metropolitan policy on colonial industrialisation again began to exercise the official mind in London. An apparently innocuous request from the West Indian governments for guidance reopened the entire question, prompting an extended debate within the Colonial Office, the first on the subject since the heady days of wartime reconstruction planning.[100] Early in 1950, following a visit by Gorell Barnes to the west Indies, the issue of industrial policy was raised and the Colonial Office decided that a memorandum shouid be drafted, discussing legislation designed to encourage industrial development that was either enacted or under consideration in the colonies. While the memorandum was primarily intended for internal use, it was felt that it might form an appropriate, if belated, sequel to Stanley's despatch of 27 February 1945.[101] At this stage, official caution on the subject was evident. For instance, when Christopher Eastwood, assistant under-secretary responsible for production and marketing, suggested that the development of secondary industries might be mentioned in the Office's annual report, Gorell Barnes advised against this since no policy on the subject had yet been accepted by Cabinet.[102]

Although it was a colonial enquiry which provided the immediate stimulus to discussion in London, the Colonial Office nevertheless had several additional reasons for reviewing its industrial policy. In some territories, notably the Gold Coast, the development of hydro-electric power seemed likely to stimulate, or at least facilitate, industrialisation; following the Anglo–American talks in Washington in September 1949, an increase in US external investment appeared possible; additional development capital was now available from the CDC; and, finally, the basic services on which industrial development would depend were being strengthened by progress, albeit limited, under the colonies' ten-year development plans, and as development gathered pace, so the possibilities for industrialisation were expected to grow.[103]

The Colonial Office's Economic General Department subsequently consulted the geographical departments on the legislation enacted by individual territories to encourage industrial development. In Nigeria's case, the only substantial measure had been the Local Development Board Ordinance of 1946, and the Gold Coast could offer only its Industrial Development Ordinance of 1947. Significantly, a number of the responses revealed a continuing imprecision over the meaning of 'industry'. Even in 1950, the term was being used to describe any economic activity not directly related to agriculture, and was clearly not synonymous with manufacturing.[104] More interesting, however, was the developing analysis of industrial policy within the Colonial Office early in 1950. This discussion involved a review of the first principles of policy, something noticeably absent in the previous five years.

Since 1945, Gorell Barnes observed, the Office had been proceeding under the 'tacit' assumption, first that the State's role should be limited to providing inducements to industrialisation such as short-term tax concessions and, secondly, that the primary object should be to establish industries geared to the use of local raw materials to produce manufactured goods for local consumption. Beyond this, officials were hesitant. For example, the operation of factories by government in their early stages, or the construction of factories by government for sale or lease to industrialists at subsidised rates had not been pursued by officials although they had been discussed by the CEAC after 1943. However, the traditional 'taboo' on industries based on imported raw materials appeared, by 1950, to be less entrenched. Nevertheless, colonial industrialisation had apparently lost little of its controversial flavour. Gorell Barnes saw little point in calling on the Board of Trade for assistance, 'since their attitude towards Colonial industrialisation is not very helpful, to put it mildly.'[105]

In April 1950, Griffiths, Dugdale and senior officials met to discuss industrial policy. This appears to have been the first such discussion at so high a level since the financial crisis of summer 1947. It was agreed that Stanley's 1945 despatch should be examined in the light of experience, with a view to reissuing it.[106] This ministerial intervention was part of a general 'stock-taking' operation, associated particularly with Dugdale, who was similarly interested in reviving the question of mining development under State auspices, an issue largely neglected since Creech Jones's circular *Memorandum on Colonial Mining Policy* of October 1946. However, the re-opening of discussions on industrial development stemmed from the Colonial Office's belief that colonial governments were eager to receive more guidance from Britain.

In May 1950, Aaron Emanuel, assistant secretary in charge of the Economic General Department, produced a detailed memorandum on 'The Promotion of "Secondary" Industry in the Colonies'. In view of growing local pressure for industrial development, and of the inadequacy of local development machinery, Emanuel argued that machinery was needed to keep developments under review. The key problem, judging from the Colonial Office's earlier experiences, was to secure ministerial approval, since only this could guarantee the kind of interdepartmental co-operation necessary for the successful implementation of policy.[107]

It remained unclear how far Stanley's despatch of 1945 had influenced subsequent development. It had been issued before the full scope of the revised Colonial Development and Welfare Act was known and, although progress had subsequently been made in establishing local departments of commerce and industry, local development corporations and the CDC, and in passing legislation to encourage industry, still not enough appeared to have been done to diversify the colonial economies or to absorb surplus populations that were dependent on agriculture. In Emanuel's view, the problem by 1950 was how to accelerate development.[108]

Officials recognised that industrialisation was not necessarily synonymous either with economic diversification or with economic progress.[109] While predominantly monocrop agriculture formed an unsatisfactory basis for development, industrialisation was not seen as the only remedy, other possibilities being the development of diversified agriculture and of mineral and forestry resources. In terms resonant of the Colonial Office's traditional concerns, Emanuel insisted that industrial development could be justified only if the resulting industries could survive in the long-term without special assistance from other economic sectors.

He was similarly cautious in his attitude towards State-assisted industrialisation, which, he noted, was often justified on the grounds that agricultural improvements would create surplus agrarian populations, which industrial development could absorb productively. Emanuel considered this claim to be economically sound only if the 'marginal productivity' of industrial workers exceeded that of agricultural workers. While he believed that

Britain would inevitably be the chief source of capital and enterprise for such development, Emanuel also warned that, however much external assistance were provided, the scope for industrial development was limited unless local conditions were favourable. The conclusion he drew was that a clear demarcation was needed between the local and central fields of responsibility, although it should permit the 'fullest collaboration' between London and the colonial governments. Hitherto, the Colonial Office had not integrated economic development sufficiently into its overall thinking on development, and consultation with territorial governments had been spasmodic. Moreover, no machinery had evolved through which accumulated experience could be transmitted to the colonies.

On the basis of the scanty information received in the Colonial Office, it appeared that most local development plans excluded industrialisation except where this was associated with providing basic services. Industries therefore emerged from no systematic plan, a consequence of the limited support given in Stanley's despatch to government participation, and the continuing belief that industry was primarily a field for private enterprise. Yet private enterprise seemed unlikely to explore colonial industrial potential unless key areas of government policy were clarified, and this required the dissemination of information on local possibilities, the provision of an adequate legislative framework, finance, government organisation and active sponsorship.

Emanuel pointed out that before an industry could be established, basic problems about the scope for development had to be addressed, involving, for example, raw materials, the labour supply and markets, after which local factors had to be assessed to determine the potential for development in specific locations. However, many of these questions could not be resolved solely through local investigation, and it was this which Emanuel saw as a key flaw in existing planning machinery. His proposed solution was the appointment of an expert advisory committee with two broad functions: first, to investigate and report on local conditions relevant to the manufacturing industries that could be established, including those based on imported materials, possibly producing for wider markets; and secondly, to make recommendations, periodically, on industries meriting detailed local investigation. Emanuel envisaged the 'closest' collaboration between this committee and colonial governments through the

Colonial Office. He also proposed the formation of a small inter-departmental committee, composed of officials and chaired by the Colonial Office, to examine existing industrial legislation and any licences and concessions which had resulted from it.

Emanuel saw the CDC as the chief prospective source of non-colonial government finance for industrial development, and he believed that the role of the Corporation should be discussed once the new machinery he suggested had been established. Regarding territorial government machinery, he noted that, despite the encouragement given in Stanley's despatch, few colonial governments had created departments of commerce and industry and that, in some cases where there was scope for industrial development, no single government department was responsible for co-ordinating the government's role. This, he felt, called for a systematic study of local development machinery by the Colonial Office. Finally, he suggested that colonial governments should consider attracting what he called industrial 'tourists', and generally publicising local development opportunities.[110]

Reactions to Emanuel's paper within the Colonial Office were mixed. H.T. Bourdillon, assistant secretary responsible for finance, hoped that his colleagues might be approaching, 'for the first time', a systematic policy on secondary industry, although he reiterated Emanuel's basic point that the essential aim of development was economic *diversification*, rather than the establishment of secondary industries as such.[111] It was the centralising thrust in Emanuel's initiative that officials considered most problematic, involving the risk of local political hostility to detailed planning of development from London. Specifically, doubts were voiced about the value of an advisory committee which might be unwieldy in size and too broad-ranging to be effective; a further drawback was that any industrial consultants engaged would probably have to be paid. More importantly, however, it was felt that the Board of Trade might be unwilling to participate if colonial industrialisation threatened metropolitan exporters, and on this the CEPS seemed likely to support the Board. Hence officials feared that a committee might retard, rather than encourage, development, and political friction was bound to develop if it seemed to colonial opinion that such a body was acting as a brake on development. As Andrew Cohen observed, 'considerable political embarrassment might result if a conflict of interests emerged between Britain and any particular colony'.[112] Cohen suggested the creation of an informal body of experts, rather than the advisory committee proposed by Emanuel. This, he believed, should be consulted on an *ad hoc* basis, but should be available to assist colonial governments as well as to advise the Colonial Secretary.[113]

Equally controversial was the assumption, implicit in Emanuel's paper, that if any colony could develop a secondary industry it should be encouraged to do so, with Colonial Office assistance. In particular, the question of encouraging industries based on imported raw materials remained sensitive. Experience led officials to doubt whether British industry would view the encouragement of such competitive production in the colonies favourably.[114] Nevertheless, any effective review of policy could not evade these questions, as was demonstrated by the Colonial Office's parallel concern to discover how far existing colonial tariffs protected British manufactures from colonial competition and the extent to which colonial tariffs had been amended in recent years to permit the safeguarding of colonial manufactures from British, Dominion and foreign competition. Similarly, the Office wanted to know how far colonial tariffs were imposed on raw materials for industry, and whether the Office itself was normally consulted by colonial governments when tariffs were amended for protective purposes.[115]

At this stage, in mid-1950, the general review of industrial policy received ministerial encouragement from both Dugdale and Griffiths. Following discussions with the Nigerian Director of Commerce and Industry, Dugdale had been impressed with the work Lagos was undertaking to promote small industries, and he proposed informing all colonial governments of the efforts being made by this and other administrations.[116] Similarly, in July 1950, Griffiths took the opportunity provided by the supply debate on the colonial estimates to restate the broad objectives of colonial economic development:

> On the economic side, our aim is to seek to build, in every one of the Territories, a stable economy by developing its agriculture, mineral or industrial resources, by improving methods of production, by safeguarding the natural wealth of the country and instilling 'good husbandry' in all economic activities, and, most important, by diversifying these activities so that development is not lop-sided, and

consequently, dependent on a few basic products.[117]

This represented no radical departure from the principles familiar from the lips of Griffiths's predecessors, especially Stanley and Creech Jones. The Colonial Office still regarded Stanley's memorandum of 1945 as the 'standard text' on industrial development and was, understandably, reluctant at that stage to issue any general 'pronunciamento' on the subject.[118] Nevertheless, Griffiths appears to have injected a degree of dynamism into official discussions, making plain his commitment to progress with diversification and industrialisation.[119]

By July 1950, therefore, two strands were feeding into the Colonial Office's review of industrial policy. First, there was a growing sense that it was important to respond to local needs, prompting the official discussions which led to Emanuel's appraisal. Secondly, there was Dugdale's enthusiasm, reinforced by Griffiths's interest. With characteristic caution, the Colonial Office preferred to delay further action until Griffiths had considered the proposals already at hand, after which the colonial governments could be informed of the policy review.[120]

Late in August 1950, Griffiths and his senior officials discussed Emanuel's proposals. Griffiths was enthusiastic and, unlike some officials, favoured the creation of a committee in London to oversee industrial policy. Furthermore, he called for consultations with the CDC and the FBI, followed by the preparation of a despatch informing colonial governments of the proposals under consideration and seeking their co-operation. Griffiths stressed the importance of promoting diversification and industrialisation as a matter of long-term policy. Consequently, it was agreed that the Board of Trade, the Treasury and the Ministry of Supply should be approached to discuss the establishment of a committee.[121]

As the policy review took shape, officials were reminded of the continuing interest which the Board of Trade was likely to show in the subject. The Board had, for example, recently decided to publish more information on colonial industries and especially on industrial legislation, in its *Journal*. When asked by Lagos for guidance on industrial development in mid-1949, the Board seemed reluctant to help: a year later, Lagos had heard nothing.[122] As Emanuel noted

in discussions with officials of the Board I have learnt that

> they are becoming increasingly perturbed about what they assert is the growth of uneconomic industries in the Colonies.

While this was seen as a 'natural' stance for the Board, the Colonial Office could not assume that the industrial projects being supported by colonial governments *were* economic, even in the long term. It was therefore essential, if the policy set out by Stanley in 1945 were to be successfully defended against criticism from Whitehall, that there should be adequate machinery to keep development under constant review.[123]

The Colonial Office realised that the question of protection would have to be handled carefully when other departments were approached, and it sought to pre-empt their probable unease.[124] It explained that it was necessary to stimulate colonial industrialisation, and to ensure that development took place on 'sound lines', so that the 'industries which are set up have a good chance of maintaining themselves in the long run on a genuine economic basis, i.e. without undue artificial protection.'[125]

The Ministry of Supply's response was guarded. Like the Board of Trade, the Ministry thought it preferable to learn more about what the colonies themselves saw as suitable development opportunities. The Colonial Office therefore decided to proceed alone with a small internal committee, chaired by Gorell Barnes, to examine local legislation designed to encourage industry, although the Office's aim was still to pursue inter-departmental consideration of the subject.[126] The Board of Trade and the Ministry of Supply subsequently relented, and agreed that a body such as the Colonial Office proposed would be desirable, and should contain representatives of metropolitan interests such as the FBI, ensuring the maximum possible co-operation from British industry.[127] Meanwhile, the Colonial Office's own committee decided that the first step was to obtain information from the colonial governments.[128]

A difficulty with Stanley's 1945 despatch was that it gave no guidance on incentives for industrial development such as granting monopolies, import restrictions and subsidies, which were left to the discretion of territorial governments. Unsurprisingly, in the view of officials, few territories had introduced any legislation at all while others had taken steps in a 'partial and piecemeal' fashion on 'quite disparate lines'. It was agreed that present practice was unsatisfactory because information and experience were not pooled effectively nor were they disseminated among the colonies, a problem aggravated by the fact that some colonies with industrial potential lacked adequate government machinery to draft appropriate incentive legislation.[129]

Early in 1951, the Colonial Office's own committee decided that the CDC should be asked for its opinions on the desirability of protection for any colonial industries in which it might participate.[130] The CDC replied that import duties were of little help in encouraging existing industries, which seemed to contradict the widespread consensus that import duties were the most flexible method of protection where the main danger of competition came from imports. Equally, the Corporation believed that exclusive manufacturing licences, while protecting the capitalist against competition within a colony, did not offer any inducement to new undertakings which required heavy capital and whose future profits were uncertain. In contrast, the Colonial Office's Economic General Department believed that where the main risk of competition was internal, an exclusive licence *would* offer a degree of encouragement because it established a monopoly.[131]

The Colonial Office decided that Poynton should discuss British industrial co-operation with Sir Norman Kipping of the FBI.[132] Officials were heartened by Kipping's reaction. The Federation appeared to be sympathetic and anxious that Britain should seize opportunities for 'sound' colonial industrialisation, rather than allowing other countries, such as the United States, to take the lead through fear of the impact of industrialisation on imports from Britain. However, the FBI advocated market research on local demand for consumer goods, enabling the Colonial Office and territorial governments to approach British industry with specific proposals.[133]

The Federation suggested that the British Export Trade Research Organisation (BETRO) could examine the colonial consumer market and the practicability of establishing local manufacturing capacity.[134] BETRO, in turn, proposed a pilot survey of Nigeria to investigate the territory's market potential for locally based industry geared to local consumer needs, possible export markets, and local resources. Its purpose was to identify and attract investors and manufacturers.[135]

The Colonial Office suspected the motives of the FBI and BETRO. Gorell Barnes feared that their attitudes stemmed from a desire to pursue consumer research in the colonies for the benefit of British exporters and warned that BETRO's proposal could be interpreted as an attempt to promote British exports, possibly by restricting local industrialisation. He questioned the value of market research in West Africa, where habits of consumption were relatively well developed, and believed the UAC could provide better information more quickly than BETRO.[136]

The Governor of Nigeria, however, welcomed the proposal for a pilot survey and promised his full assistance.[137] A divergence of views soon emerged between what Lagos and BETRO considered to be industries appropriate for encouragement. The government, it transpired, envisaged mainly the processing of raw materials, including pioneer palm-oil mills, textiles, and sackmaking. BETRO, however, was more interested in light industries requiring high levels of technical skill. Nevertheless, the government told London that it would 'welcome any sound ideas which are likely to enable us to broaden the basis of production, and to induce the investment of foreign capital in this country for productive purposes.'[138]

In June 1951, the FBI's Overseas Trade Policy Committee produced a report in response to the Colonial Office's request for advice and assistance on colonial industrialisation.[139] The Committee felt that 'political stability' was a major consideration for industrialists contemplating colonial investment, and that the perceived risk would be greatly increased by 'premature' movements towards self-government. Specifically, the Committee thought it unlikely that British interests would consider investing in colonial industries without guarantees that profits made could be remitted to Britain to a 'reasonable' degree over an extended period, since new enterprises might initially be unprofitable. Moreover, problems might arise if the management of affairs passed out of British hands, and investors' rights would have to be safeguarded adequately.[140]

The Accra authorities were interested in BETRO's work in Nigeria, and they thought that a similar study in the Gold Coast would be worthwhile.[141] The Colonial Office, however, was already having second thoughts. Its view was that some systematic machinery was required to discover suitable industries and to encourage foreign entrepreneurs to consider development in the colonies, but the entire problem was complex, and no single or easy solution seemed to exist.[142]

Rearmament and industrial policy

Early in 1951, the Colonial Office attempted to use the opportunity provided by the domestic rearmament programme to encourage further inter-departmental consideration of colonial industrialisation. In a paper for the CCD, the Office suggested that the strains that rearmament would place on metropolitan manpower resources made it necessary to examine the help that the colonies might provide in manufacturing military equipment or essential non-military goods. The Office noted that some 'advanced' territories were beginning to industrialise and could use existing factories with under-employed capacity, or new plants drawing on surplus local manpower. Although the Office admitted that little surplus machine capacity probably existed, it was thought that some existing production, for example in East and West Africa, could be transferred to more 'important' work and that, although much of the available labour was industrially unskilled, a 'nucleus' of skilled and semi-skilled labour existed among local ex-servicemen. The Colonial Office argued that the increasingly specialised division of labour in modern industrial production created opportunities for semi-skilled workers and those requiring relatively little instruction, and it cited the example of the female work-force in Britain during the last war.

Officials admitted that it would be expensive to ship heavy raw materials to overseas factories and to transport back finished goods, but they argued that the dispersal of industrial effort need not be limited to heavy metal products, but could include simple plastic mouldings such as those used in motor vehicles and wireless equipment. Some raw materials might, they added, be available locally.

The Office did not favour the establishment of 'shadow' factories, such as Lord Swinton had suggested during the war, whose labour force could be transferred to Britain if circumstances, such as shipping shortages, made it impossible to operate colonial factories in wartime. Officials pointed out that this would be an expensive way of training labour, and would not be in the colonies' long-term interests. The Colonial Office stressed the political advantages of its proposals, arguing that colonial participation in rearmament would demonstrate the British government's desire to associate with the colonial peoples in a common effort.[143]

The CCD agreed that the Colonial Office's proposal should be considered by a working party, chaired by the Central Economic Planning Service (CEPS), comprising representatives of eight interested departments.[144] When the working party met for the first time, in March 1951, it endorsed a suggestion from the CEPS that its work should be limited initially to discussing the problem of linking metropolitan needs to known colonial capacity, and to exploring how Britain's needs could be met by adapting existing colonial capacity. The working party thus avoided more speculative enquiries into the scope for colonial industrialisation from scratch. The Colonial Office's representative, Emanuel, emphasised his department's concern to dispel fears in the colonies that their economies were being developed solely for raw material production, predictably rehearsing the question's political, as well as its economic, dimensions. He also suggested that the use of small-scale workshop capacity in Nigeria and the Gold Coast might be examined. The working party agreed to ask the Colonial Office to compile a questionnaire to be sent to colonial governments, emphasising that the help which the UK supply departments could accept was limited.[145]

The Colonial Office found this approach disheartening. M.A. Willis, a principal within the Economic General Department, described the 'bleak atmosphere' of the working party's discussions. Although the Office was committed to industrialisation, other departments clearly thought differently: 'The policy in all other Departments seems to be the maintenance of full employment in the United Kingdom and it was made clear at the Working Party meetings that Colonies were expected to take second place in the competition for raw materials.' Willis continued:

> If that attitude is to be accepted, and quite frankly I doubt whether any Government at the present time could get away with a policy designed to share employment opportunities between the United Kingdom and the Colonies, then we must consider to what extent we can continue to encourage Colonial Governments to spend their time, and in some cases money, on efforts to persuade investors to set up industries in their territories.

The supply situation reinforced this pessimistic assessment. It was particularly unfortunate that the materials currently in shortest supply, such as non-ferrous metals and light alloys, were precisely those needed in the light engineering industries which the

Colonial Office proposed for the colonies:

> If the U.S.A. and U.K. are going to monopolise all available supplies of these materials up to the point where their industrial potentials are fully occupied, the outlook for the Colonies, even at their present level of industrialisation, is poor. The idea of spreading industrialisation in the Colonies in these circumstances is largely academic.

This posed the problem of whether the Office should warn the colonies of the 'futility' in existing circumstances of fostering industries dependent on scarce materials.[146] While there was sympathy in the Colonial Office with Willis's views, it was also thought that the rate of industrialisation to date had depended not on British government policy, but on basic conditions in the colonies. In other words, whether or not the metropolitan government were united on policy, efforts were apparently continuing locally to develop suitable industries, many of them based on locally available materials.[147]

Nevertheless, further disturbing evidence of the government's attitude to colonial industrialisation emerged in August 1951. Asked in the Commons about the possibility of manufacturing munitions in the West Indies, John Strachey, the Secretary of State for War, stressed the importance of the colonies concentrating on primary production, and appeared to discount the role of industrialisation in colonial development.[148] The Colonial Office was understandably anxious to establish whether Strachey had been airing personal views, or whether he was expressing opinions held generally by his Cabinet colleagues. If the latter were true, as the already despondent Willis observed, 'then we in the C.O. are working under a misapprehension and the quicker we realise it the better'. He continued:

> I have felt for some time and I have said as much on occasion, that we are fighting a lone battle in this matter of industrialisation in the Colonies. Other Departments, and the F.B.I. for that matter, seem to me to be paying only lip-service to our policy.[149]

The particular delicacy of this question was reflected in Griffiths's subsequent admonitory letter to Strachey. Reminding Strachey that it was the government's policy to encourage colonial industrialisation, Griffiths added,

> Colonial communities are aware of this and, in the present state of political consciousness, any suggestion that the development and diversification of their economy by industrial development should be held back in favour of continued concentration upon primary production for the benefit of the United Kingdom, would be liable to serious misunderstanding and criticism.[150]

These discouraging indicators were confirmed when the inter-departmental committee concluded that an investigation into a colonial contribution to rearmament would serve no useful purpose. Having examined the items which might be required from the colonial empire, the working party concluded that these were not of a broad enough range to merit asking colonial governments to survey local resources, and that the most that could be done would be to ensure that metropolitan supply departments recognised the possibility of using colonial capacity where opportunities arose.[151]

NOTES

1. Cairncross (1985), 165–211.
2. Hinds (1987), p.164.
3. Cairncross (1985), pp.22, 66.
4. Cmd.8243, *The Colonial Territories (1950–51)*, (May 1951).
5. Cairncross (1985), pp.21, 212–33; Morgan (1984), pp.456–60.
6. CAB 134/64, CD(49)9, 'Dollar situation and the colonies', 1 July 1949.
7. CO 852/1039/6, CCD Working party on submission of information to ECA, 2nd meeting, 4 July 1949.
8. Ibid., minutes by Emanuel and Gorell Barnes, 11 July 1949.
9. Ibid., minute by Poynton, 28 Sept. 1949.
10. T 229/144, letter to Cripps, 3 Oct. 1949.
11. CAB 134/65, Report of the CDWP, 11 Oct. 1948.
12. CO 852/1041/1, CEDC(49)19, 12 May 1949.
13. Morgan (1980) II, pp.23–4.
14. CAB 134/64, CCD 2nd meeting, 25 Jan. 1949.
15. CAB 134/65, CD(49)10, 'Price differentials in colonial imports', 30 Mar. 1949.
16. Ibid., CD(49)16, 11 Apr. 1949.
17. CAB 134/64, CD(49) 5th meeting, 12 Apr. 1949.
18. Buxton and Aldcroft (1979), p.44.
19. CO 852/834/3, Colonial Supplies Conference, minutes, 10 June 1949.
20. Ibid.; see also Dupree (1987) II p.503.
21. BT 175/5, CB 7860a, CB 35th meeting, 6 Sept. 1949. Fears for Lancashire's future persisted. In July 1950, the President of the Board of Trade reminded the Economic Policy Committee of the need to deal with Japanese competition in colonial markets, arguing that agreements on this reached between Japan and the sterling area late in 1948 were no longer adequate. See CAB 134/226, EPC(50)82, 'Colonial textile

requirements from Japan 1950/51', 25 July 1950.
22. CAB 134/64, CD(49) 7th meeting, 30 May 1949.
23. CAB 134/64, CD(49)9, 'Dollar situation in the colonies', 1 July 1949.
24. Morgan (1980) II, p.29.
25. CAB 134/65, CD(49)39, 'Alteration in the sterling–dollar exchange rates. Implications for the colonies', 22 Oct. 1949.
26. CAB 134/64, CCD 2nd meeting, 25 Jan. 1949.
27. Ibid., CCD 3rd meeting, 28 Mar. 1949.
28. CO 537/5194, letter to Creech Jones, 5 Apr. 1949.
29. CAB 134/65, CD(49)14, '1949 Dollar Ceilings', 8 Apr. 1949.
30. CAB 134/66, CD(50) 1st meeting, 13 Jan. 1949.
31. Morgan (1980) II, pp.25–6.
32. CAB 134/65, CD(49)27, 'Price differentials', 29 June 1949.
33. CO 852/1039/6, circular telegram, 4 July 1949.
34. Ibid., circular telegram, 18 July 1949.
35. Ibid., circular telegram, 26 Aug. 1949.
36. CAB 134/65, CD(49)36, 'Colonial dollar imports – July, 1949 to December, 1950', 20 Sept. 1949.
37. CAB 134/66, CD(50)3, '1950 Dollar Ceilings', 11 Jan. 1950; (this figure did not include expenditure proposed by the CDC or the OFC, see CD(50) 1st meeting, 13 Jan. 1950).
38. CAB 134/66, CD(50)26, 'Colonial dollar imports', 2 June 1950.
39. Ibid., CD(50)29, 'Import programmes and dollar ceilings 1951', 30 June 1950.
40. CO 852/1041/2, 'Survey of inflationary and deflationary tendencies in the colonies', 21 July 1949.
41. Cmd.8243, (May 1951).
42. CAB 134/263, ES(50)30, 'Economic implications of rearmament to the colonial territories', 23 Dec. 1950; CAB 134/264, ES(51) 1st meeting 11 Jan. 1951.
43. CAB 134/67, CD(51)5, 'Colonial dollar expenditure', 2 Feb. 1951; Cmd.8243, May 1951.
44. Rathbone (1993), pp.lv–lvii.
45. CAB 134/67, CD(51)12, 'Supplies for colonial development', 1 Aug. 1951.
46. Ibid., CD(51) 2nd meeting, 15 Aug. 1951.
47. CO 852/878/1, circular despatch, 24 Jan. 1949.
48. Morgan (1980) II, p.50–51.
49. CO 852/1325/2, 'Sources of financial assistance available to small industrial and agricultural enterprises in the colonies', 8 May 1950.
50. Morgan (1980) II, p.52.
51. CAB 134/67, CD(51)16, 'Applications to the Capital Issues Committee in respect of colonial enterprises during 1951', 1 Nov. 1951.
52. CAB 134/65, CD(49)7, 'President Truman's "Fourth Point" (Annex A)', 14 Mar. 1949.
53. Ibid.
54. Ibid.
55. Morgan (1980) II, p.102.
56. E.g. CO 537/5193, telegram from Macpherson (Nigeria), 25 Mar. 1949.
57. Ibid., minute by Gorsuch, 28 Mar. 1949.
58. CAB 134/65, CD(49)15, 'Colonial implications of President Truman's "Fourth Point"', 9 Apr. 1949; CO 852/1040/4, CEDC 2nd meeting, 23 May 1949.
59. CAB 134/65, CD(49)15, 9 Apr. 1949; Whitehall's discussions on Point Four also produced a significant, and rare, indication of a continuing metropolitan concern to protect colonial markets. In March 1949, the CCD was advised that US technical assistance in development was preferable to supplies, because the latter might compete with British exports (CAB 134/64, CD(49) 3rd meeting, 28 Mar. 1949).

60. CO 537/5192, minute by Emanuel, 14 Apr. 1949.
61. Morgan (1980) II, p.104.
62. CAB 134/222, EPC(49)74, 'Investment of foreign capital in the colonies', 5 July 1949.
63. CAB 128/16, CM 51(49)1, 29 July 1949.
64. Morgan (1980) II, p.104; CO 852/840/2, supplementary record of 14th meeting with CDC, 17 Sept. 1949.
65. CAB 134/64, CD(49) 12th meeting, 22 Sept. 1949.
66. Morgan (1980) II, p.104; the committee, chaired by the Treasury, included representatives from the Foreign Office, the Colonial Office, the Board of Trade, the Commonwealth Relations Office, the CEPS and the Bank of England.
67. Morgan (1980) II, p.105–6.
68. *PD(C)*, 476, 221–2, 28 June 1950.
69. CO 537/7233.
70. Quoted in J.M. Lee, *Colonial Development and Good Government: a study of the ideas expressed by the British official classes in planning decolonisation, 1939–1964*, (Oxford: Oxford University Press, 1967), p.112.
71. *PD(C)*, 477, 1490, 12 July 1950; P.S. Gupta, *Imperialism and the British Labour Movement* (London: Macmillan, 1975), p.243.
72. CO 852/1325/2, minute, 6 July 1950.
73. Ibid., 'Sources of financial assistance available to small industrial and agricultural enterprises in the colonies', 8 May 1950; CO 96/830/31695/1951, minute by Unsworth, 7 Feb. 1951; CO 852/1325/4, Arden-Clarke to Griffiths, 17 May 1951.
74. CO 537/5193, telegram to Creech Jones, 25 Mar. 1949.
75. CO 583/311/30699/1950, telegram to Griffiths, 21 Apr. 1950.
76. CO 852/1323/5, minute by Emanuel, 22 May 1950.
77. CO 852/1325/2, minute by Vile, 6 Apr. 1950.
78. CO 583/295/30676/1949, note on Regional Development Boards, 7 Sept. 1949.
79. CO 852/840/2, minutes of 14th meeting with CDC (12 Sept. 1949), 17 Sept. 1949.
80. CO 583/295/30676/1949, minutes of 14th meeting with CDC, 12 Sept. 1949.
81. Ibid., note on Regional Development Boards, 7 Sept. 1949.
82. A.E. Hinds, 'British imperial policy and the development of the Nigerian economy, 1939–1951', unpublished Ph.D. thesis, Dalhousie University, (1985), p.263.
83. Ekundare (1973), pp.302–303; Kilby (1969), pp.112, 312–15.
84. Ekundare (1973), p.303.
85. CO 583/311/30699/1950, 'Proposals for the expansion of the Department of Commerce and Industries', Sept. 1949.
86. Kilby (1969), pp.311–12.
87. CO 583/311/30699/1950, telegram, 21 Apr. 1950.
88. CO 852/840/2, note of meeting with CDC, 11 Apr. 1949.
89. CO 852/1325/2, 'Sources of financial assistance available to small industrial and agricultural enterprises in the colonies', 8 May 1949.
90. CO 583/307/30498/1/1950, Macpherson to Griffiths, 21 Aug. 1950.
91. CO 583/295/30676/1949, minute by Eastwood, 15 Aug. 1949.
92. CO 852/842/2, Quarterly report on schemes under active consideration No. 6, (September–November 1949), Jan. 1950.
93. CO 583/295/30676/1949, minute by Eastwood, 15 Aug. 1949.
94. CO 852/842/2, Quarterly report ... No. 6, Jan. 1950.
95. Ibid.; CO 583/307/30498/1/1950, supplementary record of meeting with CDC, 7 Feb. 1950.
96. Ibid., letter to Griffiths, 9 Aug. 1950.
97. Ibid., Mackay (Treasury) to Willis (CO), 25 Aug. 1950; Griffiths to Trefgarne, 31 Aug. 1950.
98. CO 583/307/30498/1/1951, letter from Winterbotham (CDC), 5 June 1951.

99. Ibid., minute by Willis, 3 Aug. 1951.
100. CO 852/1323/5, 'The promotion of "secondary" industry in the colonies', 22 May 1950.
101. Ibid., note of meeting in Colonial Office, 17 Feb. 1950; CO 852/1324/4, minute by Adie, 21 Mar. 1950.
102. Ibid. (both references).
103. CO 852/1323/5, 'The promotion of "secondary" industry in the colonies', 22 May 1950.
104. CO 852/1324/4, minutes by Adie, 21 Mar., Vile, 23 Mar., and Hanrott, 30 Mar. 1950.
105. CO 852/1323/5, minute, 20 Apr. 1950.
106. Ibid., minute by Roberts, 24 Apr. 1950.
107. Ibid., minute, 22 May 1950.
108. Ibid., 'The promotion of "secondary" industry in the colonies', 22 May 1950.
109. Ibid. minute by Rogers, 30 May 1950.
110. Ibid., 'The promotion of "secondary" industry ...'.
111. Ibid., minute by H.T. Bourdillon, 30 May 1950.
112. Ibid., minutes by Rogers, 30 May, Mayle, 6 June, Gorsuch, 9 June and Cohen, 10 June 1950.
113. Ibid., minute, 10 June 1950.
114. Ibid., minute by Gorsuch, 9 June 1950.
115. CO 852/1325/1, minute by Adie, 14 June 1950.
116. CO 852/1325/2, minute, 6 July 1950.
117. *PD(C)*, 477, 1369, 12 July 1950.
118. CO 852/1324/4, Emanuel to Carstairs, 14 July 1950.
119. CO 852/1323/5, note of meeting, 30 Aug. 1950.
120. Ibid., minute by Gorell Barnes, 28 July 1950.
121. Ibid., note of meeting, 30 Aug. 1950.
122. CO 852/1325/2, Cox (Nigeria) to Gorell Barnes, 28 June 1950.
123. CO 852/1323/5, minute, 22 May 1950.
124. CO 852/1325/2, minute by Gorell Barnes, 28 July 1950.
125. CO 852/1323/5, letter from Poynton, 4 Sept. 1950.
126. CO 852/1325/3, EOD No.127, 'Office committee on encouragement of industry legislation', 9 Oct. 1950; OCLI(50)3, 'Legislation in the colonies to encourage the development of secondary industries', Oct. 1950.
127. CO 852/1323/5, Rowlands (Ministry of Supply) to Poynton, 20 Sept 1950; Woods (BoT) to Poynton, 20 Oct. 1950; ibid., note of meeting in CO, 26 Oct. 1950.
128. CO 852/1325/1, OCLI 1st meeting, (23 Oct. 1950), 2 Nov. 1950; CO 852/1325/3, circular despatch, 'Industrial development in the colonies', 10 Nov. 1950.
129. Ibid., OCLI(50)2, 'The promotion of "secondary" manufacturing industry in the colonies', Oct. 1950.
130. CO 852/1325/5, OCLI(51) 3rd meeting, 8 Jan. 1951.
131. Ibid., comments on CDC memo., 'Encouragement of capital investment in the colonies by legislative action, 24 Jan. 1951', Mar. 1951.
132. CO 852/1323/5, note of meeting, 26 Oct. 1950.
133. Ibid., minutes by Poynton, 8 Dec. 1950 and Emanuel, 13 Dec. 1950.
134. CO 852/1323/6, Griffiths to Macpherson, 2 Mar. 1951.
135. Ibid.; Macpherson to Griffiths, 13 Mar. 1951; Roberts to Director General, BETRO, 17 Mar. 1951.
136. Ibid., minute, 24 Feb. 1951.
137. Ibid., Macpherson to Griffiths, 13 Mar. 1951.
138. Ibid., Macpherson to Poynton, 9 Apr. 1951.
139. CO 852/1325/6, 'Industrial legislation in the colonies affecting the establishment of secondary industries', 14 June 1951.

140. Ibid.
141. CO 852/1333/7, letter from Tours (Minister of Finance, Gold Coast), 25 June 1951; Emanuel to Tours, 27 July 1951; Tours to Emanuel, 13 Aug. 1951.
142. Ibid., letter from Emanuel, 27 July 1951.
143. CAB 134/67, CD(51)4, 'The use of colonial industrial and manpower capacity in the United Kingdom rearmament programme', 25 Jan. 1951.
144. Ibid., CD(51) 1st meeting, 6 Feb. 1951; the departments were the Treasury, the Colonial Office, the Ministry of Defence, the Admiralty, the Board of Trade, the Ministry of Supply, the Ministry of Transport and the Ministry of Labour.
145. T 229/263, minutes of working party meeting (30 Mar. 1950), 3 Apr. 1951
146. CO 852/1323/6, minute by Willis, 8 May 1951.
147. Ibid., minutes by Emanuel, 22 May 1951 and Gorell Barnes, 23 May 1951.
148. *PD(C)* 491, 1645, 2 Aug. 1951.
149. CO 852/1323/6, minute, 8 Aug. 1951.
150. Ibid., Griffiths to Strachey, 21 Aug. 1951.
151. CAB 134/67, CD(51) 2nd meeting, 15 Aug. 1951.

Conclusion

Between 1939 and 1951, the Colonial Office evolved a policy on the industrialisation of the colonies which remained broadly consistent throughout the period. This policy, growing from tentative beginnings, owed its development above all to the experience of the inter-war Depression and to the impact of the Second World War on the colonial economies. These factors convinced the Colonial Office of the need to promote the diversification of the colonial economies. The Colonial Office had little experience in dealing with such questions and, for much of the period examined in this book, lacked clear guidelines on the implications of metropolitan government economic policy for its own deliberations. Once formulated, the Office's goals remained vulnerable to a spectrum of fluctuating circumstances and deep-rooted obstacles.

While increasingly recognising a need for local industrial growth, the Colonial Office saw this as only one element in a broad strategy of economic development designed to prepare the colonies for eventual self-government. The more immediately relevant problem of promoting greater agricultural productivity remained. Similarly, officials spent much time considering a strand of policy that could potentially have conflicted with industrial development, namely the stabilisation of predominantly agricultural colonial economies through controlled primary produce marketing. Arguably, the two strands of policy were not mutually exclusive, but could be seen to be complementary. Yet the special conditions of wartime need and post-war dislocation gave stabilisation a wider appeal than industrial development: whereas the former offered an attractive supplementary role in indirectly supporting sterling, the latter could be interpreted as endangering metropolitan interests, either directly by encroaching on colonial export markets, or indirectly, by distracting colonial efforts from the primary production that was temporarily lucrative for the British economy.

Like other departments in Whitehall, especially the Board of Trade, the Colonial Office consistently sought to promote 'sound' and 'economic' industrial development, although its motives were different. The Office displayed a realism eclipsed elsewhere by an unfocused metropolitan enthusiasm for 'reconstruction'. This realism was the product of disappointing experiences of colonial development following the brief post-1918 'boom', the consequences of the Depression, and protracted negotiations with the Treasury in the later 1930s to secure colonial development and welfare funding. Moreover, the Office displayed a continuing sensitivity to the broad range of external criticism to which it was exposed and, for most of this period, it had a fear of encouraging unrealistic expectations of what was achievable in colonial development.

The successful implementation of the Colonial Office's development policies, united in their common respect for the new icon, 'planning', required a reappraisal of the machinery of colonial administration, both in London and in the colonies. The inadequacies revealed in this extended analysis were not satisfactorily resolved during this period, but they exposed and emphasised the delicate relationship between the Colonial Office and the colonial governments. Barely had the Office grasped the nettle of a greater central initiative in development when circumstances in West Africa seemed to dictate an emphasis on an authentically local contribution, avoiding any impression that London's role was to direct, rather than to guide. Moreover, the critical steps towards shaping industrial policy were taken by the Office in response to promptings from West Africa, especially during the war. Despite its transient enthusiasm for an enhanced role in promoting development, therefore, on a fundamental issue such as industrialisation, the Office found itself still reacting to local initiatives and developments which it never learned to anticipate. By the end of the period examined in this book, new political demands were being articulated within the colonies, especially in West Africa, and these demands made the development schedule that had been assumed during the 'reconstruction' debate largely redundant. Consequently, the development formulae produced by this debate had to be hastily revised, therefore, with a reversal, in West Africa's case, of the former orthodoxy that painstaking *economic* development must precede self-rule.

Similarly, during these years, the Colonial Office achieved only limited success in addressing what it perceived to be fundamental problems of promoting colonial industrialisation, namely the provision of capital, expertise and entrepreneurship. These broad questions were of extreme delicacy in the West African context. A continuing reliance on expatriate capital as the engine of development was considered by officials, and especially those with 'geographical' responsibilities, to be unwise given the extent of local hostility towards large foreign firms: a political dimension was insinuated into the arena of development which the Colonial Office dared not ignore.

The ensuing discussions on extending the legitimate boundaries of State economic intervention raised fundamental questions about the scope for direct government operation of enterprises (something which, significantly, was never greatly favoured), the role of 'development commissions' and the potential value of publicly controlled development corporations. There was a circularity in these discussions, reflecting the recurring disappointment of initial hopes. For instance, the development commission idea, an early attempt to satisfy requirements thought to be essential to progress, was translated eventually into the concept of the development corporation, itself, ironically, a vehicle increasingly attractive to big business, whose potentially unpalatable characteristics it had originally been devised to circumvent. When the development corporation, embodied in the CDC, fell short of the Colonial Office's expectations, pursuing a trajectory more in keeping with Treasury ambitions than with the Office's, the need for investigative bodies much like 'development commissions' received renewed attention from the Office.

The outward unanimity of the official voice concealed important divisions of opinion within the Colonial Office. For example, some, like Gerard Clauson, while recognising the shortcomings of pre-war policy, continued to think largely in pre-war categories, resisting potentially 'dangerous' experimentation in development, sceptical about an expanded role for the colonial State and ultimately sympathetic to expatriate capital. Political pressures, rather than ideological conviction, gradually turned the weight of official opinion in favour of greater State intervention.

The arrival of Creech Jones, a political head frankly committed to public enterprise, only accentuated a tendency that already existed among officials.

A factor tending towards cohesion in the 'official mind', however, was the Colonial Office's uneasy relationship with externally recruited 'specialist' opinion: officials often justifiably suspected outsiders' limited grasp of the complexity of colonial issues. For much of this period, officials were torn between admitting their own incapacity and lack of information and opening the development debate to uncontrollable contributions from metropolitan interest groups, whether motivated commercially or politically, or from an emerging and ascendent generation of technocrats.

It was the resilience of entrenched metropolitan attitudes towards the colonies, perhaps more than anything else, that gave the Colonial Office an external threat which encouraged internal unity. Increased contact with other Whitehall departments during this period, together with recurrent exposure to criticism, taught the Office to handle colonial questions, and especially industrialisation, with tact and caution. Attempts were made, generally without success, to tailor the presentation of the Office's policies so as to reflect dominant attitudes in Whitehall. Only briefly, at the height of the reconstruction planning debate, did the Office display much public confidence in its policy on manufacturing, and then it only did so because of the Board of Trade's apparent acquiescence.

The changing climate in Whitehall after the war, with renewed indications of metropolitan hostility, found the Office reverting to its pre-war diffidence: during 1947–48, colonial industrialisation was scarcely mentioned. Having gathered momentum during the war, officials' interest in the subject dissipated in the confusion surrounding the post-war crisis. The Colonial Office gradually resumed its discussions on manufacturing, once more in response to prompting from the periphery, only to encounter again the indifference, and even the opposition, of other departments.

The Colonial Office was commonly obliged to proceed without clear indications of the intentions of other departments. Officials sifted through fragments of information in order to construct a broad sense of predominant metropolitan attitudes to colonial industrialisation. This was made all the more difficult when contradictory signals were detected, or when the practice of other departments, especially the Board of Trade, belied stated policy.

The Colonial Office failed, in these years, to overcome a long-standing metropolitan predisposition to assume the complementarity of the British and colonial economies: such claims received new currency after 1947, when a division of labour on 'neo-mercantilist' lines held strong attractions for a British government enduring repeated financial crises while engaged in major domestic social reform. The practical consequences were seen in ever-increasing metropolitan control over colonial economic activity and imports. At the end of the period studied, the Colonial Office had not succeeded in persuading the rest of Whitehall to embrace its catholic interpretation of 'development' as a series of interlocking processes that reinforced one another towards the goal of viable nationhood: instead, attitudes of an older pedigree resurfaced, geared to the protection of sterling and British living standards.

Biographical Notes

BOURDILLON, Sir Bernard (1883–1948). St. John's College, Oxford. Indian Civil Service, 1908–17. Service in Mesopotamia and Iraq, 1918–29. Colonial and Chief Secretary, Ceylon, 1929–32. Governor, Uganda, 1932–35. Governor, Nigeria, 1935–43. Member of CEAC and CEDC. Director, Barclays Bank DCO and Barclays Overseas Development Corporation.

BURNS, Sir Alan (1887–1980). Colonial Secretary, Bahamas, 1924–29. Deputy Chief Secretary, Nigeria, 1929–34. Governor, British Honduras, 1934–40. Assistant Under-Secretary, Colonial Office, 1940–41. Governor, Gold Coast, 1941–47. Acting Governor, Nigeria, 1942. Permanent UK representative, UN Trusteeship Council, 1947–56.

CAINE, Sir Sydney (1902–91). London School of Economics. Entered Colonial Office, 1926. Secretary, West Indian Sugar Commission, 1929. Secretary, UK Sugar Industry Inquiry Committee, 1934. Financial Secretary, Hong Kong, 1937. Assistant Secretary, Colonial Office, 1940. Member, Anglo–American Caribbean Commission, 1942. Financial Adviser to Colonial Secretary, 1942. Assistant Under-Secretary, Colonial Office, 1944. Deputy Under-Secretary, Colonial Office, 1947–48. Third Secretary, Treasury, 1948. Head of UK Treasury and Supply Delegation, Washington, 1949–51. Chief, World Bank Mission to Ceylon, 1951. Director, London School of Economics, 1957–67.

CAMPBELL, Sir John (1874–1944). Glasgow University; Christ Church, Oxford. Entered Indian Civil Service, 1897. Under-Secretary to Government of United Provinces, Under-Secretary to Government of India. Director of Civil Supplies for United Provinces. Economic and Financial Adviser, Colonial Office, 1930–42.

CARSTAIRS, Charles Young (1910–93). Edinburgh University. Entered Dominions Office, 1934. Transferred to Colonial Office, 1935. Assistant Private Secretary to Colonial Secretary, 1936. Private Secretary to Permanent Under-Secretary, Colonial Office, 1937. Assistant Secretary, West India Royal Commission, 1938–39. Administrative Secretary,

Development and Welfare Organisation, British West Indies, 1947–50. Secretary, British Caribbean Standing Closer Association Committee, 1948–49. Director, Information Services, Colonial Office, 1951–53. Assistant Secretary, Colonial Office, 1953–62.

CARTLAND, Sir George Barrington (b.1912). Manchester University; Hertford College, Oxford. Entered Colonial Service, Gold Coast, 1935. Joined Colonial Office, 1944. Head of African Studies Branch and editor, *Journal of African Administration*, 1945–49. Secretary, London African Conference, 1948. Administrative Secretary, Uganda, 1949. Secretary for Social Services and Local Government, Uganda, 1952. Minister for Social Services, Uganda, 1955. Minister of Education and Labour, Uganda, 1958. Chief Secretary, Uganda, 1960. Deputy Governor, Uganda, 1961–62.

CLAUSON, Sir Gerard (1891–1974). Corpus Christi, Oxford. Entered Colonial Office, 1919. Member, UK Delegation, Imperial Economic Conference, 1932, and Monetary and Economic Conference, London, 1933. Assistant Secretary, Colonial Office, 1934. Assistant Under-Secretary, Colonial Office, 1940–51. Member, UK Delegation to Hot Springs Conference, 1943.

COHEN, Sir Andrew B. (1909–68). Trinity College, Cambridge. Entered Inland Revenue Department, 1932. Transferred to Colonial Office, 1933. Assistant Secretary, Colonial Office, 1943. Superintending Assistant Secretary, 1947. Assistant Under-Secretary, 1947–51. Governor, Uganda, 1952–57. Permanent British representative, UN Trusteeship Council, 1957–61. Director-General, Department of Technical Co-operation, 1961–64. Permanent Secretary, Ministry of Overseas Development, 1964–68. Publications include *British Policy in Changing Africa* (London: Routledge & Kegan Paul, 1959).

CREASY, Sir Gerald (1897–1983). Entered Colonial Office 1920. Chief Secretary to West African Council, 1945–47. Governor, Gold Coast, 1947–49. Governor, Malta, 1949–54. Retired 1954.

DAWE, Sir Arthur (1891–1950). Brasenose College, Oxford. Entered Colonial Office, 1918. Deputy Secretary, Imperial Economic Conference, 1923. Secretary, Commission of Enquiry into Affairs of Freetown Municipality, 1926. Secretary, Malta Royal Commission, 1931. Member, British Government delegation to International Labour Conference, 1946. Assistant Under-Secretary, Colonial Office, 1938–45. Deputy Under-Secretary of State, 1945–47. Retired 1947.

DUGDALE, John (1905–63). Wellington; Christ Church, Oxford. Attaché, British Legation, Peking, 1926–27. Private Secretary to C.R.A. Attlee, 1931–39. Member, London County Council, 1932–41. MP

(Labour), 1941–63. PPS to Deputy Prime Minister, 1945. Parliamentary and Financial Secretary, Admiralty (1945–50). Minister of State for Colonial Affairs, 1950–51.

DURBIN, Evan (1906–48). New College, Oxford. University Lecturer. Joined Economic Section, War Cabinet Secretariat, 1940. Personal Assistant to Deputy Prime Minister, 1942. MP (Labour) 1945–48. Parliamentary Secretary to Ministry of Works, 1947–48.

EASTWOOD, Christopher G. (1905–83). Trinity College, Oxford. Entered Civil Service, 1927, and appointed to Colonial Office. Private Secretary to High Commissioner, Palestine, 1932–34. Secretary, International Rubber Regulation Committee, 1934. Private Secretary to Secretary of State for the Colonies, 1940–41. Principal Assistant Secretary, Cabinet Office, 1945–47. Assistant Under-Secretary of State, Colonial Office, 1947–52, and 1954–66. Commissioner of Crown Lands, 1952–54.

EMANUEL, Aaron (b.1912). London School of Economics. Economist, International Institute of Agriculture, Rome, 1935–38. Joined Board of Trade, 1938, Ministry of Food, 1940, Colonial Office, 1943, Ministry of Health, 1961, Department of Economic Affairs, 1965, Ministry of Housing and Local Government, 1969. Under-Secretary, Department of the Environment, 1970–72. Chairman, West Midlands Economic Planning Board, 1968–72.

FIRTH, Raymond (b.1901). Auckland University College; London School of Economics. Professor of Anthropology, University of London, 1944–68. Secretary, Colonial Social Science Research Council.

GATER, Sir George (1886–1963). New College, Oxford. Assistant Director of Education for Nottinghamshire, 1912–14. Director of Education, Lancashire County Council, 1919–24. Education Officer, London County Council, 1924–33. Clerk of the Council, 1933–39. Permanent Under-Secretary of State, Colonial Office, 1939–47. Seconded as Joint Secretary, Ministry of Home Security, 1939–40. Secretary, Ministry of Supply, 1940. Secretary, Ministry of Home Security, 1940–42.

GOODENOUGH, Sir William (1899–1951). Christ Church, Oxford. Chairman, Oxfordshire County Council, 1934–37. Chairman, Barclays Bank Ltd, 1947–51.

GORELL BARNES, Sir William (1909–87). Pembroke College, Cambridge. Served in HM Diplomatic Service, 1932–39, and offices of War Cabinet, 1939–45. Personal Assistant to Lord President of the Council, 1942–45. Assistant Secretary, Treasury, 1945–46. Personal

Assistant to Prime Minister, 1946–48. Seconded to Colonial Office, 1948. Assistant Under-Secretary of State, 1948–59. Deputy Under-Secretary of State, 1959–63. Member, UK delegation for negotiations with EEC, 1962. Retired 1963.

GRIFFITHS, James (1890–1975). Trade union official, 1916–36. MP (Labour) 1936–70. Minister of National Insurance, 1945–50. Secretary of State for the Colonies, 1950–51. Secretary of State for Wales, 1964–66. Deputy Leader and Vice-Chairman, Parliamentary Labour Party, 1956–59.

HAILEY, Lord (William Michael Hailey) (1872–1969). Corpus Christi, Oxford. Entered Indian Civil Service, 1895. Chief Commissioner, Delhi, 1912–18. Governor, Punjab, 1924–28. Governor, United Provinces, 1928–30 and 1931–34. Director, African Research Survey, 1935–38. Member, Permanent Mandates Commission, League of Nations, 1935–39. Chairman, Colonial Research Committee, 1943–48. Deputy Chairman, Royal African Society, 1949–59.

HALL, George (1st Viscount Hall) (1881–1965). Trade union official, 1911–22. MP (Labour) 1922–46. Civil Lord of the Admiralty, 1929–31. Parliamentary Under-Secretary of State, Colonial Office, 1940–42. Financial Secretary to the Admiralty, 1942–43. Parliamentary Under-Secretary, Foreign Office, 1943–45. Secretary of State for the Colonies, 1945–46. First Lord of the Admiralty, 1946–51. Deputy Leader, House of Lords, 1947–51.

HALL, Noel (1902–83). Brasenose College, Oxford. Professor of Political Economy, University of London, 1935–38. Director, National Institute for Economic and Social Research, 1938–43. Joint Director, Ministry of Economic Warfare, 1940. Minister in charge of War Trade Department, British Embassy, Washington, 1941–43. Development Adviser, West Africa, 1943–45.

HANCOCK, Sir Keith (Professor. Sir William Keith) (1898–1988). All Souls, Oxford. Professor of Modern History, University of Adelaide, 1924–33. Professor of History, University of Birmingham, 1934–44. Chichele Professor of Economic History, Oxford, 1944–49. Director, Institute of Commonwealth Studies (University of London) and Professor of British Commonwealth Affairs, 1949–56. Director, Research School of Social Sciences, Australian National University, 1957–61. Appointed to Offices of War Cabinet as Supervisor of Civil Histories, 1941, thereafter editor of series.

HENDERSON, Sir Hubert (1890–1952). Emmanuel College, Cambridge. Secretary, Cotton Control Board, 1917–19. Fellow, Clare College, Cambridge and University Lecturer in Economics, 1919–23. Editor,

Nation and Athenaeum, 1923–30. Joint Secretary, Economic Advisory Council, 1930–34. Member, West India Royal Commission, 1938–39. Chairman, Royal Commission on Population, 1946. Economic Adviser, Treasury, 1939–44. Chairman, Statutory Committee on Unemployment Insurance, 1945–48. Professor of Political Economy, Oxford, 1945–51.

HINDEN, Rita (1909–71). London School of Economics. Secretary, Fabian Colonial Bureau, 1940–50. Member, Colonial Labour Advisory Committee and Colonial Economic Development Council, 1948–51. Member, British Guiana Constitutional Commission, 1950–51. Editor, *Socialist Commentary*, 1951–71.

JEFFRIES, Sir Charles (1896–1972). Magdalen College, Oxford. Entered Colonial Office, 1917 after being invalided from Army. Principal, 1920. Assistant Secretary and Establishment Officer, 1930–39. Assistant Under-Secretary, 1939–47. Joint Deputy Under-Secretary of State, 1947–56. Retired 1956. Publications include *The Colonial Empire and its Civil Service* (Cambridge: Cambridge University Press, 1938), *Transfer of Power* (London: Pall Mall Press, 1960) and *Whitehall and the Colonial Service* (London: Athlone Press, 1972).

JONES, Arthur Creech (1891–1964). Trade union official, 1919–29. Organising Secretary, Workers Travel Association, 1929–39. MP (Labour) 1935–50, 1954–64. Parliamentary Private Secretary to Bevin at Ministry of Labour and National Service, 1940–45. Co-founder and Chairman of Fabian Colonial Bureau, 1940–45. Member, (Colonial Office) Advisory Committee on Education in the Colonies, 1936–45. Vice-Chairman, Higher Education Commission to West Africa, 1943–44. Parliamentary Under-Secretary, Colonial Office, 1945–46. Secretary of State for the Colonies, 1946–50.

LEWIS, Sir William Arthur (1915–92). London School of Economics. Lecturer, LSE, 1938–47. Temporary Principal, Board of Trade, 1943, and Colonial Office, 1944. Reader in Colonial Economics, University of London, 1947. Part–time member, Board of Colonial Development Corporation, 1951–53. Professor of Political Economy, Manchester University, 1948–58. Principal, University College of the West Indies, 1959–62. Professor of Public and International Affairs, Princeton University, 1963–68; Professor of Political Economy, 1968–82. President, Caribbean Development Bank, 1970–73.

LLOYD, Sir Thomas (1896–1968). Caius College, Cambridge. Assistant Principal, Ministry of Health, 1920; transferred to Colonial Office, 1921. Principal, 1929. Secretary, Palestine Commission, 1929–30. Secretary, West India Royal Commission, 1938–39. Assistant Secretary, 1939. Assistant Under-Secretary of State, 1943. Permanent Under-Secretary of State, 1947–56. Retired 1956.

McLEAN, Sir William (1877–1967). Glasgow University. Entered Sudan Civil Service, 1906. Transferred to Egyptian Civil Service, 1913. MP (Conservative) 1931–35. Member, Advisory Committee on Education in the Colonies, 1932–38. Member, Secretary of State's Educational Commission to East Africa, 1937, and to Malaya, 1938. Colonial Office Representative, New York World Fair, 1939. Honorary liaison officer with members of Houses of Lords and Commons on Colonial Office's development work since 1931.

MILVERTON, Lord (Sir Arthur RICHARDS) (1885–1978). Christ Church, Oxford. Cadet, Malayan Civil Service, 1908. 2nd Assistant Colonial Secretary, Straits Settlements, 1920. Secretary to High Commissioner, Malay States, 1923. Acting General Adviser to Government of Johore, 1929. Governor, North Borneo, 1930–33. Governor, Gambia Colony, 1933–36. Governor, Fiji, and High Commissioner for Western Pacific, 1936–38. Captain-General and Governor, Jamaica, 1938–43. Governor, Nigeria, 1943–47. Part-time Director, Colonial Development Corporation, 1948–51.

MONSON, Sir (William Bonnar) Leslie (1912–93). Hertford College, Oxford. Entered Dominions Office, 1935, transferred to Colonial Office, 1939. Assistant Secretary, 1944. Seconded as Chief Secretary to West African Council, 1947–51. Assistant Under-Secretary, Colonial Office, 1951–64. High Commissioner, Republic of Zambia, 1964–66. Deputy Under-Secretary of State, Commonwealth Office (subsequently Foreign and Commonwealth Office), 1967–72.

MOYNE, Lord (Walter Edward GUINNESS) (1880–1944). MP (Unionist) 1907–31. Member, London County Council, 1907. Parliamentary Under-Secretary of State, War Office, 1922–23. Financial Secretary, Treasury, 1923–24 and Nov 1924–24. Minister of Agriculture and Fisheries, 1925–29. Chairman, Departmental Committee on Housing, 1933. Chairman, West India Royal Commission, 1938–39. Joint Parliamentary Under-Secretary, Ministry of Agriculture, 1940–41. Secretary of State for the Colonies, 1941–42. Leader, House of Lords, 1941–42. Deputy Minister of State, Cairo, 1942–44 (Assassinated).

ORDE BROWNE, Major Granville (1883–1947). Assistant District Commissioner, East African Protectorate, 1909. Retired from Royal Artillery, 1920. Senior Commissioner, Tanganyika, 1921. Labour Commissioner, Tanganyika, 1926–31. Undertook special studies of labour questions in Northern Rhodesia (1937), West Indies (1938), west Africa (1939) and Far East (1941). Adviser on Colonial Labour, Colonial Office, 1938–47.

PARKINSON, Sir Cosmo (1884–1967). Magdalen College, Oxford. Entered Admiralty, 1908, transferred to Colonial Office, 1909. Assistant

Secretary, 1925–31. Assistant Under-Secretary of State, 1931–37. Permanent Under-Secretary of State, 1937–40. Permanent Under-Secretary of State, Dominions Office, Feb 1940. Acting Permanent Under-Secretary, Colonial Office, May 1940. Seconded for special duty in Colonies, 1942. Retired, Dec 1944 and re–employed on special duty for Colonial Secretary, Jan–Sept 1945. Published *The Colonial Office from Within, 1909–1945* (London: Faber & Faber, 1947).

PEDLER, Frederick J. (1908–91). Caius College, Cambridge. Entered Colonial Office, 1930. Seconded to Tanganyika, 1934. Secretary, Commission on Higher Education in East Africa and Sudan, 1937. Secretary to Lord Privy Seal, 1938. Secretary to Lord Hailey in Africa, 1939–40. Chief British Economic Representative, Dakar, 1942. Finance Dept., Colonial Office, 1944. Joined United Africa Company, 1947; Director 1951 and Deputy Chairman, 1965–68. Director, Unilever Ltd & NV, 1956–68. Chairman, Council for Technical Education and Training for Overseas Countries, 1962–73. Treasurer, School of Oriental and African Studies (University of London), 1969–81.

POYNTON, Sir Hilton (b.1905). Brasenose, Oxford. Entered Department of Scientific and Industrial Research, 1927, transferred to Colonial Office, 1929. Private Secretary to Minister of Supply and Minister of Production, 1941–43. Reverted to Colonial Office, 1943. Permanent Under-Secretary of State, 1959–66. Member, Governing Body, SPCK, 1967–72.

REES–WILLIAMS, D.R. (Lord OGMORE) (1903–76). University of Wales. MP (Labour) 1945–50. Parliamentary Under-Secretary, Colonial Office, 1947–50 and Commonwealth Relations Office, 1950–51. Minister of Civil Aviation, 1951. Member, Government Mission to Sarawak, 1946. Chairman, Burma Frontier Areas Committee of Inquiry, 1947. UK Delegate to UN General Assembly, 1950. Leader, UK Delegation and Chairman, African Defence Facilities Conference, Nairobi, 1951. President, Liberal Party, 1963–64.

RICHARDS, Sir Arthur, see MILVERTON, Lord

ROBINSON, Kenneth (1914–88). Hertford College, Oxford and London School of Economics. Entered Colonial Office, 1936. Assistant Secretary, 1946. Resigned 1948. Fellow, Nuffield College, and Reader in Commonwealth Government, Oxford, 1948–57. Director, Institute of Commonwealth Studies, and Professor of Commonwealth Affairs, University of London, 1957–65. Editor, *Journal of Commonwealth Political Studies*, 1961–65.

ROSA, John Nogueira (1903–77). London School of Economics. Served in Ottoman Bank, Istanbul, 1924–28, and with Helbert, Wagg & Co.

Ltd, Private Bankers, London, 1929–41. Treasury Representative in Syria and Lebanon, 1941–42. Colonial Office, 1942–47. Member, Colonial Office Mission to East and Central Africa to investigate production of groundnuts, 1946. Rejoined Helbert, Wagg & Co. Ltd, 1947 (resigned same year). Member, Board of Overseas Food Corporation and Colonial Development Corporation, 1948–51. Deputy Managing Director, M. Golodetz Ltd, International Merchants (retired 1971).

STANLEY, Oliver (1896–1950). Called to Bar, 1919. MP (Conservative) 1924–50. Parliamentary Under-Secretary, Home Office, 1931–33. Minister of Transport, 1933–34. Minister of Labour, 1934–35. President, Board of Education, 1935–37. President, Board of Trade, 1937–40. Secretary of State for War, 1940. Secretary of State for the Colonies, 1942–45.

STOCKDALE, Sir Frank (1883–1949). Magdalene College, Cambridge. Director of Agriculture, Mauritius, 1912. Registrar, Co-operative Credit Societies, 1913. Official Member, Council of Government, 1913–16. Director of Agriculture and Registrar of Co-operative Societies, Ceylon, 1916–29. MLC, Ceylon, 1921–29. Agricultural Adviser to Colonial Secretary, 1929–40. Comptroller for Development and Welfare, West Indies, 1940–45. Vice-Chairman, Colonial Advisory Council on Agriculture and Animal Health, 1929–40. Co-Chairman, Anglo–American Caribbean Commission, 1942–45. Adviser on Development Planning, Colonial Office, 1945–48. Vice-Chairman, Colonial Development Corporation, 1948–49.

STRACHEY, John (1901–63). Magdalen College, Oxford. MP (Labour) 1929–31, 1945–63. Parliamentary Under-Secretary of State, Air Ministry, 1945–46. Minister of Food, 1946–50. Secretary of State for War, 1950–51.

SWINTON, Lord (Philip CUNLIFFE-LISTER) (1884–1972). University College, Oxford. Called to Bar, 1908. Joint Secretary, Ministry of National Service, 1917–18. MP (Unionist) 1918–35. Parliamentary Secretary to Board of Trade, 1920–21. Secretary, Overseas Trade Department, 1921–22. President, Board of Trade, 1922–23, 1924–29 and 1931. Chairman, Imperial Economic Conference, 1923. Secretary of State for the Colonies, 1931–35. Secretary of State for Air, 1935–38. Chairman, UK Commercial Corporation, 1940–42. Resident Minister, West Africa, 1942–44. Minister for Civil Aviation, 1944–45. Chancellor of the Duchy of Lancaster and Minister of Materials, 1951–52. Secretary of State for Commonwealth Relations, 1952–55.

TREFGARNE, Lord (G.M. GARRO JONES) (1894–1960). Private Secretary to Lord Greenwood at Home Office, Department of Overseas Trade and while Chief Secretary for Ireland. MP (Labour) 1924–29,

1935–45. Parliamentary Secretary to Ministry of Production, 1942–45. Member, Empire Parliamentary delegation to Nigeria, 1928. Founder Chairman, Colonial Development Corporation, 1947–50.

TRENCHARD, Hugh Montague, 1st Viscount Trenchard of Wolfeton (1873–1956). Marshal of the RAF. Chief of Air Staff, 1918–29. Commissioner, Metropolitan Police, 1931–35. Chairman, United Africa Company since 1936. Director, Goodyear Tyre and Rubber Company (G.B.) Ltd.

WILLIAMS, J.B. (1906–53). McGill University; Trinity College, Cambridge. Assistant Principal, Dominions Office, 1929, transferred to Colonial Office, 1930. Secretary, Colonial Development Advisory Committee, 1934. Seconded to Government of Northern Rhodesia, 1935–36. Colonial Adviser, Eastern Group Supply Council, New Delhi, 1941. Seconded to Ministry of Supply, 1942. Assistant Secretary, Colonial Office, 1943. Assistant Under-Secretary of State, 1949–53.

WILLIAMS, Owen G.R. (1886–1954). Hertford College, Oxford. Entered Inland Revenue, 1910, transferred to Colonial Office, 1911. Assistant Secretary, 1926–46. Retired 1946.

Bibliography

UNPUBLISHED RECORDS

(i) Public Record Office, Kew, Surrey

Cabinet Papers

CAB 65	War Cabinet Minutes
CAB 128	Cabinet Minutes
CAB 66	War Cabinet Memoranda WP and CP Series
CAB 67	War Cabinet Memoranda WP(G) Series
CAB 68	War Cabinet Memoranda WP(R) Series
CAB 129	Cabinet Memoranda
CAB 21	Cabinet Office: Registered Files
CAB 104	Supplementary Registered Files
CAB 71	War Cabinet, Lord President's Committee
CAB 123	Lord President of the Council Secretariat Files
CAB 132	Lord President's Committee and Sub-Committees
CAB 78	War Cabinet Committees, Miscellaneous and General Series
CAB 72	War Cabinet Committees on Economic Policy
CAB 87	War Cabinet Committees on Reconstruction
CAB 95	War Cabinet Committees on Middle East and Africa
CAB 117	Reconstruction Secretariat Files
CAB 124	Minister of Reconstruction, Lord President of the Council and Minister for Science: Secretariat files.
CAB 130	Ad Hoc Cabinet Committees: General & Miscellaneous Series
CAB 134	Cabinet Committees: General Series, 1945–51
PREM 8	Prime Minister's Office: Correspondence and Papers, 1945–51

Colonial Office files

CO 323	Colonies, General: Original Correspondence
CO 378	Colonies, General: Register of Correspondence
CO 537	Colonies General Supplementary Original Correspondence
CO 852	Economic: Original Correspondence

CO 859	Social Service: Original Correspondence
CO 867	Establishment: Registers of Correspondence
CO 875	Public Relations and Information Original Correspondence
CO 878	Establishment Miscellanea
CO 879	Confidential Print: Africa
CO 885	Confidential Print Miscellaneous
CO 900	Colonial Research Council
CO 901	Colonial Social Science Research Council
CO 919	Personnel: Register of Correspondence
CO 927	Research Department: Original Correspondence
CO 936	International Relations: Original Correspondence
CO 967	Private Office Papers
CO 987	Advisory Committee on Education in the Colonies: Papers and Minutes
CO 990	Colonial Economic Advisory Committee: Minutes and Papers
CO 997	Colonial Social Welfare Advisory Committee: Minutes and Papers
CO 999	Colonial Economic Development Council: Minutes and Papers
CO 847	Africa: Original Correspondence
CO 583	Nigeria Original Correspondence
CO 763	Nigeria: Registers of Correspondence
CO 96	Gold Coast Original Correspondence
CO 343	Gold Coast Register of Correspondence
CO 554	West Africa Original Correspondence
CO 555	West Africa Register of Correspondence

Board of Trade files

BT 5	Minutes
BT 11	Commercial Department: Correspondence and Papers
BT 60	Department of Overseas Trade Correspondence and Papers
BT 64	Industries and Manufactures Department: Correspondence and Papers
BT 175	Cotton Board and Textile Council: Minutes and Papers
BT 225	Export Promotion Department
BT 241	Commercial Relations and Export Division: Policy, General and Record (P, G & R) Files

Treasury files

T 161	Supply Files
T 162	Establishment Files
T 165	Blue Notes
T 220	Imperial and Foreign Division: Files
T 228	Trade and Industry Division: Files
T 229	Central Economic Planning Section: Files
T 236	Overseas Finance Division: Files

T 266 Capital Issues Committee
T 273 Bridges Papers

(ii) Rhodes House Library, Oxford

MSS Brit.Emp.s365 Fabian Colonial Bureau Papers.
MSS Brit.Emp.s332 Creech Jones Papers.
MSS Brit.Emp.s334–s340, s342–3, s357 Hailey Papers.

(iii) Bodleian Library, Oxford

MS Attlee dep.48 Attlee Papers.

(iv) Nuffield College Library, Oxford

Cripps Papers.

UNPUBLISHED THESES

Bowden, J.H., 'Development and control in British colonial policy, with reference to Nigeria and the Gold Coast, 1935–48'. (Birmingham Ph.D. 1980).

Hinds, A., 'British Imperial Policy and the Development of the Nigerian Economy, 1939–1951'. (Dalhousie Ph.D. 1985).

Kent, J., 'The International Dimensions of British West African Policy 1939–1949'. (Aberdeen Ph.D. 1986).

Meredith, D.G., 'The British Government and Colonial Economic Development, with particular reference to British West Africa, 1919–1939'. (Exeter Ph.D. 1976).

Miller, T.J., 'The Board of Trade and British economic reconstruction, 1940–9; the regeneration of exporting industries'. (Stirling M.Litt. 1986).

Nordman, C.R., 'Prelude to Decolonisation in West Africa: the development of British Colonial Policy, 1938–1947'. (Oxford D.Phil. 1976).

Parsons, G.N., 'Imperial "partnership": British colonial development and welfare policy, 1938–50'. (Oxford M.Phil. 1985).

Rampersad, D.G.M., 'Colonial economic development and social welfare: the case of the British West Indian colonies, 1929–47'. (Oxford D.Phil. 1979).

Souter, D.N., 'Colonial labour policy and labour conditions in Nigeria, 1939–45'. (Oxford D.Phil. 1981).

Stockwell, S.E., 'British business, politics and decolonization in the Gold Coast, c.1945–60'. (Oxford D.Phil. 1993).

Throup, D.W., 'The governorship of Sir Philip Mitchell in Kenya, 1944–52'. (Cambridge Ph.D. 1983).

Westcott, N.J., 'The impact of the Second World War on Tanganyika, 1939–49'. (Cambridge Ph.D. 1982).

OTHER UNPUBLISHED WORKS

Shuckburgh, Sir John, 'Colonial Civil History of the War'; mimeographed manuscript, 4 volumes; Institute of Commonwealth Studies Library, University of London.

Westcott, N.J., 'Sterling and Empire: The British Imperial Economy, 1939–1951'; seminar paper (Jan. 1983), Institute of Commonwealth Studies Library, University of London.

PUBLISHED SOURCES

Official publications

Cmd.6175, *Statement of Policy on Colonial Development and Welfare*, 1940, *PP* (1939–40) x, 25.

Cmd.6299, *Despatch from Secretary of State to Colonial Governments, regarding certain aspects of colonial war-time policy*, 1941, *PP* (1940–41) viii, 1.

Cmd.6422, *Colonial Development and Welfare Act, 1940: Report on the operation of the Act to 31st October 1942*, 1943, *PP* (1942–43) ix, 601.

Cmd.6713, *Colonial Development and Welfare. Despatch, dated November 12, 1945, from the Secretary of State for the Colonies to Colonial Governments*, *PP* (1945–46) xix, 35.

Cmd.7167, *The Colonial Empire, 1939–47*, *PP* (1946–47) x, 403.

Cmd.7433, *The Colonial Empire, 1947–48*, *PP* (1947–48) xi, 47.

Cmd.7715, *The Colonial Territories, 1948–49*, *PP* (1948–49) xiii, 641.

Cmd.5872, *Statistical Abstract for the British Empire for each of the ten years 1928 to 1937. Sixty Seventh Number*, (1938).

Cmd.7224, *Statistical Abstract for the British Commonwealth for each of the ten years 1936 to 1945. Sixty Ninth Number*, (1947).

Col.no.231, *Report of the Commission of Enquiry into Disturbances in the Gold Coast, 1948*, (8 June 1948).

Col.no.232, *Statement by His Majesty's Government on the Report of the Commission of Enquiry into Disturbances in the Gold Coast, 1948*, (8 June 1948).

H.C.181, *Fifth Report from the Select Committee on Estimates. Session 1947–48. Colonial Development*, (30 June 1948).

BOOKS AND PAMPHLETS

Addison, P., *The Road to 1945* (London: Quartet, 1975).

Adu Boahen, A., *African Perspectives on Colonialism* (Baltimore: The Johns Hopkins University Press, 1987).

Ajayi, J.F.A. and M. Crowder, (eds), *The History of West Africa. Volume Two* (London: Longman, 1974).

Aldcroft, D.H., *The British Economy: Vol. 1: years of turmoil* (Brighton: Wheatsheaf, 1986).

Arndt, H.W., *Economic Development. The History of an Idea* (Chicago : University of Chicago Press, 1987).

Austen, R., *African Economic History. Internal Development and External Dependency* (London: James Currey, 1987).

Barnett, C., *The Audit of War* (Basingstoke: Macmillan, 1986).

Berman, B., *Conflict and Crisis in Colonial Kenya. The Dialectics of Domination* (London: James Currey, 1990).

Booth, A. and M. Pack, *Employment, Capital and Economic Policy. Great Britain 1918–1939* (Oxford: Blackwell, 1985).

Bourdillon, Sir B., *The Future of the Colonial Empire* (London: SCM Press, 1945).

Brett, E.A., *Colonialism and Underdevelopment in East Africa: The Politics of Economic Change, 1919–1939* (London: Heinemann, 1973).

Butler, L.J., 'The ambiguities of British colonial development policy, 1938–48', in A. Gorst, L. Johnman and W. Scott Lucas (eds), *Contemporary British History 1931–61 Politics and the Limits of Policy* (London: Pinter, 1991).

Buxton, N.K., and D.H. Aldcroft, (eds.), *British Industry between the Wars* (London: Scolar Press, 1979).

Cain, P.J. and A.G. Hopkins, *British Imperialism Crisis and Deconstruction 1914–1990* (Harlow: Longman, 1993).

Cairncross, A., *Years of Recovery: British economic policy 1945–1951* (London: Methuen, 1985).

Cairncross, A. and N. Watts, *The Economic Section 1939–1961. A study in economic advising* (London: Routledge, 1989).

Cell, J.W., *Hailey A Study in British Imperialism, 1872–1969* (Cambridge: Cambridge University Press, 1992).

Chester, Sir D.N., *Lessons of the British War Economy* (Cambridge: Cambridge University Press, 1951).

Constantine, S., *The Making of British Colonial Development Policy 1914–1940* (London: Frank Cass, 1984).

Cowen, M. and N.J. Westcott, 'British Imperial Policy During the War' in D. Killingray and R. Rathbone (eds), *Africa and the Second World War* (Basingstoke: Macmillan, 1986), pp.40–61.

Cross, J.A., *Lord Swinton* (Oxford: Oxford University Press, 1982).

Crowder, M., *West Africa under Colonial Rule* (London: Hutchinson, 1968).

Crowther, M.A., *British Social Policy 1914–1939* (Basingstoke: Macmillan, 1988).

Dalton, Hugh, *High Tide and After. Memoirs 1945–60* (London: Frederick Muller, 1962).

Darwin, John, *Britain and Decolonisation. The Retreat from Empire in the Post-War World* (Basingstoke: Macmillan, 1988).

Dewey, Clive, 'The end of the imperialism of free trade: the eclipse of the Lancashire Lobby and the concession of fiscal autonomy to India' in C. Dewey and A.G. Hopkins, (eds), *The Imperial Impact: Studies in the Economic History of Africa and India* (London: Athlone Press, 1978).

Dobson, A. P., *US Wartime Aid to Britain 1940–1946* (London: Croom Helm, 1986).

Drummond, I.M., *British Economic Policy and the Empire 1919–39* (London: Allen and Unwin, 1972).

Drummond, I.M., *Imperial Economic Policy, 1917–1939* (London: Allen and Unwin, 1974).

Duignan, P. and L.H. Gann, *Colonialism in Africa 1870–1960. Vol. 4. The Economics of Colonialism* (Cambridge: Cambridge University Press, 1975).

Dupree, Marguerite (ed.), *Lancashire and Whitehall; the diary of Sir Raymond Streat. Volume I (1931–39), Volume II (1939–57)* (Manchester: Manchester University Press, 1987).

Ekundare, R. Olufemi, *An Economic History of Nigeria 1860–1960* (London: Methuen, 1973).

Fabian Colonial Bureau, *Domination or Co-operation?* (London: Fabian Society, 1946).

—-, *Downing Street and the Colonies* (London: Fabian Society, 1942).

—-, *Next Steps in Colonial Policy* (London: Fabian Society, 1948).

T. Falola, 'The Lebanese in Colonial West Africa', in J.F. Ade Ajayi and J.D.Y. Peel (eds), *People and Empires in African History: Essays in Memory of Michael Crowder* (London: Longman, 1992) pp.121–42.

Federation of British Industries, *Industry and the Way to Recovery* (London: FBI, 1947).

—-, *Reconstruction. A Report* (London: Macmillan, 1942).

Fieldhouse, D.K., 'Arrested Development in Anglophone Black Africa?', in P. Gifford and Wm. Roger Louis (eds), *Decolonization and African Independence. The Transfers of Power, 1960–1980* (New Haven: Yale University Press, 1988).

—-, *Black Africa 1945–1980: economic decolonisation and arrested development* (London: Unwin Hyman, 1986).

—-, *Colonialism 1870–1945. An Introduction* (Basingstoke: Macmillan, 1983).

—-, 'Decolonization, Development and Dependence: a survey of changing attitudes', in P. Gifford and Wm. Roger Louis, (eds.), *The Transfer of Power in Africa. Decolonisation 1940–1960* (New Haven: Yale University Press, 1982).

—-, 'Keith Hancock and Imperial Economic History: A Retrospect Forty Years On' in F. Madden and D.K. Fieldhouse (eds), *Oxford and the Idea of Commonwealth* (London: Croom Helm, 1982).

—-, 'The Labour Government and the Empire-Commonwealth 1945–1951' in R. Ovendale (ed.), *The Foreign Policy of the British Labour Governments 1945–1951* (Leicester: Leicester University Press, 1984).

—-, *Merchant Capital and Economic Decolonization The United Africa Company 1929–1987* (Oxford: Oxford University Press, 1994).
Floud, R., and D.N. McCloskey, (eds), *The Economic History of Britain since 1700: Volume II: 1860 to the 1970s* (Cambridge: Cambridge University Press, 1981).
Frankel, S.H., *Capital Investment in Africa* (London: Oxford University Press, 1938).
Gallagher, J., *The Decline, Revival and Fall of the British Empire* (Cambridge: Cambridge University Press, 1982).
Gann, L.H., and P. Duignan, (eds), *African Proconsuls* (New York: The Free Press, 1978).
Gifford, P. and Wm. Roger Louis, (eds), *The Transfer of Power in Africa: Decolonization 1940–60* (New Haven: Yale University Press, 1982).
Goldsworthy, D., *Colonial Issues in British Politics, 1945–1951. From 'colonial development' to 'wind of change'* (Oxford: Oxford University Press, 1971).
Griffiths, J., R. Hinden, and A. Creech Jones, *The Way Forward* (London: Victor Gollancz, 1950).
Gupta, P.S., *Imperialism and the British Labour Movement, 1914–1964* (London: Macmillan, 1975).
—-, 'Imperialism and the Labour Government' in J.M. Winter, (ed.), *The Working Class in Modern British History* (Cambridge: Cambridge University Press, 1983), pp.112–15.
Hailey, Lord, *An African Survey* (Oxford: Oxford University Press, 1938).
—-, *Britain and Her Dependencies* (London: Longman, 1943).
—-, *The Future of Colonial Peoples* (London: Oxford University Press, 1943).
—-, *Native Administration and Political Development in British Tropical Africa* (Nendeln: Kraus Reprint, 1979).
—-, *The Position of Colonies in a British Commonwealth of Nations* (London: Oxford University Press, 1941).
Hancock, W.K., *Argument of Empire* (Harmondsworth: Penguin, 1943).
—-, *Survey of British Commonwealth Affairs II. Problems of Economic Policy 1918–1939* (London: Oxford University Press, 1940–42).
—-, *The Wealth of Colonies* (Cambridge: Cambridge University Press, 1950).
Hancock, W.K., and M.M. Gowing, *British War Economy. History of the Second World War – UK Civil Series* (London: HMSO, 1949).
Hargreaves, E.L., and M.M. Gowing, *Civil Industry and Trade History of the Second World War – UK Civil Series* (London: HMSO, 1952).
Hargreaves, J.D., *Decolonization in Africa* (Harlow: Longman, 1988).
—-, *The End of Colonial Rule in West Africa* (London: Macmillan, 1979).
Havinden, M. and D. Meredith, *Colonialism and Development Britain and its Tropical Colonies, 1850–1960* (London: Routledge, 1993).
Hetherington, P., *British Paternalism and Africa, 1920–1940* (London: Frank Cass, 1978).

Hinden, R., *The Colonies and Us* (London: Fabian Society, 1942).
—, *Common Sense and Colonial Development* (London: Victor Gollancz, 1949).
— (ed.), *Fabian Colonial Essays* (London: George Allen & Unwin, 1945).
—, *Plan for Africa* (London: George Allen & Unwin, 1941).
—, *Socialists and the Empire* (London: Fabian Society, 1946).
Hopkins, A.G., *An Economic History of West Africa* (Harlow: Longman, 1973).
Howard, R., *Colonialism and Underdevelopment in Ghana* (London: Croom Helm, 1978).
Howe, S., *Anti-colonialism in British politics: the Left and the end of Empire, 1918-64* (Oxford: Oxford University Press, 1993).
Howson, S. and D. Winch, *The Economic Advisory Council, 1930–1939* (Cambridge: Cambridge University Press, 1977).
Huxley, J., and P. Deane, *The Future of the Colonies* (London: Pilot Press, 1944).
Hyam, R. (ed.), *British Documents on the End of Empire. Series A. Volume 2. The Labour Government and the End of Empire 1945–1951* (London: HMSO, 1992).
Ingham, B., *Shaping opinion on development policy: economists at the Colonial Office during World War II.* (Salford: University of Salford Papers in Economics 88–5, 1988).
Ingham, B., and C. Simmons, (eds), *Development Studies and Colonial Policy* (London: Frank Cass, 1987).
Jeffries, Sir C., *The Colonial Office* (London: George Allen & Unwin, 1956).
—, *Whitehall and the Colonial Service: an administrative memoir, 1939–1956* (London: Athlone Press, 1972).
Jones, A. Creech, *Labour's Colonial Policy* (London: Victor Gollancz, 1947).
—, *New Fabian Colonial Essays* (London: The Hogarth Press, 1959).
Kent, J., *The Internationalization of Colonialism: Britain, France, and Black Africa, 1939–1956* (Oxford: Oxford University Press, 1992).
Kilby, P., *Industrialization in an Open Economy: Nigeria, 1945–60* (Cambridge: Cambridge University Press, 1969).
—, 'Manufacturing in Colonial Africa' in P. Duignan and L.H. Gann, *Colonialism in Africa: Vol. 4, The Economics of Colonialism* (Cambridge: Cambridge University Press, 1975).
Killingray, D. and R. Rathbone, (eds.), *Africa and the Second World War* (Basingstoke: Macmillan, 1986).
Kindleberger, C.P., *The World in Depression, 1929–1939* (Harmondsworth: Penguin, 1987).
Kirby, M.W., *The Decline of British Economic Power since 1870* (London: Allen and Unwin, 1981).
Labour Party, *The Colonies. The Labour Party's Post-War Policy for the African and Pacific Colonies* (London: Labour Party, 1943).

Latham, A.J.H., *The Depression and the Developing World, 1914–39* (London: Croom Helm, 1981).
Lee, J.M., *The Churchill Coalition, 1940–45* (London: Batsford, 1980).
—-, *Colonial Development and Good Government: a study of the ideas expressed by the British official classes in planning decolonization, 1939-1964* (Oxford: Oxford University Press, 1967).
Lee, J.M. and M. Petter, *The Colonial Office, War, and Development Policy: organisation and the planning of a metropolitan initiative, 1939–1945* (London: Maurice Temple Smith, 1982).
Leys, C., *Underdevelopment in Kenya* (London: Heinemann, 1975).
Louis, W. Roger, *Imperialism at Bay: The United States and the Decolonisation of the British Empire, 1941–45* (Oxford: Oxford University Press, 1977).
Macmillan, H., *The Blast of War, 1939–1945* (London: Macmillan, 1967).
Macmillan, W.M., *Africa Emergent* (London: Faber & Faber, 1938).
Madden, F. and D.K. Fieldhouse, (eds), *Oxford and the Idea of Commonwealth. Essays presented to Sir Edgar Williams* (London: Croom Helm, 1982).
Morgan, D.J., *The Official History of Colonial Development. Vols I and II* (Basingstoke: Macmillan, 1980).
Morgan, K.O., *Labour in Power 1945–1951* (Oxford: Oxford University Press, 1984).
Morris-Jones, W.H. and G. Fischer, (eds), *Decolonization and After: The British and French Experience* (London: Frank Cass, 1980).
Munro, J.Forbes, *Britain in Tropical Africa 1880–1960. Economic Relationships and Impact* (Basingstoke: Macmillan, 1984).
Niculescu, B., *Colonial Planning* (London: George Allen & Unwin, 1958).
Ovendale, R. (ed.), *The Foreign Policy of the British Labour Governments, 1945–1951* (Leicester: Leicester University Press, 1984).
Pearce, R.D., *Sir Bernard Bourdillon: The Biography of a Twentieth Century Colonialist* (Oxford: The Kensal Press, 1987).
—-, 'The Colonial Economy: Nigeria and the Second World War', in B. Ingham and C. Simmons, (eds), *Development Studies and Colonial Policy* (London: Frank Cass, 1987).
—-, *The Turning Point in Africa: British Colonial Policy 1938–48* (London: Frank Cass, 1982).
Peden, G.C., *British economic and social policy: Lloyd George to Margaret Thatcher* (Deddington: Philip Allan, 1985).
Phillips, A., *The Enigma of Colonialism. British Policy in West Africa* (London: James Currey, 1989).
Political and Economic Planning, *The Future of the Colonies* (London: PEP, 1942).
Pollard, S., *The Development of the British Economy. Third Edition 1914–1980* (London: Edward Arnold, 3rd ed, 1983).
Porter, A.N., and A.J. Stockwell, *British Imperial Policy and Decolonization 1938–64. Volume 1, 1938–51* (Basingstoke: Macmillan, 1987).

Porter, B., *The Lion's Share* (Harlow: Longman, 1975).
Pressnell, L.S., *External Economic Policy since the War. Volume I. The Post-War Financial Settlement* (London: HMSO, 1986).
Rathbone, R. (ed.), *British Documents on the End of Empire. Series B Volume 1. Ghana. Part I. 1941–1952* (London: HMSO, 1993).
Redford, A., *Manchester Merchants and Foreign Trade. Vol II. 1850–1939* (Manchester: Manchester University Press, 1956).
Rendell, W., *History of the Commonwealth Development Corporation* (London: Heinemann Educational, 1976).
Roberts, A.D. (ed.), *The Cambridge History of Africa Volume VII from 1905 to 1940* (Cambridge: Cambridge University Press, 1986).
—, *The Colonial Moment in Africa. Essays on the Movement of Minds and Materials, 1900–1940* (Cambridge: Cambridge University Press, 1990).
Robinson, K., *Dilemmas of Trusteeship – Aspects of British Colonial Policy between the Wars* (London: Oxford University Press, 1965).
Robinson, R.E., 'Andrew Cohen and the Transfer of Power in Tropical Africa, 1941–1951', in W.H. Morris-Jones and G. Fisher, (eds), *Decolonisation and After* (London: Frank Cass, 1980), pp.50–72.
—, 'Sir Andrew Cohen Pro-Consul of African Nationalism' in L.H. Gann and P. Duignan (eds), *African Pro-Consuls* (New York: The Free Press, 1978).
Rodney, W., *How Europe Underdeveloped Africa* (Washington: Howard University Press, 1982).
Swainson, N., *The Development of Corporate Capitalism in Kenya 1918–1977* (London: Heinemann, 1980).
Thane, P., *The Foundations of the Welfare State* (Harlow: Longman, 1982).
Thorne, C., *Allies of a Kind: the United States, Britain and the war against Japan, 1941–1945* (Oxford: Oxford University Press, 1978).
Throup, D., *Economic and Social Origins of Mau Mau 1945–53* (London: James Currey, 1987).
Thurston, A., *Sources for Colonial Studies in the Public Record Office Volume 1 Records of the Colonial Office, Dominions Office, Commonwealth Relations Office and Commonwealth Office* (London: HMSO, 1995).
Tippett, L.H.C., *A Portrait of the Lancashire Textile Industry* (Oxford: Oxford University Press, 1969).
Tomlinson, J., *British Macroeconomic Policy since 1940* (London: Croom Helm, 1985).
Wilson, C., *The History of Unilever* (London: Cassell, 1954).
Winter, J.M., (ed.), *War and Economic Development* (Cambridge: Cambridge University Press, 1975).
Worswick, G.D.N. and P.H. Ady, (eds) *The British Economy, 1945–50*, (Oxford: Oxford University Press, 1952).
Wrigley, C.C., 'Aspects of Economic History', in A.D. Roberts (ed.), *Cambridge History of Africa Vol. VII from 1905 to 1940* (Cambridge: Cambridge University Press, 1986).

Articles

Abbott, G.C., 'A re-examination of the 1929 Colonial Development Act', *EcHR*, 2nd series, 24, 1, (Feb. 1971) pp.68–81.

Abbott, G.C., 'British Colonial Aid Policy during the Nineteen Thirties', *Canadian Journal of History*, 5, 1, (March 1970) pp73–89.

Aldcroft, D., 'Cotton comes to Whitehall', in *Times Higher Education Supplement*, 19 Feb. 1988, p.21.

Barker, R.S., 'Civil Service Attitudes and the Economic Planning of the Attlee Government', *Journal of Contemporary History*, 21, 3, (July 1986) pp.473–86.

Booth, A., 'The "Keynesian Revolution" in Economic Policy-making', *EcHR*, 2nd ser., 36, 1, (Feb. 1983) pp.499–522.

Bourdillon, Bernard H., 'Colonial Development and Welfare', *IA*, 20, 3, (July 1944) pp.369–80.

Brett, E.A., S. Gilliatt, and A. Pople, 'Planned trade, Labour Party policy and US intervention', *History Workshop*, 13, (Spring 1982) pp.130–42.

Buckley, S., 'The Colonial Office and the Establishment of an Imperial Development Board: The Impact of World War One', *JICH*, 2, 3, (May 1974) pp.308–17.

Cain, P.J. and A.G. Hopkins, 'Gentlemanly capitalism and British expansion overseas II: new imperialism, 1850–1945', *EcHR*, 2nd ser., 60, 1, (Feb. 1987) pp.1–26.

Cell, J.W., 'On the Eve of Decolonization: The Colonial Office's Plans for the transfer of power in Africa 1947', *JICH*, 8, 3, (May 1980) pp.235–57.

Cowen, M., 'Early Years of the Colonial Development Corporation: British State Enterprise Overseas during late Colonialism', *AA*, 83, 330, (Jan. 1984) pp.63–75.

Drummond, I.M., 'More on British Colonial Aid Policy in the Nineteen Thirties', *CJH*, 6, 2, (Sept. 1971) pp.189–95.

Dumett, Raymond, 'Africa's strategic minerals during the Second World War', *JAH*, 26, 4, (1985) pp.381–408.

Ehrlich, C.C., 'Building and Caretaking: Economic Policy in British Tropical Africa, 1890–1960', *EcHR*, 26, 4, (Nov. 1973) pp.649–67.

Flint, J., 'Planned Decolonization and its Failure in British Africa', *AA*, 82, 328, (July 1983) pp.389–411.

Hinds, A.E., 'Sterling and Imperial Policy, 1945–1951', *JICH*, 15, 2, (Jan. 1987) pp.148–64.

Holland, R.F., 'The Federation of British Industries and the international economy', *EcHR*, 2nd series, 24, 2, (May 1981) pp.287–300.

Hopkins, A.G., 'African Economic History: The First Twenty Five Years', *JAH*, 30, 1, (1989) pp.157–63.

—, 'Imperial Business in Africa Part I: Sources', *JAH*, 17, 1, (1976) pp.29–48.

—, 'Imperial Business in Africa Part II. Interpretations', *JAH*, 17, 2, (1976) pp.267–90.

Hyam, R., 'Africa and the Labour Government, 1945–1951', *JICH*, 16, 3, (May 1988) pp.148–9.

Jefferys, K., 'British Politics and Social Policy During the Second World War', *Historical Journal*, 30, 1, (March 1987) pp.123–44.

Johnson, H., 'The West Indies and the Conversion of the British Official Classes to the Development Idea', *Journal of Commonwealth and Comparative Politics*, 15, 1, (March 1977) pp.55–75.

Jones, A. Creech, 'British Colonial Policy with particular reference to Africa', *IA*, 27, 2, (Apr. 1951) pp.176–83.

—, 'The Colonial Office', *Political Quarterly*, 14, 1, (Jan.–Mar. 1943) pp.19–32.

Killingray, D., 'The Empire Resources Development Committee and West Africa 1916–20', *JICH*, 10, 2, (Jan. 1982) pp.194–210.

Lee, J.M., 'The Dissolution of the Empire Marketing Board, 1933: Reflections on a Diary', *JICH*, 1, 1, (Oct. 1972) pp.49–59.

—, '"Forward Thinking" and War: the Colonial Office during the 1940s', *JICH*, 6, 1, (Oct. 1977) pp.64–79.

Meredith, D., 'The British Government and Colonial Economic Policy 1919–1939', *EcHR*, 2nd ser., 28, 3, (Aug. 1975) pp.484–99.

—, 'The Colonial Office, British Business Interests and the Reform of Cocoa Marketing in West Africa, 1937–1945', *JAH*, 29, 2, (1988) pp.285–300.

—, 'Government and the decline of the Nigerian oil-palm export industry, 1919–1939', *JAH*, 25, 3, (1984) pp.311–29.

—, 'State controlled marketing and economic "development": the case of West African produce during the Second World War', *EcHR*, 2nd ser., 39, 1, (Feb. 1986) pp.77–91.

Munro, J. Forbes, review of S. Constantine, *The Making of British Colonial Development Policy 1914–1940*, in *JAH*, 27, 1, (1986).

Pearce, R.D., 'The Colonial Office and Planned Decolonisation in Africa', *AA*, 83, 330, (Jan. 1984), pp.77–93.

—, 'The Colonial Office in 1947 and the Transfer of Power in Africa: An Addendum to John Cell', *JICH*, 10, 2, (Jan. 1982) pp.211–15.

—, 'Governors, Nationalists and Constitutions in Nigeria, 1935–51', *JICH*, 14, 3, (May 1981) pp.289–307.

—, 'Morale in the Colonial Service in Nigeria during the Second World War', *JICH*, 11, 2, (Jan. 1983) pp.175–96.

Petter, M., 'Sir Sydney Caine and the Colonial Office in the Second World War: a career in the making', *CJH*, 16, 1, (Apr. 1981) pp.67–85.

Pim, Sir A., 'The Economic Future of Tropical Africa', *Political Quarterly*, 12, 4, (Oct.–Dec. 1941) pp.391–404.

Rimmer, D., 'The Economics of Colonialism in Africa', *JAH*, 19, 2, (1978) pp.265–73.

Robinson, R.E., 'The Moral Disarmament of African Empire 1919–1947', *JICH*, 8, 1, (Oct. 1979) pp.86–104.

Smythe, R., 'Britain's African colonies and British propaganda during World War II', *JICH*, 14, 1, (Oct. 1985) pp.65–82.

Stockwell, S.E., 'Political Strategies of British Business during Decolonization: The Case of the Gold Coast/Ghana, 1945–57', *JICH*, 23, 2, (May 1995) pp.277–300.

Winder, R., 'The Lebanese in West Africa', *Comparative Studies in Society and History*, 4, (1962) pp.296–333.

Index